JOURNAL FOR THE STUDY OF THE NEW TESTAMENT SUPPLEMENT SERIES

178

Sheffield Academic Press

Christ and Community

A Socio-Historical Study of the Christology of Revelation

Thomas B. Slater

Journal for the Study of the New Testament
Supplement Series 178

In loving memory of

Thomas J. and Thelma B. Slater
Eugene and Amanda K. Bowie
Rachel Matthews Slater Kimball
Naomi K. Donato
Ezell Charles
Doris Dean Green
Van Edward Slater
Sylvester Williams

In loving appreciation to

Cheryl A. Bowie
Vinnetta A. Cole
Joyce D. Slater
Lisa Y. Williams
Mrs Juanita K. Charles

Published by
Sheffield Academic Press Ltd
Mansion House
19 Kingfield Road
Sheffield S11 9AS
England

Typeset by Sheffield Academic Press
and
Printed on acid-free paper in Great Britain
by Biddles Ltd
Guildford, Surrey

British Library Cataloguing in Publication Data

A catalogue record for this book is available
from the British Library

ISBN 1-85075-939-1

CONTENTS

Acknowledgments

This study constitutes a revision of my doctoral thesis done under the supervision of Professor Graham N. Stanton in the Department of Theology and Religious Studies, King's College London, University of London (1992–96). I am deeply indebted to Professor Stanton for working with me, sometimes late at night, when I am sure that he would have preferred being home with his family. His faith in me often pushed and pulled me farther than I ever imagined that I could go. As I have often said, he made this the most pleasurable stressful experience of my life.

I am also most appreciative of the analyses and words of encouragement given to me, and my fellow postgraduates, by the other New Testament faculty at King's during my studies there. Professor J. Leslie Houlden consistently offered beneficial insights to all the postgraduates and a sense of humor that lightened many moments. Moreover, as my internal examiner, his probing questions and astute analyses added much to this thesis and helped greatly to improve the finished product. Since my graduation, Professor Houlden has continued to support my work and encourage my endeavors. Dr Francis Watson always provided the types of theological analyses and detailed scrutiny that proved fruitful to our work. Dr Judith Lieu's knowledge of the cultural context of early Christianity, as well as her penetrating questions during colloquia, added much to my knowledge of Roman society, in general, and early Christianity, in specific. In all these ways and more, the New Testament faculty provided a model of tutelage that was at once challenging and positive. Without a doubt, this was the most influential intellectual experience of my life. Moreover, the friendships that I established while in the United Kingdom shall last a lifetime.

Thanks also to the following for their encouragement as I embarked upon postgraduate studies in Britain: Professor John Riches of Glasgow, Professor Richard Bauckham of St Andrews, Professor James Dunn of Durham, Canon John Sweet of Cambridge, Dr John Court of Kent, Dr A.T. Lincoln, then of Sheffield, and Professor Christopher Tuckett, then of Manchester. I am especially indebted to Canon Sweet, my external examiner, whose insight and knowledge of apocalyptic literature has been invaluable to me in improving my thesis for publication. Canon Sweet has continued to dialogue with me since my graduation and his comments have pushed me at various points to clarify my positions.

I must also express special thanks to Professor William Farmer, my first New Testament Greek professor, and Professor Harold Attridge, my DMin supervisor at SMU, whose seminar on Revelation in 1978 was the genesis of my interests in Revelation. Both of them have continued to be ready resources, helpful critics and sources of encouragement. Also, I am appreciative of my colleagues at the University of Georgia for their undying faith in my abilities, especially Professors George Howard, Sandy Martin, R. Baxter Miller and John Morrow.

I must also extend a special thank you to *Technical Papers for the Bible Translator* and *New Testament Studies* for allowing me to utilize at my own discretion work that I have previously published in their scholarly journals.

Very special thanks go to Mrs Zinetta McDonald, for typing various drafts, and also to the Revd Christine Bainbridge, Dr Joan Bruggemann Rufe and the Revd Dr Mary Catherine Orr for their help in reading various drafts of this work; a most special thanks to Mrs Angela Colson who proof-read the entire final draft.

I am most appreciative to Stanley Porter and the editorial board of the JSNT Supplement Series for accepting my manuscript and to the staff at Sheffield Academic Press for their assistance in making its publication a reality. I owe a special thanks to Ms Ailsa Parkin and Mrs Vicky Acklam at Sheffield Academic Press.

And finally, to my very large family, especially those to whom this work is dedicated, and my wife Olivia Elaine, who sacrificed so much quality time so that I could finish this task, as well as my many friends in the US and the UK, whose constant encouragement, support, love and faith in me have made this book possible, 'I just want to thank you'.

Advent 1998
Oconee County, Georgia, USA

A NOTE ON TRANSLATIONS AND ABBREVIATIONS

The system of abbreviations of Sheffield Academic Press is employed throughout this study. Exceptions to the Sheffield rule will be noted in the appropriate places.

Unless stated to the contrary, all translations of the Septuagint, the Greek New Testament and Jewish and Christian pseudepigraphical writings are mine; all translations from the Hebrew Bible are from the New American Standard Bible; all translations of non-Christian Greek and Roman writings are from the Loeb Classical Library. This study has used *Biblia Hebraica Stuttgartensia* (edited by K. Elliger and W. Rudolph; Stuttgart: Deutsche Bibelgesellschaft, 1976/77, 1984) for translations of the Hebrew Bible; *Septuaginta* (edited by A. Rahlfs; 2 vols. in 1; Stuttgart: Deutsche Bibelgesellschaft, 1979) for translations of the Septuagint; *Novum Testamentum Graece* (edited by E. Nestle, K. Aland *et al.*; Stuttgart: Deutsche Bibelgesellschaft, 27th edn, 1993) for New Testament translations.

Throughout this study, I shall refer to John as the author of the book of Revelation as a matter of convenience without implying apostolic authorship.

ABBREVIATIONS

AB	Anchor Bible
ACNT	Augsburg Commentaries on the New Testament
AOT	H.F.D. Sparks (ed.), *The Apocryphal Old Testament* (Oxford: Clarendon Press, 1984)
Aug	*Augustinianum*
AUSS	*Andrews University Seminary Studies*
AUSSDS	Andrews University Seminary Studies Dissertation Series
BAGD	Walter Bauer, William F. Arndt, F. William Gingrich and Frederick W. Danker, *A Greek–English Lexicon of the New Testament and Other Early Christian Literature* (Chicago: University of Chicago Press, 2nd edn, 1958)
BASOR	*Bulletin of the American Schools of Oriental Research*
BETL	Bibliotheca ephemeridum theologicarum lovaniensium
Bib	*Biblica*
BJRL	*Bulletin of the John Rylands University Library of Manchester*
BK	*Bibel und Kirche*
BKAT	Biblischer Kommentar: Altes Testament
BNTC	Black's New Testament Commentaries
BR	*Bible Review*
BSac	*Bibliotheca Sacra*
BT	*The Bible Translator*
BZAW	Beihefte zur *ZAW*
CBCNEB	Cambridge Bible Commentaries on the New English Bible
CBQ	*Catholic Biblical Quarterly*
CD	Cairo (Genizah text of the) *Dasmascus* (Document)
CNT	Commentaire du Nouveau Testament
CTA	A. Herdner (ed.), *Corpus des tablettes en cunéiformes alphabétiques découvertes à Ras Shamra–Ugarit de 1929 à 1939* (Paris: Imprimerie nationale Geuthner, 1963)
CTM	*Concordia Theological Monthly*
CurTM	*Currents in Theology and Mission*
ETL	*Ephemerides theologicae lovanienses*
EvQ	*Evangelical Quarterly*
ExpTim	*Expository Times*
FRLANT	Forschungen zur Religion und Literatur des Alten und Neuen Testaments

GNB	Good News Bible
GNS	Good News Studies
HDR	Harvard Dissertations in Religion
HNT	Handbuch zum Neuen Testament
HNTC	Harper's NT Commentaries
HR	*History of Religions*
HSM	Harvard Semitic Monographs
HTR	*Harvard Theological Review*
IB	*Interpreter's Bible*
IBS	*Irish Biblical Studies*
ICC	International Critical Commentary
Int	*Interpretation*
JBL	*Journal of Biblical Literature*
JETS	*Journal of the Evangelical Theological Society*
JITC	*Journal of the Interdenominational Theological Center*
JRT	*Journal of Religious Thought*
JSNT	*Journal for the Study of the New Testament*
JSNTSup	*Journal for the Study of the New Testament*, Supplement Series
JSPSup	*Journal for the Study of the Pseudepigrapha*, Supplement Series
JTC	*Journal for Theology and the Church*
LCL	Loeb Classical Library
MeyerK	H.A.W. Meyer (ed.), *Kritisch-exegetischer Kommentar über das Neue Testament*
MNTC	Moffatt NT Commentary
NAB	*New American Bible*
NASB	*New American Standard Bible*
NCB	New Century Bible
NIBC	New International Biblical Commentary
NICNT	New International Commentary on the New Testament
NIV	New International Version
NJB	*New Jerusalem Bible*
NorTT	*Norsk Teologisk Tidsskrift*
NovT	*Novum Testamentum*
NRSV	New Revised Standard Version
NRT	*La nouvelle revue théologique*
NTD	Das Neue Testament Deutsch
NTS	*New Testament Studies*
OGIS	W. Dittenberger (ed.), *Orientis graeci inscriptiones selectae* (Leipzig, 1903–1905)
OTL	Old Testament Library
OTP	James Charlesworth (ed.), *Old Testament Pseudepigrapha*
OTS	*Oudtestamentische Studiën*
RB	*Revue biblique*

REB	Revised English Bible
RelSRev	*Religious Studies Review*
ResQ	*Restoration Quarterly*
RevExp	*Review and Expositor*
RHPR	*Revue d'histoire et de philosophie religieuses*
RHR	*Revue de l'histoire des religions*
SBLMS	SBL Monograph Series
SBT	Studies in Biblical Theology
ScEs	*Science et esprit*
SEG	*Supplementum epigraphicum graecum* (Leiden, 1923–)
SJT	*Scottish Journal of Theology*
SNT	Studien zum Neuen Testament
SNTSMS	Society for New Testament Studies Monograph Series
SR	*Studies in Religion/Sciences religieuses*
ST	*Studia theologica*
St Cl.	*Studi Clasice*
SUNT	Studien zur Umwelt des Neuen Testaments
TBT	*The Bible Today*
TDNT	Gerhard Kittel and Gerhard Friedrich (eds.), *Theological Dictionary of the New Testament* (trans. Geoffrey W. Bromiley; 10 vols.; Grand Rapids: Eerdmans, 1964–)
TNTC	Tyndale New Testament Commentaries
TPINTC	Trinity Press International New Testament Commentaries
TS	*Theological Studies*
TU	Texte und Untersuchungen
WBC	Word Biblical Commentary
WMANT	Wissenschaftliche Monographien zum Alten und Neuen Testament
WTJ	*Westminster Theological Journal*
ZNW	*Zeitschrift für die neutestamentliche Wissenschaft*

Chapter 1

INTRODUCTION

This study of the Christology of the book of Revelation examines the major christological images in the book, the 'one like a son of man', the Lamb and the Divine Warrior, in order to ascertain how these images functioned in the life of the community. It will demonstrate that, for the first readers of this evocative writing, the 'one like a son of man' functioned primarily in a pastoral role; the Lamb performed various functions (e.g. pastor, role model, liberator); the Divine Warrior functioned primarily as an eschatological judge. The first two images related directly to the churches by promising fellowship with God Almighty and Christ in the New Jerusalem. The Divine Warrior, conversely, judges the worldly institutions that John believed had oppressed the church, thereby vindicating the community and assuring it of its righteousness. While these christological images varied in function to some degree, this study will demonstrate that they are also interrelated. This study employs historical criticism and insights from the sociology of knowledge.

1. *Literary Genre*

Before broaching the Christology of Revelation, a few fundamental matters need to be discussed. The book of Revelation is an apocalypse. Currently, no consensus exists as to what constitutes an apocalypse or how to define apocalypticism.[1] No single definition is all-encompassing or

1. E.g. the different definitions of the genre in P. Vielhauer, 'Introduction to Apocalypses and Related Studies', in E. Hennecke, W. Schneemelcher and R.M. Wilson (eds.), *New Testament Apocrypha* (2 vols.; Philadelphia: Westminster Press, 1965), II, pp. 579-609; E. Käsemann, 'On the Topic of Primitive Christian Apocalyptic', in R.W. Funk (ed.), *Apocalypticism* (JTC, 6; New York: Herder & Herder, 1969), p. 100 n. 1; C.C. Rowland, *The Open Heaven* (New York: Crossroad, 1982),

suitable for every apocalypse. In this study, a definition that has gained a measure of international acceptance is used. However, this definition is adopted with the understanding that it is provisional even for those who have employed it for over a decade.[2] It is derived from the Society of Biblical Literature (SBL) Genre Project's Apocalypse Group: an apocalypse is

> a genre of revelatory literature with a narrative framework, in which a revelation is mediated by an otherworldly being to a human recipient, disclosing a transcendent reality which is both temporal, insofar as it envisages eschatological salvation, and spatial insofar as it involves another, supernatural world.[3]

Hellholm expands this definition by including social function. It is not enough to visualize apocalypticism and apocalypses in the abstract. Apocalypticism always reflects 'a group in crisis' undergoing persecution or impending doom. Those involved are not interested simply in receiving revelations from the supernatural world about transcendent reality and eschatological salvation. They are looking for 'exhortation and/or consolation' for a present emergency.[4]

Hellholm's point has value since so many apocalypses written between the return from Babylon and the Bar Kochba War appear on the surface to reflect a social crisis of some kind. For example, Daniel reflects the tensions between Antiochus Epiphanes and the Maccabean-led revolt; *4 Ezra* the destruction of Jerusalem and its theological implications for international Jewry. Nevertheless, caution is required in expanding the basic definition given above. Yarbro Collins, for

pp. 9-72, esp. pp. 9-11; E.P. Sanders, 'The Genre of Palestinian Jewish Apocalypses', in D. Hellholm (ed.), *Apocalypticism in the Mediterranean World and the Near East* (Tübingen: J.C.B. Mohr [Paul Siebeck], 1983), pp. 447-59; D. Hellholm, 'The Problem of Apocalyptic Genre and the Apocalypse to John', *Semeia* 36 (1986), pp. 13-64; D.E. Aune, 'The Apocalypse of John and the Problem of Genre', *Semeia* 36 (1986), pp. 65-96; L. Morris, *The Book of Revelation: An Introduction and Commentary* (TNTC; Grand Rapids: Eerdmans, 2nd edn, 1987), pp. 24-27; P.E. Hughes, *The Book of Revelation* (Leicester: Inter-Varsity Press; Grand Rapids: Eerdmans, 1990), pp. 7-11. For a historical overview of the scholarly debate, see R.E. Sturm, 'Defining the Word "Apocalyptic": A Problem in Biblical Criticism', in J. Marcus and M.L. Soards (eds.), *Apocalyptic and the New Testament: Essays in Honor of J. Louis Martyn* (JSNTSup, 24; Sheffield: JSOT Press, 1989), pp. 17-48.

2. See Sanders, Aune and Hellholm in n. 1 above.
3. J.J. Collins, 'Introduction', *Semeia* 14 (1979), p. 9.
4. Hellholm, 'The Problem of Apocalyptic Genre', p. 27; see also pp. 18-26.

example, modifies Hellholm and argues that the apocalyptic world-view may not necessarily involve anything more than a *perception* of reality. She argues that not all apocalypses were written to and for communities. Some might have been produced by individuals for their own unique purposes. In particular, she argues that the author of Revelation might have only perceived an empire-wide crisis that did not actually exist.[5]

Larkin, espousing a similar position, argues that exegetes must prove that apocalypses reflect a group's social setting and not merely take it for granted. She also insists that some apocalyptic literature may come from lone individuals and may not reflect communal perspectives.[6]

The points that Yarbro Collins and Larkin make are important and must be taken into consideration, but, in regard to Revelation, it does not seem that John wrote simply for himself. If the witness of the book is to be given due consideration, the letters to the seven churches of Asia, recorded in Revelation 2–3, demonstrate a familiarity with the social context of each church and require a community audience. Each letter has a distinctive message, often mentioning specific persons (e.g. 2.13, 20) or details (e.g. 2.6, 14) in order to convince the recipients that the Lord of the cosmos knows their individual situations and also knows what they must do to improve them.

If John's perception had been vastly different from his audience/readers, it is doubtful whether the book would have survived. Bauckham correctly notes that Revelation is a unique apocalypse in that it is also a 'circular letter'. By this, Bauckham means that the letters function both individually and collectively as introduction to the entire book: each of the seven letters provides a different introduction to the entire book, probably arranged according to the 'circuit' John took when he travelled to the churches, while simultaneously they collectively provide an introduction to the broader social setting of Asian

5. A. Yarbro Collins, *Early Christian Apocalypticism* (Atlanta: Scholars Press), pp. 1-11; cf. L.L. Thompson, *The Book of Revelation: Apocalypse and Empire* (New York: Oxford University Press, 1990), pp. 1-34, 186-201. For a critique of Yarbro Collins, see J.C. Wilson, 'The Problem of the Domitianic Date of Revelation', *NTS* (1993), pp. 587-605, esp. p. 597 n. 49.

6. K.J.A. Larkin, *The Eschatology of Second Zechariah* (Contributions to Biblical Exegesis and Theology, 6; Kampen: Kok, 1993), pp. 9-52.

Christianity. 'The special character of a letter ... is that it enables the writer to specify those to whom he or she is writing and to address their situation as specifically as he or she may wish.'[7] I agree in general with Bauckham concerning the function of the letters in Revelation.

The purpose of each letter was to show each church what it must do in order to enter the New Jerusalem. Further, the letters conveyed to the churches 'how the issues in their local context belong to, and must be understood in the light of, God's cosmic battle against evil and his eschatological purpose of establishing his kingdom'.[8] I agree and shall argue in Part I of this study that, in general, each letter tells each congregation what it needs to do in order to survive the eschatological events described in Revelation 4–19. Specifically, the promises to the conquerors at the end of each letter (2.7, 11, 17, 26-28; 3.5, 12, 21) are fulfilled in Rev. 20.1–22.21. References to conquering recur throughout the apocalyptic sections (e.g. 5.5; 6.2; 12.11; 15.2; 17.14; 21.7). In this manner, Revelation is a circular letter that speaks to both the specific and the general; the present situation and the future salvation.

Ancient Jewish and Christian apocalypses exhibited some or all of the following five general characteristics. First, they reflected crisis situations, either perceived or real, in which an oppressed group looks to God for liberation. The degree of the perception of the oppression varies and thus also the intensity of the struggle and the projected outcome. Secondly, they were pseudonymous. The writer composed the work under the name of an outstanding figure from the past, such as Noah or Enoch, giving the writing a measure of prestige and also 'enabling' the writing to 'predict' the future. Such prophecy-after-the-fact is called *ex eventu* prophecy or *vaticinia ex eventu*. The aim of *ex eventu* prophecy

7. R. Bauckham, *The Theology of the Book of Revelation* (NTT; Cambridge: Cambridge University Press, 1993), p. 13. See also, G.A. Krodel, *Revelation* (ACNT; Minneapolis: Augsburg, 1989), pp. 51-61; R.W. Wall, *Revelation* (NIBC, 18; Peabody, MA: Hendrickson, 1991), p. 10 n. 6; E. Schüssler Fiorenza, *Revelation: Vision of a Just World* (Edinburgh: T. & T. Clark, 1993), pp. 23-26.

8. Bauckham, *Theology*, p. 15. While I agree in general with Bauckham on the function of the letters, I disagree with him on how the letters relate to the apocalyptic visions. See my review in *Journal of the Interdenominational Theological Center (JITC)* 21 (1993–94), pp. 172-74.

was to assure the reader/hearer that the book's other predictions would come true, also. Hopefully, this assurance would give the reader/hearer the courage to remain true to his/her religious convictions. This is an attempt to retain persons within the community, what sociologists often term a 'maintenance strategy.' Thirdly, these books were often apocryphal: supposedly they had been hidden and had only been found immediately prior to the fulfilment of their final prophecies. This characteristic often gave apocalyptic literature a sense of urgency. Fourthly, they divided time into two epochs. The first period was ruled by evil forces, the second by God. The second era sometimes included a new creation and/or a purification of the first creation. The second period often had a final judgment that selected some persons to enter a glorious new age while casting others into eternal torment. This selection often contained deterministic elements in order to assure the chosen/oppressed of their ultimate salvation. Some sociologists refer to this as 'nihilation,' the elimination of all that is not good. Fifthly, most apocalypses contained either an otherworldly journey (e.g. *1 En.* 1–36; 1QS 3–4; *Sib. Or.* 2.34-55, 149-347) or a survey of history (*1 En.* 85–90; *2 Baruch*; *The Shepherd of Hermas*). The *Apocalypse of Abraham* (*Apoc. Abr.*) is the only known apocalypse that contained both the heavenly journey and the survey of history. Again, most apocalypses do not have all these characteristics.

It is important to note that the book of Revelation, though an apocalypse, lacks some of these distinctive apocalyptic characteristics. Unlike most apocalypses, it is not pseudonymous. The author does not appeal to the authority of an ancient worthy but is an authority figure in his own right who speaks as a contemporary to his readers/hearers in the Asian churches. The author sees himself as a prophet in the tradition of Isaiah, Ezekiel, Daniel, Enoch and others (1.3; 22.7-10). He also believes in past prophecies that will be fulfilled at a future date. Furthermore, Revelation contains little *ex eventu* prophecy. It does not predict major events that appear to have occurred already. Finally, as we have noted briefly above, Revelation is a circular letter. To the best of our knowledge, it is the only letter in the apocalyptic genre from early Jewish/early Christian times. As a result, although other Jewish and Christian apocalypses can enhance our understanding of the apocalyptic genre, the book of Revelation must be studied on its own terms. Comparisons with other apocalypses can assist our investigation, but none must be used as determinative for an interpretation of Revelation.

2. *The Social Setting of the Book of Revelation*[9]

a. *Christianity in the First-Century* CE *Roman Empire*

First-century CE Christian writers described the relations between Christians and pagans, on one front, and Jews, on another, in several early Christian writings. While these writings show that Christians in different contexts and times had different experiences, they also report that many of these experiences were negative and that in many places Christians were held in low esteem (e.g. Acts 5.17-31; 8.1-3; 1 Thess. 2.14-16; Gal. 1.13-14; cf. Acts 9.1-2; Heb. 10.32-39).

First and foremost, several writers record that Christians suffered simply because they were Christians, that is, because of the name 'Christ' that they confessed and not because of any criminal act. For example, Mt. 10.17-23 describes pagan and Jewish repression of Christians διὰ τὸ ὄνομά (see also Lk. 21.12). Mt. 24.9, Jn 15.21, Acts 5.41 and 1 Pet. 4.14, to identify but a few, follow suit. While the scholarly consensus is that Matthew and Luke used common sources, most scholars would argue that this is not the case with the other writings. This suggests that, in first-century Roman society, many Christians lived in an environment that was generally unfriendly, a context where the very names 'Christ' or 'Christian' themselves aroused ill feelings among their neighbors.

Moreover, pagan and Jewish harassment was felt so deeply by some Christians that some developed a rationale for Christian suffering (e.g. Phil. 1.12-14; Jas 1.2-3; Heb. 12.3; 1 Pet. 1.6-7; 4.12; Rev. 7.14). Others went further and related Christ's suffering to their own experiences (e.g. Jn 15.18; 1 Pet. 4.13; Rev. 5.9-10). In some instances, Christians felt ostracized by the general society and frequently placed their local problems on a cosmic scale (e.g. Jn 1.9-10; Acts 24.5; 28.22; Eph. 6.12; 1 Pet. 5.9; 1 Jn 3.13; 5.1-5). Some Christians sought and expected an imminent end to their trials that would vindicate them (e.g. Mt. 10.23; 24.9-35; 2 Cor. 4.17; 1 Pet. 1.6-12; 4.7, 17; 5.10). In this regard, the writings of Paul (1 Thess. 2.14-16; 2 Cor. 4.17; cf. Gal.

9. The remainder of this chapter is an expansion of arguments put forth elsewhere ('On the Social Setting of the Revelation to John', *NTS* 44 [1998], pp. 232-56).

1.13-14) are particularly important for they give evidence of the repression of Christians at a time when many first-generation Christians were still alive. The other writings, usually dated between 65 and 100 CE, show that some Christians continued to experience harassment, suppression and ridicule throughout the century.[10]

Revelation dealt with some of the same issues in very similar ways. Asian Christians addressed in Revelation suffered because they confessed the name 'Christ' (e.g. 2.17; 3.5, 10, 12). The book related their sufferings to those of Christ (e.g. 1.5-6; 5.9-10; 7.14-17), thereby developing a rationale for Christian distress. Revelation also expected the oppression to end soon (e.g. 1.3; 3.10; 22.10, 12, 20). Finally, Revelation placed the plight of Asian Christians on a cosmic scale (chs. 4–19).

For our purposes, the most helpful parallels are between 1 Peter and Revelation. Both books were written to Christians in the same general area of the Roman Empire (1 Pet. 1.1; Rev. 1.4, 11) and reveal something of the social status of Christians in that region. Recent scholarly opinions date 1 Peter between 50 and 100 CE.[11] While we have yet to establish a date for Revelation, a brief examination of 1 Peter might enable us to understand better the social milieu to which both books spoke.

10. On the dates of the these other writings, see, for example, discussions in the following works: W. Marxsen, *Introduction to the New Testament* (Oxford: Basil Blackwell, 1968); W.G. Kümmel, *Introduction to the New Testament* (Nashville: Abingdon Press, rev. edn, 1975); H. Köster, *Introduction to the New Testament* (2 vols.; Philadelphia: Fortress Press, 1982); E.D. Freed, *The New Testament: A Critical Introduction* (Belmont, CA: Wadsworth Press, 1986); R.A. Spivey and D.M. Smith, *Anatomy of the New Testament* (Englewood Cliffs, NJ: Prentice–Hall, 5th edn, 1995).

11. Those who argue for a pre-70 date include J.N.D. Kelly, *A Commentary on the Epistles of Peter and Jude* (HNTC; New York: Harper & Row, 1969), pp. 27-30; D.G. Miller, *On This Rock: A Commentary on First Peter* (Pittsburgh: Pickwick Press, 1993), p. 40; W. Grudem, *1 Peter* (TNTC; Leicester: Inter-Varsity Press; Grand Rapids: Eerdmans, 1988), pp. 35-37. Those who argue for a post-70 date include F.W. Beare (ed.), *The First Epistle of Peter* (Oxford: Basil Blackwell, 2nd rev. edn, 1958), pp. 9-19; J.H. Elliott, *A Home for the Homeless* (Philadelphia: Fortress Press, 1981), pp. 78-84. L. Goppelt (*Erste Petrusbrief* [MeyerK; Göttingen: Vandenhoeck & Ruprecht, 1978], pp. 43, 62-65) and D.L. Balch (*Let Wives Be Submissive* [SBLMS, 26; Chico, CA: Scholars Press, 1981], pp. 137-38) are among those who date the book between 65 and 90 CE.

Moule has identified some helpful parallels between 1 Peter and Revelation.[12] Both books exhort their readers to remain steadfast (e.g. 1 Pet. 2.20; Rev. 2.2, 3.10). Both refer to the Christian community as a royal priesthood (1 Pet. 2.9; Rev. 1.6). Both works speak of witnesses who have suffered for the kingdom (1 Pet. 5.1-2; Rev. 1.9) and promise the faithful a στέφανος (1 Pet. 5.4; Rev. 2.10; 3.11). In both books, some have definitely experienced oppression (1 Pet. 4.12–5.11; Rev. 2.13), while others are under threat (1 Pet. 2.11–4.11; Rev. 2.10). At the very least, Moule has shown that 1 Peter and Revelation share a concern for the fidelity of the Christian community as well as the need by that community to remain true to its religious beliefs under duress. While fidelity describes the group's self-image, the appeal to remain faithful under social pressure says something about the general public's perception of the group, whatever other factors might be involved.

Most scholars now believe that 1 Peter provides no evidence of an official Roman general persecution of Christians but much evidence of harassment by local Asian community leaders, especially adherents of the imperial cult, as well as harassment by Jewish groups. They argue that this mistreatment of Christians was spasmodic and periodically escalated into very serious regional pogroms.[13] For example, Elliott[14] writes that the novelty of Christianity, coupled with its exclusive attitude, was at the foundation of the social denigration of 1 Peter's original readership. Because Christians kept to themselves, pagans knew little about their religion (1 Pet. 2.15-16), creating pagan suspicions and contempt for Christians. Eventually suspicion and contempt led to slander and reproach (1 Pet. 4.4, 14). As a result, Christians became sorrowful and fearful, owing to the public ridicule they had to endure (2.19-20; 3.14, 17; 5.9-10). Some Christians considered taking a more accommodating, less exclusive stance toward pagan society because of

12. C.F.D. Moule, 'The Nature and Purpose of I Peter', *NTS* 3 (1956–57), pp. 1-11.

13. Cf. B. Reicke, *The Epistles of James, Peter, and Jude* (AB, 37; Garden City, NY: Doubleday, 1964), pp. 69-75; E. Best (ed.), *I Peter* (NCB; London: Marshall, Morgan & Scott, 1971), pp. 36-39; P.H. Davids, *The First Epistle of Peter* (Grand Rapids: Eerdmans, 1990), pp. 7-9; P. Perkins, *First and Second Peter, James, and Jude* (Interpretation; Atlanta: John Knox Press, 1995), pp. 15-16; E.G. Selwyn, *The First Epistle of St. Peter* (Grand Rapids: Baker Book House, 1981 [repr. 1947 edn]), pp. 52-56; Miller, *Rock*, p. 35; Balch, *Wives Be Submissive*, pp. 137-38; Moule, 'Purpose of I Peter', pp. 1-11; Kelly, *Peter and Jude*, pp. 27-30.

14. Elliott, *Home*, pp. 78-84.

their duress (1.14, 18; 2.11; 4.1-4). Elliott also argues that many of these Christians were immigrants.[15] If he is correct, some of the repression which they experienced might have been expressions of cultural superiority. I find Elliott's arguments generally persuasive, and with him I date 1 Peter between 73 and 92 CE, the middle Flavian years, because the book reflects a period when Christianity is emerging as a movement distinct from Judaism. While 1 Peter remains open to both Jews and Gentiles, it takes pains to reinterpret Judaism. These features reflect the context of the Christian community during the latter decades of the first century CE.

Revelation addresses similar issues. Indeed, one of the key issues was the manner in which the Christian community should relate to the imperial cult, symbolized by the beast from the land in Revelation 13.[16] Price argues that there was no Christian mechanism for showing respect to the emperor because Christianity had no role for sacrifice in its rituals. Conversely, adherents of the imperial cult expected some sign of reverence for the emperor that approximated sacrifice. At this point, Christian practice and pagan expectations caused tensions to the social detriment of Christians. Pagans would have pressured the Christians to be less exclusive and become more accommodating to ancient regional religio-political customs.[17] I concur with Price and will discuss it in more detail later. At this point, it is necessary to point out ways in which Revelation itself lends credence to Price's reconstruction. The letters in Revelation 2–3 tell us that accommodation, complacency and other forms of religious laxity were real issues within some of these congregations. Moreover, the apocalyptic visions in Revelation 4–19 relate how suspicion, contempt, slander and reproach (e.g. Rev. 3.2-3, 14-22; cf. 1 Pet. 2.15-16; 4.14) have escalated to the deaths of some Christians (e.g. Rev. 2.10-13; 6.9-11; 7.14; 16.6; 17.6; cf. 1 Pet. 1.6-7; 3.16; 4.4, 12, 16).[18] As with 1 Peter, there is no evidence that this was an official Roman imperial policy. Rather, it appears that John placed a regional oppression on a worldwide plane.

15. Elliott, *Home*, pp. 21-58.

16. S.R.F. Price, *Rituals and Power: The Roman Imperial Cult in Asia Minor* (Cambridge: Cambridge University Press, 1984), pp. 197-98; see also pp. 123-26.

17. Price, *Rituals*, pp. 220-23.

18. Price, *Rituals*, p. 197; see also pp. 78-100.

A second front was the relationship between Christians and Jewish groups. Both sides appealed to the same ancient traditions, yet in strikingly different ways. Unlike the pagans, the Jews disliked the Christians *because they understood them.* It was to the advantage of Judaism to distance itself from the Christian movement, a topic that will be fully dealt with at a later point in this chapter.

In sum, many Christian groups experienced ridicule, harassment and oppression throughout the first century CE. 1 Peter and Revelation provide evidence of this same attitude toward Christians in the Roman province of Asia in the latter decades of the first century CE.

b. *Dating Revelation*

For most of this century, biblical scholars have generally argued that the book of Revelation was written during the reign of Domitian and that Domitian instituted an empire-wide persecution of Christians.[19] Most exegetes who espouse this position have taken their cue from Irenaeus.

Irenaeus, who wrote c. 190–200 CE, is the earliest extant witness to the date of Revelation. He writes that the book was written 'near the end of Domitian's reign' (*Adv. Haer.* 5.30.3).[20] Domitian was Roman emperor from 81–96 CE. Several commentators argue that the Domitianic date is correct because, during Domitian's reign, the titles 'Savior' and 'Benefactor' and Roman claims to divine honors were applied to the emperor more frequently. During this time, there would have

19. E.g. M. Kiddle, *The Revelation of St. John* (MNTC; London: Hodder & Stoughton, 1940), pp. xxxix-xl; T.F. Glasson, *The Revelation of John* (CBCNEB; Cambridge: Cambridge University Press, 1965), pp. 6-9; G.E. Ladd, *A Commentary on the Revelation of John* (Grand Rapids: Eerdmans, 1972), p. 8; Kümmel, *Introduction to the New Testament*, pp. 458-62, 466-69; R.H. Mounce, *The Book of Revelation* (NICNT, 17; Grand Rapids: Eerdmans, 1977), pp. 32-35. Cf. Price, *Rituals*, pp. 197-98.

20. Οὐδὲ γὰρ πρὸ πολλοῦ χρόνου ἑωράθη, ἀλλὰ σχεδὸν ἐπὶ τῆς ἡμετέρᾶς γενεᾶς, πρὸς τῷ τέλει τῆς Δομετιανοῦ ἀρχῆς (*Neque enim ante multum temporis visum est, sed pene sub nostro saeculo ad finem Domitiani imperii* [*PG* 7:2, 1208]). See also Clement of Alexandria (c. 150–c. 215), *Quis Dives Salvetur?* 42; Victorinus (third century CE), *Apoc.* 10.11; 17.10; Origen (c. 185–c. 255), *In Matthaeum* 16.6; Jerome (c. 342–420), *De vir. illus.* 9; Eusebius (c. 260–c. 340), *H. E.* 3.18-25, whose primary sources were Irenaeus and Clement.

been considerable social pressure for Christians to conform to traditional Asian religio-political practices. Such pressures might have led some Christians to consider a more accommodating stance to regional religio-political traditions. Along these lines, some exegetes postulate that Christian complacency and compromise toward the imperial cult also contributed to the writing of Revelation.[21]

Others add that the use of 'Babylon' as a code name for Rome is evidence of a Domitianic date for Revelation. They note that *4 Ezra*, *2 Baruch*, *Sibylline Oracles* 5 and 1 Peter all employ 'Babylon' as a code name for Rome. More recent scholarly opinions date *4 Ezra*, *2 Baruch* and *Sibylline Oracles* 5, between 100 and 120 CE; 1 Peter, between 64 and 100 CE.[22] Thus, it is argued that the use of 'Babylon' as a code name for Rome in Revelation reflects a late first century CE development. Like the Babylon of old, Rome destroyed the Temple and the city of Jerusalem itself. Many Jews quickly made the connection between the two events. Yarbro Collins notes, 'This designation [for Rome] could not have arisen in Judaism prior to the destruction of the temple, when priests offered sacrifices for the well-being of Rome and its emperors.'[23] Price suggests that if the Domitianic date is correct, it corresponds to the date of the establishment of the imperial cult at Ephesus, an event that involved the entire province, as attested by the series of dedications by numerous cities. Such an event would have eventually 'led to unusually great pressure on the Christians for conformity'.[24]

21. E.g. R.H. Charles, *A Critical and Exegetical Comentary on the Book of Revelation of St. John* (2 vols.; ICC; New York: Charles Scribner's Sons, 1920), I, pp. 43-47; J.P.M. Sweet, *Revelation* (TPINTC; London: SCM Press, 1979), pp. 21-35.

22. See J.H. Charlesworth (ed.), *The Old Testament Pseudepigrapha* (2 vols.; Garden City, NY: Doubleday, 1983–85), I, pp. 390, 520, 615-17, and J.J. Collins, *The Apocalyptic Imagination* (New York: Crossroad, 1989), pp. 155-86 on the Jewish apocalypses; on 1 Peter, see n. 11 above.

23. A. Yarbro Collins, *Crisis and Catharsis: The Power of the Apocalypse* (Philadelphia: Westminster Press, 1984), pp. 57-58; see also Krodel, *Revelation*, p. 63; M.E. Boring, *Revelation* (Interpretation Commentary; Louisville, KY: Westminster/John Knox Press, 1989), pp. 10-12.

24. Price, *Rituals*, p. 198.

In addition, Rev. 13.3 and 17.9-11 have often been used as starting points to date the book.[25] They are examples of the *Nero redivivus* myth. Rev. 13.3 is a reference to Nero's suicide and helps the reader to identify Nero in Rev. 17.9-11.[26] Revelation 17.9-11 reads,

> Here is the mind which has wisdom: The seven heads are seven mountains upon which the woman sits. They also are seven kings. Five have fallen, one is, another has yet to appear and whenever he appears it is necessary for him to remain a brief time. And the beast who was and is not, he is the eighth and is from the seven and he goes to destruction.

The seven mountains refer to the seven hills of Rome. Roman writers often referred to Rome in this manner.[27] Do these verses refer to Roman emperors or do they refer to a succession of kingdoms (e.g. Assyria, Babylonia, Persia, Greece, Rome), with Rome being the current world power?

I believe the seven kings symbolize the imperial line because the passage refers to kings, not kingdoms. If this imagery does refer to kings/emperors, should one begin counting with Julius Caesar, or Augustus Caesar (the first true emperor) or Caligula, who was the first emperor to insist that his statue be worshiped? Perhaps, owing to the complex nature of this question, the current scholarly trend is not to count the emperors at all, but to view seven as a symbolic number here as elsewhere in Revelation. According to this viewpoint, 'seven emperors' represents the entire imperial line whatever the actual number might be. If seven is used symbolically in 17.9-11, it would connote completeness, because seven is the number of completeness in Revelation (e.g. 1.4-20; 4.5; 5.1, 6; 8.2; 15.1). Krodel writes,

25. See, for example, Yarbro Collins, *Crisis*, pp. 58-64, who accepts a Domitianic date; A.A. Bell, Jr, who accepts a c. 68 date ('The Date of John's Apocalypse: The Evidence of Some Roman Historians Reconsidered', *NTS* 25 [1978], pp. 93-102).

26. On the *Nero redivivus* myth, see R. Bauckham, *The Climax of Prophecy* (Edinburgh: T. & T. Clark, 1993), pp. 384-452 (see my review in *EvQ* 68 [1996], pp. 168-71); cf. G.B. Caird, *The Revelation of St. John the Divine* (HNTC; New York: Harper & Row, 1966), pp. 174-77; Sweet, *Revelation*, pp. 206-13, 255-59; E. Schüssler Fiorenza, *Revelation: Vision of a Just World* (Edinburgh: T. & T. Clark, 1993), pp. 83-84, 96-98; Wall, *Revelation*, pp. 167-69.

27. E.g. Virgil, *Aeneid* 6.781-84; Martial 4.64.11-12; Ovid, *Tristia* 1.5.69-70.

> When he (John) identifies the Antichrist as an eighth, then he suggests that the Antichrist will be someone so novel in evil as to signal a new beginning. But on the other hand he belonged to the seven, which means that the evil can already be detected in the imperial cult of Asia Minor.[28]

Many who interpret seven literally in 17.9-11 usually count Augustus, Tiberius, Gaius (Caligula), Claudius, Nero, then omit Galba, Otho and Vitellius, and continue with Vespasian, Titus and end with Domitian as the eighth.[29] Regardless of whether one interprets Rev. 17.9-11 symbolically or literally, the passage is one of the few examples of *ex eventu* prophecy in the book.

The passage itself suggests a symbolic interpretation. Seven heads represent seven mountains that in turn represent seven rulers. This is pure symbol. In the real world, heads and mountains and rulers have no natural connection. John created the connection in order to communicate a specific message to his original audience. Quite possibly, Revelation 17 employs seven as a symbol and also in some literal sense as a manifestation of evil. It is clear from the use of the seven heads, seven mountains and seven rulers that the Roman Empire represents the power of Satan in the world for John. If Revelation employs the number seven in Rev. 17.9-11 both symbolically and literally, which occurs often in apocalyptic writings, it may not be possible to determine the date of the writing of this book solely upon this passage, as some have suggested.[30]

28. Krodel, *Revelation*, p. 296, see also 297-98; for similar views, see Caird, *Revelation*, pp. 216-19; Mounce, *Revelation*, pp. 313-16; Morris, *Revelation*, pp. 196-207; Boring, *Revelation*, pp. 180-83; Hughes, *Revelation*, pp. 185-86; Wall, *Revelation*, pp. 207-208; cf. A. Yarbro Collins, *The Apocalypse* (NTM, 22; Wilmington, DE: Michael Glazier, 1979), pp. 121-22; H. Kraft, *Die Offenbarung des Johannes* (HNT, 16a; Tübingen: J.C.B. Mohr, 1974), pp. 220-23; Rowland, *Open Heaven*, p. 405. For alternative approaches, see G.E. Ladd, *A Commentary on the Revelation of John* (Grand Rapids: Eerdmans, 1972), pp. 228-31; J.M. Ford, *Revelation* (AB, 38; Garden City, NY: Doubleday, 1975), pp. 289-91; Schüssler Fiorenza, *Vision*, pp. 96-98. Ford, Mounce, Caird and Ladd have especially informative discussions of this topic. For arguments for a pre-70 CE date of Revelation, see J.A.T. Robinson, *Redating the New Testament* (London: SCM Press, 1976), pp. 230-53; Bell, 'The Date', pp. 93-102; J.C. Wilson, 'The Problem of the Domitianic Date', pp. 587-605. To date, Wilson has the most refined statement of this position.

29. Bell and Wilson (see preceding note) do not omit Galba, Otho and Vitellius.

30. In their attempts to date Revelation, Sweet and Rowland, for example, both examine Rev. 17.9-11 but reach different conclusions. Sweet accepts a Domitianic

I date Revelation c. 95 CE. First, the use of 'Babylon' as a code name for Rome has parallels in *4 Ezra*, *2 Baruch*, *Sibylline Oracles* 5 and 1 Peter, reflecting a late first-century CE development. I believe this is the strongest argument for dating Revelation. Additionally, I have dated 1 Peter between 73 and 92 CE. 1 Peter takes a more positive role toward the state than Revelation. Thus, since they were written to the same general area, it is more probable that Revelation reflects a later, more intense time for Christians (cf. 1 Pet. 2.13-14, 17 and Rev. 16.1–18.24). Finally, Price states that a Domitianic date would coincide with the establishment of the imperial cult at Ephesus which involved the participation of the entire province. The institution of the cult at this time might have led to increased social pressure upon Christians to conform to Asian religious customs. For these reasons, I date Revelation c. 95.

Church fathers are important witnesses; however, since Irenaeus is the earliest witness, and he is at least two generations removed from John, I consider the patristic testimonies supplementary external witnesses. Moreover, while Revelation 13 and 17 must be examined when attempting to date Revelation, the symbolic nature of these chapters can lead to conflicting reasonable conclusions. Until scholarship can obtain a better understanding of these passages, their usefulness for dating Revelation will continue to be limited.

c. *Persecution: Rhetoric or Reality?*

If, as Revelation 17 seems to stress, the power of Rome is clearly in view, are we to assume that Revelation was written to Christians facing persecution? If so, can this be squared with a Domitianic dating? Although they differ in emphases, several scholars have recently questioned the traditional depiction of Domitian as a persecutor of the Christian Church.[31] Others note that the letters speak of compromise, complacency and/or accommodation as the threats to community and say little about persecution or oppression by the Roman state.[32]

date (*Revelation*, pp. 21-35), and Rowland argues for a date in the late 60s (*Open Heaven*, pp. 405-406).

31. E.g. L.L. Thompson, *The Book of Revelation: Apocalypse and Empire* (New York: Oxford University Press, 1990), pp. 95-197. Others who question the traditional view of Domitian include Yarbro Collins, *Crisis*, pp. 54-110; Krodel, *Revelation*, pp. 35-39; Wall, *Revelation*, pp. 10-12.

32. E.g. Charles, *Revelation*, I, pp. 43-47; Sweet, *Revelation*, pp. 26-27; Bauckham, *Theology*, pp. 12-17.

Classicists have long questioned the traditional view of New Testament scholars that Domitian was an 'arch persecutor' of the Church. H.W. Pleket, for example, argued in 1961 that Domitian was loved in the provinces because he attempted to curb economic exploitation by Roman provincial governors. While the provincials held Domitian in favor, the provincial governors, who owed much to their senatorial benefactors, disliked Domitian because he hampered their economic and political agendas. Pleket concludes that Domitian was not without his faults, but he was not a second Nero.[33]

Thompson, following the classicists, is representative of many current New Testament exegetes who argue that the depiction of Domitian as a persecutor of the Church and a 'second Nero' is inaccurate.[34] Thompson, who dates Revelation late in the reign of Domitian, makes the following main points: (1) the widely held negative impression of Domitian comes from anti-Flavian writers who sought the favor of Trajan and his successors and Trajan himself, who also used to argue that his imperial family was superior to the Flavians; (2) all epigraphic, numismatic, prosopographic and biographical data contemporary with Domitian depict him more fairly. These two points are distinct but inseparable for Thompson.

The official depiction of Domitian as an evil, incompetent ruler who arrogantly demanded that he be worshiped as *dominus et deus noster* comes primarily from Pliny the Younger (c. 60–c. 115), Tacitus (c. 55–c. 120) and Suetonius (c. 75–c. 135). This circle of friends and historians heavily influenced later Roman and Christian writers concerning Domitian (e.g. Dio Cassius, Juvenal, Philostratus, Eusebius). They portray Domitian as a cunning and devious ruler (e.g. Tacitus, *Agricola* 39, 43; Pliny, *Panegyric* 90.5-7; *Epistles* 1.12.6-8) who was both tyrannical

33. H.W. Pleket, 'Domitian, the Senate and the Provinces', *Mnemosyne* 14 (1961), pp. 296-315. I am indebted to the Revd Canon John Sweet of Cambridge University for directing me to Pleket (cf. Sweet, *Revelation*, pp. 26-27). See also D. Magie, *Roman Rule in Asia Minor to the End of the Third Century after Christ* (2 vols.; Princeton, NJ: Princeton University Press, 1950), I, pp. 566-92; B. Reicke, *The New Testament Era* (Philadelphia: Fortress Press, 1968), p. 272; B.W. Jones, *The Emperor Domitian* (London: Routledge, 1992), p. 114; Krodel, *Revelation*, p. 37.

34. Thompson was a member of the SBL seminar 'Reading the Apocalypse: The Intersection of Literary and Social Methods'. Other members of this seminar who concur with Thompson's position concerning the social setting include D.E. Aune and D.L. Barr.

and insane (e.g. Suetonius, *Domitian* 1.3; Pliny, *Panegyric* 48.3-5) and had a voracious sexual appetite (e.g. Suetonius, *Domitian* 1.1; 1.3; 22.1; Tacitus, *Histories* 4.2; 4.68; cf. *Agricola* 7). He was jealous of his father Vespasian and his brother Titus (e.g. Pliny, *Epistles* 4.9.2; *Titus* 9.3; Tacitus, *Histories* 4.5, 52, 86), was an unenlightened ruler who indiscriminately murdered political opponents and placed a financial strain upon the empire (e.g. Tacitus, *Germania* 37; Pliny, *Panegyric* 11.4; 76.5; 82.4; Suetonius, *Domitian* 4.1, 4; 5; 12.1, 14.1). Thompson claims that the negative depiction of Domitian came about because of later political and practical agendas. Pliny and Tacitus had political axes to grind against Domitian. While both men had good careers under Domitian, both had relatives and/or friends who were either exiled or executed by Domitian. Both felt their opportunities for advancement and freedom of expression were hampered by Domitian (Pliny, *Epistles* 3.11.3-4; 4.24.4-5; 7.27.14; *Panegyric* 95.3-4; Tacitus, *Agricola* 2–3, 44–45). Thus they wrote to discredit Domitian, and, at the same time, they contributed to the image of the new imperial family that Trajan promulgated.

Trajan proclaimed a 'new era' (beginning with Nerva) in order to legitimize his dynastic line and also to distinguish it from the Flavians. Trajan enlisted the services of Pliny, Tacitus and others to propagate this new era throughout the empire. Thompson writes,

> The opposing of Trajan and Domitian in a binary set serves overtly in Trajan's ideology of a new age as well as covertly in his praise. Newness requires a beginning and therefore a break with the past; such a break is constructed rhetorically through binary contrast.[35]

Agreeing with Pleket, Viscusi and other classicists, Thompson argues that Domitian was no more despotic an emperor than his predecessors, and that Jews and Christians were not singled out by Domitian for persecution but enjoyed the benefits of *pax Romana* as did other groups in Roman society.[36] Thus, he concludes that no actual crisis existed but only a tension between Christian expectations and reality, a tension within the 'social location' of the minds of Christians.[37]

35. Thompson, *Revelation*, p. 115.

36. Thompson, *Revelation*, pp. 95-115.

37. Thompson, *Revelation*, pp. 171-201. For reviews of Thompson, see A. Yarbro Collins, *JBL* 110 (1991), pp. 748-50; see also my own review in *JITC* 20 (1992–93), pp. 139-41.

Thompson vigorously challenges the traditional view of Domitian as arch persecutor: he notes that almost all epigraphic, numismatic, prosopographic and biographical data contemporary with Domitian throw this negative characterization into doubt. First and foremost, with Viscusi, he notes that there are no extant inscriptions, coins or medallions from the Domitianic period that refer to Domitian as *dominus et deus noster*.[38] Moreover, he notes that Quintilian (*Inst. Orat.* 10.1.91), Martial (2.2; 8.15, 78); Statius (*Silvae* 3.3.171; 4.1.34-39; 4.3.159) and Silius Italicus (*Punica* 3.607), who wrote *during* Domitian's reign, provide more positive views of Domitian. Further, Thompson notes that these same writers did not hesitate to criticize Domitian or his politics and did not suffer as a consequence (e.g. Quintilian, *Inst.Orat.* 12.1.40; Martial 1.8; 4.54.7), evidence that they almost certainly portray Domitian more accurately.

As helpful as this new perspective might be, especially Thompson's analysis of the socio-political setting for historical writing under Trajan, a closer examination of the classical texts themselves shows that Thompson's revisionist case is not as strong as it appears initially. First and foremost, it is possible that the work of Statius and Quintilian may have been biased toward Domitian, since both men found employment with help from Domitian, Quintilian as the tutor to Domitian's great-nephews, a fact that Thompson neglects to discuss. Moreover, Statius praises Domitian excessively in the same context that Thompson cites. Finally, Thompson cites Martial as an uncensored critique of Domitian; however, Martial does not make a single explicit reference to Domitian in the passages that Thompson has identified. Martial merely praises men who happen to be Domitian's opponents. Unless Domitian was the emotionally insecure emperor that Thompson argues *that he was not*, one could not imagine these passages angering him.

Examples from Statius, Quintilian and Martial themselves will demonstrate my points. In *Silvae* 4, 1, close to passages that Thompson cites, Statius writes concerning Domitian:

> In glory the emperor's robe of office joins the sixteen terms accomplished; the conqueror of Germany sheds splendour on the year he opens; he rises with the rising sun, with the mighty constellations, shining with great brilliance, more powerful than the star of early morning.

38. P. Viscusi, 'Studies on Domitian' (PhD dissertation; Ann Arbor: University Microfilms, 1973), p. 94.

This is not the type of objective, moderate rhetoric one might expect from an unbiased, dispassionate critic. Indeed, these words, at the very least, verge on describing Domitian as one worthy of divine honors. Thus, Statius clearly is not the detached observer that Thompson would have us believe.

One finds a similar pattern in the writings of Quintilian. While Quintilian does not employ *dominus et deus noster*, he describes Domitian as one worthy of divine honors twice in *Inst. Orat.* 4, preface, 2 and 5:

> But now Domitianus Augustus has entrusted me with the education of his sister's grandsons, and I should be undeserving of the honoùr conferred upon me by such divine [*caelestium*] appreciation...
>
> Assuredly therefore I may ask indulgence for doing what I omitted to do when I first entered on this task and calling to my aid all the gods and Himself [i.e. Domitian] before them all (for his power is unsurpassed and there is no deity that looks with such favor upon learning), beseeching him to inspire me with genius in proportion to the hopes that he has raised in me, to lend me propitious and ready aid and make me even such as he has believed me to be.[39]

Thompson's insistence that Domitian was not worshiped as 'our lord and god' may be strictly true, but it is equally true that Quintilian clearly sees him as worthy of divine honors, a detail that undermines, to some degree, Thompson's point.[40] Statius's comments are almost as grandiose. Indeed, it is possible that Domitian's benefaction caused Statius and Quintilian to speak of him so highly. Thus, with these two writers, two aspects of Thompson's revisionist program, that Domitian did not receive divine honors and that Statius and Quintillian were unbiased commentators, are found to be less than satisfactory.

Thompson also argued that Martial prospered during Domitian's reign, even though he criticized him. Thompson makes reference to two passages from Martial that refer positively to Paetus Thrasea, a political opponent of Domitian, as proof that Martial criticized Domitian and did

39. 'mili quoque profecto poterit ignosci, si, quod initio, quo primum hanc materiam inchoavi, non feceram, nunc omnes in auxilium deos ipsumque in primis, quo neque praesentius aliud nec studiis magis propitium numen est, invocem, ut, quantum nobis expectationis adiecit, tantum ingenii adspiret dexterque ac volens adsit et me qualem esse credidit faciat.'

40. This is a point that Thompson does not discuss in any detail (*Revelation*, pp. 95-115).

not suffer as a consequence. In my opinion, neither passage supports Thompson's case.

> In that you follow the maxims of great Thrasea and of Cato the perfect, and yet are willing to live, and rush not with unarmed breast upon drawn swords, you do, Decianus, what I would have you do. No hero to me is the man who, by easy shedding of his blood, purchases his fame; my hero is he who, without death, can win praise (1.8).

> Though thou wert richer than Crispus, more firm of soul than Thrasea's self, more refined even than sleek Melior, yet Lachesis addeth nought to her tale of wool ... (4.54).

Both passages are merely passing references to Thrasea and neither one directly mentions Domitian. These are not clear, definitive statements denigrating Domitian but positive statements about Thrasea. The praise of Thrasea and the criticism of Domitian are not necessarily mutually inclusive. Moreover, if Domitian were the enlightened leader whom Thompson proposes, one would think that Thompson would mention criticisms that explicitly mentioned Domitian. It is quite possible that Martial never had Domitian in mind at all. Indeed, again only if Domitian were the insecure megalomaniac that Thompson argues that *he is not* could we reasonably expect Domitian to find these statements offensive. I do not find these brief statements as strong evidence that Martial criticized Domitian and was not punished. Rather, they are evidence that Martial praised Domitian's political opponents and was not punished, but it is no more than that.

In sum, Statius and Quintilian's praise of Domitian might have been influenced by his benefaction and/or status as emperor, just as Trajan's sponsorship influenced Suetonius, Pliny and Tacitus's writings. Moreover, in one passage Statius compares Domitian to the sun, an expression very close to stating that Domitian was worthy of divine honors. Further, Quintilian spoke of Domitian in a manner that connoted one worthy of divine honors. Additionally, Martial's two passing references, which Thompson lists as criticisms, do not mention Domitian. Thus, the evidence is not as clear cut as Thompson argues. A more critical reading of the classical writers themselves might have led Thompson to different conclusions concerning the status of Christians under Domitian.

According to Krodel, Domitian could be heartless, but he was no more heartless when dealing with opponents than his predecessors or his successors. 'In short, there is no evidence that Christians in Asia

Minor had it any worse under Domitian than they had it before or after him.'[41] I agree with Krodel. More importantly, even if Domitian did not demand that he be referred to as 'our lord and god', it does not mean that no one deemed him worthy of divine honors. Indeed, in the Roman province of Asia, the social setting for the Revelation to John, provincials took seriously the worship of their rulers as persons divinely appointed to rule them. We shall return to Asian religiosity later.

I accept that there is no evidence that an empire-wide persecution of Christians occurred under Domitian. In this respect, the traditional view of Domitian as an 'arch-persecutor' of Christians must be revised. However, because an empire-wide persecution did not exist does not necessarily mean that there was not a limited, regional repression of Christians during this time period. Many scholars have shown that there is plenty of evidence for the enthusiastic promotion of the imperial cult in Roman Asia. Concurrently, the repression of persons who would not support this cult was a real possibility in the first century CE.[42]

Others have also pointed to the letters as proof that Revelation is not responding to a crisis of any type, arguing that the letters do not mention persecution or oppression but complacency, compromise and/or accommodation as the chief problems for the churches in Asia.[43] These commentators have assumed that, since the letters are in prose, they represent a more straightforward version of the apocalyptic visions. However, the relationship between the letters and the apocalyptic visions is somewhat more complex than that. Scobie has shown that there are few references to the social context in the letters but much about John's relationship to those congregations. In other words, if one reads the letters in order to obtain data concerning Roman Asian society

41. Krodel, *Revelation*, p. 38.

42. My forthcoming discussion in this chapter on 'Religious Factors in Asia' will attempt to demonstrate that the Christians' refusal to participate in the imperial cult resulted in Asian pagans repressing Asian Christians (cf. Price, *Rituals*, pp. 123-26, 197-98; D.A. DeSilva, 'The Social Setting of the Revelation to John: Conflicts Within, Fears Without', *WTJ* 54 [1992], pp. 273-302, esp. 289-91; also *idem*, 'The Revelation to John: A Case Study in Apocalyptic Propaganda and the Maintenance of Sectarian Identity', *Sociological Analysis* 53 [1992], pp. 375-95, esp. 378-81).

43. E.g. Charles, *Revelation*, II, pp. 43-47; Sweet, *Revelation*, pp. 26-27; Bauckham, *Theology*, pp. 12-17. It is on this point that Bauckham and I disagree concerning the role of the letters in the overall scheme of Revelation.

in general, one will not find much of that type of data.[44] I agree with Scobie. He explains succinctly and correctly why one finds little reference to pagan attitudes toward the church in Roman Asia in these letters: the purpose of the letters was to discuss the inner religious life of each of these churches, not the relationship between church and society in each situation.

The general function of the letters is to inform each church what it needs to do in order to become spiritually strong enough to endure the coming apocalyptic trials in order to 'enter the new Jerusalem.'[45] Many exegetes have presupposed, without proving, that the letters reflect the actual broader social context; the visions, apocalyptic projections upon the social context. However, these same exegetes have failed to note that *only one* of the letters (Rev. 2.8-11) discusses the relationship between Christians and non-Christians in Roman Asia. Rather, in general, the letters focus upon issues within each church in order to improve that church's spiritual well-being. On the other hand, the apocalyptic visions that dominate chs. 4–19, in general, speak to the role of the Christian community in a non-Christian world, explaining why the letters, in general, emphasize the problems of accommodation, laxity, complacency and other internal issues, issues that receive little attention, if any, in the apocalyptic visions. John presupposes that, if the churches correct their problems, they will be able to survive the apocalyptic trials and enter the New Jerusalem.

A closer examination of the letters will demonstrate my point. The letter to Smyrna (2.8-11) is the only letter that addresses the relationship of the church to a social entity outside itself. The other six comment upon internal issues (2.2-6; 2.14-16; 2.19-25; 3.2-4; 3.8-11; 3.15-20). If these letters had been written primarily to tell us something about the wider social milieu, why is it that only one letter does this? In fact, the letters provide only passing references to the wider social milieu. Those who argue against persecution or oppression[46] as a

44. C.H.H. Scobie, 'Local References in the Letters to the Seven Churches', *NTS* 39 (1993), pp. 606-24.

45. Bauckham, *Theology*, p. 14; see also DeSilva, 'Social Setting', pp. 282-96.

46. Josephine Ford makes a helpful distinction between persecution and oppression. She says persecution refers to an official state program of systematic and consistent discrimination and harassment, while oppression is an unofficial, localized crisis (SBL Seminar, Reading the Apocalypse: The Intersection of Literary and Social Methods, Philadelphia, PA, USA, 18 November 1995). I find this distinction

contributing social factor for Asian Christians have failed to note that the letters contain only one full comment (2.8-11) and two passing references (2.13; 3.8-10) to any external issues *and that all three passages refer to the repression of Christians*. They have also failed to note that the apocalyptic visions contain little or no references to Christian complacency, compromise and accommodation. The full comment, found in the letter to Smyrna, mentions tribulation, Jewish harassment, impending imprisonment and ends with an admonition to be faithful unto death (2.9-10). The letter to Pergamum mentions the death of Antipas, 'my witness' (ὁ μάρτυς μου [2.13]), and the letter to the Philadelphians mentions Jewish harassment and Christian endurance under pressure to recant religious beliefs (3.8-10).[47]

Thus, it is not that the letters made no reference to oppression, but rather that the *only* references to external matters were to oppression. These passing references are all the more important because they are among the few references to the wider social milieu. Indeed, writers often reveal more in passing than in explicit comments. This is not to say that compromise, complacency and accommodation to Asian religion and other internal issues played little or no role in the churches. Rather, they were internal concerns, matters that represented only an aspect of John's concerns. If complacency, compromise and accommodation were the central issues in these churches, as some have argued, one would expect these issues to recur throughout the book. They do not. Indeed, DeSilva argues that the main socio-religious issues revolved around the external pressure placed upon Christians by participants in the imperial cult and by trade guilds, which expected its

helpful in general and this thesis uses oppression, suppression and repression interchangeably as references to a regional maltreatment of Christians by Jews and Gentiles alike.

47. It is quite possible that the Christians to whom John wrote saw themselves in some way connected to the synagogue. It is not certain when Jews and Christians became separate organizations, and there is no reason to believe that it occurred at the same time in every region of the Roman Empire. The fact that the Asian Jewish community feels a need to contest the Christian community indicates that the Jews themselves saw the Christians as being related to them in some way (cf. Yarbro Collins [*Crisis*, pp. 85-87] and Wall [*Revelation*, pp. 10-12] who have similar arguments). Even Rev. 2.8-11 then, from John's perspective, might be an internal matter. For a different perspective, see DeSilva, 'Apocalyptic Propaganda', pp. 383-84.

members to eat meat offered to idols. While some, such as the Nicolaitans, see no harm in accommodating to these social pressures, John sees them as practices that blur the distinctions between Christians and non-Christians. Thus, DeSilva correctly recognizes that the attempt to accommodate or modify their lifestyle by some Asian Christians is a response to external pressures upon the community to conform to normal provincial social expectations.[48] I concur completely. The problem for these congregations is not simply religious laxity, but the larger question of how to respond to the social pressures upon them to conform. Some want to be more compromising; others do not.

My socio-historical exegeses in Parts I and II of this study will argue that at the very least Revelation responds to some type of maltreatment, most probably to some type of limited, regional oppression. In my opinion, a sociological exegesis asks the appropriate questions that push us beyond the historically verifiable to the 'historically intelligible',[49] given what is known about the wider context, and provide a more thorough understanding of early Christianity.

Other writers have presented what I consider a more nuanced understanding of the social setting of the book of Revelation.[50] Classicists have argued for at least a century that in the late first/early second centuries CE Christians experienced regional, limited repression. The only question has been the legal precedents that led Roman officials in

48. DeSilva, 'Social Setting', pp. 286-96.

49. For me, the historically verifiable refers to data that can be confirmed by two or more independent sources. Historically intelligible hypotheses come into play when the data are incomplete and/or independent verification is not possible. In such cases, the exegete seeks to extrapolate from general premises, which are verifiable historically, intelligible hypotheses that are probably true though not fully verifiable. Historically intelligible hypotheses are necessary and appropriate in the present study because our knowledge of both early Christianity and the Roman Empire is incomplete, as Price states (*Rituals*, pp. 79-80).

50. E.g. Yarbro Collins, *Crisis*, pp. 84-110; Boring, *Revelation*, pp. 8-23; Schüssler Fiorenza, *Vision*, pp. 124-31; DeSilva, 'Social Setting', pp. 273-302; *idem*, 'Apocalyptic Propaganda', pp. 378-86; Krodel, *Revelation*, pp. 35-42; Wall, *Revelation*, pp. 10-12. See also the work of the classicists Price (*Rituals*, pp. 197-99) and A.N. Sherwin-White (*The Letters of Pliny: A Historical and Social Commentary* [Oxford: Clarendon Press, 1966], pp. 772-87).

different regions to act as they did.[51] The earliest Roman references to Christianity are negative ones, lending support to an argument for a regional suppression of Christians.

Some classicists have argued that the Romans punished Christians because they viewed Christianity as a social movement that disturbed Roman sensibilities, especially with regard to religious customs. Sherwin-White argues that previously the Romans had become intolerant of the Bacchanalians (second century BCE) and the Druids (first/second centuries CE) for what the Romans considered anti-social acts, *scelera* or *flagitia,* associated with human sacrifice.

> When cult and *scelera* appear inseparable, a total ban, or strict control, may be placed upon a particular cult. So because of the *flagitia*, the *nomen*, active membership of a criminal organization without further proof of individual guilt is constituted a capital charge, by direct magisterial action ... with or without support of a senatorial decree.[52]

He argues that there was no official imperial persecution of Christians, but that Christians were held in low social esteem in the empire. While some provincial governors punished Christians, others chose not to do so. Thus, he argues, the plight of Christians depended upon the attitude of the Roman authority before whom Christians were tried.[53] An examination of Tacitus, Suetonius and Pliny, discussed earlier in our analysis of Thompson, is instructive.

The writings of Tacitus, to which Sherwin-White does not appeal, support his argument. In describing the repression of Christians, following the burning of Rome in 64, Tacitus has an enlightening passage on Roman attitudes toward Christians.

> Therefore, to scotch the rumour [that the fire had been started intentionally] Nero substituted as culprits, and punished with the utmost refinements of cruelty, a class of men, loathed for their vices, whom the crowd styled the Christians [*quos per* flagitia *invisos vulgus Christianos appellabat*]. Christus, the founder of the name [*nominis*], had undergone the death penalty in the reign of Tiberius, by sentence of the procurator Pontius Pilate, and the pernicious superstition [*superstitio*] was checked for a moment, only to break out once more, not merely in Judaea, the

51. E.g. W.M. Ramsay, *The Church in the Roman Empire* (London: G.P. Putnam's Sons, 1893); E.G. Hardy, *Christianity and the Roman Government* (London: S. Sonnenschein, 2nd edn, 1906); Sherwin-White, *Letters*.

52. Sherwin-White, *Letters*, pp. 780-81.

53. Sherwin-White, *Letters*, pp. 696, 781-84.

> home of the disease [*mali*], but in the capital itself ... First, then, the confessed members of the sect were arrested; next, on their disclosures, vast numbers were convicted, not so much on the count of arson as for hatred of the human race [*odio humani generis*] (*The Annals of Imperial Rome*, 15.44).

While Tacitus clearly decries Nero's action, he has no respect for Christians. He uses *flagitia* to refer to Christianity, supporting Sherwin-White's argument. He calls it a superstition and a disease. More so, Christians were deemed guilty simply because they were Christians, that is, because of the *nomen*, also supporting Sherwin-White's argument.

Suetonius makes a similar comment in his *Nero*: 'Punishment was inflicted on the Christians, a class of men given to a new and mischievous superstition' (16.2).[54]

These highly anti-Christian sentiments probably reflect a general lack of respect for Christians altogether in Roman society. They are so corrupt, in Roman eyes, that they deserve punishment merely for being Christians. Christian writings give a similar account (e.g. Mt. 10.17-23; Jn 15.21; Acts 5.41; 1 Pet. 4.14; Rev. 2.17; 3.5, 10, 12). Thus, there is evidence from Christian and Roman sources describing the type of public ridicule and harassment that first-century Christians endured.

One might argue against my position that Tacitus and Suetonius are second-century CE writers whose comments may not reflect the sentiment of the citizens of Rome in 64 CE. This is true, but both men came into adulthood in the first century CE, when their ideas and opinions were formulated. Moreover, they reached adulthood in the late first/early second century CE at approximately the same time Revelation was written. It is also noteworthy that both writers denigrate Christianity without feeling the need to support their position with proof. Persons often take this attitude when their opinions reflect the perspective of society in general.

On the other hand, if one argues that Christians were often held in moderate to high social esteem, one has to deal with the fact that our earliest extant pagan references to Christianity are negative. Similarly, how does one explain the ease with which Nero persuaded the Roman

54. 'afflicti suppliciis Christiani, genus hominum superstitionis novae ac maleficae.'

population of Christian culpability? If Christians were respected after 64 CE, how does one explain Tacitus's attitude early in the second century CE? The absence of extant pagan witnesses for the propriety of Christianity does not mean that such witnesses did not exist. Rather, it suggests that those non-Christians who held any respect for Christianity were in the minority and that their opinions held little public sway. Moreover, the paucity of any references to Christianity, either positive or negative, at best, suggests that Christianity was an insignificant movement within the Roman Empire that received little note from first-century CE pagan authors. My argument that Christianity was often held in low social esteem in the first century CE is not historically verifiable, given our limited knowledge of this period of time; however, given what is verifiable from both Christian and Roman writers, my argument is historically intelligible.

Pliny's correspondence with Trajan provides another example of the Roman attitude toward Christianity. Pliny, a Roman provinical governor under Trajan, writes a letter to the emperor Trajan. This letter and Trajan's response share with Tacitus and Suetonius a disdain for Christians. Written c. 112 CE in the province of Bithynia, north of Asia, *Letter* 10.96-97 states that Christians have been tried previously. Although Pliny gives no date for the beginning of this practice, his statements read as if this is one of many givens in provincial administration, and at no point is he decrying Christian trials.[55] His purpose in writing to the emperor is to be sure that he has done it properly!

What has Pliny done? He has led a regional oppression of Christians after *local residents* have informed him that the Christians are seditious persons. Initially, Pliny *assumed*, without verifying it, that Christians were criminal by nature and thus executed them upon their Christian confession of faith (just as Tacitus says occurred in Rome in *Annals*) and their refusal to worship the traditional gods and the emperor. Pliny refers to their refusal to worship the traditional gods and the emperor as 'obstinance and stubbornness'. In interrogating some persons, he learned that they were once Christians but had left the movement, some as long ago as 20 years earlier, during the reign of Domitian. They told Pliny that Christianity was not a seditious, immoral movement, but was somewhat benign in its religious practices and beliefs. Instead of being immoral, Christians actually took oaths to act honorably.

55. Sherwin-White, *Letters*, pp. 694-96.

Seeking verification, Pliny tortures two Christian women and learns that Christianity was indeed the ethical movement that the former Christians described. He then writes Trajan, 'I found nothing more than a vulgar, excessive superstition' (*superstitionem pravam inmodicam*). He continues, 'The plague [*contagio*] of this superstition has spread not only in the cities, but through villages and the countryside.'[56] He concludes that, since his pogrom, the temples are gaining more and more people, the sacred feasts are being observed again and the sacrificial meat is being purchased once more.

Trajan responds by applauding Pliny's actions, not exactly how one might expect him to respond to a respected movement. While there is no norm for such cases, Trajan states that Christians should not be sought out. Trajan states further that if Christians do not recant their faith and worship the traditional gods, then they should be punished, that is, executed.

It is noteworthy that Pliny executed Christians for not participating in the traditional religious practices. He writes, 'If they persist [in worshipping Christ], I order them to be led away for execution; for whatever the nature of their admission, I am convinced that their stubbornness and unshakeable obstinancy ought not to go unpunished.' Again, as with Tacitus and Suetonius, Pliny assumed that they were a seditious, criminal social movement without any proof of their culpability. Pliny could hardly have drawn this conclusion if Christian practices and beliefs had been well-known and understood and/or well-respected in Roman society, a point that Elliott makes about the recipients of 1 Peter.[57] Indeed, even when he learns the truth, Pliny continues to describe the movement in derogatory terms. Such an attitude usually does not develop within months but over years of denigration and mistrust.

Pliny's reaction to this 'mischief' was a religio-political attempt to maintain social institutions at the expense of Christian lives. The fact that Pliny knows so little of Christian values, values extremely close to Roman values,[58] means that the contempt for Christians is probably

56. M.E. Boring's translation (*Revelation*, p. 15).

57. Elliott, *Home*, pp. 78-84.

58. See, e.g., the lists of virtues and duties in Cicero, *The Ends* 19-20; *The Duties* 1.2.7–3.10; 1.17.53-58; Epictetus, *Discourses* 2.10.7-23; 2.14.13; 3.7.26-27; compare with Rom. 13.1-7; Mk 12.13-17; Eph. 5.21–6.9; Col. 3.18–4.1; 1 Tim. 5.1–6.2; 1 Pet. 2.13-17. I have chosen the Romans Cicero and Epictetus because they

very deep and reflects the low regard with which the general society viewed Christianity. Pliny's actions and statements do not reflect a social setting where Christians have prospered and been respected, but, rather, one in which they have been deemed unworthy of any social respect. This negative attitude toward Christianity probably has deep historical roots because, even when both Pliny and Trajan learn that Christianity is not immoral and has ethical ideals in common with Roman ideals, neither man feels any remorse for the loss of Christian lives. Such prejudices have long histories. Heller states the case accurately: 'In vain do we confront the established prejudices with reality: they are unshakeable.'[59]

It is quite possible that Revelation, written to churches in the same general region of the Empire approximately 20 years earlier, responds to a similar localized oppression. Local adherents of the imperial cult, a practice that we shall show began under Caesar Augustus, would see Christians as social malcontents who were unlawful and/or unpatriotic, and as people who refused to participate in the traditional religious customs.[60] When taken before provincial governors, Christians would unwittingly confirm for the Roman official their guilt by not worshiping the traditional gods and the emperor. The provincial governor would then execute the 'guilty'. From a Roman perspective, Christians are obstinate and stubborn; from a Christian perspective, faithful witnesses (e.g. Rev. 2.10; 17.14).

I believe that this is a historically intelligible argument that explains the images of persecution in the apocalyptic visions and also explains why John identifies the Roman Empire as the earthly manifestation of Satan. Moreover, the exegeses of pertinent passages in this study will demonstrate that a key issue in the link between Christ and community is the question of what it means to be a faithful witness, as with Antipas

reflect the types of ethical mores common to their culture and also because Cicero pre-dates Christianity and Epictetus's life and career overlaps the writing of Revelation. They represent established expectations of social behavior, modes of behavior that Christians shared with the broader society.

59. A. Heller, 'Toward a Sociology of Knowledge of Everyday Life', *Cultural Hermeneutics* 3 (1975), pp. 7-18 (7-8).

60. Cf. DeSilva, 'Apocalyptic Propaganda', pp. 378-82; Price, *Rituals*, pp. 197-98; Yarbro Collins, *Crisis*, p. 100; Rowland, *Open Heaven*, pp. 412-13.

(2.13), an issue that recurs throughout the book, indicative of its importance for its original audience (e.g. 1.5; 2.10, 13; 3.14; 17.14; 19.11).[61]

Several New Testament commentators have argued that, because there was no empire-wide persecution as envisioned in Revelation, it does not mean that there was no social crisis at all, but that a limited, localized oppression of Christians c. 95 CE is historically intelligible.[62] Furthermore, these exegetes state that such limited actions could be as horrific as an imperial persecution to those who suffered its effects. They postulate that John placed a limited repression of Christians on a cosmic scale in order to explain the plight of his fellow Christians within the wider perspective of the divine plan.

I agree with this position because it provides a needed corrective to the assumption that since there was no empire-wide persecution then there was no suffering. Further, this position relates the book of Revelation to first- and second-century CE Christian and Roman writers who describe the low social status of Christians. Indeed, Christians suffered not because of their criminality but often because of the name alone. Additionally, our sources indicate that both Jews and pagans had reasons to resent Christians and to see them as social deviants. Jews disliked their belief that Jesus was worthy of divine honors; pagans their refusal to participate in traditional Asian religio-political customs. Paul tells us that initially he persecuted the church and that in this endeavor he was the best among his peers (Gal. 1.13-14), clearly implying that he was not the only Jewish persecutor of Christians. Conversely, there is also little evidence that Christians received a great of deal of respect in Roman society during this time (see Heb. 10.32-39; 12.4; Lk. 21.12; Ign., *Magn.* 8).

Several New Testament writings, dated variously by scholars from 55 to 125 CE, describe the Christian perspective of the relationship of the Christian community to Judaism: Christians saw themselves as the True Israel/New Israel that continues the task that the Old Israel had left undone (e.g. Acts 13.46-48; 14.27; 24.10-16; 28.17-30; Gal. 3.7-9; 6.16; Rom. 4.13-17; Jas 1.1; cf. 1 Pet. 1.1; 2.9-10; Rev. 7.4-9). This Christian

61. Cf. Schüssler Fiorenza, *Vision*, p. 127.

62. E.g. Schüssler Fiorenza, *Vision*, pp. 62-69; Yarbro Collins, *Crisis*, pp. 84-110; Boring, *Revelation*, pp. 8-23; Krodel, *Revelation*, pp. 35-42; Wall, *Revelation*, pp. 10-12; DeSilva, 'Social Setting', pp. 286-91; cf. Price, *Rituals*, pp. 123-26; Sherwin-White, *Letters*, pp. 772-87.

self-image would not have endeared Christianity to other movements within Judaism. Other forms of Judaism would have re-asserted their own claims to election, probably themselves excluding Christians. Moreover, by the time Revelation was written, Christianity was a predominantly Gentile movement.[63] Gentiles claiming to be God's true people would have upset more traditional Jewish persons, many of whom probably thought of Gentiles as inherently impure. Rev. 2.9 and 3.9 may reflect such a social context or a similar one: 'Jews', treated as an honorific name and pointed to as the religious ideal, indicates that both sides took this name and thought of themselves as the elect people of God.[64] Our exegesis of these passages will develop this point in more detail later.

d. *Religious Factors in Asia*

While the aforementioned section discussed the social status of Christians in Asia, this section will demonstrate that both the novelty of Christianity and its Asian religio-political setting would have caused significant tension between Christians and pagans. Price points out that Christians were perceived negatively because of their refusal to participate in the traditional religions and in the imperial cult.[65] I agree.

Greco-Roman society in general had little respect for new movements. The Roman state in particular was suspicious of any new assembly or association lest it might develop into a political organization in conflict with the Roman state.[66] Secondly, and perhaps more importantly, the Asian religio-political setting itself could produce tensions between non-Christians who participated in the imperial cult and Christians who did not. In the eastern region of the Mediterranean, the worship of the emperor was not mandated by the emperor himself, but was a grassroots movement among the common people, who traditionally believed that the king was a son of the nation's god.[67] Alexander

63. See S.G. Wilson, *Related Strangers* (Minneapolis: Augsburg–Fortress, 1995), pp. 1-35.

64. Cf. Rowland, *Open Heaven*, p. 409; also DeSilva, 'Social Setting', pp. 287-89.

65. Price, *Rituals*, pp. 123-26; cf. DeSilva, 'Social Setting', pp. 289-91.

66. E.g. Pliny, *Letter* 10.96-97. See also R. Stark, 'The Class Basis of Early Christianity from a Sociological Model', *Sociological Analysis* 47 (1986), pp. 216-25.

67. See Price, *Rituals*, pp. 123-26, 197-98, 220-22.

received such treatment after conquering these countries as had his Seleucid and Ptolemaic successors.

When the Romans conquered the eastern Mediterranean, their emperors received similar divine honors.[68] The Roman imperial cult began in Asia in the first century BCE. Dio Cassius writes that, early in Augustus's principate, Roman citizens in Asia were required to worship the divine Julius Caesar and the goddess Roma, while the provincials were required to worship Augustus and the goddess Roma.[69] Pausanias mentions a temple to Octavia, Augustus's sister, in the first century BCE. Reynolds argues that, by the middle of the first century BCE, Aphrodisias had a temple dedicated to Rome; by 14 BCE, one to Augustus.[70] Claudius's living grandmother was worshiped as *Thea Antonia*.[71] Although Caligula might have been the first living emperor to require that he be worshiped, he was not the first living member of the imperial family to receive divine honors. Price's comment is important:

> Though I would not wish to return to the old picture of a clash between Christ and the Caesars, the imperial cult was clearly one of the features of the contemporary world that troubled the Christians. Their responses during the first three centuries of the empire consisted essentially of passive resistance.[72]

I concur. Parts I and II of this study will show that Revelation is a form of passive civil disobedience that advocates faithfully waiting for an imminent divine deliverance (see Rev. 22.7-20).

The imperial cult was practiced strongly in Asia and in most of the eastern Mediterranean regions of the Roman Empire, and, more importantly, cities competed vigorously for the privilege of being declared

68. See, e.g., W. Dittenberger (ed.), *Orientis graeci inscriptiones selectae* (*OGIS*) (2 vols.; Leipzig: S. Hirzel, 1903–1905), I, pp. 215-19; A.G. Hunt and G.C. Edgar (eds.), *Select Papyri* (LCL; 2 vols.; London: Heinemann, 1932–34), I, p. 208; F.W. Walbank, *The Hellenistic World* (Cambridge, MA: Harvard University Press, 1982), pp. 209-26; Price, *Rituals*, pp. 25-47. This is not to say that there was an unbroken, identical tradition between the Hellenistic ruler-cults and the imperial cult without any differences. Rather, I am here referring to continuities between the two (cf. Price, *Rituals*, pp. 23-25).

69. *Roman Histories* 51.20.6-7; cf. *SEG* 23.206.

70. J.M. Reynolds, 'Further Information on Imperial Cult in Aphrodisias', *St. Cl.* 24 (1986), pp. 109-17.

71. *IGRR* 4.1608c; see also N. Kokkinos, *Antonia Augusta: Portrait of a Great Lady* (London: Routledge, 1992), pp. 158-62.

72. Price, *Rituals*, p. 123.

neokoros, an official center for the imperial cult. All seven cities addressed in Rev. 2.1–3.22 received the neokorate in the late first and/or early second century CE.[73] In the first century CE, Ephesus (see Rev. 2.1), which received the neokorate more than once, had a cult to Roma and Julius Caesar and later added a temple to Tiberius. Caesarea had a temple to Augustus and Roma. Pilate dedicated a shrine in Caesarea to Tiberius. Augustus was worshiped in Antioch-near-Pisidia in his lifetime. Other first-century CE neokorate cities included Pergamum, Smyrna, Sardis, Laodicea, Philadelphia (all mentioned in Rev. 2–3), Cyzicus and Ancyra. In the next century, Magnesia-on-the-Maeander had a cult to Nero, a testimony to the esteem in which the eastern provinces held him. Thyatira and Tralles also received the neokorate in the second century.[74]

The neokorate symbolized for these cities civic pride and devotion to their religious traditions. Perhaps more importantly, the imperial cult established a means by which these once proudly autonomous cities came to understand their relationship to the new Roman imperial power by representing it to themselves in the forms long established for the gods.[75] The imperial cult played a key role in the establishment of the new symbolic universe for the Roman province of Asia. Christians who denied the validity of these religio-political traditions constituted an affront to Asian pagan social sensibilities. Christian religious impiety, from a pagan perspective, left them open to reprisals from the gods through natural disasters and social anarchy. While some local Roman officials did not seek out Christians, as Trajan advised Pliny, they held them in low esteem and would not hesitate to execute Christians if they did not adhere to the normal religio-political customs of the day, including worshiping the emperor, again reflecting Trajan's sentiments to Pliny. The writings of Tacitus and Suetonius also support this observation.

I propose a socio-religious setting for the book of Revelation in which Asian Christians endured a limited regional oppression in the early nineties for their religious beliefs and their refusal to worship the

73. See, e.g., Price, *Rituals*, pp. 24-25, 249-74; J. Ferguson, *The Religions of the Roman Empire* (London: Thames & Hudson, 1970), pp. 93-98.

74. See Price, *Rituals*, pp. xxii-xxvi, 64-65 n. 47, 66-67, 249-74.

75. Price, *Rituals*, pp. 25, 51-52, 56-58, 171, 225-27, 239-48.

traditional gods.[76] Several Christians have been executed (see 2.13; 6.9-11; 7.13-14; 20.4-6) and John believes that more executions will follow before the end comes (see 16.6; 17.6).

Several additional points support this conclusion. First, both Christian and Roman writers tell us the very name 'Christian' had negative connotations in Roman society (e.g. Lk. 21.12; Jn 15.21; Acts 5.41; Tacitus, *Annals* 15.44; cf. Pliny, *Letter* 10). Some leading Roman writers considered Christianity a social vice (*flagitia*) without any attempt to substantiate this opinion (Tacitus, *Annals* 15.44; Suetonius, *Nero* 16.2; cf. Pliny, *Letter* 10.96-97).[77] Indeed, Roman leaders felt no remorse in punishing Christians who had not committed a crime, even when they learned that Christians were not malevolent persons (Pliny, *Letter* 10.96-97). This is all the more significant given the similarity between Roman and Christian ethics,[78] giving support to Elliott's argument that the exclusiveness of the Christian community led to a general ignorance about Christian beliefs and practices as well as a suspicion of the Christian movement. Finally, 1 Peter, Revelation and Pliny all give evidence of the regional oppression of Christians in the eastern region of the Roman Empire. If our dating of these works is correct, these three writings demonstrate that Christians suffered in this region for approximately 50 years. Our discussion of the religious traditions of the eastern areas of the Roman Mediterranean world support a regional suppression of Christians owing to differences with pagans, as well as Roman officials and Jewish leaders. Classical and biblical scholars who reach this conclusion are able to base it on an abundance of solid evidence.[79]

76. Sherwin-White, *Letters*, p. 774; Price, *Rituals*, pp. 123-26, 197-98. Many New Testament commentators hold a similar view concerning 1 Peter (e.g. Selwyn, *First Peter*, pp. 52-56; Kelly, *Peter and Jude*, pp. 5-11; Balch, *Wives Be Submissive*, p. 138; Elliott, *Home*, p. 87; Perkins, *Peter, James and Jude*, pp. 15-16).

77. Cf. Sherwin-White, *Letters*, pp. 696, 780-84.

78. See, e.g., Cicero, *The Ends* 19-20; *The Duties* 1.2.7-13; Epictetus, *Discourses* 2.10.7-23; 3.7.26-27; and Rom. 13.1-7; Eph. 5.21–6.9; 1 Tim. 5.1–6.2; 1 Pet. 2.13-17.

79. E.g. *OGIS* 54, 212, 245; Dio Cassius, *Roman Histories* 51.20.6-7; *SEG* 23.206; Tacitus, *Annals* 15.44; Pliny, *Letter* 10.96-97; see also Sherwin-White, *Letters*, pp. 772-87; Price, *Rituals*, pp. xxii-xxvi, 123-26, 197-98, 220-22, 249-74; Yarbro Collins, *Crisis*, pp. 84-100; Rowland, *Open Heaven*, pp. 403-13; DeSilva, 'Social Setting', pp. 286-96; Boring, *Revelation*, pp. 8-23; Krodel, *Revelation*,

The exegeses in Parts I and II of this study will argue that John placed a regional oppression on a cosmic scale in order to understand the role of the Church in the divine plan for the cosmos. Since Revelation communicates its message predominantly through its images, an approach that attempts to understand how images function within a given community is preferable to others in order to interpret it. It is to such a method that I now turn.

3. *Symbolic Biblical Language and Sociological Interpretation*

Religious communication is distinctive because it refers to a transcendent truth that is beyond total human comprehension. This incomprehensibility carries with it a sense of mystery and awe. Thus, the need arises for symbolic forms of communication, by means of analogy and comparison, in order to overcome these difficulties.[80] Moreover, there is also a need for a method of interpretation appropriate to interpret the symbols. This study employs sociology of knowledge as its method for the task of interpreting the symbolic language of Revelation. This method has the benefit, when practiced properly, of asking how symbols function within a community without imposing value judgments upon those symbols.

Religious discourse attempts to give meaning and purpose to life, that is it attempts to inspire and inform human existence. One may distinguish these functions, but one should not attempt to separate them within the context of religious communication where they rightly function hand-in-hand. Religious discourse employs symbols and/or images as abbreviated messages that communicate data already known in a more complete form or a more complete sense. They provide pathways to the beliefs and values that contribute to the structure of a particular symbolic universe.

As well as symbols and images, religious communities also use metaphors, parables and stories as primary means of symbolic discourse. Stories are the most highly developed and complex forms of symbolic

pp. 35-42; Wall, *Revelation*, pp. 10-12; Elliott, *Home*, pp. 78-84; Balch, *Wives Be Submissive*, pp. 137-38.

80. See P. Tillich, *Dynamics of Faith* (New York: Harper & Row, 1957), pp. 41-54; L.S. Cunningham *et al.*, *The Sacred Quest* (Englewood, NJ: Prentice–Hall, 2nd edn, 1995), pp. 61-77; J.C. Livingston, *Anatomy of the Sacred* (New York: Macmillan, 2nd edn, 1993), pp. 74-103.

communication. They may be historical, ahistorical or both to some degree. They may employ several different literary forms (e.g. myth, legend, epic, encomium, historiography, parable or drama), or may combine forms or include different forms within a greater formal framework (e.g. a parable within a legend). Since stories function within a narrative framework that recognizes past actions; present realities and future possibilities, they possess a sense of realness that coheres with the narrative quality of life itself. For this reason, common stories within a given social group may provide extraordinary means of social cohesion and identity. Stories may simultaneously constitute the reason for being for nations, cultures and individuals, performing three functions: (1) giving meaning to life for the group as well as for each person within the group; (2) providing a sense of corporate and individual identity; (3) creating a sense of purpose both collectively and personally. Similarly, stories help to indoctrinate new members into the social order. The social value of stories lies in their ability to inspire and inform.[81]

The two basic types of symbols are representational symbols and presentational ones. Representational symbols bring together two objects that have no natural connection or relationship. Their association derives from a given socio-historical context and continued use within that context, that is, through custom and tradition. Presentational symbols participate in and/or may be similar to that which they symbolize. Because of the similarity between the symbol and its referent, presentational symbols can become powerful icons that are strongly resistant to change. In many religious groups, followers may believe that this type of symbol actually brings them into contact with their god/goddess.[82]

Revelation employs myth as its primary mode of narrative. Religious myth should not be evaluated solely upon whether it is factual but upon its communicative power. A myth is a narrative that describes the heavenly/transcendent realm and relates the activities of a heavenly/transcendent being, or an agent of that transcendent being, in ways that

81. Cf. T. Hoyt, Jr, 'Interpreting Biblical Scholarship for the Black Church Tradition', in C.H. Felder (ed.), *Stony the Road we Trod: African American Biblical Interpretation* (Minneapolis: Augsburg–Fortress, 1991), pp. 34-39.

82. Livingston, *Anatomy*, pp. 78-82.

human beings can appropriate. Some scholars argue that actual occurrences lie behind many myths.[83] With Malinowski, I would argue that a myth must be understood as it functions within its own cultural setting.[84]

Myths perform three functions. First, they provide a model for structuring the social order. Cosmogonic myths relate how the universe came into being or how a pivotal social event occurred. These data in turn influence social structures and social institutions. Such myths serve to unify diverse elements in a given society and establish a cultural identity for an ethnic group. Secondly, myths explain what cannot be easily explained, both the good and the bad, and often relate what needs to be done to renew the social order. This renewal may be termed either 'liberation' or 'salvation' and may be viewed as a political act, a religious one, or both. Finally, myths provide models of behavior and a sense of one's role and identity within a social group. Outstanding individuals become role models and their recorded deeds, or stories about their deeds, become criteria by which to judge human behavior. Myths sanction some forms of behavior, tolerate others and condemn still others. Important events associated with a group's mythology are commemorated on special days and these events reinforce social norms and social expectations.[85] This present study will demonstrate how myths function similarly in Revelation.

Images are symbols that represent in abbreviated form the fuller metaphor, parable, myth and/or story. Images may be representational or presentational. They provide a means of communicating, in an expedient but thorough fashion, important concepts and messages. They possess the power to inspire and inform their readers/hearers. 'Images address the person in the concreteness of life, putting one in touch with the senses in a holistic manner.'[86] Within Revelation's mythic framework, select images function as literary symbols, abbreviated forms of

83. See M. Dibelius, *From Tradition to Gospel* (London: Nicholson & Watson, 1934), pp. 266-86; R. Bultmann, *A History of the Synoptic Tradition* (Oxford: Basil Blackwell, rev. edn, 1968), pp. 244-317; Tillich, *Dynamics*, pp. 41-54; Cunningham *et al.*, *The Sacred Quest*, pp. 28-37, 62-65, 70-81; Livingston, *Anatomy*, pp. 78-82; cf. A. Farrer, *A Rebirth of Images* (Westminster: Dacre, 1949), pp. 13-35.

84. B. Malinowski, *Myth in Primitive Psychology* (New York: W.W. Norton, 1926), pp. 81-83.

85. Livingston, *Anatomy*, pp. 78-82.

86. Hoyt, 'Black Church Tradition', p. 37.

the larger narrative, that remind the hearer/reader of the details behind the image. Some images in Revelation are representational (e.g. the Lamb), while others are presentational (e.g. 'one like a son of man', the Divine Warrior). All provide John with means of communicating an important concept quickly and, like the stories that they represent, possess the power to inspire and inform.[87]

Since Revelation conveys its messages primarily through its symbols and mythology, an approach that enables one better to interpret symbolic language is preferable. Sociology of knowledge is suited to this task because it attempts to examine the analogies and symbols that help to structure human societies.[88]

The task of sociology of knowledge is two-fold: to uncover (1) 'whatever passes for "knowledge" in a society' and (2) the process of its development, transmission and maintenance through social institutions.[89] 'The theoretical formulations of reality (in whatever forms) ... do not exhaust what is "real" for the members of a society.' Sociology of knowledge then must concern itself with 'common-sense "knowledge" ' that constitutes 'the social structure of reality' for a given society or culture.[90] Sociology of knowledge must also concern itself with the

87. See Thompson, *Revelation*, pp. 4-6, 46-50, esp. the excellent discussion of puns and word plays on pp. 49-50.

88. H.E. Remus, 'Sociology of Knowledge and the Study of Early Christianity', *SR* 11 (1982), pp. 45-56, esp. pp. 45-47.

89. P. Berger and T. Luckmann, *The Social Construction of Reality: A Treatise in the Sociology of Knowledge* (Garden City, NY: Doubleday, 1966), p. 15; cf. Remus, 'Sociology', pp. 45-47; Thompson, *Revelation*, pp. 7-8, 25-34, 95; see also K.H. Wolff, 'Introduction to Fifty Years of "Sociology of Knowledge" ', *Cultural Hermeneutics* 3 (1975), pp. 1-5; E.E. Hindson, 'The Sociology of Knowledge and Biblical Interpretation', *Theologia Evangelica* 17 (1984), pp. 33-38; D.J. Tidball, 'On Wooing a Crocodile: An Historical Survey of the Relationship between Sociology and New Testament Studies', *Vox Evangelica* 15 (1985), pp. 95-109; Heller, 'Towards a Sociology', pp. 7-18; V. Meja, 'The Sociology of Knowledge and the Critique of Ideology', *Cultural Hermeneutics* 3 (1975), pp. 57-68; see also broader discussions in R. Scroggs, 'The Sociological Interpretation of the New Testament: The Present State of Research', *NTS* 26 (1979–80), pp. 164-79; J.H. Elliott, *What Is Social-Scientific Criticism?* (Minneapolis: Augsburg–Fortress, 1993); T.B. Slater, 'Sociological Methodology and the New Testament', *Bible Bhashyam* 19 (1993), pp. 237-48.

90. Berger and Luckmann, *Social Construction of Reality*, p. 27; see also Tidball, 'Crocodile', pp. 95-96; Heller, 'Everyday Life', pp. 7-18.

analysis of the process of the construction of reality in human societies. Berger, Luckmann, Wolff, Hindson and others correctly describe reality and knowledge functionally, enabling the sociologist to analyze without judging the validity of a given social reality or concept of knowledge. Indeed, structuralist-functionalist views of religion have become the dominant methods employed by sociologists of religion.[91] The work of Abraham Malherbe, Gerd Theissen and Wayne Meeks are prime examples among New Testament exegetes.[92]

'Knowledge' connotes 'the certainty that phenomena are real and that they possess specific characteristics'.[93] The sociologist then asks if two different perceptions of reality might reflect two different societal settings. This is particularly true in conflict situations.[94] 'The need for a "sociology of knowledge" is thus already given with the observable differences between societies in terms of what is taken for granted as "knowledge" in them.' Moreover, the need arises by a recognition of 'the general ways by which realities are taken as "known" in human society'.[95]

Every group, society or culture constructs a 'symbolic universe'[96] that provides its constituents with an ideal, prototypical society that gives legitimation and rationality to every aspect of human existence by explaining and justifying the given social order. This occurs in the following manner. Initially, the existing social order should make sense to the majority of persons in different social roles. Next, the social order must make all of life a meaningful process. As a result, the social order gives cognitive value to its meaningful process. Social knowledge leads to social values, and those values then indicate proper social behavior.

91. Tidball, 'Crocodile', pp. 96, 105.

92. E.g. A. Malherbe, *Social Aspects of Early Christianity* (Baton Rouge, LA: LSU, 1977); G. Theissen, *The Social Setting of Pauline Christianity* (Philadelphia: Fortress Press, 1982); W. Meeks, *The First Urban Christians* (New Haven: Yale University Press, 1983).

93. Berger and Luckmann, *Social Construction*, p. 15; cf. Hindson, 'Sociology', p. 35; Thompson, *Revelation*, pp. 176-85.

94. Cf. Tidball, 'Crocodile', p. 103.

95. Berger and Luckmann, *Social Construction*, p. 15; see also Tidball, 'Crocodile', pp. 105-106; Heller, 'Everyday Life', p. 10.

96. One might use 'sacred realm' or 'sacred cosmos' or a similar phrase to describe a symbolic universe from a religious perspective. See also J. Camery-Hoggatt, *Irony in Mark's Gospel* (SNTSMS, 72; Cambridge: Cambridge University Press, 1992), pp. 16-17, 26-30; Thompson, *Revelation*, pp. 33-34, 95.

Subsequently, the social order provides four different levels of legitimation. Often these levels overlap both in method and time of use. The incipient level begins with the transmission of 'linguistic objectifications of human experience',[97] that is, oral traditions intended to explain life's purpose and meaning. The next level, rudimentary theoretical proposition, deals with the more pragmatic side of life. It transmits proverbs, myths, legends and folk-tales. The third level relates to advanced theories which explain and justify social institutions by means of complex theories. This level is entrusted to specialists (e.g. economists, lawyers, philosophers, theologians). The final level of legitimation is the symbolic universe itself. It contains traditions 'that integrate different provinces of meaning and encompass the institutional order of a symbolic totality'.[98] The symbolic universe includes both collective and individual histories and represents the ultimate fulfillment of institutional processes.[99] The conceptualization of a symbolic universe involves objectivation, sedimentation and accumulation of knowledge. Objectivation consists of the common expressions and concepts valued and adhered to at all social levels. Sedimentation refers to memorable experiences that help to form one's self-consciousness and perception of reality. Accumulation of knowledge occurs when the data of the first two steps are brought together and assimilated into a meaningful, coherent whole.[100]

Symbolic universes have three general roles: (1) they legitimize individuals; (2) they legitimize societies/cultures; and (3) they present a society's version of the ideal human society. First, symbolic universes legitimate individuals by giving order to one's life. They validate, or invalidate if one chooses poorly by its standards, one's choices at the highest level of existence. They make life intelligible and liveable. Moreover, they may help certain persons to return to normality when

97. Berger and Luckmann, *Social Construction*, p. 112; see also Heller, 'Everyday Life', pp. 11-12.

98. Berger and Luckmann, *Social Construction*, p. 113.

99. Berger and Luckmann, *Social Construction*, pp. 110-15; cf. Tillich, *Dynamics*, pp. 41-54; N.T. Wright, *Christian Origins and the Question of God*. I. *The New Testament and the People of God* (London: SPCK, 1992), pp. 45-61, 112-30. See my review of Wright in *JRT* 51 (1994), pp. 111-12.

100. Berger and Luckmann, *Social Construction*, pp. 49, 85, 115.

their behavior has strayed too far from the social norm. Symbolic universes also provide a way of integrating the discrepant meanings encountered regularly in life. Furthermore, one's self-identity receives validation by its place within the universe, that is even when no one else understands me, God does. Finally, symbolic universes make death something with which one can live by giving death a meaningful purpose. Berger and Luckmann state that this final element is the most potent legitimation of the symbolic universe.[101]

Secondly, symbolic universes legitimate cultures/societies by providing protection for institutions and set limits to social interaction and social reality. They also structure social history by giving all events a cohesive unity (e.g. Dionysius of Halicarnassus's *Roman Antiquities*, or the nineteenth-century US doctrine of manifest destiny, or a Chinese Maoist interpretation of history). In addition, symbolic universes integrate all discrete institutional processes, making the entire social operation coherent and, in doing so, preventing social chaos.[102]

Finally, human societies construct symbolic universes in order to represent the ideal human society.[103] In this manner, a symbolic universe provides a strong sense of cosmic security for its members, even in the face of a competing, more technologically advanced symbolic universe.

Symbolic universes usually develop maintenance strategies[104] in order to react to both interior and exterior threats. Societies maintain their symbolic universes in several ways. Mythology, a narrative that embodies ideas rather than history,[105] is one maintenance strategy, the most archaic one, according to Berger and Luckmann. They define mythology as 'a concept of reality that posits the ongoing penetration of the world of everyday experience by sacred forces'.[106] A myth is a symbolic story that expresses a group's, or a society's, or a culture's identity in part or *in toto*. Myths depict how things should be and not

101. Berger and Luckmann, *Social Construction*, pp. 115-19; see also Heller, 'Everyday Life', p. 9.

102. Berger and Luckmann, *Social Construction*, pp. 120-21.

103. Berger and Luckmann, *Social Construction*, pp. 121-22; Heller, 'Everyday Life', p. 9; Schüssler Fiorenza, *Vision*, pp. 129; Wright, *People of God*, pp. 112-30.

104. In this study, 'maintenance strategy' and 'maintenance technique' will be used interchangeably.

105. Remus, 'Sociology', p. 55.

106. Berger and Luckmann, *Social Construction*, p. 128. See also my earlier discussion of myth.

always how things are. I find Berger and Luckmann, at this point, showing too little appreciation for the social need for mythic language. Tillich provides a more cogent discussion.[107]

Tillich writes that symbols and myths are closely related for they both constitute the language of faith for which science is ill-equipped. He defines myth as a 'combination of symbols of our ultimate concern'.[108] By this, Tillich means that myths represent, either through narrative or symbol, that which a society or culture values most dearly. A myth is a symbolic presentation of divine figures/divine agency figures and their actions in human history. Myths will always be present because faith can only be expressed through symbolic language. Myths may either respond to a need and grow and develop or die and become forgotten when their usefulness has passed. However, they are invaluable as means of expressing the highest values and goals of a society.[109] At this point, the theologian informs the sociologists.

As a form of social maintenance, mythologies contain little theoretical deliberation save one's claim to a superior mode of life. They convey the connection between the human world and the transcendent world. A universe based primarily upon myth has specialists who best understand the tradition, but their knowledge is rather commonplace and non-technical.[110] Again, although very helpful, one notes a certain elitist bias in Berger and Luckmann's comments concerning myths as forms of social maintenance. Mythology is a major maintenance strategy in Revelation and is closely related to the book's theology.

Like mythology, theology, the second maintenance method, also functions as a mode of contact between the human realm and the heavenly, transcendent realm, but it requires specialists with more technical skills than mythology requires.[111] The acquisition of such skills often distances these specialists from everyday, commonplace life. These skills (e.g. translating the Greek New Testament) then become more and more difficult to obtain and may even seem extremely difficult to grasp

107. For a critique of Berger and Luckmann on this point, see N. Smart, *The Science of Religion and the Sociology of Knowledge* (Princeton, NJ: Princeton University Press, 1973), pp. 74-91. I am grateful to Alan Godlas of the University of Georgia for directing me to Smart.

108. Tillich, *Dynamics*, p. 50.

109. Tillich, *Dynamics*, pp. 41-54.

110. Berger and Luckmann, *Social Construction*, pp. 128-29.

111. Berger and Luckmann, *Social Construction*, p. 129.

by non-specialists. Often, however, mythology and theology coexist, each supporting the same symbolic universe within different social circles, affecting one another very little. Revelation, however, most often presents its theological content within a mythological framework. In this way, mythology and theology work together in maintaining church order.

Philosophy is the third means of maintenance. It may be viewed as a secularized version of theology (or theology may be viewed as a religious version of philosophy). Philosophy removes the means of maintenance farther from everyday life.[112] The symbolic universe is taken for granted totally. In extreme cases, it may come to dominate every aspect of one's life (e.g. Communist China under Chairman Mao). Determinism is the most frequently employed philosophical argument employed by Revelation (e.g. 13.8).

The final major means of maintaining a symbolic universe is modern science. Berger and Luckmann describe this as an extreme step that totally removes the sacred and knowledge concerning it from everyday life.[113] In other words, scientists become the specialists who keep the system running. In such social schemata, specialists in other fields rank beneath the scientists in importance. At its worst, this mode of maintenance can degenerate into a dehumanizing symbolic universe where the end result becomes more important than how people are treated by the process.

Two maintenance techniques that address minor situations, according to Berger and Luckmann, are therapy and nihilation. Therapy keeps people within the system and from entering other competing symbolic universes. Nihilation is a negative form of legitimation wherein everything outside the system is liquidated in some way. Deviant behavior is given an inferior status or incorporated within the system itself.[114] However, Revelation employs therapy as a major maintenance strategy. Often, mythology, theology and nihilation function conjointly in order

112. Berger and Luckmann, *Social Construction*, pp. 129-30.

113. Berger and Luckmann, *Social Construction*, p. 130.

114. Berger and Luckmann, *Social Construction*, pp. 130-34. A brilliant and gifted person may have no role in a given society. Berger and Luckmann refer to such an individual as an 'intellectual', one 'whose expertise is not wanted by the society at large' (p. 143). Anyone who has been so designated at any time in their life knows how valid this definition can be.

to perform therapeutic tasks in Revelation. These maintenance strategies are prevalent in the letters to the seven churches (Rev. 2.1–3.22) as means of retaining the connection between Christ and community. In particular, this study will demonstrate that the promise of an unbroken fellowship between Christ and community, principally as priest-kings with Christ in the New Jerusalem, is the primary maintenance strategy throughout the book of Revelation.

Harvey and Smart have been particularly critical of the work of Berger and Luckmann from different disciplines. On theological grounds, Harvey argues that their work relativizes contrasting views while claiming a value-free and objective perspective, a position that Berger and Luckmann themselves question in others. Furthermore, Harvey notes that Berger does not provide any norms or criteria that justify one type of religious faith rather than others. Smart, writing as a sociologist of religion, states that Berger and Luckmann reduce religion to a human construction within a supposedly neutral universe. Smart argues that they have not demonstrated that the experience of the numinous is a product of human society. Moreover, many objects in Berger's construction of the universe are not human products (e.g. the sun) but are grouped with human products nonetheless. Berger should revise his metaphysics and/or abandon his concept of a neutral universe.[115] While these critiques deserve serious consideration by sociologists of knowledge, Harvey's second critique is less convincing. Sociologists of religion do not provide criteria to justify one type of religious faith over against others. Their task is to describe these religious traditions objectively.

Vorster makes some interesting comments on Revelation and the manner in which it creates a sacred cosmos. It narrates 'otherworldly realities to a subculture whose members have to overcome the pressures of their society'. The reader accepts 'the authority of these visions' and is 'an insider in apocalyptic imagery and symbolism, a believer in the triumph of God in the second coming of Christ'. This process creates 'an image of the reader in the text which directs the actual reader'.[116] Indeed, Parts I and II of this study will substantiate Vorster's statements

115. See V. Harvey, *RelSRev* 5 (1979), pp. 1-10; Smart, *The Science of Religion*, pp. 74-91.

116. W.S. Vorster, 'The Reader in the Text: Narrative Material', *Semeia* 48 (1990), pp. 31-32.

with respect to the three major christological images in Revelation. In particular, it will argue that Jewish and pagan pressures caused internal and external pressures upon the churches in Asia, pressures that led some to a more relaxed attitude toward pagan religious customs and Jewish traditions and led others to ask how the Church could survive in a hostile environment. Moreover, it will suggest that Revelation was written to churches with competing prophetic/apocalyptic movements (John's movement, the Nicolaitans, the Jezebel movement) and that this context assured John an astute audience that presumed that God communicated to prophetic figures.[117] My use of the terms 'reader', 'hearer', 'reader/hearer', 'hearer/reader', 'original audience' or 'original recipients', or similar expressions, connotes persons within the Christian community who may or may not be 'insiders' (to use Vorster's expression) in apocalyptic visions, images and symbols, but who nonetheless have a sound knowledge of the message of a given image or symbol owing to its currency in early Christianity.

With regard to sociology of knowledge, I am conscious of the limitations of the method. Along with the aforementioned criticisms of Berger and Luckman, it can be said of the method itself that it is often difficult to determine with certainty whether the relationship between symbol/image and community is symmetrical or asymmetrical or whether it intensifies or denies an empirical experience. Mythic symbols present more unique problems. They often reflect an earlier stage in the life of the community than the time when the document under examination was written. Moreover, they often alternate between description and prescription to varying degrees without noticing any tension in doing so. Additionally, social paradigmatic mythic symbols may

117. See Bauckham's insightful discussion of the possibility of Christian prophetic circles in Asia Minor in *The Climax of Prophecy*, pp. 83-91. See also Farrer, *The Rebirth of Images*; A. Satake, *Die Gemeindeordnung in der Johannesapokalypse* (WMANT, 21; Neukirchen–Vluyn: Neukirchener Verlag, 1966); F.D. Mazzaferri, *The Genre of the Book of Revelation from a Source-Critical Perspective* (Berlin: W. de Gruyter, 1989); D. Hill, 'Prophecy and Prophets in the Revelation of St John', *NTS* 18 (1971–72), pp. 401-18; M.D. Goulder, 'The Apocalypse as an Annual Cycle of Prophecies', *NTS* 27 (1981), pp. 342-67; D.E. Aune, 'The Social Matrix of the Apocalypse of John', *BR* 26 (1981), pp. 16-32; *idem*, 'The Prophetic Circle of John of Patmos and the Exegesis of Revelation 22.16', *JSNT* 37 (1989), pp. 103-16.

provide a sense of the direction, motivation and rationale for the community but miss the unique features of the specific context.[118] Furthermore, a religious symbol may reflect an ideal situation for which the author hopes and not the real situation. The author may have an inaccurate perception of reality. I will attempt to minimize these limitations by comparing passages in Revelation that rely on symbols to communicate their messages with those that do not rely on symbols to communicate. In this way, hopefully, the shortcomings of the method may be minimized.[119]

4. *Previous Studies: A Historical Overview*

The major studies of the Christology of Revelation in this century have been heavily theological in nature and have not engaged in detailed discussions of the possible sociological dimensions. These studies have focused upon the titles and names that can be catalogued, examined and explained within a theological tradition-history with minimal reference to their social impact.[120]

Büchsel (1907) developed the first modern, extensive study of the Christology of Revelation by describing the function of its christological titles and themes. Although Büchsel's work is dated due to subsequent research, its focus upon the christological titles has provided a model for others to follow (e.g. Comblin, Ellwanger, Feuillet, J. Giblin, Holtz, Jankowski, Jonge, Mounce and Müller). I would argue, against Büchsel's approach, that the foundational christological meaning of the book of Revelation, a book of visions, is in the symbols and images expressed through its visions. Only after examining those symbols and images, can one appreciate and understand the christological agenda in Revelation and then go on to make statements about christological titles.

Comblin (1965) argued that the main innovation of Revelation is the identification of the two figures of the Son of Man and the messianic

118. Cf. Tidball, 'Crocodile', p. 101.

119. Cf. Scroggs, 'Sociological Interpretation', pp. 166-67, 176.

120. F. Büchsel, *Die Christologie der Offenbarung Johannis* (Halle: Druck von C.A. Kammerer, 1907); J. Comblin, *Le Christ dans l'Apocalypse* (Paris: Desclèe, 1965); T. Holtz, *Die Christologie der Apocalypse des Johannes* (TU, 85; Berlin: Akademie Verlag, 1971). See Hindson's comments on these types of studies ('Sociology', pp. 33-34).

king of Israel in the person of Jesus of Nazareth. While the concepts of the Son of Man and king of Israel derive from Jewish apocalypticism, the ministry of the historical Jesus constitutes a singularly Christian contribution to Revelation. This is comprehensible if one starts with the concept of Isaiah's transcendent suffering servant of God, a prophecy fulfilled in Jesus. If Jesus is the servant of God, then one should expect him also to be the Son of Man and the king of Israel. Comblin states that this Christology was present in the Christian community from a very early date (e.g. Paul). The Church continues Christ's servanthood in the interim between the ascension and the second coming. Similarly, the faithful Christian witnesses will live again with Christ in the New Jerusalem. Christians enjoy that bliss proleptically in the interim. Jesus guides the Church from heaven. The title of the exalted and sacrificial Lamb is subsumed under the Son of Man and King of Israel titles.

Comblin's work, though outstanding at many points, has two shortcomings. First, as we shall see, Revelation does not contain a 'son of man' Christology, but employs the comparison 'one *like* a son of man' motif. The latter comes from Second Temple Judaism, with examples in Ezekiel, Daniel, *1 Enoch*, *4 Ezra*, the *Apocalypse of Abraham,* the *Testament of Abraham*, Philo's *On Abraham* and the *Martyrdom and Ascension of Isaiah*, not Isaiah in the Hebrew Bible, as a means of denoting heavenly beings in human likeness. Early Christian writers continued the tradition (e.g. Acts 14.11; Phil. 2.7-8; Rev. 1.13).[121] Just as myths are stories about a transcendent being in human terms, such comparisons are descriptions of transcendent beings in human likeness. Secondly, if Comblin had been more sensitive to the sociological function of the christological images and symbols, he might have noted that the king of Israel motif plays a small role in Revelation. Unlike *4 Ezra* 11–13, which stresses the king of Israel through the symbol of the lion, Revelation places much more emphasis upon the slain Lamb who has become Sovereign of the universe (not only Israel; cf. Rev. 5.5-10; 17.14; 19.16). Thus, the way to dominion and salvation, two inseparable concepts in Revelation, is through faithful witnessing, even unto death (e.g. 1.5-6; 20.4-6). The kingship of Israel theme has been overshadowed by the slain Lamb, who has become the role model for

121. This point will be demonstrated in Chapter 2 of the present study, a more developed version of my 'One Like a Son of Man in First-Century CE Judaism', *NTS* 41 (1995), pp. 183-98. See also my 'Comparisons and the Son of Man', *Bible Bhashyam* 24 (1998), pp. 67-78.

Christian witnessing in Revelation. This study argues in Part II that the slain Lamb of Revelation is a Christian adaptation of Jewish traditions.

Like Büchsel, Holtz (1971) concentrates on the christological titles. Holtz has done an outstanding job of describing what John and his original audience believed. His understanding of the interrelated nature of the doctrines of Christology, soteriology, eschatology and ecclesiology provides helpful insights into the community's theology. However, he has not shown clearly the interrelationships among the various aspects of John's theology, often addressing topics in isolation from related materials. For example, he does not recognize the high status of priest-kings consistently presented in connection with 'one like a son of man' and with the Lamb. Furthermore, by concentrating rather on the theological background and not on the socio-historical foreground, he fails to recognize what the former christological tradition has contributed to the latter. Thus, while Holtz has made the initial steps in helping us to understand the relationship between Christology and ecclesiology, his work provides little data on how these images might have influenced John's readers/hearers in Asia and fails to provide an integrated christological study.

The present work will focus upon christological symbols and images because prophetic and/or apocalyptic writings communicate primarily through visions and not theological expositions, a fact recognized by Beck but not developed by him.[122] Visions have the power to affect both one's emotionality and rationality simultaneously, that they can inspire and inform.

Keck correctly warns us that the study of christological titles has many shortcomings.[123] First, title-centered studies cannot adequately explain important christological passages that do not include titles. He notes that some scholars even provide titles that are not there (e.g. Comblin's the king of Israel thesis concerning Revelation). I agree with Keck. Rev. 1.7 is an example of an important christological passage in Revelation without a title or a name. Its relevance will be explored

122. D.M. Beck, 'The Christology of the Apocalypse of John', in E.P. Booth (ed.), *New Testament Studies: Critical Essays in New Testament Interpretation with Special Reference to the Meaning and Worth of Jesus* (New York: Abingdon–Cokesbury, 1942), pp. 253-77.

123. L.E. Keck, 'Toward the Renewal of New Testament Christology', *NTS* 32 (1986), pp. 362-77, esp. 365-75.

later. Secondly, title-centered studies do not adequately address the phenomenon of a plurality of titles in a given passage or pericope. He notes that the biblical writers themselves show no embarassment about using many titles within one context, but scholars feel the need to instruct the reader how these titles relate to one another. I concur with Keck and would suggest that, because no single title exhausted what Jesus meant to the early church, a plurality of titles may indicate a search for the combined images that would convey all that Jesus represented. Thirdly, title-centered studies can miss the Christology in the text. For example, Keck notes, correctly in my opinion, that nothing Paul says about the importance of Jesus depends upon a christological title. Subsequently, christological elements are either underappreciated or overlooked entirely. Fourthly, title-centered studies often elucidate only half the Christology in a given text. Jesus interprets the titles and not vice versa, that is, who Jesus was for the early church determined what the title meant. Again, I agree. The Lamb who conquers through suffering leads the community and destroys evil in Revelation (John's contribution without a titular history) is an image that takes its cue from the history of Jesus in order to explain the history of the community. For example, while Rev. 5.5 mentions the lion, a traditional Davidic messianic image, it then replaces the lion with the slain Lamb, an image with a tradition history, but one re-defined in Revelation in light of the crucifixion of Jesus. More will be said concerning this in Part I. Moreover, Part II of this study will demonstrate how an examination of the symbolic names alone in Rev. 19.11-21 misses key christological issues, that the symbolic names and images complement one another and their interrelationships are crucial if one is to fully understand the passage.

In addition to the general weaknesses that Keck identified, studies of the Christology of Revelation based primarily upon titles suffer from three basic problems. The first problem is that many writers recognize the implications for a sociological understanding of Revelation but do so through theological categories that speak to academic questions (e.g. Holtz and Comblin), that is, the question of what people believed. Sociological realities and academic questions do not always go hand-in-hand. Sociological inquiries ask why people believed certain things and how their lives were affected by their beliefs. Such questions are vitally important when studying a work that offers an alternative world-view, as an apocalypse does.

The second problem is that even more narrowly focused studies (e.g. Lietzmann on the son of man; Hillyer on the Lamb) often spend more time discussing the ANE/Jewish background at the expense of an examination of the social foreground.[124] As a result, their studies provide substantial information about the history of an idea but little about the social setting and perspective of its proponents. As a corollary, the function of symbolic discourse (stories, symbols, images, etc.) for the ongoing life of a given community goes underappreciated at best, unnoticed at worst.

The third problem, a by-product of theological interests, is that previous studies have failed to notice the sociological function of the major christological images in Revelation and thus failed to make vital connections that reveal important sociological data about the community. While we are indebted to these works for recovering the tradition-history of many passages, they have often overlooked John's creativity in re-fashioning older imagery to suit the pastoral task before him.

The present study employs a different approach. First of all, it isolates the distinctive apocalyptic 'one-like-a-son-of-man' tradition in first-century CE Judaism and demonstrates how Revelation incorporates this tradition. It also demonstrates how John reinterprets the 'one like a son of man' in distinctively Christian ways. This continues some of my earlier work.[125] Secondly, it identifies the social function of this tradition in Revelation and demonstrates how this tradition has influenced the Lamb imagery in Revelation. This has rarely been noted previously by New Testament scholars. Thirdly, it shows how the fullest christological expression is found in the Divine Warrior image (19.11-21) and how the 'one like a son of man', the Lamb and the Divine Warrior images are interrelated. This last point has been noted previously by Laws, but, in my opinion, she undervalues the importance and influence of the other two christological images in the fashioning of the Divine

124. E.g. H. Lietzmann, *Der Menschensohn* (Freiburg: Mohr, 1896); N. Hillyer, ' "The Lamb" in the Apocalypse', *EvQ* 39 (1967), pp. 228-36.

125. See T.B. Slater, ' "*Homoion huion anthropou*" in Rev 1.13 and 14.14', *BT* 44 (1993), pp. 349-50; 'One Like a Son of Man in First-Century CE Judaism', *NTS* 41 (1995), pp. 183-98; 'More on Rev 1.13 and 14.14', *BT* 47 (1996), pp. 146-49; 'Comparisons and the Son of Man', pp. 67-78.

Warrior.[126] This study concurs with Laws and attempts to go beyond her work to substantiate her earlier thesis. Finally, this study will detail the sociological implications of these images for a more complete understanding of the book of Revelation.

The methodology employed will involve a combination of historical criticism and insights from the sociology of knowledge. Since I have discussed historical criticism in detail elsewhere, I will not burden the reader unduly presently.[127]

The main ways in which the Christology of Revelation has been studied have been noted above. This particular study will conduct a socio-historical study of the Christology of Revelation using historical criticism and insights from the sociology of knowledge. The strengths of this approach are threefold. First and foremost, it emphasizes the need for a thorough knowledge of the socio-historical context that gives meaning to expressions, symbols, myths, stories and rituals. It also investigates the ways in which what passes as 'knowledge' or 'reality' in a given social setting is transmitted from place to place and generation to generation and acknowledges that literature plays a role in this transmission. This thesis will demonstrate the ways in which the pagan sacred cosmos and the Christian sacred cosmos came into conflict in Roman Asia.

Secondly, historical criticism attempts to ascertain the context of a given document by identifying its author, locating its historical setting and stating the significance of social, cultural, economic and political references. It also attempts to determine the meaning of the original document for the original readers and its original purpose and function for those readers. Sociology of knowledge begins with the assumption that groups, societies and cultures create symbolic universes, or sacred cosmoses, that provide a cosmic rationale for the way things function in society, legitimize the social institutions that support the social order and create a framework from which individual identities come into formation. In the dynamic relationship between social reality and psychological development, there exists an unconscious validation system in

126. S. Laws, *In Light of the Lamb* (GNS, 31; Wilmington, DE: Michael Glazier, 1988).

127. See T.B. Slater, 'Leading a Bible Study: Explorations in the Historical-Critical Method' (Doctor of Ministry [DMin] thesis; Southern Methodist University, Dallas, TX, 1981), pp. 13-16.

which the social order validates personal behavior that falls within the accepted norms and adheres to the standard values. Likewise, personality characteristics that conform to social expectations reinforce the correctness of the perception of reality in a given social community. Historical criticism provides a means to determine the historical background for the reconstruction of the social setting. Sociology of knowledge then attempts to ascertain the manner in which traditional materials have been incorporated by the group under study. Since the aims of the two methods complement one another so well, the two can naturally work hand in hand in historical research.

Because of these similar concerns, sociology of knowledge and historical criticism can function together. They will be especially helpful in this study, which has the following two overall objectives: (1) to ascertain the role and function of Christ within Revelation's symbolic universe through its use of the 'one like a son of man', the Lamb and the Divine Warrior images; (2) to understand how these images affected the life of the Christian communities in Asia in the first century CE.

Part I

ONE LIKE A SON OF MAN

Chapter 2

THE JEWISH BACKGROUND

Part I will examine the one-like-a-son-of-man tradition in Judaism from Ezekiel to apocalyptic Jewish writings in the early decades of the second century CE and will conclude with a detailed exegesis of the role of the tradition in the book of Revelation.

The preceding chapter discussed the characteristics of apocalyptic literature, the date and social setting of Revelation and commented on recent studies on the Christology of Revelation. It also discussed the research methods, historical criticism and aspects of the sociology of knowledge, to be employed conjointly in order to ascertain in what ways christological imagery helped to maintain a particular communal world-view.

Part I, encompassing Chapters 2–4 of this study, will examine the 'one like a son of man' tradition, identify its roots and development in exilic and postexilic Judaism and demonstrate how Rev. 1.1–3.22 and 14.14-16 fit within this tradition. In particular, Chapter 4 will conclude with a detailed exegesis of Rev. 2.1–3.22 and 14.14-16, demonstrating the manner in which Revelation's Christology incorporates the human-like redeemer imagery and relates it directly to the life of the community by means of the promise of an eternal fellowship with God Almighty and Christ in the new age. This promise established the chief point of contact between Christ and community in Revelation. My discussion of the letters in Revelation 2–3 in Chapter 4 will substantiate this point. Revelation does not merely promise the faithful an eternal fellowship but one as priestly co-regents (i.e. priest-kings) with Christ, a maintenance strategy aimed at sustaining Revelation's symbolic universe. The promise of a priest-kingship is an eschatological exodus motif depicting the Christian Church as the New Israel on the verge of entering the New Jerusalem.[1]

1. I am indebted to Canon John Sweet for pointing out to me in private conversation the importance of exodus motifs in Revelation.

Our discussion of the 'one like a son of man' found in Rev. 1.13 and 14.14 in Part I of this study necessarily also studies the letters to the seven churches (Rev. 2–3), because these letters contain the messages that the 'one like a son of man' sends to the churches and, in turn, reveal something of the Christology of those communities. It would not be enough simply to examine the description, call and commission in 1.13-20 without also examining what Christ instructed John to write. Thus, as Mk 1.1 serves as a programmatic statement to the entire gospel, Rev. 1.13-14 serves as a *superscription* to Revelation 2–3.

Chapter 1 of this study argued that the purpose of the seven letters, with one exception, is to address internal issues within each congregation by stating what constitutes a faithful Christian witness in each context. In this way, the instructions within the letters are aimed at preparing the churches spiritually so that they might endure and overcome the perceived crises envisioned in Rev. 4.1–19.21. If Christians held fast to their faith, they would become priest-kings in the next age. If they did not hold fast to their faith, they could not become priest-kings. Since Christians valued life in the next age more, Rev. 1.5b-6, with its reference to 'the one who loves us and freed us from our sins by means of his blood and made us a kingdom, priests to his God and Father', could be a powerful therapeutic maintenance technique.

1. *The Scholarly Interpretation of Daniel 7.13* [2]

Daniel 7.13a reads, 'As I looked in the night visions, I saw one like a son of man coming with the clouds of heaven' (translation mine).[3] This passage of Scripture has created an enormous amount of secondary literature. Although scholarly comment upon it has been extensive, there is no consensus as to its origin or its original meaning and referent. Our task will not be an exhaustive history of the critical scholarship. Others

2. The remainder of this chapter is a more developed version of my 'One Like a Son of Man in First Century CE Judaism', *NTS* 41 (1995), pp. 183-98.

3. The issue of the mode of transportation by the 'one like a son of man' need not detain us here. Our primary concern is to identify the origin and purpose of the expression 'one like a son of man', an issue that is independent of the former one. Those who espouse a Canaanite setting for the mode of transportation are probably correct, but that need not determine our position on every aspect of Dan. 7.13.

have done so ably.[4] Rather, we shall ask and attempt to answer two questions: (1) What did this expression 'one like a son of man' mean originally in Daniel? (2) To whom did it refer? These two questions are interrelated, if not inseparable.

Generally, scholarly opinion has taken its point of departure from one of six general perspectives. Often methods, ideas and conclusions overlap. However, most scholars make the same error of failing to adequately distinguish the different ways in which the Hebrew Bible and Second Temple Jewish writings employed generic expressions (e.g. 'son of man/sons of men') on the one hand, and the description of heavenly beings by means of comparison to human beings (e.g. 'one like a son of man'), on the other.

1. The messianic interpretation is the earliest extant interpretation of Dan. 7.13. 'Conservative scholars are agreed that the Son of Man is a picture of the Lord Jesus Christ ...'[5] According to this school of interpretation, the setting for Daniel is the Babylonian exile of the sixth century BCE; the 'one like a son of man' referred prophetically to the first coming of Jesus in the first century CE; and the transportation upon clouds connotes his role as a divine being. This school argues that 'Son of Man' was a messianic title for Daniel. Walvoord, for example, writes that 'the frequent introduction of this term in the New Testament referring to Jesus Christ is the divine commentary on the phrase.' He claims that the Son of Man in Daniel 'corresponds clearly to other Scriptures which predict that Christ will rule over all nations (Ps. 72:11; Rev. 19:15-16)'. Walvoord finds confirmation in the fact that Christ 'took the title Himself in the New Testament'.[6] Walvoord has interpreted the Hebrew Bible/Old Testament in light of the New Testament. If he had not, he might have realized that Dan. 7.13 has the comparison 'one *like* a

4. E.g. J. Day, *God's Conflict with the Dragon and the Sea: Echoes of a Canaanite Myth in the Old Testament* (University of Cambridge Oriental Publications, 35; Cambridge: Cambridge University Press, 1985), pp. 151-78; J.E. Goldingay, *Daniel* (WBC, 30; Dallas: Word Books, 1989), pp. 137-72.

5. J.F. Walvoord, *Daniel: The Key to Prophetic Revelation* (Chicago: Moody, 1971), p. 167; see also C.A. Briggs, *Messianic Prophecy* (New York: Charles Scribner's Sons; Edinburgh: T. & T. Clark, 1886), p. 240. For an alternative, see S.R. Driver, *The Book of Daniel* (Cambridge: Cambridge University Press, 1922), pp. 212-50.

6. Walvoord, *Daniel*, p. 168.

son of man' and not the titular 'the son of man'. He presupposes that all prophecies in the Hebrew Bible are predictions concerning Jesus in the first century CE without allowing the prophets to speak for themselves. Finally, many Hebrew Bible scholars question the Babylonian captivity as the true historical setting of Daniel.[7]

2. Other scholars have tended to pinpoint ancient Near Eastern (ANE) parallels as the source of the 'one like a son of man' tradition.[8] For example, in his discussions of Ugaritic, Egyptian, Gnostic and Iranian texts, Mowinckel concluded that the Son of Man concept did not develop within Judaism but developed as a Jewish variant of the ANE concept of the cosmic Primal Man. In the Jewish version, soteriological and eschatological elements replaced the cosmological ones.[9] Similarly, Cullmann argued that a concept of an Original Man existed in oriental religions and that Judaism attempted to relate this concept to Adam, the first human. One result of this attempted merger was the Danielic Son of Man.[10] However, our knowledge of the origin and geographical extent of the *Urmensch* traditions is limited, and thus this tradition cannot be assumed with certainty to be a model for the book of Daniel. This approach also misses entirely the distinction within the tradition between the generic and comparative expressions. While the generic expressions (e.g. 'son of man' or 'sons of men') function as circumlocutions, the comparisons (e.g. 'like that of a man' [Ezek. 8.2] or 'one

7. For example, Shea accepts the Babylonian provenance ('The Neo-Babylonian Historical Setting for Daniel 7', *AUSS* 24 [1986], pp. 31-36), while Collins espouses a second century Syrian-occupied Palestine provenance ('Daniel and his Social World', *Int* 39 [1985], pp. 131-43).

8. E.g. C.H. Kraeling, *Anthropos and Son of Man* (New York: Columbia University Press, 1927); S. Mowinckel, *He That Cometh* (New York: Abingdon Press, 1954); M. Noth, 'Die Heiligen des Höchsten', *NorTT* 56 (1955), pp. 146-61; J.A. Emerton, 'The Origins of the Son of Man Imagery', *JTS* 9 (1958), pp. 225-42; J. Morgenstern, 'The "Son of Man" of Dan 7:13f.: A New Interpretation', *JBL* 80 (1961), pp. 65-77; O. Cullmann, *The Christology of the New Testament* (Philadelphia: Westminster Press, rev. edn, 1963); F.H. Borsch, *The Son of Man in Myth and History* (Philadelphia: Westminster Press, 1967); *idem*, *The Christian and the Gnostic Son of Man* (Naperville, IL: Allenson, 1970); H.S. Kvanvig, *Roots of Apocalyptic: The Mesopotamian Background of the Enoch Figure and the Son of Man* (Neukirchen–Vluyn: Neukirchener Verlag, 1988).

9. Mowinckel, *He That Cometh*, pp. 346-450.

10. Cullmann, *Christology*, pp. 142-43. For critiques of Mowinckel and Cullmann, see F.M. Wilson, 'The Son of Man in Jewish Apocalyptic Literature', *Studia Biblica et Theologica* 8 (1978), pp. 28-52.

like a son of man' [Dan. 7.13]) describe heavenly beings in human likeness.

3. Colpe is among those who argue for a Canaanite background to the son of man image in Daniel. He argues that the Ras Shamra texts describe Baal, the young god who replaced the chief god El, as one who rides upon the clouds. He also notes other borrowings from the Canaanites, for example, in Isa. 19.1, 27.1; Ps. 74.13-14; Job 9.13 and 26.12. In this way, he hopes to demonstrate how these non-Jewish traditions survived in the Jewish community up to the second century BCE.[11]

The parallels identified by Colpe are generally sound, but they may reflect a more general ANE tradition lost to us. One should note, however, that Dan. 7.13 does not tell of a young god replacing an older god, as with Baal and El, but rather a god giving authority to a heavenly being. If Canaanite religiosity is the source of Dan. 7.13, it has been demythologized considerably. In addition, Colpe's explanation provides little information as to how the figure functions in Daniel 7. Moreover, this interpretation fails to appreciate the traditional distinction made between the generic expressions and the descriptive comparisons.

4. Many commentators look more to the biblical tradition itself. Hooker, for example, argues that in both Daniel and *1 Enoch* the 'Son of Man' represented the faithful remnant within the people of God in both suffering and glorification.[12] 'The fact that the phrase "Son of

11. C. Colpe, 'ὁ υἱός τοῦ ἀνθρώπου', *TDNT*, VIII, pp. 406-30; see also J.J. Collins, *The Apocalyptic Vision of the Book of Daniel* (HSM, 16; Missoula, MT: Scholars Press, 1977), pp. 123-47; *idem*, *The Apocalyptic Imagination* (New York: Crossroad, 1984), pp. 78-86; see also Day, Emerton and Morgenstern cited above. For a critique of this position, see Wilson, 'Son of Man', p. 36.

12. M.D. Hooker, *The Son of Man in Mark* (Montreal: McGill University Press, 1967). Scholars with similar views include S.R. Driver (mentioned above); T.W. Manson, 'The Son of Man in Daniel, Enoch and the Gospels', *BJRL* 32 (1949–50), pp. 171-93; J. Muilenburg, 'The Son of Man in Daniel and the Ethiopic Apocalypse of Enoch', *JBL* 79 (1960), pp. 197-209; C.F.D. Moule, *The Origin of Christology* (Cambridge: Cambridge University Press, 1977), esp. pp. 11-22; *idem*, ' "The Son of Man": Some of the Facts', *NTS* 41 (1995), pp. 277-79; M. Casey, *Son of Man: The Interpretation and Influence of Daniel 7* (London: SPCK, 1979); A.A. DiLella, 'The One in Human-Likeness and the Holy Ones of the Most High in Daniel 7', *CBQ* 39 (1977), pp. 1-19; D.S. Russell, *Daniel* (Philadelphia: Westminster Press, 1981); R.A. Anderson, *Signs and Wonders* (International Theological Commentary; Edinburgh: Handsel; Grand Rapids: Eerdmans, 1984).

man" is used here as a comparison suggests that, whatever else he may or may not be, he is not a mere "Son of man".'[13] Against Schmidt, who argues that 'one like a son of man' is a comparison that refers to angels, she argues, 'Such reasoning presents a too-neat solution to our problem. The useful convention that animals represent men and men represent supernatural beings no doubt holds good for later apocalyptic, but it is doubtful whether it was already a recognized formula when Dan. 7 was composed.'[14] She finds two themes in Daniel 7. First, there is a conflict between the people of Israel and their foes and, secondly, the conquest of chaos by their god. 'Yahweh's struggle with the monster and the people's battle with their enemies are one, and it is God's victory which ensures the well-being of the people.'[15] The Son of man represents the faithful remnant of Israel who received dominion. Israel is 'the true Son of Man to whom dominion belongs by right.'[16]

Hooker notes a shift in the Similitudes of Enoch (*1 En.* 37–71) and 2 Esdras/*4 Ezra* 13. In the Similitudes, the Son of Man is more an individual, while not losing his function as a representative figure. He is the Righteous One who represents the righteous ones; the Elect One who represents the elect ones.[17] In 2 Esdras 13, the Danielic Son of man has become an individual Man, possibly under the influence of an *Anthropos* tradition.[18]

Hooker's argument has several strengths. First and foremost, she correctly recognizes that Dan. 7.13 contains a comparison, is not a formula and is not a title. Moreover, she properly discerns the representational function of both the Danielic and the Enochic figures. Finally, Hooker correctly identifies the shift of meaning from a representative heavenly figure in Daniel to the Messiah in the Similitudes and 2 Esdras 13. However, Hooker argument is not flawless. For example, she fails to appreciate the change that the comparison creates when joined with the generic phrase. It is no longer a generic phrase in Daniel, the Similitudes of Enoch or 2 Esdras but becomes a description of a heavenly being in human likeness. Thus, she also fails to identify the use of comparisons in *1 Enoch* 46 and 2 Esdras (*4 Ezra*) 13 as descriptions of

13. Hooker, *Son of Man*, p. 11; see also n. 1.
14. Hooker, *Son of Man*, p. 14.
15. Hooker, *Son of Man*, pp. 20-21; quote from p. 21.
16. Hooker, *Son of Man*, pp. 23-29; quote from p. 29.
17. Hooker, *Son of Man*, p. 46.
18. Hooker, *Son of Man*, pp. 49-56.

heavenly beings totally consistent with Dan. 7.13. Indeed, her contention that humans did not represent heavenly beings when Daniel was written cannot be sustained. Daniel 9.21 and 12.5 refer to angels as human beings, when it is clear from the literary context that they are not. Earlier, Ezek. 9.2-3 and 10.1-8 described angels similarly. Schmidt's solution may be 'too-neat' simply because it is correct. The 'one like a son of man' in Dan. 7.13 is more than a representative figure. He is also an individual heavenly being who has received the dominion in heaven that will come soon to the faithful remnant of Israel on earth, according to Daniel 7–12.

5. Like Hooker, DiLella argued that the son of man was a symbol of the faithful. The Aramaic כְּבַר אֱנָשׁ (one like a son of man) and the Hebrew בֶּן אָדָם (son of man) are figures of speech that merely mean 'a human being' or 'a person'. The 'one in human likeness' is not a real person but

> a symbol of 'the holy ones of the Most High', a title given, ... to the faithful Jews ... who courageously withstood the persecution of Antiochus IV Epiphanes. Hence, there seems to be no mystery at all as to the meaning and background of the 'one in human likeness'.[19]

First of all, against DiLella, I would argue that there is a 'mystery' simply because this figure is not named explicitly in Daniel. Secondly, Dan. 7.13 does not simply read בַּר אֱנשׁ but כְּבַר אֱנָשׁ. In both its Hebraic and Aramaic forms, 'son of man' is merely a figure of speech denoting human beings; however, the comparison changes the meaning significantly, conveying to its original readers that the figure only has a human appearance.

Indeed, what sense would it make to describe a human being with the expression 'like a human being'? It would convey that the being in question only looked human, or had a human appearance, but was not actually human. This is exactly how the four beasts are described in Dan. 7.1-8. The reader knows that these descriptions are nothing but analogous representations. Thus, the 'one like a son of man' is not a human being but a description of another type of being, a heavenly being (as traveling via clouds connotes in the Hebrew Bible [e.g. Exod. 13.21; 16.10; Num. 11.25; Ps. 104.3; Isa. 19.1]) in human form.

19. DiLella, 'One in Human-Likeness', p. 3; cf. Moule, 'Purpose of I Peter', p. 278.

6. The final position was first put forth by Nathaniel Schmidt in two journal articles late in the nineteenth century.[20] In his first article, Schmidt argued that 'son of man' was not a messianic title. In the later article, developing his earlier one somewhat, Schmidt argued that 'one like a son of man' did not refer to the Messiah but to the archangel Michael. Schmidt argued that in Dan. 8.15, Gabriel is described as 'one having the appearance of a man'. Daniel 10.16 later described another angel as 'one in the likeness of the sons of men' and Dan. 10.18 a third time described an angel as 'one having the appearance of a man'. Furthermore, coming with clouds suggests a heavenly being (see my comments above concerning DiLella's position). Finally, Dan. 10.21 identified Michael as the heavenly prince of Israel. Thus, Schmidt concluded that 'one like a son of man' in Dan. 7.13 functioned similarly and described an angelic being. Since Michael is the angelic prince for Israel, he would be the logical referent of 'one like a son of man'.

Others have followed Schmidt's lead. For example, Leitzmann argued that, since Daniel and Revelation both use comparisons and the Gospels do not, Revelation depends upon Daniel and knows nothing of the synoptic son of man tradition.[21] Others have identified 'the holy ones of the Most High' as the angelic army that followed Michael in battle at the celestial level. Both Michael and the holy ones would be the heavenly counterparts to the faithful Jews under Antiochus's persecution.[22] Day argues, for example, that except in Psalm 34, 'holy ones' always refers to angels in the Hebrew Bible, Qumran and the intertestamental

20. N. Schmidt, 'Was *bar nash* a Messianic Title?', *JBL* 15 (1896), pp. 36-53; *idem*, 'The "Son of Man" in the Book of Daniel', *JBL* 19 (1900), pp. 22-28. It is this Schmidt to whom Hooker referred whose solution was 'too neat'.

21. H. Lietzmann, *Der Menschensohn* (Freiburg: Mohr, 1896), pp. 56-57; also Krodel, *Revelation*, p. 322; T.B. Slater, ' "*Homoion huion anthropou*" in Rev 1.13 and 14.14', *BT* 44 (1993), pp. 349-50; *idem*, 'More on Revelation 1.13 and 14.14', *BT* 47 (1996), pp. 146-49. See also J.J. Collins's helpful discussion (*Daniel* [Hermeneia; Minneapolis: Augsburg–Fortress, 1993], pp. 304-10).

22. E.g. Emerton and Noth cited above; L. Dequeker, 'Daniel vii et les Saints du Très-Haut', *ETL* 36 (1960), pp. 353-92; *idem*, 'The Saints of the Most High in Qumran and Daniel', *OTS* 18 (1973), pp. 108-87; Collins, *Vision of Daniel*, pp. 96-101; cf. H. Sahlin, 'Wie wurde ursprünglichlich die Benennung "Der Menschensohn" verstanden', *ST* 37 (1983), pp. 147-79; R. Kearns, *Die Entchristologisierung des Menschensohnes* (Tübingen: Mohr Siebeck, 1988). For a contrasting view, see G.F. Hasel, 'The Identity of the "Saints of the Most High" in Daniel 7', *Bib* 76 (1975), pp. 173-92.

literature.[23] Collins notes similar roles for Michael in the Qumran literature (QL) (e.g. 1QM 17.7-8) and the New Testament (e.g. Rev. 12.7-12) and notes similar heavenly figures in 11QMelch 8-15; *T. Mos.* 10; Mt. 16.27; Mk 8.38; 1 Thess. 4.16; and 2 Thess. 1.7. For him, the Danielic figure is a variant version of a Second Temple Jewish belief in a heavenly savior.[24]

I agree with the position taken by Schmidt and followed and developed by others. First, it does justice to Daniel by not reading the New Testament back into it, but reads Daniel on its own terms. Secondly, those who have followed Schmidt's lead have shown parallels in other Jewish writings without overlooking Daniel's place within the tradition. Collins especially has shown parallel developments in Second Temple Judaism and early Christianity that elucidate Daniel's use and concept of the expression. Thirdly, Schmidt correctly perceives the distinctive manner in which Daniel 7–12 uses comparisons.

Why then have so many gone wrong on this topic? With few exceptions, regardless of the point of departure, most scholars have made the same three errors. First, the synoptic son of man tradition is either in the foreground and/or the background of the thinking of many exegetes. Either they want to argue that Dan. 7.13 refers to Jesus (e.g. Walvoord) or they want to argue that 'one like a son of man' is merely a generic reference (e.g. DiLella). The distinction between generic expressions and descriptive comparisons was recognized by both Second Temple Jewish and early Christian writers. For example, Mark uses a generic expression (υἱοῖς τῶν ἀνθρώπων [3.28]) to denote human beings, while using ὁ υἱὸς τοῦ ἀνθρώπου as a technical term to denote the Messiah (e.g. 8.38). Similarly, *1 Enoch* makes a similar distinction, using son of man/sons of men to refer to human beings (39.1); comparisons to refer to the Messiah (45.1). Secondly, while exegetes consistently recognize that the beasts are described by means of comparisons and are symbolic dynastic representations, they rarely recognize the use of the comparison in the presentation of the human-like heavenly creature and the relevance of this fact when interpreting 7.13, almost certainly owing to the

23. Day, *God's Conflict*, p. 168, esp. n. 81.

24. Collins, *Vision of Daniel*, pp. 123-47; *idem*, *Apocalyptic Imagination*, pp. 84-86; cf. Day, *God's Conflict*, pp. 167-78. For a critique of these writers, see A.J. Ferch, 'Daniel 7 and Ugarit: A Reconsideration', *JBL* 99 (1980), pp. 75-86.

influence of the synoptic traditions.[25] Finally, they do not realize the degree to which Daniel is dependent upon Ezekiel for its comparisons, primarily due to an overemphasis on the question of the relationship between Dan. 7.13 and the synoptics. Subsequently, they fail to perceive how comparisons function in the Hebrew Bible, Second Temple Jewish literature and Revelation.

These errors are interrelated. Several persons have recognized the dependence of Daniel 7 upon Ezekiel 1.[26] For example, Bowman notes the throne on wheels aflame (cf. Ezek. 1.4, 15-16, 21, 26; Dan. 7.6); God enthroned in human likeness (cf. Ezek. 1.26-27; Dan. 7.9-10); a great cloud (Ezek. 1.4; Dan. 7.13); and four great beasts (Ezek. 1.5-14; Dan. 7.3-8). This listing, however, is but partial. I have identified four other elements that Daniel borrows from Ezekiel that enable us to understand better the role and function of the comparisons and the relationship between the two books. First and most importantly, the setting for both books is the Babylonian captivity in the sixth century BCE, in actuality for Ezekiel; in imagery for Daniel. This cannot be overstated. The author of Daniel uses Ezekiel's context as a symbolic metaphor, a mirror for his own time. As in Ezekiel's time, faithfulness to God cannot be taken for granted in the face of an oppressive foreign ruler but must be shown constantly. *4 Ezra*, Revelation, *Sibylline Oracles* 5 and the *Apocalypse of Abraham*, all thought to have been written about 100 CE, also use 'Babylon' as a code name for the oppressor and use Ezekiel's time as a symbolic metaphor.

Secondly, both books contain symbolic messages of hope in order to encourage the faithful in their struggle against oppression (e.g. Ezek. 37; Dan. 7).

Thirdly, in the books of Ezekiel and Daniel alone in the Hebrew Bible, 'son of man' functions as a means of address to a human being (e.g. Ezek. 2.1; 5.1; 11.2; 15.2; 22.23; 30.21; 37.3; 40.4; Dan. 8.17 [cf.

25. J.J. Collins is among the few who recognize the employment of comparisons in all cases in Dan. 7.1-13 (*Daniel*, pp. 304-10).

26. E.g. J. Bowman, 'The Background of the Term "Son of Man" ', *ET* 59 (1947–48), pp. 283-88 (285); A. Feuillet, 'Le Fils de l'homme de Daniel et la tradition biblique', *RB* 60 (1953), pp. 180-89; R.B.Y. Scott, 'Behold, He Cometh with Clouds', *NTS* 5 (1958–59), pp. 127-32; M. Delcor, *Le livre de Daniel* (Paris: Gabalda, 1971), pp. 302-304; Day, *God's Conflict*, pp. 157-58; F.M. Wilson, 'Son of Man', p. 37.

Dan. 10.19]).[27] The only other extant occurrence of 'son of man' as a means of address in early Judaism is in *1 En.* 60.10: 'And he said to me, "Son of man, you here wish to know what is secret." '[28]

Fourthly, in the Hebrew Bible both Ezekiel and Daniel describe heavenly beings by means of comparison. Schmidt correctly noted this in Dan. 7.13; 8.15; 10.16, 18 (see also 12.6-7). Parallels in Ezekiel include 1.26-28, which describes the appearance of the Lord; 8.2-4, which may describe either God or an angel; 9.2-11, which describes an angel as a 'man clothed in linen' (see Dan. 10.5 and 12.6-7; also compare Ezek. 9.4-6 with Rev. 7.3); 40.3-4 describes an angel who acts as Ezekiel's heavenly guide (cf. Dan. 10.10-21).

These parallels in and of themselves may not persuade everyone; however, one should note that 'son of man/sons of men' never functions as a description of a heavenly being but only as a reference or means of address to a human being in the Hebrew Bible. The same is also true in Second Temple Judaism. Some might argue that the title 'that/this Son of man' in *1 Enoch* 37–71 is an exception to this rule. It is not. In *1 Enoch* 37–71 'that/this Son of man' is not the primary referent. The primary referent is one 'whose face had the appearance of a man' (46.1). In other words, in *1 Enoch* 37–71 'that/this Son of man' always refers back to the figure introduced with a comparison in 46.1 and not vice versa.[29] That is to say, the phrase 'whose face had the appearance of a man' is the image for which 'that/this Son of Man' is the symbol. Additionally, the Ethiopic translation of *1 Enoch* employs three different expressions for 'that/this son of man', suggesting that it was not a technical term or a title in the earlier document of which the Ethiopic version is a translation. This entire matter is difficult to clarify because Ethiopic has no definite article. However, it is certain that 'this/that Son

27. Cf. Driver, *Daniel*, p. 215; W.S. Towner, *Daniel* (Interpretation; Atlanta: John Knox Press, 1984), pp. 90-103; J.J. Collins, *Daniel, with an Introduction to Apocalyptic Literature* (FOTL, 20; Grand Rapids: Eerdmans, 1984 [hereafter Collins, *Daniel*, FOTL]), p. 87.

28. I am using M.A. Knibb's translation of *1 Enoch* in H.F.D. Sparks (ed.), *The Apocryphal Old Testament* (Oxford: Clarendon Press, 1984); B.M. Metzger's translation of *4 Ezra* (2 Esdras) in J.H. Charlesworth (ed.), *The Old Testament Pseudepigrapha* (2 vols.; Garden City, NY: Doubleday, 1983–85). A good selection of apocalyptic writings can also be found in M.G. Reddish (ed.), *Apocalyptic Literature: A Reader* (Nashville: Abingdon Press, 1990).

29. Cf. J.J. Collins, 'The Son of Man in First-Century Judaism', *NTS* 38 (1992), pp. 452-53.

of Man' is not a mere mortal, but a heavenly being who possesses extraordinary powers and duties.[30]

Furthermore, even though there is no consensus among scholars concerning the origin, meaning and function of Dan. 7.13, there is a broad consensus that Ezekiel has influenced Daniel's presentation of heavenly beings[31] and that Dan. 8.15, 10.16 and 10.18 refer to heavenly beings.[32]

We began this section by asking what the expression 'one like a son of man' meant and to whom it referred originally. Our research has shown that this expression was one of several descriptions by comparison that the books of Ezekiel and Daniel employed to designate heavenly beings, either God (e.g. Ezek. 1.26-28) or angels (e.g. Dan. 10.16-18). Although absolute literary dependence has not been established, nowhere else does one find these same aforementioned literary parallels. My research does not deny other parallels, but those parallels, for example in Canaanite traditions, have not adequately examined the function of these comparisons in the Hebrew Bible.

2. *The Interpretation of Daniel 7.13 in First-Century* CE *Judaism and Christianity*

a. *The Similitudes of Enoch*

1 Enoch 37–71, also known as the Similitudes of Enoch, *4 Ezra* 13, the *Apoc. Abr.* 10.1-4 and the *Mart. Isa.* 4.1-2 provide important examples of the interpretation of Dan. 7.13 in first-century CE Judaism and independent, parallel Christian traditions.[33]

30. Cf. Wilson, 'Son of Man', pp. 40-42.

31. E.g. DiLella, 'One in Human-Likeness', pp. 10-11; Walvoord, *Daniel*, p. 191; Towner, *Daniel*, p. 103; Emerton, 'Origin', pp. 236-38; Feuillet, 'Le Fils', pp. 181-191; Russell, *Daniel*, pp. 119, 124-25; J.A. Montgomery, *A Critical and Exegetical Commentary on the Book of Daniel* (ICC, 22; Edinburgh: T. & T. Clark, 1960), p. 346; N.W. Porteous, *Daniel: A Commentary* (OTL; Philadelphia: Westminster Press, rev. edn, 1979), pp. 108, 127.

32. E.g. A. Lacocque, *The Book of Daniel* (Atlanta: John Knox Press, 1976), pp. 167-73, 206-13; Goldingay, *Daniel*, pp. 213-15, 290-92; Anderson, *Signs*, pp. 99-103, 124-28; Driver, *Daniel*, pp. 212-14, 256-64; Collins, *Daniel*, FOTL, pp. 87, 96-104; Walvoord, *Daniel*, pp. 191, 248-49; Towner, *Daniel*, pp. 117, 152-53; Russell, *Daniel*, pp. 152-58, 195-202; Manson, 'Son of Man', p. 177; Porteous, *Daniel*, pp. 127-30, 154-56; Casey, *Son of Man*, pp. 27-28.

33. Collins, 'Son of Man', pp. 452-59; Reddish, *Apocalyptic Literature*, pp. 163-66. For different points of view on the Similitudes and *4 Ezra*, see J.Y.

It is generally acknowledged that *1 Enoch* is a composite of several Enoch books written at different times and places. These books are (1) The Watchers (1–36), (2) The Similitudes (37–71), (3) The Astronomical Writings (72–82), (4) The Dream Visions (83–90) and (5) The Epistle (91–107). The Similitudes have five parts: (1) an introduction (37.1-4); (2) the first similitude (chs. 38–44); (3) the second similitude (chs. 45–57); (4) the third similitude (chs. 58–69); (5) two epilogues (chs. 70–71).

The Similitudes were not found in the Qumran collection and this fact has led many scholars to date the Similitudes after the death of that community in 70 CE. Milik, for example, has argued for a pre-Christian Enochic Pentateuch at Qumran with a longer version of the astrological writings and a 'Book of Giants' instead of the Similitudes. Milik did not work closely with the Ethiopic translations. He discovered late additions in 61.1 in Aramaic that refer to angels flying with wings. He concluded that the Similitudes was a Christian work that eventually replaced the Giants in the Enoch tradition. He dated the Similitudes in the late third century CE.[34]

Milik has been soundly criticized by other leading scholars studying *1 Enoch*. Some have argued that, if Milik had worked more closely with the Ethiopic translations, he would have found that the addition in 61.1 was not in the Ethiopic and would have dated the Similitudes in the first century CE.[35] Reddish argues that the earliest possible date would be 40 BCE if 56.5-7 refers to an attack on Palestine by the Parthians at that time. He also notes that 67.5-13 refers to hot springs where the affluent sought cures from illnesses. This could refer to the springs at Callirhoe,

Campbell, 'The Origin and Meaning of the Term Son of Man', *JTS* 48 (1947), pp. 145-55; J.C. Hindley, 'Towards a Date for the Similitudes of Enoch: An Historical Approach', *NTS* 14 (1967–68), pp. 551-65; D.C. Sim, 'Matthew 22.13a and 1 Enoch 10.4a: A Case of Literary Dependence?', *JSNT* 47 (1992), pp. 3-19. *4 Ezra* and the *Apocalypse of Abraham* do have Christian interpolations but not in the verses which we shall examine.

34. J.T. Milik, *The Books of Enoch: Aramaic Fragments from Qumran Cave 4* (Oxford: Clarendon Press, 1976), pp. 4-135.

35. See J.H. Charlesworth, 'The SNTS Pseudepigrapha Seminars at Tübingen and Paris on the Books of Enoch', *NTS* 25 (1978–79), pp. 315-23; G.W.E. Nickelsburg's major review of Milik in *CBQ* 40 (1978), pp. 411-19; M.A. Knibb, *The Ethiopic Book of Enoch* (2 vols.; Oxford: Clarendon Press, 1978); *idem*, 'The Date of the Parables of Enoch: A Critical Review', *NTS* 25 (1978–79), pp. 345-59; C.L. Mearns, 'Dating the Similitudes of Enoch', *NTS* 25 (1978–79), pp. 360-69.

to which Herod travelled prior to his death in 4 BCE. Moreover, Reddish also notes parallels between the New Testament and the Similitudes (Mt. 19.28 and *1 En*. 45.3; Jn 5.22 and *1 En*. 61.8).[36] In general, I agree with Reddish. However, the New Testament parallels may simply reflect dependence upon a common Jewish religious milieu. I would argue for a date in the first six decades of the Common Era, because the Similitudes do not contain any reference to the Jewish War of 66–72 CE but allude to events at the close of the previous century. It would be difficult for a Jewish writer not to mention the destruction of Jerusalem after the fact, as *4 Ezra*, *2 Baruch* and the *Apocalypse of Abraham* attest.[37]

1 En. 46.1 describes one with the Head of Days 'whose face had the appearance of a man and his face [was] full of grace, like one of the holy angels', that is, he is a heavenly being. This text clearly picks up where Dan. 7.13 ends. The 'Ancient of Days' is now the 'Head of Days', the 'one like a son of man' is now one 'whose face had the appearance of a man' who is identified as 'that Son of Man'. As noted earlier, *1 En*. 46.1 introduced the human-like figure with a descriptive comparison, in keeping with Dan. 7.13 and Ezek. 1.26. In other words, the comparison becomes the point of reference for 'this/that Son of Man' and not the reverse (see also *1 En*. 46.2, 3, 4; 48.2; 60.10; 62.7, 9, 14; 63.11; 69. 26, 27 (twice); 70.1; 71.14, 17). 'This/That Son of Man' is the Messiah, the Elect One, the Chosen One (e.g. chs. 51–52).[38] 'This/That Son of Man' sits on a throne (e.g. 45.3; 55.4; 61.8; 62.5; 69.27, 29), acts as a judge (e.g. 45.3; 46.2) and gathers a community of the faithful to himself (e.g. 48.4 and 62.12-13); is righteous (e.g. 46.3; 62.2), has a mysterious dimension (e.g. 48.3; 62.7), functions as a revealer (e.g. 46.3), rules the cosmos (e.g. 62.6-7; 71.15-17) and is an object of adoration (e.g. 48.5; 62.9).

In contrast, *1 Enoch* 37–71 has ten generic sayings that do not describe or refer to heavenly beings but to human beings. *1 Enoch* 39.1 provides an excellent example, for it contrasts heavenly beings with human beings. 'And it will come to pass in these days that the chosen and holy children [i.e. angels] will come down from the high heavens,

36. Reddish, *Apocalyptic Literature*, pp. 164-65.

37. See discussion in Collins, *Apocalyptic Imagination*, pp. 155-86.

38. Cf. C.C. Caragounis, *The Son of Man: Vision and Interpretation* (Tübingen: Mohr Siebeck, 1986), pp. 116-19.

and their offspring will become one with the sons of men' (cf. 39.5; 42.2; 64.2 [twice]; 69.6 [twice]; 69.12; 69.14 [v. 69.15 in *OTP*]).

1 Enoch 60.10 stands out for it provides a parallel to Ezekiel's and Daniel's use of 'son of man' as a means of address: 'And he said to me, "Son of man, you here wish to know what is secret." '[39] One finds in *1 Enoch* 37–71 the same literary feature that one finds in the Hebrew Bible with respect to the generic son of man/sons of men phrases referring to humans and comparisons referring to heavenly beings.

b. *4 Ezra/2 Esdras*

4 Ezra is a composite Jewish-Christian work. Chapters 3–14 contain the original Jewish work, also known as *2 Esdras*. Chapters 1–2 and 15–16 are later Christian additions. Chapters 3–14 contain seven visions: (1) 3.1–5.20; (2) 5.21–6.34; (3) 6.35–9.25; (4) 9.26–10.59; (5) 11.1–12.51; (6) 13.1-58; (7) 14.1-48.[40] Most scholars date *4 Ezra* c. 100 CE. *4 Ezra* 3.1 laments the destruction of the city by the Babylonians 30 years earlier (cf. Ezek. 1.1). However, this is probably a symbolic reference to the Romans' destruction of Jerusalem in 70 CE. In *4 Ezra* 11–12, the eagle vision presents an eagle with 12 wings and 3 heads. The 12 wings probably symbolize the 12 Roman emperors, from Caesar to Domitian; the 3 heads, the Flavians Vespasian, Titus and Domitian. Indeed, the symbol of the Roman Empire was the eagle, the very symbol used for the oppressor in chs. 11–12. Thus, New Testament scholars generally agree that *4 Ezra* 3.1 refers to the siege of Jerusalem in 70 CE by Vespasian and Titus.[41]

4 Ezra 13 interprets Dan. 7.13 in a manner similar to *1 Enoch* 46 by employing a comparison to present a heavenly being: 'And I looked, and behold, this wind made something *like* the figure of a man come up out of the heart of the sea. And I looked, and behold, that man flew with the clouds of heaven … (*4 Ezra* 13.3; italics added).' As with Ezekiel, Daniel and *1 Enoch*, a heavenly being is described in human likeness

39. Collins agrees and argues that *1 En.* 71.14 may also be a form of direct address ('Son of Man', p. 456). I am open to that possibility.

40. Seven is a holy number in both Revelation and *4 Ezra* (see Bauckham, *Theology*, pp. 16-17, 26-27, 40-42, 79-83, 109-19; Collins, *Apocalyptic Imagination*, pp. 49-52).

41. Cf. Collins, *Apocalyptic Imagination*, p. 156; Reddish, *Apocalyptic Literature*, p. 58.

by means of a comparison.[42] With regard to qualities and/or functions, there are strong parallels with *1 Enoch* 37–71, suggesting a common tradition of interpretation in first-century CE Judaism. In *4 Ezra* 13, this human like figure is unknown (v. 52; cf. 7.28; 12.31-39; *1 En.* 48.3; 62.7); pronounces judgment (vv. 37-38; cf. 12.32-33; *1 En.* 46.4-6; 62.3-16; 69.27-29), gathers an elect community (vv. 12-13, 39-50; *1 En.* 48.4 and 62.12-13) and is the messiah (*4 Ezra* 12-13; *1 En.* 52–53). Finally, as with Dan. 7.13, the human-like figure of *4 Ezra* 13 rides upon the clouds. These parallels strongly support an argument for *1 Enoch* and *4 Ezra* sharing in a common exegetical tradition.

c. *The Apocalypse of Abraham and the Martyrdom and Ascension of Isaiah*

Two other writings also deserve attention, the *Apocalypse of Abraham* and the *Martyrdom and Ascension of Isaiah*. These two works do not employ descriptive comparisons to present messianic figures, but they do use them to describe the appearance of heavenly beings.

Most scholars date the *Apocalypse of Abraham* around 100 CE on the grounds that, like *4 Ezra* and *2 Baruch*, it attempts to understand the meaning behind the destruction of Jerusalem in 70 CE.[43] I am persuaded by this argument.

Apoc. Abr. 10.1-4 describes how God sent an angel to Abraham to restore his strength. In ch. 9, God has given Abraham a vision. Abraham becomes faint in 10.1-2 (cf. Rev. 1.17a). God sends an angel to strengthen him (v. 3). The seer describes the angel in this manner (v. 4): 'The angel he sent to me *in the likeness* of a man came, and he took me by my right hand and stood me on my feet' (italics added).[44] Here we have a clear example of a heavenly being described in human likeness. Although this being is not the Messiah, this tradition agrees with examples presented in Ezekiel, Daniel, *1 Enoch* and *4 Ezra*, which describe God, the Messiah and angels in this same manner. This verse, without Christian influence and employing a comparison to describe an angel

42. For contrasting views, see G.H. Box (ed. and trans.), *The Ezra Apocalypse* (London: Pitman & Sons, 1912), p. 286; M.E. Stone, *Fourth Ezra* (Hermeneia; Minneapolis: Fortress Press, 1990), pp. 207-13; Kvanvig, *Roots*, pp. 522-31.

43. *OTP*, I, p. 683 nn. 15-16. See also Collins, *Apocalyptic Imagination*, pp. 180-86.

44. Rubinkiewicz's translation in *OTP*, I, pp. 681-705.

instead of the Messiah, in contrast to the Similitudes of Enoch and *4 Ezra*, still shares with them the use of comparisons to describe heavenly beings. Rowland argues that *Apoc. Abr.* 10.4 based its description of the angel upon Ezekiel and Daniel.[45]

The Martyrdom and Ascension of Isaiah is a composite work whose various parts need not detain us.[46] We shall focus upon *Mart. Isa.* 3.13–4.22, also known as the *Testament of Hezekiah*, a Christian work. Knibb, correctly in my opinion, dates it between 68–100 CE. *Mart. Isa.* 4.2 describes Beliar/Satan:

> And after it has been brought to completion, Beliar will descend, the great angel, the king of this world, which he has ruled ever since it existed. He will descend from his firmament *in the form of a man*, a king of iniquity, a murderer of his mother—this is the king of this world (italics added).

Originally, the tradition probably only recounted Satan's fall from heaven in human likeness (cf. Lk. 10.18; Rev. 12.7-9). However, after Nero's persecution of Christians, *Mart. Isa.* 4.2 identified Satan with a specific human being. What is of importance for our study is the use of the descriptive comparison 'in the form of a man' to present a heavenly being (cf. *Mart. Isa.* 9.12-13).

d. *Other Comparisons: The Testament of Abraham and Philo's On Abraham*

The *Testament of Abraham* (c. first century BCE–second century CE) uses a comparison with regard to the archangel Michael: 'The Prince Michael was approaching, when lo, Abraham saw him in the distance looking *like* a most handsome soldier' (2.3; italics added).[47] The author uses a comparison to convey to the reader that the archangel Michael appeared in human likeness. The likeness is so convincing that Abraham, according to the narrative, mistakes the archangel for a human being. Verse 6 confirms this interpretation. 'Abraham said to the Prince, "Greetings, most honourable soldier, [whose face] shines like the sun and [whose form is] more handsome than any other sons of men: you

45. Rowland, 'Vision of the Risen Christ', pp. 1-11.
46. On these matters and the translation, see M.A. Knibb in *OTP*, II, pp. 143-76.
47. I am using Nigel Turner's translation of *The Testament of Abraham* in *AOT*.

are welcome indeed!" ' This second passage is significant. In it 'sons of men' is clearly a generic reference and to read it in any other way is to misread it. It demonstrates clearly that 'son of man/sons of men' were generic references; however, it is just as significant that the author used a comparison in introducing the archangel Michael.

Philo has a similar passage in *Abraham* 118:

> It is a marvel indeed that though they neither ate nor drank they gave the appearance of both eating and drinking. But that is a secondary matter; the first and greatest wonder is that, though incorporeal, they *assumed human form* to do kindness to the man of worth.[48]

Philo's point is that the angels feigned human activities and assumed human forms when they came to visit Abraham. In other words, the angels assumed human likeness.

This passage from Philo's *On Abraham* is all the more important because it is not apocalyptic. Indeed, Philo is a well-educated Diaspora Middle Platonist Jewish apologist. Moreover, The *Testament* also uses 'sons of men' as a generic reference while still reserving the comparison for the archangel, clearly giving support to my thesis concerning the use of generics and comparisons in the traditions.

3. *Summation*

Several elements stand out from this survey. First and foremost, we have discovered the consistent use of descriptive comparisons to designate heavenly beings in Ezekiel, Daniel, *1 Enoch*, *4 Ezra*, the *Apocalypse of Abraham*, the *Testament of Abraham*, Philo's *On Abraham* and the *Martyrdom and Ascension of Isaiah*.[49] Secondly, Ezekiel, Daniel and *1 Enoch* use 'son of man' as an address to a human being. Thirdly, both *1 Enoch* 37–71 and *4 Ezra* 13, along with employing comparisons, understand those comparisons to refer to the messiah in Dan. 7.13.[50] In these two books, the Messiah has five common features/functions: (1) he acts as an eschatological judge; (2) he gathers to himself an elect

48. I am using F.H. Colson's translation, Loeb Classical Library.

49. Kraeling notes the use of comparisons in Daniel, *1 Enoch* and *4 Ezra* but not in Ezekiel and the other books (pp. 142-44).

50. Cf. Collins, 'Son of Man', pp. 464-65.

community; (3) he makes war against the enemies of God; (4) he possesses an element of mystery; (5) he is pre-existent. These common messianic expectations suggest a common tradition in first-century CE Judaism from which both writings have drawn in regard to the exegeses of Dan. 7.13. This similarity is all the more striking since there is no evidence of any literary relationship between *1 Enoch* and *4 Ezra*.[51] Finally, the *Apocalypse of Abraham*, the *Testament of Abraham*, Philo and the *Martyrdom and Ascension of Isaiah* show no relationship to *1 Enoch*, *4 Ezra* or to each other, but they also use comparisons to describe heavenly beings, a technique probably based upon the use of comparisons in Ezekiel and Daniel. This final point proves that these late first/early second-century Jewish and Christian apocalypticists consciously and consistently employed comparisons as a traditional means of describing heavenly beings.

Revelation belongs to this tradition. In Chapters 3 and 4 of this study, we shall discuss the pertinent passages in Revelation and demonstrate the similarities between Revelation and *1 Enoch* 37–71, *4 Ezra* 13, the *Apoc. Abr.* 10 and the *Mart. Isa.* 4 as well as the distinctively Christian aspects of John's use of comparisons.

One fact that could easily be overlooked is the use of the generic phrase in Mk 3.28 and the title in Mk 8.38. The evangelist clearly employed these terms differently and did not confuse them, a signal to us that Second Temple Judaism and early Christianity understood and used the generic expressions in a singularly distinctive manner. Elsewhere I have argued that at least some of the synoptic eschatological titular son of man sayings derive from the same tradition that gives us the comparisons (cf. Dan. 7.13; *4 Ezra* 13.3; Mt. 24.30; Mk 14.62; see also Lk. 17.22-24).[52] Similarly, New Testament exegetes have overlooked the

51. Cf. Wilson, 'Son of Man', pp. 49-50; J.M. Myers, *I and II Esdras* (AB, 42; Garden City, NY: Doubleday, 1974), pp. 302-16; Collins, 'Son of Man', pp. 464-66, who states that *4 Ezra* 13 is reminiscent of traditional theophanies of the divine warrior. If Collins is correct, there may have been in Second Temple Judaism a tradition that joined the concept of heavenly saviors in human likeness and divine warriors. Chapters 4 and 6 of the present study shall argue that John understands the two images to refer to the messiah.

52. 'A New Approach to the Son of Man Debate', Society of Biblical Literature International Meeting, Dublin, Ireland, 21–24 July 1996. I hope to develop this presentation into a scholarly article at some point in the future.

role of comparisons to denote heavenly beings in the New Testament itself. For example, Rom. 8.3 and Phil. 2.7 are two examples of the use of comparisons to connote a heavenly being in human likeness and both passages are clearly not generic expressions.[53]

53. I recently presented papers at the 1997 SBL International Meeting in Lausanne, Switzerland ('More on the Son of Man') and the SBL/SE regional meeting in Knoxville, TN, USA (22 March 1998) on this topic ('Comparisons and the Son of Man') in which I identified the use of comparisons to denote heavenly beings in human likeness in Second Temple Jewish and early Christian non-apocalyptic writings. A revised version of the second paper appears as 'Comparisons and the Son of Man', *Bible Bhashyam* 24 (1998), pp. 67-78.

Chapter 3

THE PRESENTATION OF THE MESSIAH IN REVELATION 1

The preceding chapter argued that Ezekiel, Daniel, *1 Enoch* 37–71, the *Apocalypse of Abraham*, *4 Ezra*, the *Martyrdom and Ascension of Isaiah*, the *Testament of Abraham* and Philo's *De Abrahamo* all employed comparisons to denote heavenly beings in human likeness. This chapter will discuss the role and function of comparisons in Revelation and show that there is a marked similarity with *1 Enoch* 37–71 and *4 Ezra* 13. It also will demonstrate the centrality of the 'one like a son of man' Christology to the life of the Christian community in Asia.

Revelation employs comparisons in 1.13 and 14.14 (ὅμοιον υἱὸν ἀνθρώπου) in order to describe the Messiah. Rev. 1.13 functions as a superscription for Rev. 1.14-20 and the letters in Rev. 2.1–3.22. That is to say, the 'one like a son of man' in 1.13 becomes the authority figure for the Asian Christians who reveals to them what they must do in order to enter the New Jerusalem. Revelation 2–3, in turn, provides the necessary instructions that will enable the churches in Asia to withstand the apocalyptic trials presented in Rev. 6.1–19.10. Thus, in this way, Rev. 1.13 functions as a key passage in the overall structure of the book of Revelation.

Lietzmann first noted the similarity of expression in Dan. 7.13 and Rev. 1.13 and 14.14, on the one hand, and their dissimilarity with the synoptic gospels, on the other. While Daniel and Revelation employ comparisons, the synoptics do not (ὁ υἱὸς τοῦ ἀνθρώπου). He also noted that, while the Synoptics have the definite article, neither Daniel nor Revelation has it. Lietzmann concluded that son of man was not a title in Daniel and Revelation and that John the apocalypticist depends totally upon Dan. 7.13.[1] We turn now to a discussion of the one in

1. Lietzmann, *Menschensohn*, pp. 56-57. Like Lietzmann, many recognize the dependence upon Dan. 7.13 but not its significance (e.g. T. Holtz, *Die Christologie*

human likeness in Rev. 1.1-20 and 14.14-16.[2]

1. *Revelation 1.1-8: The Introduction of the Author*

Although our primary concern is with the 'one like a son of man' in Rev. 1.13, one cannot fully appreciate vv. 9-20 without first examining vv. 1-8. Within these verses, one finds key themes which recur throughout Revelation: God shares divine honors with Christ by sharing authorship of the apocalypse (vv. 1-2; cf. 5.13; 7.10; 12.10; 14.4; 20.6; 22.1); the death of Christ has soteriological significance (vv. 5-6; see, e.g., 1.18; 2.8; 5.6, 9-10; 13.8; cf. 7.13-14; 22.14); and Christ's second coming is expected soon (v. 7; cf. 1.3; 3.11; 14.6; 22.12). Rev. 1.1-8 may be divided into two distinct parts: a superscription in vv. 1-3 and an epistolary greeting in vv. 4-8.

Revelation begins by asserting the origins and authorship of the vision: 'An apocalypse of Jesus Christ which God gave to him (v. 1).' This apocalypse must be shown to his (God's or Christ's) servants so that they might be prepared for the events coming soon. The usual means of transmitting visions has been supplemented in v. 1. Normally, in visions and apocalypses in the Jewish tradition, God gives the vision to an interpreting angel who then mediates it directly to a human seer (e.g. Dan. 8.15-26), such as Enoch, Isaiah or Abraham. In Revelation, God gives it to Jesus Christ, who gives it to an angel, who gives it to John. For John, however, God Almighty has entrusted the vision to

der Apokalypse des Johannes [TU, 85; Berlin: Akademie-Verlag, 2nd edn, 1971]), pp. 116-28; M. Rissi, *Time and History* (Richmond, VA: John Knox Press, 1966), pp. 56-57, esp. n. 9; Krodel, *Revelation*, pp. 94-95, 274; H.B. Swete, *The Apocalypse of St. John* (London: Macmillan, 3rd edn, 1909), pp. 16-17; G.R. Beasley-Murray, *The Book of Revelation* (NCB; Grand Rapids: Eerdmans, 1978), pp. 66-67; E. Lohse, 'Der Menschensohn in der Johannesapokalypse', in R. Pesch and R. Schnackenburg, in collaboration with O. Kaiser (eds.), *Jesus und der Menschensohn: für Anton Vögtle* (Freiburg: Herder, 1975), pp. 415-20; G.E. Ladd writes, 'The present reference goes back directly to Daniel ...' (*A Commentary on the Revelation of John* [Grand Rapids: Eerdmans, 1972], p. 32).

2. Some exegetes argue that the Son of Man title must have been known to John (e.g. Schüssler Fiorenza, *Vision*, p. 148; cf. W. Bousset, *Die Offenbarung Johannis* [Göttingen: Vandenhoeck & Ruprecht, 1906], p. 194). However, for the reasons already stated, I doubt that such a position is tenable.

Christ. Christ, not God Almighty, becomes the authoritative, authenticating figure behind the apocalypse, a pronounced Christian development in the history of Jewish apocalypses.[3] This development enables Christ to participate in divine honors with God Almighty.[4] Furthermore, the revelation of the risen, heavenly Jesus also verifies the witness of the pre-Easter, earthly Jesus, an important fact for Revelation expressed through 'confirmation statements'.

Christ's participation in divine honors as God Almighty's agent occurs in several ways in Revelation. One is by the use of confirmation statements,[5] which convey to the reader that God will faithfully execute his divine plan, that Christ has accurately and thoroughly presented the contents of that plan to humankind and that they who live in accord with Christ's witness to God are the victors/conquerors who shall inhabit the New Jerusalem. These confirmation statements are therapeutic maintenance strategies employed to retain persons within Revelation's symbolic universe.[6] One such confirmation statement is found in the superscription: 'the word of God and the testimony [or witness] of Jesus Christ' (τὸν λόγον τοῦ θεοῦ καὶ τὴν μαρτυρίαν Ἰησοῦ Χριστοῦ [v. 2]).

The expression the 'testimony of Jesus (Christ)' has generated a considerable amount of secondary literature,[7] but little attention has been

3. Krodel, *Revelation*, pp. 78-79; Beasley-Murray, *Revelation*, pp. 50-51; M. Kiddle, *The Revelation of St. John* (MNTC; London: Hodder & Stoughton, 1940), p. 4; E. Corsini, *The Apocalypse* (GNS, 5; Wilmington, DE: Michael Glazier, 1983), pp. 66-68.

4. Cf. Bauckham, *Theology*, pp. 26, 54-65.

5. Cf. Thompson's 'confirmatory statements' (*Revelation*, p. 40; see also p. 178).

6. On the use of maintenance strategies to support a symbolic universe, see Berger and Luckmann, *Social Construction*, pp. 128-34.

7. E.g. P. Ellingworth, 'The *marturia* Debate', *BT* 41 (1990), pp. 138-39; J.M. Ford, 'Persecution and Martyrdom in the Book of Revelation', *Bible Today* 28 (1990), pp. 141-46; F. Mazzaferri, '*Martyria Iesou* Revisited', *BT* 39 (1988), pp. 114-22; M.G. Reddish, 'Martyr Christology in the Apocalypse', *JSNT* 33 (1988), pp. 85-95; B. Reicke, 'The Inauguration of Catholic Martyrdom According to St. John the Divine', *Aug* 20 (1980), pp. 275-83; A.A. Trites, '*Martys* and Martyrdom in the Apocalypse: A Semantic Study', *NovT* 15 (1973), pp. 72-80; P. Vassiliadis, 'The Translation of *Martyria Iesou* in Revelation', *BT* 36 (1985), pp. 129-34; B. Dehandschutter, 'The Meaning of Witness in the Apocalypse', in J. Lambrecht (ed.), *L'Apocalypse johannique et l'Apocalyptique dans le Nouveau Testament*

given to the phrase 'the word of God'. In Revelation, 'the word of God' and 'the testimony of Jesus (Christ)' are parallel statements. These statements convey to the reader that they who are faithful to God's word and Jesus' witness, even unto death, are special.[8] Those special people include John (1.9) and the martyrs, or saints (20.4; cf. 6.9), and find fulfilment in Christ himself (19.13). Similar confirmation statements, key technical terms in Revelation, are found in 6.9 (διὰ τὸν λόγον τοῦ θεοῦ καὶ διὰ τὴν μαρτυρίαν ἣν εἶχον), 12.17 (τῶν τηρούντων τὰς ἐντολὰς τοῦ θεοῦ καὶ ἐχόντων τὴν μαρτυρίαν Ἰησοῦ) and 14.12 (οἱ τηροῦντες τὰς ἐντολὰς τοῦ θεοῦ καὶ τὴν πίστιν Ἰησοῦ).[9] Set within the superscription of the document, Jesus' role as the heavenly authority behind Revelation, coupled with a reference to his earthly role as faithful witness to God, assures the reader that faithfulness to Jesus ensures a heavenly reward. It also establishes Jesus' role as the 'trustworthy and true' (see 3.14; 19.11) witness. The text expects the readers to respond with a renewed faith and religious vigor (see 17.14; 19.10).[10]

Verse 3 should then be seen as more than a beatitude.[11] It contains parallel expressions (οἱ ἀκούοντες τοὺς λόγους τῆς προφητείας καὶ τηροῦντες τὰ ἐν αὐτῃ γεγραμμένα) and serves as a powerful exhortation to the reader to adhere completely to the dictates of the vision 'for the time is near'. Thus ends the superscription.

In the next section, vv. 4-8, we have a second example of John presenting Jesus Christ as God Almighty's agent and representative. John moves from a purely apocalyptic format to a more epistolary one. First, in v. 4 he identifies himself and follows with a distinctly Christian

(BETL, 53; Leuven: Leuven University Press, 1980), pp. 283-88; cf. Charles, *Revelation*, I, p. 7.

8. On a slightly different aspect of the relationship between God and Christ in Revelation, Boring concludes that the voices of God and Jesus are interchangeable for John ('The Voice of Jesus in the Apocalypse of John', *NovT* 34 [1992], pp. 334-59).

9. Cf. Rev. 19.10 and 19.13. Dehandschutter (see n. 7 above) has a similar argument but only concerns himself with μαρτυρέω and its cognates. For contrasting positions, see A. Satake, *Die Gemeindeordnung in der Johannesapokalypse* (WMANT, 21; Neukirchen–Vluyn: Neukirchener Verlag, 1966), pp. 97-99; T. Zahn, *Die Offenbarung des Johannes* (2 vols.; Leipzig: Deichert, 1924–26), pp. 185-87; H. Kraft, *Die Offenbarung des Johannes* (HNT, 16a; Tübingen: J.C.B. Mohr, 1974), pp. 26-27.

10. Cf. Bauckham, *Theology*, pp. 66-108, 118-19.

11. Note the other six beatitudes in 14.13; 16.15; 19.9; 20.6; 22.7, 14.

greeting made popular by Paul (e.g. Rom. 1.7; 1 Cor. 1.3; cf. 1 Pet. 1.2 and Jude 2).[12] He then refers to God in a manner that demonstrates that for John the figures of God Almighty and Christ are closely related. The apocalypse is from the God 'who is and who was and who is coming,' a present-past-future continuum.

This is not a normal temporal sequence or mode of expression from one point in time to a future point. The more normal mode of expression is found in Isa. 44.6: 'I am the first and I am the last, And there is no God besides Me' (see also Isa. 41.4; 43.10; 48.12). Similar temporal expressions abound in Greco-Roman literature. For example, Pausanias 10.12 reads, 'Zeus who was, Zeus who is, and Zeus who will be.' Similarly, Plutarch quotes Isis as saying, 'I am all that has been and is and shall be' (*On Isis and Osiris* 9). Both Greco-Roman statements have a past-present-future sequence that is more to be expected over against the present-past-future one in Rev. 1.4 and 1.8.[13]

John has reversed the first two temporal dimensions of the past-present-future continuum to make it consistent with the life, death and life again of Jesus. Rev. 11.17 is similar: 'We thank you, Lord God Almighty, who is and who was, for you took your great power and ruled.' This verse refers to God, not Christ, clearly indicated by the term παντοκράτωρ, which only refers to God in Revelation (see 4.8; 11.17; 15.3; 16.7; 19.6). Just as Christ has become the guarantor of the apocalypse and not God, just as 'word of God' and 'testimony of Jesus' are synonymously parallel confirmation statements, so too Christ functions in God Almighty's stead as God's agent in the world.[14]

After mentioning the seven spirits (v. 4) before the throne of God,[15] John moves to Christ Jesus, 'the faithful witness, the first-born of the dead and the ruler of the kings of the earth' (v. 5; cf. Ps. 89.27). Antipas, the martyr (2.13), is also referred to as a 'faithful witness'. It

12. On this topic, see the interesting discussion in E. Corsini, *The Apocalypse* (GNS, 5; Wilmington, DE: Michael Glazier, 1983), pp. 73-79.

13. Charles (*Revelation*, I, p. 20) and Beasley-Murray (*Revelation*, pp. 59-63) have identified similar statements in non-biblical Jewish writers of this same period.

14. For a contrasting view, see Bauckham, *Theology*, pp. 27-30.

15. Charles believes the reference to the seven spirits before God is an interpolation (Rev. 1.9). One must ask who would make such an addition and why. This image goes back to Isa. 11.2 LXX. For more balance discussions, see Beasley-Murray, *Revelation*, pp. 54-56; Krodel, *Revelation*, p. 83; R.H. Mounce, *The Book of Revelation* (Grand Rapids: Eerdmans, 1977), pp. 69-70; Hughes, *Revelation*, p. 18.

refers to those who were faithful in spite of the circumstances. It conveys to the reader that just as Jesus was exalted, so too will others, like Antipas, who are faithful. Charles argues that 'first-born of the dead' has messianic implications.[16] If nothing else, it connotes the pre-eminence of Christ among the children of God. It clearly refers to the resurrection.[17] 'Ruler of the kings of the earth' must be defined more fully later for the readers/hearers (17.14; 19.11-21), but already they can perceive that Christ, the crucified one, has become the Lord of the cosmos.[18] John's references to Christ do not stop here. Christ's love has freed us from sin through Christ's blood, another reference to the crucifixion (v. 5). John views the crucifixion as a sacrificial act by Christ on behalf of humankind. This point is continued in the next verse, where the kingdom is composed entirely of priests to his (Christ's) God and Father, followed by a doxology (1.5b-6; cf. 5.10).[19] 'The allusion to Israel's deliverance in the exodus is ... obvious ... Blood is the symbol of life. Freedom from sin and guilt means to be rightly related to God and enfolded by the love of Christ [realized eschatology!].'[20]

Although it does not contain any of the three christological images under examination in this study, Rev. 1.6 is a christological statement on the work of Christ creating priest-kings, constituting a link between Christ and community in Revelation. The image of priest-kings in a passage without reference to 'one like a son of man', the Lamb or the Divine Warrior illustrates the consistency of Revelation's Christology and indicates the appropriateness of the method and argument of the present study. What, then, is the source of the priest-kings imagery?

Exod. 19.6 is the source of this imagery: 'but you [i.e. Israel] will be for me a kingdom of priests and a holy nation' (NIV). Whereas the elect community is composed of priests in Exod. 19.6, Revelation states that the elect community will be composed of priest-kings who reign with

16. Charles, *Revelation*, I, p. 15.

17. Cf. Corsini, *Apocalypse*, pp. 68-71.

18. See A.J. Bandstra, 'A Kingship and Priests: Inaugurated Eschatology in the Apocalypse', *Calvin Theological Journal* 27 (1992), pp. 10-25. In private conversation, Bruce Malina told me that his research concurs with mine on this point. See his *On the Genre and Message of Revelation: Star Visions and Sky Journeys* (Peabody, MA: Hendrickson, 1995).

19. See also Hughes, *Revelation*, pp. 19-20; Morris, *Revelation*, pp. 49-50.

20. Krodel, *Revelation*, p. 85.

God and Christ in the new age (1.6; 5.10; 20.4-6). 1 Peter addresses Christians in the same general region of the Roman Empire and uses similar language: 'But you are a chosen race, a royal priesthood, a holy nation, a people for God's own possession' (2.9). Both passages incorporate an exodus typology in order to create fictive Christian families. Both relate to persons who have suffered for their religious convictions under the hands of local residents adhering to Greco-Roman religious traditions (see discussions of the social setting in Chapter 1 of this study). By referring to the new age, Revelation's exodus motif takes on eschatological dimensions as well.[21]

Sweet notes that there is exodus imagery throughout Revelation, with frequent allusions to Isa. 40–66, which heralds the new exodus from Babylon. He argues that Christians rule over earthly kings in Christ's stead; their priestly office represents God to the world and also offers the world's worship to God. This priesthood belongs to the entire Christian community.[22] I agree. The purpose of this priest-king imagery is to convey to the readers that God Almighty will initiate a new exodus, a new saving event for a new people, Israel.[23] The leader and role model of this new community is Christ (e.g. 17.14), that is, the priest-king imagery is a primary example of the relationship between Christ and community in Revelation. Indeed, it is as priestly lord of the community to whom they must remain faithful and loyal that Christ addresses the seven churches in Asia, a point that I will demonstrate in my exegesis of Rev. 1.13-20 later in this study.

Verse 7 continues the sacrificial theme. First, borrowing an element from Dan. 7.13, Christ will be seen by all coming upon clouds. Traveling upon clouds denoted that one's origins are from the heavenly realm (e.g. Exod. 13.21; 16.10; Num. 11.25; Ps. 104.3; Isa. 19.1; cf. Mt. 17.5 and Acts 1.9). Thus, Christ, who was crucified, will return to earth as God's regent, and the event which should have been his humiliation has become his exaltation and the means of redemption for all humanity.

21. I am indebted to Professor H.W. Attridge for originally pointing out to me the significance of Revelation's employment of exodus typology with regard to this passage (Revelation seminar lectures, SMU, Dallas, TX, summer 1978; see also Bauckham, *Theology*, pp. 70-72).

22. Sweet, *Revelation*, pp. 60-68.

23. Cf. Bauckham, *Theology*, pp. 70-72.

This scene is one of many reversals of expectation throughout Revelation. The greeting ends in v. 8 with God stating his eternal sovereignty over creation, which we discussed above.

Verses 4-8 contain more than a greeting. The cosmology in these verses has presented Christ as a participant in divine honors with God.[24] Christ takes a place of pre-eminence as God's first-born and ruler of the earth. Christ has faithfully *re-presented* the word of God to humanity and now *represents* that very word of God in his person (cf. Rev. 19.13). He also has faithfully discharged his responsibility, even to the point of giving his own life, and has been elevated by God to the position of Sovereign Lord of the universe. Christians may feel safe, for their lord and master rules the universe. Eventually, Christ's sovereignty will be acknowledged by all humanity (v. 7). Thus, these verses also convey to the reader the certainty of God's eternal blessings to his 'faithful witnesses.' This verse is a mythological maintenance strategy that establishes a concrete connection between Christ and community.[25]

Christ Jesus provides the model for Christian behavior: just as Christ suffered, they will suffer; just as he remained faithful, they must remain faithful; just as God rewarded him, God will reward them. God Almighty will demonstrate this in public for all persons to see (v. 7). Verse 7 would carry added meaning for Christians who might have suffered public ridicule and repression for their religious beliefs before Roman officials. These verses attempt to elicit a faithful response on the part of its readers/listeners, a response consistent with 'the word of God and the testimony of Jesus'.

2. *Revelation 1.9-20: The Call and Commission of John*

Rev. 1.9-20 records the calling and commissioning of John. Verses 9-11 describe the call itself; 12-20, the commissioning. Verse 12 is an interlocking, transitional statement. An interlock is a literary device that overlaps and connects one series of images, events, teachings or visions to another series.[26]

24. See preceding discussion of v. 4; cf. Thompson, *Revelation*, pp. 64-66.

25. On the social function of myth, see Berger and Luckmann (*Social Construction*, pp. 128-34); Tillich, *Dynamics*, pp. 41-54; Livingston, *Anatomy of the Sacred*, pp. 86-96; Cunningham *et al.*, *The Sacred Quest*, pp. 61-75.

26. Cf. Yarbro Collins, *The Combat Myth in the Book of Revelation* (ed. C. Bynum and G. Rupp; HDR, 9; Missoula, MT: Scholars Press, 1976), pp. 16-29.

Verses 12-20 can be divided further into two parts: (1) the vision of the 'one like a son of man' and its effect upon John (12-17a) and (2) the response, commission and explanation given to John by Christ (17b-20). These symbols attempt to establish Jesus' authority to write to the churches and to expect their compliance. As we shall see, these symbols also function as mythological maintenance strategies and indicate to the reader a link between Christ and community.

a. *Verses 9-12*

In v. 9, John identifies himself by name. To the best of our knowledge, Revelation is the only Jewish or Christian apocalypse from this period that is not pseudonymous. Apocalypticists wrote under pseudonyms in order to give their documents more credence.[27] John probably was known personally to these congregations. It also means that John himself believed that ancient worthies, such as Daniel, Isaiah, Enoch and Ezekiel, had indeed written prophetic books; John works on the assumption that at least some of the recipients of his own book of prophecy had that same belief. John moves quickly in an attempt to authenticate his vision. He writes that faithfulness requires steadfastness in the midst of tribulation in order to enter the kingdom. John's faithfulness to 'the word of God and the testimony of Jesus' has caused his exile to Patmos.[28] This confirmation statement communicates to the reader that John has consistently held fast to his Christian beliefs even through tribulation and that John's witness is trustworthy.

This term is Yarbro Collins's adaptation of Allo's *loi de l'emboîtement*. Yarbro Collins uses the term more narrowly than does Allo (see n. 64). See also Thompson, *Revelation*, pp. 37-52; Bauckham, *Climax*, pp. 2-22.

27. On pseudonymity in Jewish apocalyptic literature, see D.S. Russell, *The Method and Message of Jewish Apocalyptic* (OTL; Philadelphia: Westminster Press, 1964), pp. 127-39; Collins, *Apocalyptic Imagination*, pp. 30-31; Reddish, *Apocalyptic Literature*, pp. 19-24.

28. Many scholars appeal erroneously to Pliny's *Natural History* 4.12.23 and/or 4.69, Tacitus's *Annals* 3.68, 4.30, 15.71 and/or Juvenal's *Satire* 1.73, 6.563-64 and 10.170 as proof that Patmos served as a Roman place of exile. While Pliny merely describes Patmos, Tacitus and Juvenal confirm that exile to islands occurred in imperial Rome, Tacitus and Juvenal naming some places of exile; however, none of the writers identifies Patmos as a place of exile. This does not mean that Patmos was not a place of exile for Roman offenders, for the data concerning that era is far from complete. It only means that the above references do not identify Patmos as such a place and should not be used for that specific purpose.

Verse 10 states that John received the revelation 'on the Lord's Day'. Whether the reader should understand 'the Lord's Day' to refer to a specific day of the week (e.g. Sunday or Friday) or a specific religious holiday (e.g. Easter) is not important for our purposes. The reception of this vision on the Lord's Day should further confirm to the reader both its heavenly origins and its faithful reception and transmission by John and attempt to bring about an appropriate response of compliance with its demands. Next John hears a loud voice, like a trumpet, instructing him (v. 11) to write what he sees in a book and to send it to seven churches in Asia (Ephesus, Smyrna, Pergamum, Thyatira, Sardis, Philadelphia and Laodicea). This command will be repeated in v. 19. When John turns, he sees seven golden lampstands and 'one like a son of man' (vv. 12-13). Verse 12 is a typical reversal of expectation common to Revelation, where the vision prepares the hearer/reader for one thing but provides another instead. In v. 12 one expects to see a voice but sees seven lampstands instead.[29] Similarly, in Rev. 5.5, for example, one expects to see a lion (cf. *4 Ezra* 11) and sees instead a lamb. These reversals function in two ways. First, their very unexpectedness tends to grab one's attention. Secondly, they serve as transitions to more important matters. In Rev. 1.12, as in 5.5, the more important matter is the introduction of the Messiah (cf. the reversal in 1.7).

b. *Verses 13-20*

First of all, the 'one like a son of man' stands among the seven golden lampstands introduced in v. 12 and explained in v. 20. These lampstands represent the seven churches to whom Christ has instructed John to write (vv. 9-11 [and 19]). This vision in vv. 13-20 is related directly to what precedes it and what follows it. This point deserves closer attention. Revelation 1.7 employs an element of Dan. 7.13 omitted by 1.13, while 1.4 and 1.8 are recapitulated in 1.18. Revelation 1.1 identifies the one who sent the letters and his identity is confirmed in 1.8, 13, 17-20 as Jesus the Christ. In this manner, John has created numerous interlocks which hold Rev. 1.1–3.22 together as one distinct unit of the

29. J.H. Charlesworth, 'The Jewish Roots of Christology: The Discovery of the Hypostatic Voice', *SJT* 39 (1986), pp. 19-41, argues that vv. 10-12 may represent a movement toward hypostasis. However, Rev. 4.1 makes it clear that the voice in vv. 10-12 is either an angel's or Christ's.

book.[30] The purpose of these interlocks is to ensure that the readers/ hearers of Revelation understand that the apocalypse comes from Christ and not John. Thus, the Christ presented in 1.1-8 is identical to the 'one like a son of man' in vv. 13-20 instructing John to write the seven letters that comprise Rev. 2.1–3.22.

Farrer noted that the golden lampstands of Rev. 1.12-13 come from Zech. 4.1-2 (see also Exod. 25.31-40). The lampstands represent the seven-branched candelabrum of the Jewish sanctuary. In Second Temple Judaism, Zechariah 4 was a prophetic vision. 'The seven lamps of Zechariah stand for the temple worship …'[31] In Revelation, John sees the lampstands in the heavenly temple with Jesus functioning as high priest. Moreover, Christ standing in the midst of the lampstands symbolized Christ's involvement and concern for the seven churches that the lampstands represent, symbolizing the bond between Christ and community.[32]

Next in 1.13 comes the comparison 'one like a son of man', the one to whom God Almighty has given the apocalypse (1.1), the faithful witness who frees humankind from sin by means of his blood (1.5), who thereby bestowed upon humankind simultaneously royal and priestly statuses, a maintenance strategy to keep secure the bond between Christ and community (1.6), the one who comes with clouds as a triumphant heavenly being for all to see (1.7).[33] Thomas writes, 'The comparison

30. Similarly, Rev. 1.9 reiterates 1.2; 1.11, 1.4-5a; 1.12, 1.6. Other interlocks can be found in the opening lines of six of the seven letters in chs. 2–3.

31. A. Farrer, *The Revelation of St. John the Divine* (Oxford: Clarendon Press, 1964), p. 65.

32. Cf. J.F. Walvoord, *The Revelation of Jesus Christ* (Chicago: Moody, 1966), pp. 44, 49; W.J. Harrington, *The Apocalypse of St. John* (London: Geoffrey Chapman, 1969), p. 79; Corsini, *Apocalypse*, pp. 94-95; Beasley-Murray, *Revelation*, p. 70.

33. Harrington (*Apocalypse*, p. 79), Charles (*Revelation*, I, p. 27) and Hughes (*Revelation*, pp. 25-26) argue that 'one like a son of man' echoes the synoptic tradition. I believe it only echoes the eschatological synoptic son of man statements, a figure that probably goes back to Dan. 7.13. T.F. Glasson argues that the comparison in Rev. 1.13 'simply means man, here and in Dan. 7' (*The Revelation to John* [CBCNEB; Cambridge: Cambridge University Press, 1965]), p. 21; cf. Lohse, 'Menschensohn'. See my opposing argumentation above on this position. On the different types of synoptic son of man statements, see R. Rhees, 'A Striking Monotony in the Synoptic Gospels', *JBL* 17 (1898), pp. 87-102; G.N. Stanton, *The Gospels and Jesus* (Oxford: Oxford University Press, 1989), pp. 230-35.

(i.e. 'one like a son of man') sets forth essentially the human appearance, and thus the humanity of the one who John saw.' He further states that the messianic title 'son of man' is not used here, but it doubtless refers to the same messianic figure found in Rev. 19.11-16.[34] Similarly, Seiss writes that this passage focuses on Christ's humanity, 'for it is in his human nature that his redemptive work is conducted and his victories achieved'.[35] According to him, the term 'like' connotes 'something higher than humanity'. This human likeness 'presupposes some modification of what properly is not human'.[36] Thomas and Seiss do not recognize how these distinctive descriptive comparisons function in apocalyptic literature, thus giving the term a soteriological function that the original writers did not give it. These comparisons were merely traditional means of describing heavenly beings.

The second half of v. 13 describes the attire of the one in human likeness in a fashion strongly suggesting a priestly role. Thomas notes that in the LXX ποδήρης is found in passages dealing with the high priest (e.g. Exod. 28.4; Ezek. 9.2; Zech. 3.4). He also notes that ἐνδεδυμένον ποδήρη, which is found in Rev. 1.13, also occurs in Ezek. 9.2 LXX. A similar phrase is found in Dan. 10.5 LXX.[37] He concludes, however, that this verse focuses upon Jesus' 'activity in extending mercy' rather than 'a priestly capacity'.[38]

Thomas strongly denies that there is any attribution of a priestly role to the Messiah based upon this verse and wants 'to limit the significance of the symbol to the aspect dealing with judgment'.[39] His conclusion does not have sufficient argumentation. How does Rev. 1.13 relate to 1.5, 5.10 and 20.6? If Christ enables one to become a priest in the heavenly temple (1.5-6), cannot Christ himself be *the* high priest? If not, why not? Thomas is silent here. Others are less reserved. Ladd and Hughes merely state that the robe and girdle denote Christ as one with

34. R.L. Thomas, 'The Glorified Christ on Patmos', *BSac* 123 (1966), pp. 334-41. In general, Krodel agrees (*Revelation*, pp. 94-95, 274).

35. J.A. Seiss, *The Apocalypse* (Grand Rapids: Zondervan, 1957 [1909]), p. 72; cf. J. F. Toribio, 'La recepcion de Dn 7,13 en Ap 1,7', *Mayèutica* 18 (1992), pp. 9-56.

36. Seiss, *Apocalypse*, p. 73; also Ladd, *Revelation*, p. 32.

37. Thomas, 'Glorified', pp. 242-43, esp. nn. 4 and 5.

38. Thomas, 'Glorified', p. 243; cf. Charles, *Revelation*, I, pp. 27-28.

39. Thomas, 'Glorified', p. 243 n. 6. So, too, Beasley-Murray, *Revelation*, pp. 66-67; Morris, *Revelation*, p. 65.

an exalted status. Krodel states that the attire probably symbolizes his high priestly dignity (cf. Exod. 28.4; Dan. 10.5).[40] Corsini goes further. He states that v. 13 describes Christ as both king and priest (citing Exod. 28.4; 29.5 and Lev. 8.7). Angels functioned as priests, prior to Christ. Christ perfects that task. Christ belongs to a higher order than the angels. 'He is "clothed with a long robe," a technical term referring to the priestly garment.'[41] Christ is the heavenly high priest-king whose life and ministry are paradigmatic for the Asian Christians, an image discussed earlier in comments on 1.6.

Indeed, Thomas's own comments on the position of the golden girdle, placed in a footnote, and Revelation 15 argue against him. He writes in a footnote,

> Josephus gives information that the high priest wore the high girdle and that it was not adaptable to laborious servce [sic] (*Antiquities*, Book III, Chap. VII, Paragraph 2). Thus to be girded about the breast was a mark of dignity while girding about the loins signified service or activity.[42]

Along with the quotation from Josephus and the points made by Corsini, I would argue that the placement of the golden girdle around the chest and the use of the phrase ἐνδεδυμένον ποδήρη depicts the one in human likeness as a priestly messiah. What would be the point of presenting the Messiah in a manner equal to any dignified person in the midst of a temple context? Moreover, Rev. 15.6 has angels who exit the temple 'dressed [ἐνδεδυμένοι] in pure bright linen … dressed … around the chest with a golden girdle'. Jesus' sacrifice led to the salvation of the faithful, but the work of these angels leads to the plagues upon those who persecuted the faithful. Both Jesus and the angels function as priests in their respective contexts, but the result differs.[43] Finally, Second Temple Judaism and early Christianity have many examples of a priestly messiah (e.g. CD 12.23–13.1; 14.19; *T. Dan* 5.10; *T. Naph.* 8.2; *T. Gad* 8.1; Heb. 4.14–5.10; 8.1-13).

40. Ladd, *Revelation*, pp. 32-33; Hughes, *Revelation*, p. 26; Krodel, *Revelation*, p. 95; cf. p. 96.

41. Corsini, *Apocalypse*, pp. 91-93; quote from p. 92. See also Mounce, *Revelation*, pp. 77-79; Rissi, *Time and History*, pp. 56-57.

42. Thomas, 'Glorified', p. 243 n. 7; cf. Farrer, *Revelation*, p. 66.

43. See, e.g., Lev. 16.4; *m. Yom.* 3.6-7; Philo, *Vit. Mos.* 2.17; Josephus, *War* 5.230-37.

Verses 14 and 15 can be discussed together in that they describe further the appearance of the one in human likeness. They also draw upon different passages in Daniel in order to do so. First, v. 14 draws upon Dan. 7.9, which describes the Ancient of Days, God Almighty. In the Danielic passage the Ancient of Days has clothing white as snow, hair like pure wool and a throne like fiery flames. Revelation 1.14 borrows elements from this description and gives them not to God Almighty but to the Messiah. It also employs them differently. For example, in Revelation the human-like Messiah's head and hair, not clothing and hair, are white and the eyes are like fiery flames (Dan. 10.6; cf. *2 En.* 1.5), not the throne as in Dan. 7.9. Verse 15 does likewise. The descriptive elements in v. 15, the feet like polished brass refined in a furnace and a voice like the sound of many waters, come from Dan. 10.6. The vision in Dan. 10.6 describes an interpreting angel; in Revelation, the Messiah. Furthermore, John does not utilize the descriptions of the angel's body, face and eyes because he has already described the Messiah's eyes in v. 14 and now applies those elements which describe the angel's arms and legs in Daniel to the Messiah's feet. The sound of the voice is not like the roar of a multitude, as in Daniel, but like many waters as in Ezek. 43.2.[44] Once again we have an example in Revelation of the Christ participating in divine honors.

The subtle differences between Daniel and Revelation provide useful information about how John's vision developed. First, the freedom with which he employed Scripture, re-applied it and gave it new meaning probably indicates someone rather well-versed in Jewish religious literature. Terms, phrases, images are literally at his command, and he uses them at will. At the same time, his freedom with tradition does not degenerate into a self-centered license. The book of Revelation is not from John but Jesus (from John's point of view) (e.g. 1.4-5, 9-16; 2.1, 8, 12, 18; 3.1). However, John's command and use of these traditions do not consistently follow either the Hebrew Bible or the LXX. John does not simply repeat older traditions but employs them as media for his new prophetic message.

44. See also Ezek. 1.7 and 8.2. Cf. Corsini, *Apocalypse*, pp. 88-91; Beasley-Murray, *Revelation*, p. 67; Krodel, *Revelation*, p. 95; Hughes, *Revelation*, p. 27. Against Thomas ('Glorified', p. 245), who argues that 'the sound of many waters' is not at home in Revelation, it is also found in 14.2 and 19.6. All major extant textual witnesses contain it in all three verses.

In his use of Scripture John relies on his memory, for there are many more allusions to Scripture than quotations.[45] It is not impossible that both the Hebrew Bible and the LXX traditions have influenced John's recollection and employment of Scripture. Nor is it impossible that John may rely upon two different versions of one book in the same language. For example, Qumran's Hebrew Jeremiah has a different wording at some points to convey the same message as in copies of Jeremiah in other textual traditions. Indeed, we often find the same church father quoting Scripture from two different text families. However, John relies upon his memory more than on any written tradition. For example, Rev. 1.14-15 has strong parallels in Ezekiel 1 and 42 and Daniel 7 and 10 without directly quoting either. Traditional materials serve as media for a new message. Such is the norm in Revelation. Moreover, the description of the Messiah with elements from a description of an angel suggests that John does not have the literature before him but rather through memory draws from a tradition describing heavenly beings in glorious terms. Again, Dan. 10.6 is the obvious source for Rev. 1.15, but just as obviously the Danielic description has not been taken over *in toto*. For instance, John does not use Dan. 10.6 and then provide a rationale for its re-interpretation, as if correcting Daniel in some way. John simply employs a resource to communicate the vision. For John, this vision of the Messiah with white hair and fiery eyes connotes the ultimate purity and awesome powers of perception possessed by the Messiah in order that he might judge human behavior.

Secondly, Jesus, the Messiah in human likeness, functions as God Almighty's eschatological agent. To some degree this point contradicts the preceding point on John's use of Dan. 10.6. It may be argued that I apply a different criterion when relating Jesus to God Almighty than to angels. However, my means of arriving at this conclusion is not based upon v. 14 alone, but the many times throughout the book that the Messiah is presented as one who participates in divine honors with God Almighty (e.g. 4.11; 5.13; 7.10; 12.10; 21.22) and also the explicit association John himself makes between the two in vv. 14-15.

45. P. Gaechter, 'The Role of Memory in the Making of the Apocalypse', *TS* 9 (1948), pp. 419-52; cf. G.B. Caird: 'His aim is to set the echoes of memory and association ringing' (*A Commentary on the Revelation of St. John the Divine* [HNTC; New York: Harper & Row, 1966]), p. 25; W.G. Kümmel, *Introduction to the New Testament* (Nashville: Abingdon Press, rev. edn, 1975), pp. 464-65; Farrer, *Rebirth*, p. 315; Kiddle, *Revelation*, p. 15-16; Thompson, *Revelation*, pp. 51-52.

Verses 16-17a bring us to the seven stars and their meaning. The seven stars are the angelic patrons in heaven who protect the churches (cf. Dan. 10.21). The image of the sharp, double-edged sword protruding from Christ's mouth connotes Christ's authority to judge the world (cf. 2.12, 16; 19.15).[46] Isa. 49.2 is probably John's source: 'He made my mouth like a sharp sword' (cf. Isa. 11.4; *4 Ezra* 13.4). The Lord's sword 'never fails to cut. If it does not cut with the edge of salvation it cuts with the edge of condemnation ...'[47] The brightness of Christ's face is reminiscent of Judg. 5.31, which celebrates an Israelite victory over Canaanite king Jabin (see also *2 En.* 1.5; 19.1). Farrer thinks the shining of Christ's face should be compared to the shining of the stars.[48] Morris disagrees and insists the purpose is to terrify his foes.[49] However, it probably merely refers to Christ's purity and fidelity (cf. Mk 9.2-3). At this point (v. 17a), the seer falls to his feet overwhelmed with awe and emotionally drained by what he has seen. This is a typical response by a holy man to a vision (cf. Josh. 5.14; Ezek. 1.28; Dan. 8.17-18; 10.8-10; *Apoc. Abr.* 10.1-3).

Verses 17b-20 conclude this vision. The Messiah reassures John (cf. Dan. 8.19) and then identifies himself in a mode reminiscent of God Almighty's self-identification in v. 8, substantiating my earlier point that Christ functions as God Almighty's divine agency figure, and continues by identifying himself with the historical Jesus of Nazareth, who was born, died and raised to eternal life. In 1.17, 2.8 and 22.13, these words, 'the first and the last,' which refer to Christ, come from Isaiah, where they refer to Yahweh (cf. Rev. 1.8; 21.6).[50] Again, we note that Christ participates in divine honors. Finally, the Messiah has control over who might die and might descend into eternal punishment, that he is the Lord of Hades (v. 18). This last factor coheres with the Messiah's stewardship of the book of life (see 13.8; 17.8).

46. Cf. Walvoord, *Revelation*, pp. 45-46.

47. Hughes, *Revelation*, p. 27; cf. Ladd, *Revelation*, p. 33; Charles, *Revelation*, I, p. 30; Mounce, *Revelation*, p. 79; Sweet, *Revelation*, p. 72; Krodel, *Revelation*, pp. 95-96; and Corsini, *Apocalypse*, p. 93.

48. Farrer, *Revelation*, p. 68.

49. Morris, *Revelation*, p. 55; cf. Charles, *Revelation*, I, pp. 30-31; Mounce, *Revelation*, pp. 78-80; Ladd, *Revelation*, pp. 33-34; Hughes, *Revelation*, pp. 27-28; Krodel, *Revelation*, p. 96.

50. Charles, *Revelation*, I, p. 31; cf. Yarbro Collins, *The Apocalypse*, p. 13.

Verses 17b-18 are loaded with every type of symbol and imagery. First, comfort comes to the seer's psyche when his strength wanes. There is no need to fear. The Messiah is in control. Secondly, the authority of the speaker is transhistorical, spanning time (ὁ πρῶτος καὶ ὁ ἔσχατος) and therefore nothing within time escapes his purview. This expression is synonymous to the Alpha-Omega saying in v. 8, providing yet another example of the way Revelation tells the reader that Christ shares divine honors with God Almighty. This reference to Christ attempts to convince the reader to conform his/her life to the contents of the prophecy. It may be a mythological maintenance technique.[51] Thirdly, the vision is not ahistorical, for it also relates to a specific person and a specific event within human history (καὶ ἐγενόμην νεκρὸς), the crucifixion of Jesus, yet confirms the overcoming of that historical event (ἰδοὺ ζῶν εἰμι εἰς τοὺς αἰῶνας τῶν αἰώνων).[52] The purpose of this maintenance strategy is to convince the reader that they too can overcome history if they remain faithful to God (cf. Rev. 2.7). In so doing, the echoes of 1.8 come through again very clearly (see also Rev. 22.13). Finally, the cosmological dimensions state that the one in human likeness judges who will die and suffer eternally in Hades. Within these two short verses, John has identified the Jesus of history with the cosmic Christ who reigns over all temporal events in this world and the underworld. Does Christ's dominion extend upwards? Indeed it does!

Verses 19-20 confirm that Christ reigns in Hades, on earth and in heaven as well. In v. 19 John is told to write all that he has seen, is seeing and will see (with the exception of 10.4; cf. Dan. 8.26; 12.4, 9) and Christ explains the mystery of the seven stars and seven golden lampstands. The reference to 'things you saw, see and which are about to occur after these things' conveys to the reader that the author of the vision, Christ, controls past, present and future events.[53] Some scholars

51. On maintenance strategies, see Berger and Luckmann, *Social Construction*, pp. 128-34.

52. Cf. R. Morton, 'The "One Like a Son of Man" in Daniel 7:8-13 Reconsidered in Revelation 1:13-18', *Kardia* 5 (1990), pp. 23-27, esp. p. 26; cf. Beasley-Murray, *Revelation*, p. 66; Ladd, *Revelation*, p. 34; Krodel, *Revelation*, pp. 96-97; Morris, *Revelation*, p. 55; Hughes, *Revelation*, pp. 28-29; Charles, *Revelation*, I, pp. 31-32.

53. Note here John returns to a past-present-future temporal sequence, while in describing the attributes of God earlier (vv. 4, 8), he employed a present, past,

have claimed that these words revealed the overarching outline of the book of Revelation.[54] However, I think that one should expect an apocalypse supposedly from God to make such explicit claims. Verse 19 is not so much about the vision as about the one who sends it.[55]

The seven stars are the angelic messengers who represent the churches in Asia and the lampstands represent the churches themselves. Many scholars have had difficulty understanding why John addresses the letters to the angels in heaven and not directly to the churches on earth. A representative selection of their explanations might prove helpful.

Sweet writes, 'Angels are the spiritual counterparts of earthly realities; here (in Rev. 1.19-20) they represent the churches seen as spiritual entities.'[56] Some argue that the angels are actually leading members of the earthly churches themselves and not heavenly beings at all.[57] Others argue that the angels are heavenly counterparts of the earthly congregations who are spiritually in heaven but living physically on earth. This passage proclaims the sovereignty of Christ over creation.[58] Finally, still others argue that the angels are actually bishops or pastors in the earthly congregations themselves and not heavenly beings.[59]

All the commentators attempt to address why these letters to earthly communities are sent to heavenly beings. Several questions arise. If the angels are spiritual counterparts of earthly realities, why are the letters addressed to them at all? How would they have been delivered? Furthermore, what proof is there in Revelation that these angels are human leaders, bishops, priests or otherwise? If they reside materially on earth, why write to them in heaven at all?

While all the commentators attempt to explain how the stars and angels are symbolic, none of them has any trouble accepting the lampstands as the seven churches. For example, Morris states that the lampstands are the actual existing churches. 'The churches are no more than

future sequence. The latter form clearly relates only to God Almighty and Christ for John.

54. So argue Charles, *Revelation*, I, p. 33, and Walvoord, *Revelation*, p. 48.

55. Cf. Mounce, *Revelation*, pp. 81-82.

56. Sweet, *Revelation*, p. 73; see also Swete, *Apocalypse*, pp. 21-22; Morris, *Revelation*, pp. 56-57; Charles, *Revelation*, I, p. 34.

57. E.g. Hughes, *Revelation*, pp. 30-31; cf. Morris, *Revelation*, p. 57.

58. Beasley-Murray, *Revelation*, pp. 69-70; Mounce, *Revelation*, p. 83.

59. See Morris, *Revelation*, p. 57.

lampstands. The light is Christ, and they are to show forth.'[60] No one has trouble accepting the lampstands at face value, but the stars-angels pose a different problem, for they receive the messages that Christ gives to John.

Schüssler Fiorenza[61] and Enroth[62] argue that the angels of the churches might be human prophets within the congregations. John might be their leader. The angel functions as a 'visionary counterpart of the other prophets in the community, has the same function as the other Christian prophets: to make known the testimony of Jesus'.[63] This thesis represents the best argument thus far because it answers the question on John's prophetic terms. As we noted earlier, many New Testament commentators have argued for the prophetic character of Revelation (1.3; 22.18). We can now go a little further: these communities probably held prophets in high esteem and understood them to be messengers from heaven, that is, angels.[64]

In any event, the point of vv. 19-20 is that Christ has dominion over the celestial entities in the cosmos that parallel the earthly congregations. Christ is lord of heaven, earth and Hades.[65] As Farrer has noted, 'In St. John's picture the single figure of Jesus, both priestly and royal, takes the centre; the churches burn as candles around him, but his own radiance is greater.'[66] I agree with Farrer. This priestly and royal Jesus would be a point of contact with the eschatological exodus motif in 1.5b-6, where the promise of being priest-kings is held out as a salvatory reward to the faithful, thus another link between Christ and community.

What type of world-view does John present here? How does he hope this world-view will influence the Asian Christians to whom he writes? What is the relationship between Christ and community presented in

60. Morris, *Revelation*, p. 57; cf. Krodel, *Revelation*, p. 98, and Corsini, *Apocalypse*, pp. 94-95.

61. Schüssler Fiorenza, *Vision*, pp. 145-46.

62. A.-M. Enroth, 'The Hearing Formula in the Book of Revelation', *NTS* 36 (1990), pp. 598-608, esp. pp. 603-604.

63. Enroth, 'Hearing Formula', p. 604.

64. E.g. Hill, 'Prophecy and Prophets', pp. 401-18; Goulder, 'Annual Cycle', pp. 342-67; Rowland, *Open Heaven*, pp. 9-22; Bauckham, *Climax*, pp. 83-91.

65. Morton, 'One Like a Son of Man', p. 26.

66. Farrer, *Revelation*, p. 66.

these verses? Rev. 1.13-20 presents the 'one like a son of man' who is the heavenly high priest, the authoritative Lord of the seven churches in Asia who shares divine honors with God Almighty. Moreover, he is also Lord Supreme from the beginning of time, within time (as Jesus of Nazareth) and until the end of time. He is also Lord Supreme of the cosmos, including heaven, earth and Hades. As John received the apocalypse from Christ and Christ received it from God Almighty, so too Christ received universal dominion from God Almighty over all creation eternally. Heavenly beings and human beings serve both God Almighty and Christ. This is the world-view created by this passage. This vision (vv. 9-20), with its accompanying world-view, is a myth, a maintenance strategy that expects increased religious fidelity and spiritual perseverance (1.9a). It assures the reader/hearer of Christ's complete sovereignty. It expects the original audience to re-commit itself to its Christian beliefs and not waver, assured that its Lord governs the universe.

What type of reader does the material require, and what do these verses tell us about the community for which this book was written? The reader understands Second Temple Jewish religiosity in general, and messianic expectations in particular, as well as early Christian proclamation. One familiar only with Judaism or only with Christianity would not be able to decipher all the allusions in the passage. For instance, those only familiar with the Jewish elements could not perceive the allusions to the historical Jesus of Nazareth as proclaimed in the early church.[67] However, someone only familiar with the Christian traditions would not be able to recognize and appreciate the priestly traditions in the passage and could not appreciate the use of Danielic imagery, the double-edged sword, to describe the Christ and the theophanic brilliance employed in describing the Christ. Additionally, the reader understands how apocalyptic literature functions in general. In discussing the seven letters, I will argue that John's principal rivals, 'Balaam', 'Balak', the Nicolaitans and 'Jezebels,' might actually be rival prophetic groups. Such an atmosphere of competing prophetic–apocalyptic preaching movements would provide fertile ground for a

67. For example, C.H. Dodd, *The Apostolic Preaching and its Development* (London: Hodder & Stoughton, 1944) and G.N. Stanton, *Jesus of Nazareth in New Testament Preaching* (Cambridge: Cambridge University Press, 1974). On the distinctive features of early Christian apocalypticism, see Rowland, *Open Heaven*, pp. 351-57.

biblically based message and/or apocalyptic vision.[68] Thus, I believe that the reader is open to the possibility that God reveals hidden mysteries to holy persons (cf. 1.1-3, 20). Moreover, I suggest that heavenly angels have human counterparts in the churches who function as prophets. Paul's congregations in this same region had such persons (1 Cor. 12–14; 2 Cor. 12). If not, an apocalypse has no power beyond any other literary form and may even be unintelligible, ultimately discarded by the community to which it was sent originally. The reader need not experience an apocalyptic vision but only believe in them.

Furthermore, such a reader expects such a vision that would relate to the return of the Christian Messiah in light of Jewish messianic expectations. Whether or not the reader expects a priestly or political Messiah is not important since for Revelation Jesus fulfils both. This messianic expectation of both types in one person was also found at Qumran (e.g. CD 20.1). Finally, the reader accepts Jesus as the Messiah, the Lord of life. The text provides assurances that Christ has the right to address matters in the Asian congregations because of his sacrificial death on their behalf. The expected responses would be belief that the vision truly comes from Christ and not John, trust in Christ as Lord of the church and the cosmos, obedience to his word through his prophet John and confidence in his power to rule the cosmos within and beyond time. These are the connections between Christ and community in Revelation 1 and the means of persuasion employed by John. This is a Christian community with strong prophetic/apocalyptic traditions.

3. *Summation*

The presentation of the Messiah in Rev. 1.1-20 has parallels with the messianic figures in the Similitudes of Enoch and *4 Ezra*. First of all, each employs a comparison (Rev. 1.13). The description in each case interprets Dan. 7.13. Secondly, in all three, the Messiah judges the acts of humans (symbolized by the sword from his mouth in v. 16). Thirdly, he gathers the elect to himself (symbolized by his presence among the lampstands in vv. 13, 20). Fourthly, he makes war against the enemies of righteousness (vv. 7, 16b) and, fifthly, possesses an element of mystery that only he can reveal (vv. 13, 16, 20).

68. Cf. Bauckham, *Climax*, pp. 83-91; Rowland, *Open Heaven*, pp. 9-22.

In addition to these features, the Messiah of Rev. 1.1-20 also has features in common with one of those books. As in *1 Enoch*, the Messiah is a revealer (Rev. 1.19; cf. *1 En.* 46.3) and rules the universe (Rev. 1.13, 16a, 18, 20; cf. *1 En.* 62.6-7). Both Revelation (v. 7) and *4 Ezra* 13 (v. 3) depict the human-like Messiah riding on clouds. The following features are unique to Rev. 1.1-20: the Messiah serves as a sacrifice for human sin (v. 5; cf. 1 Jn 2.2); functions as a high priest in heaven (v. 13; cf. Heb. 7–8) and is God's divine agent (vv. 1, 4-6, 14-20; cf. Jn 14; 20.28). The similarities among all three works and between Revelation and at least one of the other two indicates that they share a common exegetical tradition. The traits peculiar to Revelation are ones that would be central to the proclamation of the early Christian community.

Let us turn now to discern the specific connections between Christ and community in the seven letters in Revelation 2–3 and attempt to learn to what degree Revelation's Messiah functions in a fashion similar to the parallels in *1 Enoch* 37–71 and *4 Ezra* 13 deduced earlier.

Chapter 4

ONE LIKE A SON OF MAN IN REVELATION 2–3 AND 14.14-16

1. *The Nature and Purpose of the Letters*

The 'one like a son of man' functions primarily as the pastoral leader of the community who directs it from the present age into the next. The 'one like a son of man', the heavenly lord who commends, exhorts, threatens, encourages and redeems, sends the letters to tell each church what, if anything, it needs to do in order to be spiritually strong so that it may endure the coming apocalyptic trials. In this manner, each letter functions as an introduction to the entire book. However, one should not assume that the letters are merely prose versions of the apocalyptic visions. Rather, the letters address internal communal issues that must be corrected in order that the churches may withstand social pressures to conform their religious practices and also what they must do in order to be able to endure the coming apocalyptic trials.

The arrangement of the letters may be geographically significant. The seven cities form a circuit on a major Roman road of that time. One could travel from Ephesus north to Smyrna; farther north to Pergamum; southeast to Thyatira; farther south to Sardis; southeast to Philadelphia; farther southeast to Laodicea and almost due west back to Ephesus. This route might have been the one John took when visiting these churches, and may explain the order of the letters in Rev. 2.1–3.22. With the exception of the journey from Laodicea to Ephesus, about 95 miles, the average distance between the other cities would be approximately 35 miles.[1]

1. Cf. Bauckham, *Theology*, pp. 12-17.

In each letter, the reader/hearer can identify Christ as the sender. John merely serves as a secretary. This is accomplished usually by describing the sender in an introductory title in terms drawn from earlier portions of the book.

Letter 1: the introduction in 2.1 recalls 1.13
2: the introduction in 2.8 recalls 1.17-18
3: the introduction in 2.12 recalls 1.16
4: the introduction in 2.18 recalls 1.14-15 (see also 19.12)
5: the introduction in 3.1 recalls 1.4, 16, 20; 2.1; see also 4.5; 5.6
6: the introduction in 3.7 recalls 1.18
7: introduction in 3.14, cf. 1.5; 2.13; 19.11.

Only the letter to the Philadelphians (3.7-13) does not adhere to this pattern strictly.[2] These introductions, in general, interlock ch. 1 with chs. 2–3. However, some also point back to an earlier letter and forward to other sections (3.1, cf. 2.1, 4.5 and 5.6; 2.18, cf. 19.12; 3.14, cf. 19.11), attesting to the unity of the book as a whole. In each letter, Christ comments with authority upon the quality of Christian behavior in each community (2.2-4, 6, 9, 13-15, 19-20; 3.1b, 4, 8, 10, 15, 17), that is, the purpose of the letters individually and collectively is the improvement of the internal spiritual life of the Christian community in order to maintain the bond between Christ and community. Rev. 1.13 is the superscription not only for Rev. 1.14-20 but also for Rev. 2.1–3.22, and it establishes Christ as the Lord of the community, who expects absolute and complete adherence to his word. Therefore, it is necessary to study these seven messages to ascertain the manner and extent of Christ's lordship over these congregations. These letters constitute a mythological maintenance strategy aimed at substantiating Christ's authority and maintaining order within the sacred cosmos.

Each letter also contains an exhortation to hear near its end (2.7, 11, 17, 29; 3.6, 13, 22). First, since these exhortations are always in the imperative mood—'Let the one who has an ear hear what the Spirit is saying to the churches'—they place the burden of action upon the hearer, since everyone, presumably, has ears or the faculty of hearing. Secondly, these exhortations to hear go not to a single church but to all

2. See Isa. 22.22; cf. Job 12.14. Rev. 1.18 might be the point of contact between ch. 1 and the title in the letter to the Philadelphians.

churches wherever they might exist, that is, the exhortation to adhere to the Spirit's message is universal. Thirdly, John does not differentiate sharply between the Spirit who speaks to the churches and the Christ who sends the letters to the churches (cf. 19.10). Finally, the exhortations to hear and the promises jointly function as maintenance strategies to encourage the readers/hearers to remain in the sacred cosmos so that Christ might protect them during the coming apocalyptic cataclysms and establish them in the New Jerusalem (e.g. 2.7, 11; 3.5-6, 10-13, 21-22).

In Revelation, both Christ and the Spirit convey data from the heavenly sphere to the earthly one. This is not Christ's only function, nor is it the Spirit's.[3] One should note that each letter begins with Christ identified as the sender and ends with an exhortation to hear 'what the Spirit says to the churches'. In other words, the Spirit transmits to each church the same message that Christ sends to them. Enroth, arguing (correctly in my opinion) that the two are not identical, still writes, 'The author [of Revelation] connects this phrase [the exhortation to hear the Spirit] with the introduction of the letter ... identifying the Spirit and the risen Lord by one or more epithets.'[4] Revelation 19.10 clearly substantiates it: 'For the witness of Christ is the spirit of prophecy' (cf. Rev. 1.1, 19 and 22.16-17 read in this light). While the Spirit functions as the medium of revelation to prophets in Revelation, revelation only involves one aspect of the work of Christ, who also serves as an expiation for human sin (1.5) and judges humanity (19.11-21), among other tasks, as well as the work of the Spirit, who guides the ongoing life of the Christian community, among other tasks. Finally, these exhortations to hear are powerful maintenance strategies aimed at sustaining the Christian community's positive relationship with its exalted Lord and Christ.

Since all the exhortations to hear are identical in each letter, nothing further need be said concerning them.

Before discussing the letters themselves, one must first discuss to what degree these seven letters are true letters. Charles stated that these seven letters addressed issues that typified life in first-century Christianity as a whole.[5] Many agree that the letters have a universal appeal.[6] Charles

3. Cf. Bauckham, *Climax*, pp. 118-73; *idem*, *Theology*, pp. 109-25.
4. Enroth, 'The Hearing Formula', p. 601.
5. Charles, *Revelation*, I, p. 37.
6. Cf. Mounce, *Revelation*, pp. 83-85; Kiddle, *Revelation*, p. 18; Ladd, *Revela-*

also argues that the letters were written approximately two decades before the apocalyptic section and circulated independently as authentic letters. Later, they were re-edited and added to Rev. 4.1–22.5. He noted that the letters omit any reference to the imperial cult or to an empire-wide persecution and contain a parousia hope common among first-century Christians. According to Charles, later additions include the promises in each letter, the proclamation of the resurrected Christ and Rev. 3.10.[7]

Charles's position has not gone unchallenged. Many have argued that Rev. 2.1–3.22 does not contain authentic letters at all. For example, Beckwith calls them 'special words'; Lohse, 'literary epistles'.[8] They all recognize that these letters do not follow the epistolary conventions of the time. However, one might argue that neither did Paul follow those conventions when he combined Greco-Roman and Jewish greetings at the beginning of his letters. Letters do not have to conform slavishly to current conventions to be letters. Moreover, these letters, as many have noted, contain specific details that would be relevant in each context.[9] Although the arguments for some details are often slender,

tion, p. 36; Morris, *Revelation*, p. 87-88; Sweet, *Revelation*, pp. 65, 77-78; Krodel, *Revelation*, p. 100; J.M. Court, *Myth and History in the Book of Revelation* (London: SPCK, 1979), pp. 22-25.

7. Charles, *Revelation*, I, pp. 43-47.

8. For more in depth discussions on this topic, see I.T. Beckwith, *The Apocalypse of John* (New York: Macmillan, 1919), pp. 446-47; E. Lohse, *Die Offenbarung des Johannes* (NTD; Göttingen: Vandenhoeck & Ruprecht, 1976), p. 21; K. Berger, 'Apostelbrief und apostolische Rede: Zum Formular frühchristlicher Briefe', *ZNW* 65 (1974), pp. 212-19; G. Rudberg, 'Zu den Sendschreiben der Johannes-Apokalypse', *Eranos* 11 (1911), pp. 170-79; E. Stauffer, *Christ and the Caesars: Historical Sketches* (London: SCM Press, 3rd edn, 1955); F. Hahn, 'Die Sendschreiben der Johannesapokalypse: Ein Beitrag zur Bestimmung prophetischer Redeformer', in G. Jeremias, H.-W. Kuhn and H. Stegemann (eds.), *Tradition und Glaube: Das frühe Christentum in seiner Umwelt* (Göttingen: Vandenhoeck & Ruprecht, 1971), pp. 370-77; W.H. Shea, 'The Covenantal Form of the Letters to the Seven Churches', *AUSS* 21 (1983), pp. 71-84; J.T. Kirby, 'The Rhetorical Situations of Revelation 1–3', *NTS* 34 (1988), pp. 197-207; D.E. Aune, 'The Form and Function of the Proclamations to the Seven Churches (Revelation 2–3)', *NTS* 36 (1990), pp. 182-204; cf. C.J. Hemer, *The Letters to the Seven Churches of Asia* (Grand Rapids: Baker Book House), pp. 14-20; Court, *Myth*, pp. 21-22.

9. W.M. Ramsay, *The Letters to the Seven Churches of Asia* (Grand Rapids: Baker Book House, 1963 [1904]); W. Barclay, *The Letters to the Seven Churches* (London: SCM Press; New York: Abingdon Press, 1957); Hemer, *Letters*.

these exegetes and others have shown that John knew something of the geography, the social milieu and the nature of the Christian life in each of these churches. The letters are not 'form letters' but real letters that addressed real problems.[10] Indeed, Christ's knowledge concerning the social situation in each community would attest to the specificity that accompanies most genuine letters and also to Christ's omniscience (a mythological maintenance technique aimed at sustaining order).

Others argue, against Charles, that chs. 2–3 relate directly and naturally to the rest of the book. Sweet, for example, argues that ch. 1 provides Christ's title in each letter.[11] He also notes that the promises to the victors at the end of each letter find fulfillment in chs. 19–22. He concludes that the letters constitute an integral section of Revelation. With one partial exception, this is the case; the promise of the white stone with the new name is only fulfilled partially in Revelation. Rev. 22.4 only mentions the new name. I also agree that the promises that are fulfilled in chs. 19–22 argue for the unity of the book against Charles. Moreover, certain images recur throughout the book (e.g. the sword in 1.16; 2.12; 19.15; the sevenfold formula in 1.4; 2.1–3.22; 6.1–8.5; 8.2–11.19; 15.1–16.21; the word of God in 1.2; 1.9; 6.9; 19.13; 20.4).

Many have argued that the letters contain a prophetic element.[12] For example, Beasley-Murray notes parallels between Amos 1–2 and Rev. 2.1–3.22. He claims that both have seven messages of judgment with no indication that any of these messages circulated independently.[13] Feuillet adds that τάδε λέγει at the beginning of each letter should be translated 'Thus saith', a phrase that precedes divine speech in the prophetic

10. Cf. Ladd, *Revelation*, p. 36; Caird, *Revelation*, pp. 27-28; Sweet, *Revelation*, p. 77; Mounce, *Revelation*, pp. 84-85.

11. Many argue that the titles come from the son of man vision in 1.9-20. The titles, more precisely, come from ch. 1, with the possible exception of the Philadelphian letter, which paraphrases Isa. 22.22. However, 1.18 may have brought this paraphrase to mind.

12. E.g. Hahn, 'Sendschreiben'; Bauckham, *Climax*, pp. 83-91; *idem*, *Theology*, pp. 2-22, 121-25; Rowland, *Open Heaven*, pp. 9-22. I use 'prophetic' here to mean like or similar to the prophets in the Hebrew Bible in form and purpose and not in the sense of prediction. See Corsini's instructive comments on the disadvantages of the 'prophecy-as-prediction' point of view (*Apocalypse*, pp. 103-104).

13. Beasley-Murray, *Revelation*, p. 72; cf. Bauckham, *Theology*, pp. 1-2. Amos 1–2 actually has eight oracles, not seven as Beasley-Murray stated.

oracles in the Hebrew Bible/LXX.[14] Krodel goes further. He notes parallels between Rev. 2.1–3.22 and 2 Chron. 21.12-15 and Jer. 29.1-23 (Jer. 36.1-23 in the LXX).[15] These prophetic parallels are persuasive, especially in light of John's self-conscious identity as a prophetic figure (Rev. 1.3; 22.7, 10, 18-19).

Aune has a more convincing approach because he allows the letters to interpret themselves without imposing artificial categories on them. He defines the seven letters as a mixed genre created by John that he calls 'parenetic salvation-judgment oracles'.[16] These oracles combined aspects of Jewish prophetic speech and imperial edicts. From the prophetic speeches, they took the three-part parenetic sermon with its accusation, admonition and conditional threat of judgment. From the imperial edicts, they took the juxtaposition of commendation and censure and the use of τάδε λέγει to introduce royal correspondence. John employed these elements in the letters in varying degrees, depending upon the context. Aune's argument, which I find convincing,[17] also supports my argument concerning the general purpose of the letters: the internal edification of the churches in order to ensure their participation in the new age. The great pre-exilic prophets (e.g. Amos, Micah, Isaiah) were preachers who denounced unrighteousness and proclaimed the need for righteous repentance, that is, they sought the internal edification of the people Israel. John continues this tradition in Revelation within the Christian community (Rev. 2.1–3.22) and within the broader society as well (Rev. 18.1-24). Moreover, John's use of the 'Thus saith' formula connects him with Jewish prophetic traditions.

14. Feuillet, 'Le Fils', pp. 48-49; see also Beasley-Murray, *Revelation*, p. 72; Boring, *Revelation*, pp. 85-86; cf. Isa. 22.25 LXX.

15. Krodel, *Revelation*, pp. 99-100.

16. 'Proclamation', p. 198, and *Prophecy in Early Christianity* (Grand Rapids: Eerdmans, 1983), p. 326; so too Schüssler Fiorenza, *Vision*, pp. 45-57.

17. However, the question still remains, 'What did John call them?' He called them 'letters'. Despite all our form-critical analyses, they remained for John letters, special ones but letters nonetheless. As such, he would have understood them to convey specific messages for specific locales and our exegeses of the letters will confirm this fact. It is important to remember that John did not call them prophecies, oracles or edicts, even though they might function as such. Perhaps in this way the research process does not eliminate the need for the substantive answers to the very questions that gave rise to the research in the first place: (1) What do they say? (2) What do they mean?

Many have also argued that the letters have a universal appeal.[18] The letters cover every aspect of first-century CE Christian living, in particular the relationship between Christ and community, according to this argument. The letters do indeed cover a variety of topics, but our limited knowledge of first-century Christianity prevents us from saying conclusively that they cover every major issue for first-century Christians. How did John come to select these churches, both for their location and for the quality of their spiritual lifestyle? How can one say that the letters are making a catalogue of the leading first-century Christian issues when overlaps exist among them? For example, two separate letters mention the Nicolaitans (2.6; 2.15). While 'Balaam/Balak' (2.14) and 'Jezebel' (2.20) may refer to two different prophetic movements that oppose John's own ministry, many commentators argue that they are the same movement. Still others argue that the Nicolaitans, Balaam/Balak and Jezebel all refer to the same movement. How can these repetitions exist and the letters still have a universal appeal?[19]

Some see the universality of the letters in their intentional grouping in a certain scheme. Kiddle, for example, argues that letters one and seven go to churches that lack the appropriate Christian virtues; letters two and six go to healthy churches; letters three, four and five to impaired but not destroyed churches.[20] On Kiddle's theory, the letter to Ephesus is dominated by a lack of spiritual virtue. This does not, however, do justice to this letter in which Christ commends the congregation for its steadfastness (v. 2), patience (v. 2), fidelity to his name (v. 3) and disdain for the Nicolaitans (v. 6).

Corsini argues that the letters are not true letters but represent 'a summary of the history of salvation through seven successive portraits'.[21] These letters correspond to the structure and message of sevens in Revelation. They all refer not to the end of the world but to the end of

18. E.g. Charles, *Revelation*, I, p. 37; Kiddle, *Revelation*, p. 18; Ladd, *Revelation*, p. 36; Court, *Myth,* pp. 22-25; Mounce, *Revelation*, pp. 83-85; Sweet, *Revelation*, pp. 65, 77-78; Krodel, *Revelation*, p. 100; Morris, *Revelation*, pp. 57-58.

19. One might also wonder why John would employ so many names for the same movement.

20. Kiddle, *Revelation*, pp. 19-20. See also Morris, *Revelation*, p. 58; cf. Caird, *Revelation*, p. 27 and Ladd, *Revelation*, p. 36.

21. Corsini, *Apocalypse*, p. 109.

Judaism.[22] The specific socio-historical references in each of the letters mentioned previously argue against Corsini's historico-theological interpretation. Corsini stands at the theological extreme; Ramsay, Hemer and Court at the social-scientific. The relevance and meaning of the seven letters is somewhere between the two positions.

Although I have not found the preceding arguments themselves persuasive, for the reasons already mentioned, I believe that the letters do have a universal appeal.[23] This appeal is not centered on the content of the letters but by the fact that there are only seven. Seven functions as a perfect, complete number in Revelation. No other explanation is necessary.[24] In this manner, the content of the letters speaks to the context, while the number of the letters symbolizes their universal appeal. Furthermore, as I stated earlier, each letter ends with an exhortation to hear what the Spirit says to the churches. Thus, the letters are at once specific messages to individual congregations and also communications to all Christians wherever they may be.

Finally, the letters follow the same general structure: (1) an address to the patron angel; (2) the title and presentation of the Christ as the sender and author of each letter; (3) an evaluation of the spiritual life of the church addressed, including exhortations and/or warnings of judgment; (4) a promise to the victors/conquerors; (5) an exhortation to listen to the Spirit.[25]

The exhortations, warnings, judgments, admonitions and promises in Rev. 2.1–3.22 will consume the bulk of our attention because they are the maintenance strategies employed in order to influence behavior and devotion to the faith. In these words, the fullness of Christ's lordship as the leader of the Christian communities in Asia becomes clear. The letters have the same general purpose: they communicate to each church what it must do in order that the union between Christ and community might be maintained (see 2.5). Moreover, Christ speaks through the letters as the Lord of the cosmos to whom the Christians give homage

22. Corsini, *Apocalypse*, pp. 105-17.

23. I make a distinction here between the position taken and the supporting arguments for that position.

24. On the significance of seven in Revelation, see, for example, 1.12, 20; 5.1, 6; 8.2; 15.1; Yarbro Collins, *Combat*, pp. 13-19; Bauckham, *Theology*, pp. 16-17.

25. Cf. Beckwith, *Apocalypse*, p. 260; Glasson, *Revelation*, p. 23; Sweet, *Revelation*, pp. 77-78; Yarbro Collins, *Apocalypse*, pp. 13-14; Krodel, *Revelation*, pp. 100-102; Aune, 'Proclamation', pp. 183-94.

and divine honors. In this way, the letters conveyed to the Asian Christians that the primary concern of the 'one like a son of man', who commissions John to write the letters, was the spiritual well-being of their communities.

2. *The Letters*

a. *To Ephesus (2.1-7)*

The letter to the Ephesians commends and censors the church, exhorting it to work toward its spiritual maturity. The letter begins with a title describing Christ as the author and sender of the letter (2.1; cf. 1.12-13, 16, 20): 'Thus says he who holds the seven stars in his hand and walks among the seven golden lampstands' (cf. Exod. 25.31; Heb. 9.2). It is fitting that the series of letters starts with this description for it connotes Christ's lordship over the seven churches and also over the entire universe. The letter continues by depicting Christ as an omniscient, omnipresent divine agency figure.[26] This depiction is a myth aimed at securing their continued allegiance and fidelity to Christ.

Many commentators concern themselves with the identity of the false apostles in v. 2. Moffatt and Beckwith argue for travelling evangelists; Hughes, Judaizers; Hemer, libertarians; Bousset, Charles and Sweet, the Nicolaitans or a similar group; Beasley-Murray, Gnostics.[27] Court postulates that both the Nicolaitans and the false apostles might provide 'local opposition' to John.[28] In actuality, the data are so sparse that all these answers, except that of Moffatt and Beckwith, depend upon speculation. Rev. 2.1-7 does not provide enough information to identify conclusively the false apostles in any way.[29] At the very least, the so-called false apostles of Rev. 2.2 were ministers whose ministry obtained a degree of success. Their ministry differed from John's in some way.

26. Cf. Yarbro Collins, *Apocalypse*, p. 13.

27. J. Moffatt, 'The Revelation of St. John the Divine', in *The Expositor's Greek New Testament* (5 vols.; Grand Rapids: Eerdmans, 1951), V, pp. 279-494, quote from p. 349; Beckwith, *Apocalypse*, p. 449; Hughes, *Revelation*, pp. 33-35; Hemer, *Letters*, pp. 40-41; W. Bousset, *Die Offenbarung Johannis*, p. 204; Charles, *Revelation*, I, p. 50; Sweet, *Revelation*, p. 81; Beasley-Murray, *Revelation*, p. 74.

28. Court, *Myth*, p. 29.

29. Cf. Hemer (*Letters*, pp. 40-41) on the difficulty of identifying the 'false apostles'.

John does not decry the use of the title 'apostle' to non-members of the 12 but its application to these specific persons.

Christ commends the Ephesians for their endeavors, their steadfastness and resisting evil (v. 2). He reiterates their steadfastness and abiding devotion to be recognized as his followers (v. 3). These verses speak to the social setting of Revelation. If they were complacent or lax, it would be difficult to explain the commendations for their steadfastness and resistance to evil. These words indicate that the social circumstances are the opposite, a setting in which Christians have had to withstand some type of social threat to their spiritual well-being. Verse 6 follows suit.

Other actions, however, receive condemnation. They have fallen from their first love, their first works (vv. 4-5). These two verses confirm that these were genuine letters to a specific community: the original reader knows exactly to what 'first love' and 'first works' refer. If these letters were merely artificial literary devices, one would expect a more explicit reference to the reader, but since the Ephesians knew to what John referred there was no need for an explanation.

However, scholars have attempted to discern to what 'first love' and 'first works' referred. Charles claims that brotherly love is referred to here. He argues that, in contrast to the earlier harmonious days recorded in Acts 20.37, controversies had led to censoriousness, factiousness and divisions.[30] Caird, agreeing with Charles, writes that their intolerance of impostors, their loyalty and their disdain for heresy has 'bred an inquisitorial spirit which left no room for love'.[31] Indeed, the removal of the lampstand, i.e. excommunication, is an immediate threat which will occur before the eschaton.[32] Given the scant evidence, this is a plausible argument. Some in this church might have become so ardent in resisting evil that they repressed other Christians who were not as zealous as they. On the other hand, the Ephesians might have become lax and the

30. Charles, *Revelation*, I, p. 50.

31. Caird, *Revelation*, p. 31; so too, e.g., Ladd, *Revelation*, p. 39; Moffatt, 'Revelation', p. 351; Kiddle, *Revelation*, pp. 23-24; Beasley-Murray, *Revelation*, pp. 75-76; Mounce, *Revelation*, pp. 88-89; Krodel, *Revelation*, pp. 107-108.

32. E.g. Mounce, *Revelation*, p. 89; Yarbro Collins, *Apocalypse*, p. 15. Court's argument that the movement of the lampstand alludes to the necessity of moving the city itself for political and geological reasons is at best a secondary factor (*Myth*, p. 29).

reference to first love is a call to repentance, to return to their previous Christian lifestyle.

Next comes a command to hear and a promise to the faithful that they might have the right to eat from the tree of life (v. 7; see Gen. 2.9; 3.22, 24; *T. Levi* 18.11). Rev. 22.14 fulfils this promise. Rev. 22.2 states that the tree of life produces fruit each month for the healing of the nations (cf. Ezek. 47.12). Rev. 22.14 states that those who washed their robes have a right to the healing produce of the tree of life in the New Jerusalem. The reference to washing their robes in 22.14 relates to another 'New Jerusalem' passage in Rev. 7.14: 'These are the ones who have come out of the great tribulation and they have washed their robes and made them white in the blood of the Lamb.' Thus, the washing of the robes refers to giving one's life in emulation of the Lamb, Christ Jesus, and attaining victory through suffering as did Christ. This is the means of conquering evil in the world (cf. 5.9-10). The promise in 2.7 attempts to demonstrate the salvific power of the blood of Christ; to show the Ephesians the stringent demands of Christian discipleship; and to persuade them that the salvific rewards will more than compensate them for their sufferings. Thus, Rev. 2.7 is a therapeutic maintenance strategy[33] with the purpose of persuading the reader to remain within the sacred cosmos (cf. *T. Dan* 5.12; *4 Ezra* 8.52). We will find in Part II of this study that the *victory-through-suffering* motif recurs throughout the book by means of the image of the slain Lamb. Moreover, the use of this imagery suggests a setting where Christians have suffered for their religious convictions. This promise attempts to bring solace to those who have been repressed for their beliefs.

Following Ramsay, both Hemer and Court argue that the primary referent of the tree of life was the tree-shrine of Artemis.[34] Hemer writes that the Artemis cult was a perfect analogue with the Genesis tree of life. The tree-shrine served as the point at which divinity and humanity met. If they are correct, the Artemis cult would serve Christians as a negative parallel to the tree of life imagery from Genesis. As the Artemis tree cult symbolized the connection between heaven and earth for pagans, so too did the tree of life for John's audience. If Ramsay, Hemer and Court are correct, the Ephesian church may be resisting

33. See Berger and Luckmann (*Social Construction*, pp. 128-34) and Chapter 1 of this study.

34. Court, *Myth*, pp. 30-31; Hemer, *Letters*, pp. 41-52.

pagan repression and the tree of life imagery might be a means of contrasting the competing symbolic universes.

As stated previously, John's reader perceives a three-tiered universe. This promise guarantees entry into life's highest tier, healing from suffering incurred at the earthly level and avoidance of the dreaded lowest tier. In this manner, John's vision connects the beginning of the book with the end, as well as the beginning of the Bible in Genesis and the end presented in Revelation.[35] The reader must also be familiar with the Genesis story to appreciate adequately the vision.[36] This promise would assure the faithful of security in the next age. What then does Christ say to this community?

The exhortation and warning function as powerful maintenance strategies to retain the community under Christ's control. The loss of their 'first love' attempts to motivate the Ephesians to return to their former way of Christian behavior or lose their place in the Christian community. On the negative side, Revelation uses nihilation by threatening excommunication. On the positive side, Christ offers a reward: eternal fellowship with God Almighty and Christ. This promise, a form of therapy,[37] is also part of the maintenance strategy of Revelation. These strategies may be responses to pagan attacks upon Christianity if the tree of life is being consciously contrasted with the Artemis tree-cult.

This letter contains three main points. First, Christ knows both the good and the bad that has transpired in this congregation. Secondly, Christ's exhortation attempts to redirect the congregation to its original activities and perspectives. Thirdly, Christ, Lord of heaven, earth and Hades, has communicated to John, knows the local situation, is worthy of reverence and has the power to execute judgment. The Lord of the church in Ephesus is also Lord of the universe.

b. *To Smyrna (2.8-11)*

This letter responds to a local repression and Christ's victory-through-suffering becomes the model for their victory as well.[38] The letter be-

35. I am indebted to seminar lectures on Revelation by Professor H.W. Attridge for this insight (Perkins School of Theology, Southern Methodist University, 1978 Summer Session).

36. Note the different forms of promises in 2.7b, 17b; 3.12, 21, on one hand, and 2.11b, 26-28 and 3.5, on the other.

37. On nihilation and therapy, see Chapter 1 of this study.

38. Cf. M.G. Reddish, 'The Theme of Martyrdom in the Book of Revelation'

gins by referring to Christ's suffering, attempting to inspire the Christians in Smyrna to remain faithful to Christ through their trials just as Christ was faithful to God Almighty. The title refers to Christ as 'the first and the last, who was dead and was made alive' (see Rev. 1.17-18; 2.13). The letter then speaks of the tribulations of the church in Smyrna. This is another example of the connection between Christ and community as envisioned by John, that is, Christ's faithfulness to God through suffering functions as a model for the church in Smyrna. As Christ overcame death (v. 8), so can they (v. 11b).[39] The letter then states that they will suffer for 'ten days'. Some argue that 'ten days' refers to a brief local oppression,[40] while others interpret it to refer to a regional oppression that may not be brief.[41] Still others offer a third interpretation, that the ten days would have designated one's imprisonment prior to one's execution.[42] Indeed, Rev. 2.9 makes it clear that Christians experienced some type of oppression from 'the synagogue of Satan'. Chapter 1 of this study postulated such action by Jewish opponents to Christianity (cf. 1 Pet. 4.4, 14). More traditional Jewish persons have misrepresented the Christians and these false Jewish testimonies will lead to the coming tribulations (vv. 9-10; cf. 1 Pet. 4.12–5.11).

Hemer, Court and Sweet[43] argue that the title in v. 8 refers to the rebuilding of Smyrna under Antigonus and Lysimachus. While Rev. 2.8 refers back to Rev. 1.17-18, it is also possible that local history might have influenced John's choice of title for this letter, as Hemer, Court and Sweet argue, particularly since images tend to be open-ended.[44] The first phrase, 'the first and the last', is an exact quotation of 1.17; the second, an allusion to 1.18.

(PhD thesis, Southern Baptist Theological Seminary, Louisville, KY, 1982), pp. 104-22.

39. Cf. Yarbro Collins, *Apocalypse*, pp. 17-18.

40. E.g. Charles, *Revelation*, I, p. 58; Caird, *Revelation*, p. 35; Court, *Myth*, p. 30; Krodel, *Revelation*, p. 113.

41. E.g. R. Summers, *Worthy Is the Lamb* (Nashville: Broadman, 1951), p. 113; Mounce, *Revelation*, p. 94; Hughes, *Revelation*, p. 41-42.

42. E.g. Hemer, *Letters*, pp. 69-70. Hemer's support for this argument is rather weak.

43. Hemer, *Letters*, pp. 60-65; Court, *Myth*, p. 30; Sweet, *Revelation*, p. 84.

44. I am grateful to Canon John Sweet of Cambridge University for this insight in private conversation.

In this letter, the exhortation and warning are again closely related (v. 10). This is one of only two letters without negative comments (see also 3.7-13). This congregation has suffered and is not prosperous in material terms, but is rich. However, nothing is revealed concerning the content of their affluence. Perhaps, the following comment about the so-called Jews and Satan's synagogue, which supposedly makes libelous accusations against Christians, stands in contrast to the followers of Christ. Thus, the reference to the latter's affluence probably refers to spiritual richness.

Spiritual richness defined by suffering and poverty has a long history in some forms of Judaism and early Christianity (e.g. Prov. 3.4; Isa. 25.4; Jer. 22.16; Eccl. 4.13; 9.15; cf. Jas 2.5; 4.6; 1 Pet. 5.5). By turning negatives into positives, the letter prepares the reader/listener for the exhortation and warning in v. 10: 'Do not fear the things you are about to suffer. Be watchful; the devil is about to throw some of you into prison in order that you might be tested and ... have tribulation ...' (cf. 1 Pet. 5.8-10). The two promises that follow the exhortations point toward a single reward: eternal life with Christ.

The first promise offers the crown of life to those who are faithful unto death (v. 10c). Being faithful unto death also connotes a tense situation where Christians have suffered. While it could function as an exhortation to repentance, the context of Rev. 2.8-11 suggests conflicting truth claims. Hemer lists eight possible interpretations for 'crown of life'.[45] It could mean (1) a gift presented to a champion at athletic games; (2) an adornment for a presiding Dionysian priest; (3) a civic honor; (4) an adornment for pagan priests; (5) an adornment for the eponymous priestly magistrates of a city; (6) a symbol of spiritual bliss worn by Christians; (7) a symbol for the city of Smyrna; and (8) a presentation to a human potentate at his arrival into a city. Hemer himself prefers the first, third and seventh options. I believe the first option is the most probable one for the Christians in Smyrna. Morris states that this promise would have been a fitting image in Smyrna, 'a city famous for its Games'.[46]

45. Hemer, *Letters*, pp. 72-75.

46. Morris, *Revelation*, p. 65.

> Crown (*stephanos*) means a wreath or chaplet, and is to be distinguished from the royal crown (*diadema*). The *stephanos* was ... awarded to the victor at the games, and the same word was used of the festive garland worn at banquets by all the guests.[47]

Krodel writes that the conditional promise in v. 10 'contains the same life/death contrast as the messenger formula (v. 8). Christ's fate remains ... a source of undefeatable fortitude ...'[48] The promises to the 'victors'[49] are that their richness increases as their sufferings increase. The hearer/reader living under local religious oppression would recognize this image and would be expected to respond by living faithfully. The crown makes one a victor in the game of life eternal, the central point of the second promise, a promise which is not explicitly fulfilled in Revelation. The unfulfilled promise might not be a part of the book's theological agenda but a specific promise to a specific situation.

The second promise guarantees that the faithful will escape the second death and thereby attain resurrection to life eternal. Revelation 2.11b should be translated, 'The one who conquers will *certainly never* be harmed by the second death.'[50] Krodel notes that this is the only conqueror saying stated negatively and argues that the reason for this is the conflict with the synagogue.[51] Given Rev. 2.9 and the fact that a concept of a second death was widespread in Judaism (e.g. *1 En.* 69.27-28; *T. Abr.* 12-14; 1QS 4.2-14; *4 Ezra* 7.32-44; 12.33-34; cf. *Pss. Sol.* 3.3-12; *2 Bar.* 54.15-22), this is a very strong possibility. In any event, Jewish repression has misrepresented Christianity to pagans, leading to Christian suffering, and clearly demonstrates that the letters reflect Christian suffering.

The second death is discussed in Rev. 20.6, 14 and 21.8. In Rev. 20.6, the second death is defined in contrast to the eternal bliss of the first resurrection; however, 20.14 explicitly defines the second death as

47. Morris, *Revelation*, p. 64.

48. Krodel, *Revelation*, p. 113.

49. The Greek word νικάω, the primary verb in each promise in these letters, can mean either to conquer, to overcome or to be victorious.

50. F. Blass and A. Debrunner, *A Greek Grammar of the New Testament and Other Early Christian Literature* (Chicago: University of Chicago Press, 1961), p. 184.

51. Krodel, *Revelation*, p. 113. However, the promise may not be against an opposing religious movement but merely an exhortation to the Christians in Smyrna. The reference to the second death could merely be the employment of a Jewish tradition.

the lake of fire. Rev. 21.8 states that the lake of fire, the second death, was reserved for cowards, unbelievers, corrupt persons, murderers, sexually immoral persons, sorcerers and idolaters.[52] Therefore, this second promise simultaneously states the escape from the second death and also affirms their spiritual richness stated in v. 8.[53] The second death denotes complete exclusion 'from the incomparable glory and perfection of the new heaven and earth. From this appalling end the Lord's redeemed have been saved.' This redemption is equivalent to 'receiving the crown of life and eating from the tree of life'.[54] Indeed, both promises assure Christ's followers in Smyrna of their selection, if not election, at the Judgment.[55]

Christ's message to this church is succinct. First of all, he asserts their spiritual affluence, which exceeds their poverty and suffering, and encourages them to remain faithful. Next, he gives two promises that have the same purpose: eternal life with God. These exhortations and promises encourage the church to maintain its level of devotion. The letter indicates a social context where Jewish persons pressure Christians to recant. Accusations from Jews, of the kind postulated in Chapter 1 of this study, probably led to Christians being imprisoned as social threats of some type. John prophesies that some Christians will be imprisoned but delivered eventually. That is to say, based upon their current problems, John perceives a future crisis. This action seems to be a local conflict, probably similar to the one described in Pliny's letter to Trajan (*Letter* 10).

52. This list is similar to virtue–vice lists made popular by the Stoics (e.g. Epictetus, *Discourses* 1.3.7-9: 'crafty, mischievous, wild, savage, untamed, degraded, slanderous and ill-natured'; cf. 1.7.30; 1.12.20; 2.1.11; 2.10.17-18). For virtues, see Seneca, *Letters* 88.29-30: 'courage, confidence, temperance, cultural refinement, candor, modesty and moderation, frugality and parsimony, compassion' (cf. *Letters* 113.24; Cicero, *On the Duties* 3.3.13; Stobaeus 2.59.4–60.24; 2.63.6-24; also Gal. 5.13-26; 1 Cor. 12–14). The cardinal Stoic virtues were justice, courage, temperance/moderation and wisdom/prudence. Perhaps John borrows this technique from Stoicism, a topic that I hope to investigate at a later date.

53. Cf. Morris, *Revelation*, p. 65.

54. Morris, *Revelation*, p. 63.

55. On the concept of the second death in early Judaism, see *Pss. Sol.* 3.9-12; 1QS 4.6-14 (both first-century BCE works) and *4 Ezra* 7.32-44, a work contemporary with Revelation. Also, see Hemer, *Letters*, p. 75-76; Bauckham, *Theology*, pp. 45-51.

John provides only meager data about the social circumstances of this specific congregation: it is experiencing poverty; it seems to have few, if any, materially affluent members. There are Jewish pressures on it. John contrasts its material poverty with its spiritual affluence; its present suffering with its future bliss; death with life. These therapeutic maintenance strategies are aimed at maintaining the Christian 'sacred cosmos' intact and maintaining the union between Christ and community by persuading the Christian community that religious fidelity and life in the New Jerusalem must be their focus, not their present sufferings.[56]

c. *To Pergamum (2.12-17)*

This letter mentions in passing the death of Antipas and also the need for religious fidelity. The letter comes from him who has the sharp, double-edged sword (2.12; cf. 1.16; 19.15). The letter contains a distinctive note of judgment in its title and its body (2.12, 16) by describing Pergamum negatively as the place 'where the throne of Satan' is (2.13). This could be a reference to the imperial cult[57] and also to the many pagan temples in Pergamum and their extensive influence there.[58] Christians in Pergamum stood firm in the face of intense competition for adherents and against outside oppression. Antipas, 'my faithful witness', has even died for the faith (2.13).

We should note several elements at this point. First, the exhortation in the immediately preceding letter to be faithful unto death (2.10) has already been achieved by Antipas (2.13) in Pergamum. Christians living there may have a justifiable concern for their own lives and fear that Antipas might be the first of many. Secondly, Antipas is referred to as 'my faithful witness' (ὁ μάρτυς μου ὁ πιστός μου). μάρτυς (and its cognates) and πιστός (and its cognates) function as technical terms in Revelation. Much attention has been given to μάρτυς as a technical term, little to πιστός.[59] In fact, μάρτυς/μαρτυρία and πίστις/πιστός

56. On maintaining a sacred cosmos, see 'Sociology of Knowledge' in the opening chapter of this study.

57. E.g. Ladd, *Revelation*, p. 45; Sweet, *Revelation*, pp. 87-88; Beasley-Murray, *Revelation*, p. 84; Krodel, *Revelation*, p. 114.

58. E.g. Hughes (*Revelation*, pp. 43-44) and Lohmeyer (*Offenbarung*, pp. 24-25).

59. E.g. P. Vassiliadis, 'Translation', pp. 129-34; P. Ellingworth, 'The *martyria* Debate', pp. 138-39; Lohmeyer, *Offenbarung*, p. 25; Morris, *Revelation*, p. 66;

occur together three times in Revelation (1.5; 2.13; 3.14). In each instance, the words function as synonymous Christian virtues that the Christian must maintain regardless of the cost, even one's life. 'By standing faithful to the point of death and suffering martyrdom, the Christian bore his most effective witness to his Lord.'[60] Verse 13 clearly states that Antipas has died a faithful Christian witness. The reference to his death is placed between two references to Satan. Given the preponderance of Greco-Roman religions and the importance of the neokorate to the city of Pergamum, 'Satan' probably symbolized for John the imperial cult and/or Greco-Roman politico-religious customs.[61] In either case, the death of Antipas is a sign that the situation is not good for Christians, and John only anticipates it getting worse. Rev. 2.13 is a clear example that some measure of oppression of Christians existed in Roman Asia at this time.[62]

The Christian community in Pergamum is not free from fault (vv. 14-15). The community has withstood external threats but succumbed to internal ones.[63] Christ criticizes their acceptance of false teachers and doctrines, as evidenced by the references to 'Balaam', 'Balak' and the Nicolaitans. The reference to Balaam and Balak is a symbolic employment of Num. 22.41–31.24. Balaam represents the prototypical false teacher in Second Temple Judaism and early Christianity (e.g. Philo, *Vit. Mos.* 1.53-55; Josephus, *Ant.* 4.6.6). King Balak of Moab hired Balaam to pronounce curses upon Israel. Instead, Balaam blessed Israel four times (Num. 22–24). However, Balaam fell into disrepute when, after his counsel, Israelite men committed fornication with Moabite women (see Num. 31.16). Swete, for example, notes that in Numbers 25 and several New Testament passages (e.g. Acts 15.28-29; 1 Cor. 6–10) sexual fornication was associated with idolatry and actions perceived idolatrous, such as eating meat offered to idols.[64] Ladd argues that some in Pergamum had 'a lax attitude toward pagan customs,

Sweet, *Revelation*, p. 88; Beasley-Murray, *Revelation*, p. 85; Hughes, *Revelation*, p. 44; Ladd, *Revelation*, pp. 46-47; Krodel, *Revelation*, p. 115.

60. Ladd, *Revelation*, p. 47. See also 2.19, 13.10 and 14.12.

61. See 'The Social Setting of the Book of Revelation', Chapter 1 of this study.

62. Cf. Reddish, 'Martyrdom', pp. 123-32.

63. Sweet, *Revelation*, p. 36. Note also my comments in Chapter 1 of this study on the primary purpose of the letters being internal issues.

64. Swete, *Revelation*, pp. 36-37.

including both temple feasts and sexual immorality'.[65] A lax attitude by Christians is possible, given the seriousness with which non-Christian/non-Jewish persons in the eastern Mediterranean region took their religious practices. Some scholars might argue that, since the letter only mentions the death of Antipas, no other Christians have suffered in any way and that religious laxity is the key issue in the Asian congregations.[66] If, however, other Christians died after Antipas, Revelation would have gained status as a prophetic book and would have been cherished and retained by the Asian Christian community, a possible reason for its survival. Furthermore, while religious laxity is a concern in Pergamum (vv. 14-15), John gives no indication that Antipas was lax. Rather, John gives the impression that the opposite is the case in regard to Antipas, 'the faithful witness'.

Other exegetes have argued that the Balaam/Balak movement was Gnostic;[67] still others that 'Balaam' and 'Balak' were figurative references to the Nicolaitans.[68] Hemer, in an attempt to clarify matters, defined Nicolaitanism as 'an antinomian movement like that which Paul had faced at Corinth, whatever else it may have been otherwise'.[69]

The passage does not provide enough data to enable us to draw any confident conclusions about the practice and/or theology of the Nicolaitans. John could have misunderstood them, or he could have given a biased report. Further, John is more conservative than other early church leaders on this matter (cf. 1 Cor. 8.1-6; Rev. 2.14). One could just as easily argue that John is conservative and the Nicolaitans moderate.[70] Moreover, there is insufficient data to state conclusively if Balaam/Balak and the Nicolaitans are one group or two.

Stimulating though some of these ideas may be, many are speculative. The Gnostic thesis is indefensible given that the scant data in Rev. 2.12-17 could relate to any number of Greco-Roman cults or move-

65. Ladd, *Revelation*, p. 48.

66. E.g. Bauckham, *Theology*, pp. 12-17.

67. E.g. Charles, *Revelation*, I, p. 63; Beasley-Murray, *Revelation*, pp. 83-89.

68. E.g. Kiddle, *Revelation*, pp. 32-33; Caird, *Revelation*, pp. 38-39; Mounce, *Revelation*, p. 98; E. Schüssler Fiorenza, 'Followers of the Lamb: Visionary Rhetoric and Social-Political Situation', *Semeia* 36 (1986), pp. 123-46, esp. p. 138; Yarbro Collins, *Apocalypse*, pp. 19-20.

69. Hemer, *Letters*, p. 91.

70. I am indebted to Professor H.W. Attridge's seminar lectures on Revelation, 1978 Summer Session, Perkins School of Theology, Southern Methodist University, for this insight.

ments. Moreover, while Balaam/Balak may refer to the Nicolaitans, it is by no means certain. It is worth noting that the Nicolaitans are mentioned in the Ephesian letter, but Balaam/Balak is not. One could argue then that the Nicolaitans and 'Balaam/Balak' refer to two groups, not one.

This passage tells us something of its reader and, in turn, the social context of the general readership. The lack of detail regarding John's opponents suggests that the original recipients knew to whom John referred. The reader must be familiar with ongoing first-century Jewish exegesis of Numbers 22–31 and, in this particular case, must be able to apply this negative metaphor to the appropriate group that has forsaken its ancestral traditions. Furthermore, eating meat offered to idols and fornication often referred metaphorically in early Judaism and early Christianity to actions that have led people to religious infidelity (cf. Rev. 18.3, 9). In sum, John has used two Jewish metaphors to refer to the same, in his eyes, religiously incorrect behavior. These metaphors are therapeutic maintenance strategies, aimed at creating a sense of guilt within the person/persons who have committed this offense and bringing about their repentance. Since John has employed standard negative Jewish and Christian metaphors to describe rival groups, one cannot be certain at this point to what degree the passage is purely metaphorical or may actually reflect Christian conduct in Pergamum.

Verse 16 contains an exhortation, indeed a command, to repent immediately. Christ's punishment for non-compliance, a form of nihilation, would be the sword from his mouth (vv. 12, 16). Nihilation is a maintenance strategy that attempts to eradicate everything outside the sacred cosmos.[71] This would be a fitting punishment if John's competitors actually did eat meat offered to idols, and if John is not using meat-eating as a pure symbol. The first of two promises in v. 17 may confirm this suspicion: the right to eat the hidden manna. This is the second promise not explicitly fulfilled in Revelation (cf. the crown in 2.10), suggesting that it might have been a response to a genuine issue in Pergamum and not a part of Revelation's overall theological message. It could have been suggested by the actions of those who actually ate meat offered to idols and/or by the Exodus episode from Numbers recounted earlier. In a city such as Pergamum, with its many different religious cults,[72] meat offered to idols would be a principal source of

71. See Berger and Luckmann, *Social Construction*, pp. 130-34.

72. Hemer, *Letters*, pp. 78-87.

protein. It is understandable that some Christians might not see any harm in eating such meat, since those gods did not exist (cf. 1 Cor. 8.4).[73] It is possible that a real dispute arose among Christians in Pergamum as to whether or not they should eat meat offered to idols. This dispute probably revolved around proper Christian conduct within Greco-Roman society. Some Christians probably believed some accommodation with the broader society was possible, but John felt that any accommodation was apostasy.[74] If they continued to eat such meat, Christ would punish them. If they did not, they would be rewarded with heavenly food. This crisis probably led to the martyrdom of Antipas.

On the other hand, the Balaam–Balak story might have also brought to John's mind Exodus 16.[75] Some traditions stated that Jeremiah had hidden the manna that had been kept in the Temple and that it would reappear during the messianic era (see 2 Macc. 2.4-8; cf. *Sib. Or.* 7.148-49; *2 Bar.* 29.8). Charles, however, argues that the hidden manna refers to 'bread from heaven', which nourishes the angels.[76] The hidden manna of the Jeremianic tradition is the primary referent for Revelation's 'hidden manna', because the bread from heaven to which Charles referred was not hidden. Against Charles, Hemer correctly notes that the word κεκρυμμένου clearly refers to the Jeremiah tradition.[77] John believed that the messianic age would come soon (1.1, 19; 22.6-7, 10) and that this manna would nourish the people of God.

The reader of this passage must possess a knowledge of the manna traditions, believe in miraculous feedings during the Exodus travels and look forward to a similar experience during the messianic era. It also presumes a strong hope for a messianic era when these things would be fulfilled. The manna tradition requires an acquaintance with a particular Jewish tradition-history. Such knowledge is not impossible for non-Jews but would be expected more in a Jewish context. The apologies of Philo and Josephus, from Egyptian and Roman contexts, respectively,

73. Cf. Sweet, *Revelation*, p. 89; Ladd, *Revelation*, pp. 47-49; Krodel, *Revelation*, pp. 115-21.

74. Cf. D.A. DeSilva, 'The Social Setting of the Revelation to John: Conflicts Within, Fears Without', *WTJ* 54 (1992), pp. 273-302 (286-96).

75. See Charles, *Revelation*, I, p. 65; Ladd, *Revelation*, p. 49; Beasley-Murray, *Revelation*, p. 87.

76. Charles, *Revelation*, I, p. 65.

77. Hemer, *Letters*, p. 95; cf. Philo, *Rer. Div. Her.* 39.191 and *Leg. All.* 3.59.169; see also 3.61.174-76.

suggest that rather detailed knowledge of Judaism in Greco-Roman society was not widespread.

While the hidden manna imagery requires a knowledge of Jewish traditions, the source of the imagery of the second promise, the white stone with a new name, does not and it has provoked substantial debate.[78] If the white stone image comes from Exodus, as with earlier images in this letter, then the use of Urim and Thummim in reaching decisions is the most probable source of the white stone imagery (Exod. 28.30). Glasson mentions a Targum tradition that said God's name was on these stones,[79] but another tradition held that the names of the 12 tribes were on the stones.[80] Regardless of its source, the white color conveyed purity, blessedness, righteousness and similar virtues (e.g. 6.11; 7.9; 19.11, 14).[81]

Some argue that the secret name reflects the popular religious belief in Greco-Roman society that to know a deity's name created an intimate relationship between deity and devotee, or even power over that deity.[82] This position is supported by Rev. 3.12, 14.1 and 19.12. Some commentators argue that the name on the stone is either God's name or Christ's name,[83] while others argue that the new name bestowed upon the conqueror is one given by God/Christ.[84]

78. Hemer provides a helpful list of possible sources for the white stone imagery (*Letters*, pp. 96-102).

79. Glasson, *Revelation*, p. 29.

80. E.g. Charles, *Revelation*, I, pp. 66-67; Corsini, *Apocalypse*, p. 106.

81. On the color, see also Sweet, *Revelation*, p. 90; Caird, *Revelation*, p. 42; Corsini, *Apocalypse*, p. 106; Ladd, *Revelation,* p. 49; Beasley-Murray, *Revelation*, p. 88; Mounce, *Revelation*, p. 99; Hughes, *Revelation*, p. 46. Hemer rejects the idea that the color of the stone carries any importance, but the evidence indicates otherwise.

82. E.g. Charles, *Revelation*, I, pp. 66-67; Caird, *Revelation*, p. 42; Ladd, *Revelation*, p. 49; Corsini, *Apocalypse*, p. 106.

83. E.g. Caird, *Revelation*, p. 42; Ladd, *Revelation*, p. 49; Beasley-Murray, *Revelation*, p. 88.

84. E.g. Mounce, *Revelation*, p. 100; Hughes, *Revelation*, p. 47; Morris, *Revelation*, p. 68. In particular, Morris argues strongly for this position, pointing out that there is no reference to Christ's name being secret, the point of Rev. 2.17. However, in commenting upon Rev. 19.12, Morris states, 'John may well be saying that no-one has power over Christ. He is supreme. His name is known only to himself' (p. 223). Is Morris not saying that the name of Jesus is secret and beyond human exploitation? He is indeed.

However, I prefer a fourth explanation. First of all, Rev. 14.1 and 19.12 provide near perfect parallels to 2.17. Both 2.17 and 19.12 contain the words γεγραμμένον ὃ οὐδεὶς οἶδεν εἰ μή. The parallel between them is clear. In 2.17 Christ promises the secret name to the conqueror. Rev. 14.1 states that the new name is the Lamb's name and God the Father's name placed upon their foreheads. In 19.12, God bestows a secret name upon the one who has already conquered.[85] In 2.17, 14.1 and 19.12, γεγραμμένον is a key word. Rev. 22.4 is the fulfillment passage: 'And they shall see his [God's] face and his name upon their foreheads.' Rev. 22.4, then, restates 14.1.[86] If these passages interpret one another and collectively provide a fuller interpretation of the significance of 'the name' in Revelation, and I believe they do, then the name on the white stone would be *God's name and Christ's name.*

This suggestion requires explanation. If God Almighty and Christ share functions, then one name would designate both. Rev. 22.4 would be the fulfillment passage of the promise in 2.17, 14.1 and 19.12, important verses in understanding 22.4. Rev. 3.12 says as much: 'I will write upon him my God's name and the name of my God's city, the New Jerusalem ... and my new name.'

Secondly, the victor receives a *new* name. Revelation associates newness (καινός) with righteousness, holiness and election. The heavenly court sings a new song (5.9); as do the Lamb's followers (14.3). A new creation comes from God (21.1, 2, 5). In all these passages, newness has positive connotations. Thus, the new name conveys the saintliness of the victor. Isa. 62.2 and 65.15 may be the source/sources of this image. Interestingly, while the new name recurs in 22.4, there is no further mention of the white stone in Revelation. These promises function as powerful therapeutic maintenance strategies aimed at motivating Christians in Pergamum to remain faithful. Moreover, the use of the eschatological exodus motif (Balaam/Balak, manna), a therapeutic mythology, identifies the church as the New Israel that will be saved in the new dispensation. These passages suggest that the name 'Christian' was a disparaging label in the larger society and that Christians suffered simply because of the name. The significance of the name is hidden from non-Christians and is only known by the Christians. Other early

85. This parallel between Rev. 2.17 and 19.12 will be examined more closely in Chapter 6 of this study.

86. Repetition is an important technique in Revelation, and I hope at some point in the future to discuss its function in more detail.

Christian communities had similar experiences (e.g. Lk. 21.12; Jn 15.21; Acts 4.41; 1 Pet. 4.14; cf. Tacitus, *Annals* 15.44; Pliny, *Letter* 10.96-97), which I noted in Chapter 1 of this study.

How does Christ relate to this community? Initially, he comes as a judge (the sword in vv. 12, 16). He commends their steadfastness against external threats, noting especially the death of Antipas. However, he condemns their succumbing to internal threats (vv. 14-15). He offers two promises. Both contain soteriological imagery and serve the same purpose: the assurance of salvation and eternal life to the faithful, sustaining the bond between Christ and community. The new name contains an apologetic element that explains the rejection of Christians by the larger society: just as the world did not recognize the Christ, no one recognizes his elect followers. Thus, their rejection by society is explained. This same *apologia* is behind the unrevealed name in 19.12 (to be discussed in more detail in Chapter 6 of this study). Thus, the reception of the faithful in the new age is assured, a maintenance strategy discussed earlier.

In sum, pressures from both Jews and pagans have had negative effects upon Christians in Pergamum. First and foremost, conflicts with a group deemed Satanic by John has contributed to the death of Antipas and posed a real threat to other Christians as well who did not abandon the faith even after Antipas was killed. Pergamum was a center of Greco-Roman emperor worship, as well as other Greco-Roman religious traditions, and it is quite possible that 'Satan' also refers to these religious traditions for John. Ladd's comments that this letter refers to a lax attitude toward Greco-Roman religious traditions (see vv. 14-15) may be correct. On the other hand, 'Satan' could refer to Jewish persons who repress Christians, as in 2.9 and 3.9. The Balaam–Balak imagery could refer to those same Jewish persons who have led some Christians to return to more traditional forms of Judaism, or to Christian Jews who have a different understanding of the faith than John. The Nicolaitans could refer to either Gentile Christians or Christian Jews. The data are too sparse to make a definitive statement. The unknown name imagery strongly suggests a social context where Christians espouse that they are the elect but society at large has little or no esteem for them. This apologetic element explains the readers's social circumstances, making their social status understandable and worth bearing. Whether the pressures are from pagans, or Jews, or from both those groups, Christ becomes the role model for those Christians enduring repression in Pergamum. As I argued previously, these comments are all the more important because they are among the few comments upon the relationship between an Asian congregation and its relations with the wider social context. Those relationships are far from pleasant, according to this letter.

d. *To Thyatira (2.18-29)*

This letter contains an extensive discussion of an internal struggle between John and 'Jezebel'. In this letter, the title of Christ, 'the one who has eyes like a flame of fire and who has feet like burnished brass', comes from 1.14-15 ('his eyes are [like] flames of fire and his feet like burnished brass') and will be repeated partially in 19.12 ('his eyes [are] [like] a flame of fire'). Added to it is ὁ υἱὸς τοῦ θεοῦ. Rev. 1.6 clearly presupposes the title 'son of God' ('and he made us a kingdom, priests to his God and Father'; see also 2.27-28; 3.5, 21; 14.1). Rev. 2.18 constitutes the only use of this title in Revelation. Kiddle argues that in the early days of the imperial cult devotees often proclaimed the emperor 'Apollo incarnate' (the tutelary god of Thyatira) 'and hailed [him] appropriately as the son of God'. John might be alluding to the Apollo tradition there while affirming that 'Christ is the true son of God'.[87] Similarly, Caird writes, 'The title Son of God prepares the way for the quotation from Psalm ii, the psalm in which the messiah is addressed by God as "my son".'[88] I agree with Kiddle and Caird on this point.

The 'eyes like flames of fire and the feet like burnished brass' communicated to the reader the power of total and thorough perception (the eyes) and the ability to trounce falsehood (the feet).[89] Krodel adds that the description of the eyes established a contrast with the sun god Helios.[90] If Krodel is correct, this is another possible contact with Thyatiran culture. If Kiddle, Caird and Krodel are correct, this letter employs images as reactions to Greco-Roman religion in general and the imperial cult in specific. These are indications that religious tensions existed between Christians and their non-Christian Greco-Roman neighbors.

87. Kiddle, *Revelation*, p. 37.

88. Caird, *Revelation*, p. 43.

89. Cf. Morris, *Revelation*, p. 70; Sweet, *Revelation*, p. 93; Beasley-Murray, *Revelation*, p. 90.

90. Krodel, *Revelation*, p. 122.

Hemer provides an interesting discussion of χαλκολιβάνῳ, a *hapax legomenon* in the entirety of ancient Greek literature.[91] He argues that the term would have been intelligible to its original readers as a high-quality metal, a copper alloy with zinc. He believes it was a special product of Thyatira's local smelting industry. If Hemer is correct, John has employed a term with local significance drawn from the economic life and commercial prestige of the community in order to convey Christ's judicial grandeur and strength. The title 'son of God', the allusion to Helios and the reference to burnished brass could provide vivid local images for Thyatiran Christians to contrast their religion with the imperial cult.

The heart of the letter begins in v. 19 with a commendation of the Thyatiran Christians. Their virtues include love, fidelity, service and steadfastness. Moreover, their recent efforts have exceeded their earlier ones. The later works are not mentioned specifically. The Thyatiran Christians, however, have not attained spiritual perfection. They have tolerated the ministry of 'Jezebel' (vv. 19-21), clearly a symbolic reference to the wife of King Ahab who was a patroness of the Baal cult, a Canaanite religion (see, e.g., 1 Kgs 16–21). John's opponent, like Queen Jezebel, 'constituted a threat to the continuance of true religion among the people of God'.[92] 'Jezebel' competes with John on his own terms as a prophetic figure. John does not question her authority to be a prophetess but the content of her prophecies (v. 20). At least in Thyatira, two competing Christian prophetic movements sought adherents, lending support to the earlier suggestion that John operates in a context accustomed to prophetic ministries.[93] 'Jezebel' is a false prophetess, comparable to the false apostles in Ephesus (2.2), whose teachings led to fornication and eating meat offered to idols (v. 20; cf. 2.14).

Is John's accusation figurative or literal? Is it describing one or two misdeeds? Thyatira's economic livelihood revolved around its metal industry and that industry, in turn, gave birth to trade guilds. The guilds traditionally required attendance at banquets at which meat had first been offered to idols. These meals often ended in licentious conduct. Non-attendance and/or non-participation when attending banquets might result in the loss of income and/or social status. John was probably

91. Hemer, *Letters*, pp. 112-17.

92. Beasley-Murray, *Revelation*, p. 90.

93. E.g. Hill, 'Prophecy and Prophets', pp. 401-18; Rowland, *Open Heaven*, pp. 9-22; Bauckham, *Climax*, pp. 83-91; Aune, 'Proclamations', pp. 182-204.

addressing a genuine issue for the church in Thyatira. Sexual licence and eating meat offered to idols, customary Jewish criticisms of Gentiles, could have become inseparable for him (cf. Acts 15.19; see also 1 Cor. 8.1-11.1).[94]

However, it is quite possible that 'Jezebel' might not have been the evil person John described. It could have been that 'Jezebel' stood closer to Paul and that John considered anyone who was not as rigorous as himself a religious infidel. If the Jezebel movement is directly related to eating meat offered to idols, it is quite possible that 'Jezebel' saw no harm in eating such meat since idols do not exist (cf. 1 Cor. 8.4). John, however, may not have made such a distinction and could not separate eating meat offered to idols from idolatry itself.

Sweet argues that in Revelation πλανάω (v. 20) relates 'to Satan and his imperial minions' (see 13.14; 18.23).[95] Sweet's argument is sound. I would add 12.9 to the list. In v. 20 it describes how false prophecy has led good people astray into immorality. 'Jezebel' has not won over everyone in the church in Thyatira, but it is clear that she has established a prophetic movement that rivals John's ministry.[96] Since John describes both the Balaam–Balak and Jezebel movements in similar terms, it is possible that both were prophetic movements.[97] Clearly, insufficient data exist to support this hypothesis. If it is correct, John would have had to compete with one and perhaps two rival Christian prophetic movements in Roman Asia, making the Christians in that social context well-accustomed to early Christian prophetic and apocalyptic discourse. Several commentators identify the Jezebel movement with the Nicolaitans.[98] Since we know nothing of the teachings or practices of either movement, such an identification is highly speculative. What is clear is that two opposing prophetic movements exist in Thyatira. Further examination elucidates this fact.

Christ has given the Thyatiran prophetess an opportunity to repent, but she has chosen not to do so (v. 21). Judgment (remember the title of v. 18) is rendered. First, she will become ill, her sympathizers will suffer mercilessly, if they do not repent, and her followers will die (vv. 22-

94. Cf. DeSilva, 'Social Setting', pp. 292-96.

95. Sweet, *Revelation*, p. 94.

96. Cf. Krodel's three Thyatiran groups (*Revelation*, pp. 126-27).

97. Cf. Bauckham, *Climax*, pp. 83-91; *Theology*, pp. 17-22.

98. E.g. Hemer, *Letters*, p. 122; Beasley-Murray, *Revelation*, p. 90; Charles, *Revelation*, I, p. 70; Ladd, *Revelation*, p. 52; Caird, *Revelation*, pp. 43-44.

23). Many have noted that 'to throw on a bed' is a Hebraic expression meaning to cause an illness as a form of punishment for sinfulness.[99] This expression is followed by the parallel expression '(to throw) into great tribulation' which also connotes suffering as a result of one's sins. A third expression then follows: 'I will kill by means of death', a Hebraism found in Ezek. 33.27 LXX. It means 'I will kill with pestilence'.[100] Several interpreters have also noted the double entendre wherein the bed of pleasure becomes a bed of pain.[101] These images are examples of nihilation: if all else fails, the evildoers will be eradicated.[102] This form of maintenance suggests a considerable degree of enmity between John and 'Jezebel'.

Charles argues that 'those who commit adultery with her' and 'her children' referred to her sexual partners in the first instance, and her actual offsprings in the second.[103] It is more likely that 'those who commit adultery with her' represented those who sympathized with her and that 'her children' were her disciples.[104] That would explain why the followers die while the sympathizers merely suffer mercilessly. These judgments come about so that 'all the churches' might know that Christ is the one who examines human motivations and he will 'give to you individually according to your works (or deeds)' (v. 23b; cf. Rev. 18.6; 20.12-13; 22.12; see also Mt. 16.27; Rom. 2.6; 14.12; 2 Cor. 5.10; cf. 1 Cor. 3.13; Eph. 6.8). Christ wants all the churches to recognize his omniscience and his role as eschatological judge (cf. v. 18 with Jer. 11.20; 17.10; 20.12 and Ps. 7.9). This letter contains another example of privileges previously associated only with God Almighty but now associated by John with the Messiah, again an example of the manner in which in Revelation Christ participates in divine honors. One might compare, for example, Rev. 2.23b with similar prophetic oracles in Isa. 14.22-27, Ezek. 37.1-14 and Joel 3.9-17.

99. See esp. Charles, *Revelation,* I, pp. 71-72, and Beasley-Murray, *Revelation*, pp. 91-92.

100. See Beasley-Murray, *Revelation*, p. 91; Sweet, *Revelation*, p. 95; Ladd, *Revelation*, p. 52; Morris, *Revelation*, p. 72.

101. E.g. Krodel, *Revelation*, p. 125; Hughes, *Revelation*, p. 49.

102. On nihilation, see Berger and Luckmann, *Social Construction*, pp. 130-34.

103. Charles, *Revelation*, I, p. 72.

104. Cf. Krodel, *Revelation*, p. 126.

On the other hand, a different judgment awaits those persons who have not associated or affiliated with the Jezebel movement. These persons will not suffer any punishment (v. 24) and are admonished to remain consistent in their beliefs until the parousia of Christ (v. 25). Some exegetes argue that 'another burden' (v. 24) refers to the requirements of the Apostolic Decree in Acts 15.28-29.[105] However, the letter makes no appeal to any church teaching or agreement to resolve the situation but receives direct instruction from its risen Lord mediated through John (cf. Rev. 1.9-20). Mounce accurately states, 'It is possible that the apostolic decree (Acts 15:28-29) is in mind, although apart from *baros* there are no linguistic parallels: the verb is *ballo* rather than *epitithemi*, and is followed by *eph hymas* rather than *hymin*.'[106] Not experiencing another burden means that those who have remained faithful will not encounter the punishments visited upon Jezebel and her followers and sympathizers, in addition to the oppression from local residents who adhere to Greco-Roman religious traditions.

This brings us to the promises to the victors. Christ promises (1) authority over the nations (v. 26) and (2) the morning star, two maintenance techniques. Mythologically, they depict life in the new age. Theologically, they relate directly to soteriology. The first promise in vv. 26-27 is a free rendering of Ps. 2.8-9 LXX. *Ps. Sol.* 17.23-24, a first-century CE Jewish writing, interpreted Ps. 2 messianically.[107] Ps. 2.9 in the Hebrew Bible reads, 'You shall break them with a rod of iron; you shall shatter them like earthenware.' Ps. 2.9 LXX reads, 'You shall shepherd them with an iron rod; you shall shatter them like an earthen vessel.' The context of the Thyatiran letter requires us to translate ποιμανεῖ 'will rule'. Thus, Christ promises to share his authority with the conquerors. The fulfillment passage is Rev. 20.4-6 (also see 19.15).[108] Here is another example of an Exodus motif in Revelation in the reference to priest-kings in the new age (Exod. 19.6). Most importantly, Christ promises to share his dominion with his faithful followers, a means of sustaining the bond between Christ and community in Revelation.

105. E.g. Charles, *Revelation*, I, p. 74; Ladd, *Revelation*, p. 53; Morris, *Revelation*, p. 73; Sweet, *Revelation*, pp. 95-96.

106. Mounce, *Revelation*, p. 105 n. 63.

107. For a text-critical history of this psalm, see Charles, *Revelation*, I, 75-76.

108. Cf. Mounce, *Revelation*, pp. 106-107, and Caird, *Revelation*, pp. 45-46. Chapter 6 of this study will discuss Ps. 2.9 LXX in more detail.

The second promise is a slightly different version of the first. Krodel correctly notes, 'The emphasis in Christ's [first] promise ... does not lie on the fate of the nations but on the privilege granted the conquerors to be co-regents with Christ (20:4-6).'[109] In agreement, Hughes writes, 'What is promised ... here is really union with Christ in his universal authority, as is plain from the explanation *even as I have received authority from my Father*' (emphasis as in the text).[110] The morning star is Christ himself: 'I am ... the bright morning star' (Rev. 22.16). To possess the morning star, the fulfillment of the second Thyatiran promise, means to have an intimate fellowship with the Lord. Thus, both promises would have conveyed to the reader the certainty of fellowship with Christ. The expected response would be repentance and faithfulness to Christ and the Christian gospel in its proper form.

This letter promises co-regency with Christ to the victor (vv. 26-27). This promise comes from the sovereign Son of God, the eschatological judge (v. 18). Christ commends (v. 19), but he also reproves (vv. 20-23) and exhorts (vv. 24-25). In all, Christ functions as an omniscient being who promises eternal life with God to the faithful victors, a maintenance strategy employed to maintain an unbroken relationship between Christ and community.

What social details are revealed in this letter? The religious metaphors employed as maintenance strategies suggest a culturally mixed context. The title 'Son of God' would probably be more familiar in settings where persons either considered some past worthy a son of a god or goddess or in cultures where the ruler was considered in some way a son of the national god.[111] The description of Christ's feet as a high-quality metal might reflect knowledge of Thyatira, a city where the smelting industry was a major part of the economy. 'Jezebel', the reference to fornication, eating meat offered to idols and the expressions used in describing the punishment of the Jezebel movement, however, have been correctly identified by many commentators as distinctly Jewish expressions. Their use strongly suggests that John's original audience understood this imagery and its punitive implications. Moreover, the Thyatiran church has two competing prophetic movements. John's is less accommodating to Greco-Roman culture than Jezebel's.

109. Krodel, *Revelation*, p. 129. For a different position, see Caird, *Revelation*, pp. 45-46.

110. Hughes, *Revelation*, p. 52.

111. See Walbank, *The Hellenisitic World*, pp. 209-26. Cf. Ps. 2.7.

The central issue is probably whether and/or to what degree Christians should accommodate to Greco-Roman culture (e.g. the imperial cult, trade guilds, eating meat offered to idols).[112] John employs various maintenance techniques to persuade people to continue their Christian practices. These maintenance strategies are aimed at Greco-Roman and Jewish persons, suggesting either attacks from both these groups or an ethnically mixed church in Thyatira, or both attacks from two sides and a mixed Chritian congregation. In Chapter 1 of this study, I argued that we should expect such social tensions in an eastern Mediterranean Roman province.

At the center of this conflict is the question of how best to witness in a larger non-Christian society, an issue we also noted in our discussion of 1 Peter (5.1-2). Religious laxity is a genuine issue, as several letters make plain, and it probably developed as a response to pagan and Jewish repression.[113]

e. *To Sardis (3.1-6)*

Again, we note that a letter in this series addresses an internal issue. In this case, it is the spiritual life of the congregation. Accommodation and laxity are the key elements in this debate.

The letter to Sardis describes Christ as the one who has complete authority over the spiritual representatives of the seven churches in Asia. Thus, this title asserts the complete cosmic lordship of Christ and would expect appropriate acknowledgement by the original audience.[114]

Most commentators state that the titles of Christ in the letters come from the vision in Rev. 1.9-20, but I have argued that they come from the entirety of Rev. 1.1-20. This title is a perfect example in that 'he who has the seven spirits of God' comes from Rev. 1.4,[115] not the vision in 1.9-20. The seven stars imagery comes from vv. 16 and 20. Thus, this title demonstrates the unity of Rev. 1.1–3.22 as one series of interrelated visions. The introduction and salutation (1.1-8), the vision of the

112. DeSilva, 'Social Setting', pp. 286-96.

113. Pliny, *Letters* 10; cf. Krodel, *Revelation*, pp. 30-40; DeSilva, 'Social Setting', pp. 286-96.

114. Hemer notes that both this letter and the one to the Ephesians both mention Christ holding seven stars; both congregations have fallen; and both promise life (*Letters*, p. 141).

115. Krodel correctly argues that this title forms an interlock with the next major section at 4.5 and 5.6 (*Revelation*, pp. 130-31).

'one like a son of man' (1.9-20) and the seven letters (chs. 2–3) comprise the first major section of the book.

The body of the letter begins forthrightly. 'I know your works; that you have a name that you are alive, but you are dead.' Sardis has traded on its name, not its works (v. 1). Kiddle correctly argues that this verse refers to spiritual life and death.[116] Through the seven spirits, Christ has looked beyond their reputation to their deeds. They are exhorted in v. 2 to become alert and strengthen those areas of their spiritual life that are about to die, for their deeds fall far short of completion.[117] Some argue that their fault was quiescence and accommodation in the presence of Jewish and Roman oppression.[118] Others argue that Christ does not censure Sardis for its lack of action but for its pseudo-spirituality.[119] Instead of the virtues of faith, love, service and patient endurance, commendable Thyatiran traits, the Christians in Sardis possess false piety and substandard religious morals.

The first position espoused by Kiddle and others has merits that its proponents have failed to articulate. If quiescence and accommodation to Jewish and/or Gentile religious pressure have caused their downfall, vv. 3-5 contain expressions that might substantiate that argument. In v. 3, Christ exhorts Sardis to 'Remember, therefore, in what way you have received and heard and keep it and repent.' What they have received and heard is most likely the Christian gospel. This verse may contain, therefore, an exhortation not to accept or tolerate Greco-Roman religio-political practices in any manner. Conversely, those who have not 'soiled their garments' (v. 4) could refer to persons who have not compromised their Christian beliefs. Thus, Christ's confession in v. 5 on behalf of the conquerors would have had a very powerful impact in Sardis. As some had confessed him on earth, he would confess them in heaven; if they have not, he would not (a form of maintenance). We have here a beautiful image of the Christ witnessing in the heavenly court concerning the fidelity of earthly beings. Normally, one expects the reverse: the human confession of faith in Christ on earth. Again, it

116. Kiddle, *Revelation*, pp. 44-45.

117. Several note how appropriate an exhortation to alertness would have been in Sardis, a city captured twice because its defenders were taken by surprise (e.g. Court, *Myth*, p. 36; Ladd, *Revelation*, p. 56; Morris, *Revelation*, p. 75).

118. Kiddle, *Revelation*, pp. 44-45; cf. Caird, *Revelation*, pp. 47-48; Ladd, *Revelation*, p. 56.

119. Krodel, *Revelation*, pp. 131-32; Hughes, *Revelation*, pp. 53-54.

is noteworthy that Christ is the role model for Christian conduct. This is a poignant means of maintaining the connection between Christ and community. The desired response from the reader would be one of increased love and devotion to this Lord, of whom one should bear witness, who witnesses on behalf of the faithful on earth in the heavenly court of justice. We must point out that the promise of Christ's confession is not fulfilled in Revelation. This differs slightly from the promise of the white stone with the new name (2.17) which is partially fulfilled in 22.4. Christ's confession, therefore, probably is not a part of the theological interlocks of the vision, but a specific message to the church in Sardis that spoke to an actual issue in that Christian community: public Christian confessions of faith or the lack of same. This letter may contain another reference to a need for a more faithful witness in the greater society. If this hypothesis is correct, witnessing in a hostile setting is at the foundation of the conflict. Indeed, if this is not an issue in some way, why is it an issue for John at all?

On the other hand, because the letter lacks more explicit details, this reconstruction could possibly 'over-interpret' the data. For this reason, the caution shown by Krodel and Hughes is warranted. As they argue, 'works' and 'name' in v. 1 could refer to their shallowness. If that interpretation is correct, then the phrase 'for I have not found your works completed before God' (v. 2) would mean that their Christian efforts have been woefully inadequate. However, against this hypothesis, no data exist to support it. One could just as easily argue (correctly in my opinion) that inscription in the book of life and Christ's confession of their names in heaven actually constitute one promise to combat a laxness with regard to public confessions of faith by Christians in Sardis. Whatever the case, the church in Sardis receives a severe judgment from its Lord and an exhortation to witness more faithfully and completely.

At another level, this letter includes some of the most striking and well-coordinated images in the entire book. First, those who appear to be spiritually alive are actually spiritually dead (v. 1). Christ expects them to keep the faith and repent or he will come 'like a thief' to judge them. Two things are noteworthy here. First and foremost, the life/death imagery in vv. 2-3 is a means of sustaining the sacred universe, attempting to persuade Christians in Sardis to live up to their name and remain in communion with their Lord. Secondly, the thief image continues that strategy by exhorting the church to adhere to Christ's command. This unexpected comparison of the Messiah to a thief makes this image all the more striking.[120] The reversal of expectations is a key motif in Revelation (e.g. 5.4-10). Another reversal appears in v. 4, where the 'deserved names' who have not soiled their garments stand in contrast with the 'undeserved name' of Sardis. The deserved names will walk with Christ in white garments 'because they [i.e. the people, not the garments] are worthy' (vv. 4-5; cf. 6.9-11; 7.9; 19.14). Those who deserve a name 'shall never be stricken from the book of life' (v. 5). This promise is fulfilled in 20.11-15 (see also 13.8; 17.8; cf. Exod. 32.32-33; Ps. 69.28; Dan. 7.10; 10.21; 12.1-2; Mal. 3.16-18; Lk. 10.20; Heb. 12.23; *Mart. Isa.* 9.19-23). Those who deserve a name shall have their names confessed by Christ in heaven (v. 5). Several have noted a possible allusion to the Asian custom of striking a convicted criminal's name from the citizenship roll. Hemer correctly notes that the same technical term, ἐξαλείφω, is used.[121] The use of this technical term demonstrates John's familiarity with the local setting and supports the argument that Rev. 2.1–3.22 contain genuine letters to real situations.

The color white also plays a key therapeutic role in this letter. The color white occurs 15 times in Revelation, more frequently than any other New Testament book. In every instance except 6.2, it has positive associations with the elect community (e.g. 7.9-14; 19.11, 14). Its function within this letter is to persuade the hearers/readers to remain within the sacred cosmos.

Central to this letter is the significance of 'the name'. We have noted this issue on earlier occasions in this study. The situation in Sardis appears to be slightly different. While in Pergamum Christians have withstood social pressures because of the name, the Christian community in Sardis has a reputation for religious faithfulness that it does not deserve. Christ says that it is better to have a name confessed in heaven, inscribed forever in the book of life (v. 5), than an outstanding

120. See similar imagery in Mt. 24.43-44; Lk. 12.39-40; 1 Thess. 5.2-4; 2 Pet. 3.10; Rev. 16.15. For a discussion of the nuances involved, see also Moffatt, 'Revelation', p. 448; Charles, *Revelation*, I, pp. 80-81; Sweet, *Revelation*, p. 100; Morris, *Revelation*, pp. 75-76. Moffatt ('Revelation', p. 448) and Charles (*Revelation*, I, pp. 80-81) insert Rev. 16.5 between the two sentences in v. 3. Beasley-Murray (*Revelation*, pp. 96-97) and Hemer (*Letters*, pp. 145-46) point out the weaknesses in their positions.

121. Hemer, *Letters*, pp. 148-52; see also Moffatt, 'Revelation', p. 365; Sweet, *Revelation*, p. 100.

reputation on earth that is not valid (v. 1). If the church in Sardis does not change, most of the names of its constituents will not be recorded in the book of life (cf. Rev. 20.11-15). Indeed, if they do not confess Christ's name on earth, Christ will not confess their names in heaven. For these reasons, I favor the interpretation that Christ censures them for their unchallenging and accommodating attitude toward local religio-political social pressures. Christ also exhorts them to live up to their reputation. Since the issues are rather understated, the reader must possess a detailed knowledge of the situation and the issues to which the letter alludes. Nevertheless, the mixing of exhortation and condemnation serves as a powerful maintenance strategy to ensure proper, faithful Christian witnessing in Sardis.

f. *To Philadelphia (3.7-13)*

The letter to the Philadelphians begins with a title of Christ ('The Holy One, the True One, who has the key of David, who opens and no one will close, and closes and no one opens') that does not explicitly connect with Rev. 1.1-20. Rather, it reflects Jewish traditions (e.g. Isa. 22.22; 40.25; Hab. 3.3) that John employs for this specific letter. Charles correctly notes the double epithet in Rev. 3.7 and its similarity to those in *1 En.* 1.3, 10.1, 14.1 and 84.1. Multiple epithets also play key roles in Revelation (e.g. 1.5, 8; 6.10; 19.11). Charles states that v. 7 ascribes to Jesus the qualities 'holy and true', which 6.10 ascribes to God Almighty. 'Hence, ἀληθινός implies that God or Christ, as true, will fulfil His word.'[122] As in many other passages in Revelation, Christ shares God Almighty's powers and privileges. Secondly, the remainder of the title in v. 3.7 appears to paraphrase Isa. 22.22 in the Hebrew Bible. Revelation 1.18 might have influenced the seer to employ this quotation. On the other hand, the message itself might have brought the quotation to mind. Quite possibly, both Rev. 1.18 and the situation might have jointly brought this passage from Isaiah to mind.

Kiddle argues that point by point the letters to Smyrna and Philadelphia are complementary. They should be read side by side. He identifies seven parallels. (1) Both confirm the faithfulness of each community. (2) Both communities must confront slanderous allegations from the synagogue. (3) Each church faces Roman persecution. (4) Each letter describes the Jewish opponents as Satanic. (5) Christ promises spiritual

122. Charles, *Revelation*, I, p. 86.

security to both. (6) A final reward, in the form of a crown, awaits the faithful from each church. (7) Although both churches have socially inferior statuses, their lowliness actually enhances their spiritual statuses.[123] Krodel accepts these observations but correctly stresses that, though the two letters contain similar features, they have different emphases. While the letter to Smyrna focused upon political tensions, the one to Philadelphia discussed theological issues.[124] I am persuaded by Krodel's argument.

Morris, who also rejects Kiddle's position, states that a conflict with the Jews was not the central issue. 'More probably it is admission to the city of David, the heavenly Jerusalem, that is in mind, and this Christ alone gives or withdraws.'[125] Similarly, Hemer finds no evidence of a Jewish community in Philadelphia. He states that 'Jew' was an honorable title usurped by John's opponents.[126] Against Morris, one might ask who would engage in a dispute over entrance into 'the city of David', a thoroughly Jewish concept, and not do so by engaging Jews? Who else would care enough to argue about it? Against Hemer, who but Jewish persons would engage in such a debate and to whom but Jewish persons would 'Jew' be an honorific term? The apologies of Artapanus, Philo, Josephus and other Jewish writers during the Second Temple period suggest strongly that 'Jew' was something less than an honorific title.

This letter reflects a conflict between Christians and Jews. The latter half of v. 9 ('Look! I will make them bow down before your feet, and know that I have loved you.') suggests that the struggle has been intense. The next verse contains a prophetic promise, a pledge aimed at keeping the Philadelphian church faithful and within the Christian sacred cosmos. In v. 10, John acknowledges the Philadelphians' endurance under Jewish pressure and he prophesies a worldwide conflict in the near future. However, he also foresees that Christ will protect them during these trials. References to present trials, visions of perceived future crises and a promise of protection from the Messiah (cf. 7.13-14; 14.1-3) and the employment of Jewish terms strongly suggest

123. Kiddle, *Revelation*, p. 48; cf. Ladd, *Revelation*, pp. 58-64; Wall, *Revelation*, p. 84.

124. Krodel, *Revelation*, pp. 136-37.

125. Morris, *Revelation*, p. 78.

126. Hemer, *Revelation*, pp. 159-64.

that Christians in this church are being repressed for their beliefs by Jewish persons.

The open door mentioned in v. 8 has caused an extensive debate among New Testament commentators. According to Moffatt, it refers to Christ himself.[127] Moffatt reads this verse in light of Ignatius, *Phld.* 9.1 ('he was the door of the Father' [translation mine]) and Jn 10.7, 9 ('the door of the sheep'). Moffatt's interpretation has two weaknesses. First, Ignatius' letter may reflect only the fourth gospel and not Revelation, or alternatively Ignatius could be reading Revelation in light of the fourth gospel and not on its own terms. Even if the Gospel of John and the Revelation to John come from the same John, that would not preclude John from using the same image differently. Secondly, Revelation may not depend upon the fourth gospel tradition for this image.

Kiddle offers two other possible interpretations. The door may symbolize access to God either through martyrdom or through prayer.[128] Several argue that the door symbolizes missionary opportunities.[129] However, the letter does not develop either theme. Finally, Bousset argues that the door represents entry into the messianic age (see Isa. 26.2; 60.11).[130] I agree with Bousset that the letter develops this vein of thought.

The open door of v. 8 parallels the image of Christ opening and closing solely on his own discretion in v. 7. In v. 7, Christ possesses the authority to control who does or does not enter into the heavenly kingdom. In v. 8, Christ has chosen to admit the Philadelphians because they 'kept my word and did not deny my name'.[131] Here again is a confirmation statement, a synonymous parallel. We note further the central issue is witnessing to Christ, as in previous letters (2.3, 13; 3.5; cf. 2.25; 3.10). Two expressions confirm this position. The first phrase, 'you kept my word', is essentially the same as '[you] did not deny my name', connoting to the readers the correctness of their unswerving fidelity to Christ. We have already noted how the phrases 'the word of

127. Moffatt, 'Revelation', pp. 366-67.

128. Kiddle, *Revelation*, pp. 49-50.

129. Ramsay, *Letters*, pp. 404-405; Charles, *Revelation*, I, p. 87; Caird, *Revelation*, pp. 51-52; Hemer, *Letters*, pp. 162-65; Court, *Myth*, p. 38; Hughes, *Revelation*, p. 59.

130. Bousset, *Offenbarung*, pp. 226-27.

131. See Beasley-Murray, *Revelation*, p. 100; Krodel, *Revelation*, pp. 137-38; cf. Morris, *Revelation*, p. 78.

God' and 'the testimony of Jesus' function in the same manner in 1.2 and 1.9 (see similar expressions in 2.13, 6.9, 12.17, 14.12 and 20.4).[132] Again, we note 'the name' is a central concern, suggesting that Christians have suffered simply because of their religious affiliation. This is not an isolated case (e.g. Mt. 10.17-23; Jn 15.21; 1 Pet. 4.14; Tacitus, *Annals* 15.44).

The remainder of the letter supports my argument. Verses 9-10 contain three prophetic promises. The Philadelphians will be vindicated in front of their opponents (v. 9), delivered through their trials (v. 10), and protected in the coming age (v. 10). Although the synagogue closed its doors to the Christians (v. 9), Christ opens the door to eternal life that none can close (see vv. 9-10).[133] Why does Christ make these promises? 'Since you kept the word of my steadfastness, I will also keep [i.e. protect] you from the hour of testing that is about to come upon the entire world to test the earth's inhabitants' (v. 10). In other words, their past faithful *witness* has insured Christ's future protection (cf. Mk 13.14-23; 2 Thess. 2.1-12). The Philadelphians are exhorted to maintain their present level of faithfulness in order that they might sustain their place in the sacred community. Krodel states that the crown in 3.11 'is a metaphor for the redemption already achieved (cf. 1:5-6) in distinction from the future crown of 2:10'.[134] I concur completely. Christ will come soon, conveying to the hearers/readers that the trials from which he will protect them will come soon as well. This is a strategy intended to assure the Philadelphians of their ultimate reward in the next age and to motivate them to maintain their level of religious devotion in the present one. At the very least, these passages indicate a setting where Jewish repression has had negative effects for Christians, some of whom might have been tempted to become more open to other ways of being religious.

Verse 12 constitutes a single promise expressed in two ways. First, Christ promises that he will make the conqueror a pillar in God's temple that will never be removed from God's presence. This conveys to the hearer/reader that an eternal fellowship with God and his Christ awaits the faithful. Christ expects a faithful response in both practice and belief. This promise reverses the earthly exclusion of the Christians

132. One finds seven such 'faith' confirmation statements in Revelation. This number may not be accidental.

133. Mounce, *Revelation*, pp. 117-19; Krodel, *Revelation*, pp. 137-39.

134. Krodel, *Revelation*, p. 139.

from the synagogue with inclusion in heaven as a guarantee of permanence in the presence of God Almighty.

Secondly, Christ promises to provide a new name for the conquerors. In Ezek. 9.4, God directs an angel to place a protective mark on the foreheads of the faithful so that they will be shielded from the coming catastrophe.[135] Similarly, this sealing protects the Philadelphians from eternal damnation. The reader would understand this new name to signify the legitimacy of the witness of the Philadelphian church on earth and that their witness has ensured their citizenship and entry into the gates (cf. vv. 7-8) of the New Jerusalem (see 22.4).[136] The reader would also understand the sealing of the saints to be an act of God's salvific love. This letter attempts to encourage the reader to respond courageously and hopefully when pressed by Jewry concerning their religious affiliation. Both promises are strategies to maintain the Christian symbolic universe and to sustain the bond between Christ and community.

The reader must possess a sound knowledge of Jewish Scripture and understand how characteristics formerly attributed to God Almighty have now been attributed to Christ, another example of Christ acting as God's agent in Revelation. Such a reader would understand that this theology would not be welcome in many Jewish circles. Therefore, the person who would make this claim about Jesus must be aware of the difficulties to be faced from Jewish persons. The promises would then attempt to enable the Christians in Philadelphia to look beyond the problems that their religious affiliation would cause to the promise of eternal fellowship with their Lord. This Lord holds the key of David, perhaps the key to the New Jerusalem, which determines who will or will not enter that city (cf. 13.8; 17.8).[137] This is another example of the relationship between Christ and community in Revelation and the maintenance strategies employed to keep that relationship intact.

135. The sealing of the saints may be a transformation of the Passover tradition found in Exod. 11–12. If so, it is an example of the transformation of older traditions and would connote to the reader that the Christian community is on an eschatological exodus with its destination the New Jerusalem.

136. Cf. Mounce, *Revelation*, pp. 119-21; Krodel, *Revelation*, pp. 138-40; Beasley-Murray, *Revelation*, pp. 101-103.

137. Cf. Wall, *Revelation*, p. 83.

g. *To Laodicea (3.14-22)*

In the letter to the Laodiceans, the key concern is not external pressure upon the church but the loss of religious zeal within it.

The title of Christ in this letter contains one unparallelled aspect in Revelation and another from Rev. 1.5 (cf. 2.13). Christ identifies himself as 'the Amen, the faithful and true witness' (cf. 19.11; 21.5; 22.6). The first expression, 'the Amen', may reflect the influence of Isa. 65.16, 'the God of Amen', rendered 'the true God' in the LXX (cf. NASB, NIV). Normally, 'amen' denotes that which is authentic and obligatory. The Isaianic passage conveys God's faithfulness, reliability and trustworthiness.[138] Thus, 'the Amen' is defined by the words 'the faithful and true witness'. Faithfulness can refer to Christ's witness (1.5; 19.11) and also to Antipas's witness (2.13). Each witness has given his life for his religious convictions. One who bears witness in this same manner will come as a Divine Warrior and eschatological judge in 19.11. In this way, John exhorts his readers to be willing to witness as Christ and Antipas have witnessed. The concluding titular phrase, 'the first of God's creation', probably goes back to 1.5, too ('the first-born of the dead and the ruler of the kings of the earth').

Next, Christ addresses the spiritual state of the Laodicean church. Since they are neither hot nor cold, that is lax in their devotional life, Christ is about to spit them out of his mouth (vv. 15-16), excommunication imagery.[139] Furthermore, although they describe themselves as materially affluent,[140] they actually are spiritually miserable, pitiable, poor, blind and naked (v. 17). Krodel astutely notes the contrast with the Christians in Smyrna, who are materially poor but spiritually rich, and those in Laodicea for whom the reverse is true. He further notes an admonition that seeks a transformation by the hearer/reader.[141] Poverty, blindness and nakedness allude to Laodicea's influential roles as a financial center, a noted center of ophthamological research and an outstanding clothing industry.[142] Christ exhorts the Laodicean Christians to purchase from him gold refined by fire so that they might acquire the

138. H. Schlier, *TDNT*, I, pp. 335-38; cf. Ladd, *Revelation*, pp. 64-65.

139. Hemer has an outstanding discussion of the neither hot-cold image and its referent in the locale (*Letters*, pp. 187-91).

140. On the affluence of Laodicea, see Hemer (*Letters*, pp. 193-96).

141. Krodel, *Revelation*, p. 143.

142. Many have made this same point (e.g. Krodel, *Revelation*, p. 144; Court, *Myth*, pp. 40-41; Sweet, *Revelation*, p. 100; cf. Hemer, *Letters*, pp. 196-201).

spiritual goods and obtain spiritual affluence. These images, with clear local socio-historical references, communicate to the reader that spiritual prosperity comes only from Christ, the one who provides the true salve that enables them to live by heavenly standards and not earthly appearances, and who also provides the means to purchase the true garments of salvation that cover their shame. In love, Christ exhorts his church to live zealously and repent (v. 19; cf. Prov. 3.11-12).

Sweet argues that v. 20 contains three 'interlocking allusions'.[143] First is the allusion to the crisis of the final judgment (cf. Mk 13.29; Jas 5.9). Next is the allusion to the synoptic bridegroom parables (Lk. 12.35-48; Mt. 25.1-13). Finally, there is the allusion to the bridegroom of Cant. 5.2 LXX. Sweet might be correct. However, the first two allusions might merely be current symbols and/or metaphors in first-century Judaism and Christianity conveying fellowship with God in the next age. This purpose would be to assure the Laodiceans that, if they turn to Christ and from the world (vv. 18-19), Christ will reward them for their obedience.

Exegetes are divided almost evenly on the question of whether or not the salvation offered in v. 20 is individual and present, or communal and eschatological. The first interpretation reads v. 20 in light of v. 19, connecting v. 20 with the call to repentance in the preceding verse.[144] The eschatological interpretation reads v. 20 in light of the eschatological promise in v. 21 to reign with Christ at the end of time.[145] In fact, vv. 19-21 have both individual and communal, present and future connotations and must be read as a unit. The 'anyone' in v. 20 clearly has implications for the individual in the present as well as the future. If enough individuals come together, a community will exist, a fact that vv. 19-21 do not preclude. Verse 19 speaks of election, a communal concept in biblical times, and the idea of an elect people held present and future implications during the Second Temple period. While v. 21 speaks of one person sitting on the throne with Christ, it clearly has implications for 'anyone' and everyone in the community. John would not have made the distinctions that his recent interpreters have made.

Finally, the promise to the victor (v. 21) continues the previously mentioned soteriological theme (v. 20) and assures the reader that as

143. Sweet, *Revelation*, p. 109; cf. p. 110.

144. E.g. Charles, *Revelation*, I, pp. 100-101; Beasley-Murray, *Revelation*, p. 107; Morris, *Revelation*, p. 83; Ladd, *Revelation*, pp. 67-68.

145. E.g. Moffatt, 'Revelation', p. 373; Krodel, *Revelation*, p. 145.

Christ conquered evil through suffering (cf. 1.5) so too could they. Again, we note that Christ is the role model for Christian deportment. The throne symbolizes a royal honor, an honor that Christ will share with the faithful conquerors (see fulfillment in 20.4-6).[146] Sharing Christ's throne is another example of the connection between Christ and community in Revelation. The purpose of this letter's maintenance strategy, the promise of co-regency, is to encourage the Laodiceans to follow Christ with their entire being and, in so doing, obtain spiritual goodness. As Christ conquered through suffering, so will they. As God shares his reign with Christ, God and Christ will share their reign with the victorious saints who witness faithfully to the word of God and the witness of Jesus. Again we note that witnessing is a central issue and that co-regency with Christ and/or God plays a key role in maintaining the sacred cosmos by relating Christ and community in Revelation. However, in this instance, the central concern is not local oppression but religious laxity.

h. *A Summary of the Letters*

First and foremost, the letters assume the lordship of Christ, the 'one like a son of man', to give directions and to judge these communities. The letters are natural extensions of Rev. 1.13-20. While 1.13-20 present the task, Rev. 2.1–3.22 comprise the task itself. To study the letters in isolation from the call and commission of John, or vice versa, misses a vital part of the total vision. Furthermore, the letters incorporate mythology, theology, therapy and nihilation as maintenance strategies in order to maintain a Christian symbolic universe. The letters were written primarily to strengthen the inner spiritual lives of the churches. A faithful witness would bring co-regency as priest-kings in the new age. This promise, an Exodus motif, is a maintenance strategy aimed at sustaining the union between Christ and community.[147]

Mythology and theology are inseparable in Revelation. Both describe the connection between the divine and human realms, a key concern of this study. In Revelation, the mythological framework contains the theological message. First, as stated previously, every letter assumes the lordship of Christ. Christ is God's divine agency figure who sends God's message through John to the churches (1.9-20). He is the Son of God (2.18), possesses the Spirit of God (3.1), maintains a faithful

146. Cf. Mounce, *Revelation*, pp. 83-84.

147. Cf. Reddish, 'Martyrdom', pp. 123-60, 217-20.

and true witness to God and rules the universe (3.14). Christ, God Almighty's co-regent, stands at the apex of the cosmos. Christ has supra-human powers. He is omniscient, able to see past, present and future (e.g. 2.20-23). He judges and administers justice (e.g. 3.9-10, 19). Yet Christ does not force anyone to repent (e.g. 3.20). As their Lord, Christ evaluates the behavior of the churches and applies different therapeutic strategies in order to correct different situations. He exhorts (e.g. 2.5, 7, 9-11, 12, 17, 19; 3.13, 18, 22), chastens and warns (e.g. 2.4-6, 14-16; 3.1-2, 15-17), praises (e.g. 2.2-3, 6, 13; 3.4, 8) and promises to save (2.7, 10, 11, 17, 26, 28; 3.5, 12, 21, 26-28; 3.5, 12-13, 21). His purview of the community is complete; his authority to act unquestionable. Furthermore, the letters contain a promise of a co-regency in the New Jerusalem as priest-kings with Christ. Christ's life is the prototype for this promise (2.26-28; 3.21). Possibly, John understands God Almighty to share divine honors with Christ and Christ similarly shares authority with the faithful in the New Jerusalem.

Maintenance strategies were aimed at bolstering the faith of those Christians pressured by Jewry, on one hand, and local adherents to Greco-Roman religious traditions, on the other, and to encourage others who had gone astray to return to the fold. Faithful Christian witnessing is the key issue in each letter and each letter expounds what form a faithful Christian witness should take in each context, whether facing Jewish or Greco-Roman pressures.

Our sociological examination of the letters has indicated some other possible social details. First and foremost, our exegesis has demonstrated that six of the seven letters addressed issues internal to the churches. The exception, the letter to Smyrna, speaks to Jewish oppression of Christians. It appears as though the Christians in Smyrna have been misrepresented to Roman authorities as a social menace, and John anticipates the Christians' eventual imprisonment. In Chapter 1 of this study, I argued that such actions by Jews during this period are intelligible given the religio-political context. Additionally, I argued that Roman political concerns and the indigenous religious traditions of the eastern Mediterranean would contribute to the repression of Christians by local inhabitants and Roman authorities. The reference to imprisonment might constitute an awareness of Roman attitudes, local religious suspicions and/or the religio-political reality of the situation (see 2.10).

This is a regional oppression of Christians by Jews and pagans. From the pagan side, it centers on the lack of participation by Christians in Greco-Roman religio-political activities and practices, what Pliny and Trajan would refer to as 'obstinance'; Sherwin-White, 'contumacy'. The laxity identified in some of these settings could well be a response to pagan social pressures (e.g. 2.10, 13; 3.1-3, 15-17). More than once, the letters identify Jewish oppression as a cause for concern and appropriate witness (2.9; 3.9-10). From the Jewish perspective, Christians are polytheists because in Christian doctrine Christ shares divine honors with God Almighty. From the Christian perspective, it is a matter of remaining faithful to one's religion. Against pagans and Jews, the letters exhort Christians to remain faithful. This occurs in several ways. First, it occurs in the heart of the letters themselves (2.5, 10, 16, 24-25; 3.3-4, 10-11, 18-20). Secondly, it occurs through the promises to the victors (2.7, 11, 17, 26-28; 3.5, 12, 21). Finally, it occurs through the emphasis upon the significance of the name.[148] For example, Christ says to Ephesus 'you have perseverance and have not become weary because of my *name*' (2.3); to Pergamum 'you hold fast to my *name* and did not deny my faith' (2.13); to Sardis 'I shall certainly never strike his *name* from the book of life and I shall confess his *name* before my father and before his angels' (3.5). These passages suggest that 'Christ/Christian', or a similar form of identification of Christians, had become a social stigma. The first instance has a commendation for not denying one's convictions even in the face of oppression. The second is associated with the death of Antipas, a faithful witness. The third is an exhortation to those Christians who have not been as faithful as Christians in the preceding two instances. In each case, fidelity to the name is central. Finally, the letter to Pergamum is an example of a letter that addresses both pagan (2.13) and Jewish (2.14) threats to and/or attacks upon Christianity.

Moreover, John is a prophet in these communities, but his is not the only prophetic Christian movement in the region. Rival groups, the Balaam–Balak movement (2.14), the Nicolaitans (2.6, 15) and the Jezebel movement (2.20-24) differ from John's. The letters give no clear, definitive information concerning the first two movements. John describes the Jezebel movement as a prophetic movement and saves his most extended comments for it. If the Balaam–Balak movement and the Nicolaitans

148. At some point, I hope to develop a more detailed study of the significance of name in Revelation.

are also prophetic movements, these seven churches would be accustomed to prophetic-apocalyptic preaching and the original recipients would be accustomed to this form of discourse. At the very least, this can be said for the Thyatiran Christians, where two prophetic Christian movements compete for followers. It is interesting to note that Jezebel is not condemned for her gender but for her message.

If nothing else, the letter to Smyrna at once proves my points that the letters address internal problems and that Christians were oppressed in the region. *The oppression in Smyrna is itself an internal problem that requires instruction from the Lord of the church* (2.10-11). Moreover, if the Christians and the Jews saw themselves related in some way, they could understand their disputes to be internal to some degree. This discussion has also shown that laxity, complacency, compromise and/or accommodation to Greco-Roman religions are some of the key issues addressed in Pergamum, Sardis and Laodicea. Most probably, they constitute responses to various forms of repression placed upon Christians by both Jews and pagans to force them to conform socially. There is no extant evidence that Christianity received a degree of social acceptance in the late first/early second centuries CE. In fact, the Roman sources we examined in Chapter 1 indicate that the Christians received little or no social esteem during this period. Indeed, during this general period, 1 Peter and Pliny provide evidence of pressures upon Christians in the region to conform to provincial religio-political practices.

Previously, we noted five features associated with the human-like Messiahs in *1 Enoch* and *4 Ezra*. We find these same features in Revelation 2–3. First, the Messiah introduced by means of a descriptive comparison in 1.13 (and also in 14.14) is the sender of the letters in Rev. 2.1–3.22. Secondly, the Messiah functions as an eschatological judge (e.g. 2.5, 12, 14, 16, 18-19, 22-24; 3.1, 17; 14.14-16). Thirdly, the Messiah gathers together an elect community by exhorting the Christians to hear the Spirit (e.g. 2.7, 17; 3.13, 22) and by promising blissful communal life in the New Jerusalem (e.g. 2.7, 10-11, 17; 3.12, 21). Fourthly, Christ makes war against the enemies of God (e.g. 2.6, 14-16, 20-23). Finally, there is an element of mystery associated with the Messiah (e.g. 2.17). Revelation 2–3 also shares christological features with other early Christian literature: (1) Christ has cosmic authority (e.g. 2.1; cf. Jn 1.1-3); possesses power over death (e.g. 2.7-11; cf. 1 Cor. 15); is omniscient (e.g. 2.2, 18; cf. Mk 8.31; 9.7); is a divine agency figure (e.g. 3.7; cf. Phil. 2.5-11); provides salvific benefits for the human community (e.g. 2.18-23; cf. Heb. 10.19-21). In sum, in Rev. 2.1–3.22 Christ speaks as the Lord of the churches who instructs, commends, censures and promises in order to communicate to the churches what they must do in order to enter the New Jerusalem.

This chapter would be incomplete without an examination of the other 'one like a son of man' passage in Rev. 14.14-16.

3. *On Revelation 14.14-16*

Rev. 14.14-16 is the second 'one like a son of man' passage in Revelation. In it, the figure is transported via a cloud (see Dan. 7.13; *4 Ezra* 13.3) and is harvesting the earth. Who is this being and what does the harvest symbolize?

Some argue that the figure on the cloud is Christ. For example, Prigent argues, 'The person who appeared initially is clearly the same one from the inaugural vision (Ap 1,13): the same words are employed in both cases.' Agreeing with him, Lohmeyer concludes, 'Therefore, any doubt about the identity of the figure here (in 14.14) and there (in 1.13) is indefensible.'[149] Similarly, Mounce argues that the figures in 1.13 and 14.14 both depend upon Dan. 7.13. The golden wreath, also worn by the 24 elders in Rev. 4.4, singles out the 'one like a son of man' as the Messiah, who has conquered and achieved judicial authority. The son of man's use of the sickle symbolizes righteous retribution. Most who hold to this position also identify several New Testament passages where transportation on a cloud connotes Christ's messianic glory.

Others argue that in 14.14 the 'one like a son of man' is an angel. The determinative factor for this interpretation is the angel's command to the figure on the cloud (14.15). They argue that it would be inconceivable for an angel to address the Messiah in this manner. Morris adds that Revelation refers to 'a son of man' and not the synoptic 'the son of the man'.[150]

The 'one like a son of man' in Rev. 14.14 is the Messiah. Along with the arguments put forth above, I would add that the figure being transported on a cloud in Rev. 1.7, the human-like figure standing among the

149. P. Prigent, *L'Apocalypse de saint Jean* (CNT, 2nd series, 14; Paris: Delachaux & Niestlé, 1981), p. 233; Lohmeyer, *Offenbarung*, p. 127 (translations mine in both cases). See also Corsini, *Apocalypse*, pp. 267-75; Morris, *Revelation*, p. 199; Schüssler Fiorenza, *Vision*, p. 90; Wall, *Revelation*, pp. 187-88.

150. E.g. Morris, *Revelation*, pp. 178-79; cf. Kiddle, *Revelation*, pp. 284-95.

lampstands in Rev. 1.13 and the human-like figure being transported on a cloud in Rev. 14.14 are all representations of the Messiah that depend upon Dan. 7.13. There is a similar messianic representation in *4 Ezra* 13.3. Moreover, the command in 14.15 comes from God Almighty in the Temple, God's heavenly residence. The angel is merely a messenger. Furthermore, Revelation does not confuse angels and divine agency figures (see 19.10; 22.8-9). To employ the same description to refer to Christ and an angel would confuse the matter unnecessarily. It is noteworthy that the being in 14.14 is *not* identified as an angel. Finally, against Morris and others, Revelation does not read 'son of man' but 'one like a son of man'. The use of these comparisons for heavenly beings has been discussed in Chapter 2 of this study and will not be repeated here.[151]

The human-like being on the cloud is the Messiah, but are his actions positive or negative? Commentators usually take one of four positions to explain the harvesting of the earth. Many argue that the harvest symbolized the gathering of the saints in early Christianity (e.g. Mt. 9.37). John has implied this in 14.4 by referring to the 144,000 as the 'first fruits'. The song of Moses and the Lamb, a song of salvation (15.3-4), follows the harvesting. In addition, vv. 14-16 contain no references to God's wrath or to a horrific judgment upon the unjust. All these details indicate that 14.14-16 relate the eschatological harvesting of the saints, while vv. 17-20 describe the punishment of the unjust.[152]

Another view holds that frequently John's symbols and images cannot be easily interpreted. Rev 14.14-20 would be one such passage. This passage incorporates Joel 3.13, a description of the punishment of a people for their wickedness. These commentators argue that vv. 14-16 do not refer to the saints, indicating one judgment upon God's enemies in vv. 14-20.[153]

A third view argues that vv. 14-16 and 17-20 constitute two presentations of the same message. The one message would refer to the eschatological judgment of saint and sinner alike. The harvest would then include all human beings.[154]

151. Cf. Mounce, *Revelation*, p. 279.

152. E.g. Caird, *Revelation*, pp. 190-92; Ladd, *Revelation*, pp. 198-200; Schüssler Fiorenza, *Vision,* pp. 90-91.

153. E.g. Yarbro Collins, *Apocalypse*, p. 105; Wall, *Revelation*, pp. 187-90.

154. E.g. Beasley-Murray, *Revelation*, pp. 228-29; Morris, *Revelation*, pp. 179-80; Kiddle, *Revelation*, pp. 288-89.

A fourth approach argues that 14.14-20 comprises a prolepsis of 20.4-6, 11-15. The 144,000 are also the saints who reign with Christ for a millennium. They are not subject to the judgment in 14.14-20 or 20.11-15. Thus, the harvest in 14.14-16 and the vintage in 14.17-20 are for everyone except the followers of the Lamb. They come alive during the first resurrection.[155]

I believe there are two visions in 14.14-20. Verses 14-16 describe the ingathering of the saints; vv. 17-20 the punishment of the enemies of God. While vv. 17-20 use language that in Revelation conveys the punishment of the enemies of God (14.19: τὴν ληνὸν τοῦ θυμοῦ τοῦ θεοῦ; cf. 14.10: τοῦ οἴνου τοῦ θυμοῦ τοῦ θεου ... τῆς ὀργῆς αὐτοῦ; 19.15: τὴν ληνὸν τοῦ οἴνου τοῦ θυμοῦ τῆς ὀργῆς τοῦ θεοῦ), it is noteworthy that vv. 14-16 contain none of this language but employ harvest language as an image of salvation for the saints, a practice consistent with other New Testament witnesses (see Mt. 9.37; Mk 4.26-29; Lk. 10.1-12, esp. v. 2; Jn 4.38). Furthermore, the LXX rarely uses θερίζω or θερισμός to connote judgment against the unjust (e.g. Isa. 63.1-6 LXX).[156] Revelation 14.14-16 is a prolepsis of 20.4-6, 11-15, the ingathering of the elect community of saints, a messianic function in Revelation that also is found in *1 En.* 48.4 and *4 Ezra* 13.12-13. Moreover, the preceding exegeses have demonstrated that the overall function of the 'one like a son of man' passages has been the pastoral oversight and care of the churches so that they might obtain an eternal fellowship with God and Christ in the new age. In keeping with that role, 14.14-16 contains a proleptic vision of the eschatological ingathering of the saints.

3. *Conclusion to Part I*

Part I has identified several common features among Ezekiel, Daniel, *1 Enoch*, *4 Ezra* and Revelation that have been only partially noted previously. Especially in *1 Enoch*, *4 Ezra* and Revelation, the principal purpose of these features is to maintain the spiritual well-being of the community addressed by the individual books. This has been demonstrated in several ways.

155. Cf. Krodel, *Revelation*, p. 273.

156. Cf. Caird, *Revelation*, pp. 190-92; Boring, *Revelation*, pp. 168-72; Krodel, *Revelation*, pp. 271-75.

1. Chapter 2 examined the 'one like a son of man' of Dan. 7.13, concluding that Ezekiel's use of comparisons to describe heavenly beings in human likeness was the source for Daniel's descriptions of God and angels in Daniel 7–12 in human likeness. Chapter 2 also examined the exegesis of Dan. 7.13 in Jewish and Christian pseudepigraphical writings roughly contemporaneous with Revelation (*1 En.* 37–71; *4 Ezra* 13; *Apoc. Abr.* 10; *Mart. Isa.* 4) and discovered that the first three maintain the use of comparisons when interpreting Dan. 7.13. While *1 Enoch* and *4 Ezra* describe the Messiah, the *Apocalypse of Abraham* and the *Martyrdom and Ascension of Isaiah* describe angels. While the functions of these beings so described showed a degree of variety, five features common to *1 Enoch* and *4 Ezra* were identified: (1) the use of comparisons in presenting the Messiah; (2) the Messiah as judge; (3) the Messiah as one who gathers an elect community to himself; (4) the Messiah as one who makes war against the enemies of God; (5) the Messiah as one surrounded by an element of mystery. Subsequently, Chapters 3 and 4 of this study revealed these same features in Revelation 1–3 and 14.14-16, along with others held in common with each individual writing. The additional messianic features unique to Revelation were identified as distinctively Christian elements. Furthermore, the use of comparisons to depict heavenly beings in *The Testament of Abraham* and Philo's *On Abraham* substantiates our argument concerning the use of comparisons for just this purpose during the Second Temple period.

2. Chapter 3 also demonstrated that in Rev. 1.1-8 Christ became for John the author and guarantor of the vision, a role formerly held by God Almighty in Jewish apocalypses. We also noted other ways that Christ participates in divine honors with God Almighty. Christ has received these honors because he has died for human sin and has faithfully represented *through his witness* the will of God. In this manner, Christ has provided a model for Christian witnessing in the Roman province of Asia. Revelation 1.1-8 attempt to elicit a faithful response from the readers/hearers of the book that is consistent with the word of God. Christ, through his prophet John, exhorts them to be true to their calling and to remain firm in their faithful witness, even unto death (2.5, 10, 13, 25; 3.2-3, 8, 18).

3. Revelation 1.9-20 reports the calling and commissioning of John to write to the seven churches in Asia. These passages accomplish four things. First, they establish Christ's role as the Lord of the churches,

one who has the authority to direct human behavior within the churches. Secondly, they establish John as Christ's authentic spokesman over against John's opponents. Both Christ and John have suffered for their witnesses (e.g. 1.5-7, 9) and Christ is a role model for John. John might be attempting to convey to his readers that his life best emulates the life of Christ. Thirdly, Christ is not only lord of the churches but lord of the universe and human history as well. His authority is comprehensive (1.13-20). Fourthly, Christ is the one who will redeem the saints and lead them in the New Jerusalem (e.g. 2.7, 10-11, 17; 14.14-16; cf. 20.4-6). These passages are maintenance strategies aimed at convincing the readers to listen to prophets like John who proclaim Christ's message among them. The book of Revelation assumes that the churches knew whom those prophets were.

4. Christ is the messiah described in human likeness (v. 13) who authorizes the seven letters and gathers, protects and leads the faithful at the eschaton (e.g. 3.12, 21; 14.14-16; cf. 7.13-17). The titles in six of the seven letters explicitly refer back to Rev. 1.1-20, where Christ's authority has been established as lord of these churches (vv. 1-3, 5, 7, 11, 17b-20). Christ performs many of the same messianic functions we have noted in *1 Enoch* and *4 Ezra*. First, he judges these churches (e.g. 2.5, 12, 14, 16, 18-19, 22-24; 3.1, 17). Secondly, he gathers together the churches through his exhortations to all the churches to hear the Spirit (e.g. 2.7, 17; 3.13, 22), through his promises to the conquerors (e.g. 2.7, 10-11, 17; 3.12, 21) and through his harvesting the saints in the end-time (14.14-16), constituting an elect Christian community. Thirdly, he makes war against his enemies (e.g. 2.6, 14-16, 20-23; cf. 14.17-20).[157] Fourthly, he possesses an element of mystery (2.17). Finally, the author employs a comparison to present the messiah (1.13; 14.14). Thus, we have noted the same five common features in Rev. 1.1–3.22 and 14.14-16 that we found between *1 En.* 37-71 and *4 Ezra* 13.

Rev. 2.1–3.22 also has other messianic features peculiar to it. The Messiah has cosmic authority (2.1; 3.1; cf. Jn 1.1-3); power over death (2.7-11; Jn 11.28-44); is an omniscient being (e.g. 2.2, 18; cf. Jn 2.23-25; Mt. 21.23-27) who participates in divine honors (cf. 3.7; 6.10; cf. Phil. 2.5-11) and holds the keys to salvation (e.g. 3.5, 9-10, 12; cf. Jn 6.22-33) or damnation in his hands (e.g. 2.18-23; cf. Jn 14.6-7). Again,

157. The fullest christological expression of making war is found in Rev. 19.11-21, the focus of Chapter 6 of this study.

the features peculiar to Revelation were central elements of early Christian preaching.

5. The 'one like a son of man' Christology relates directly to the saints' priestly co-regency with Christ (2.26-28; 3.21), establishing through the promises, for all who remain faithful to the Christian witness, an unbroken relationship between Christ and community. The promises in Revelation are the primary means through which the churches remain in the symbolic universe and sustain the union between Christ and community. Priest-kingship, the basic means of maintaining the union, is an eschatological exodus motif that goes back to Exod. 19.16.

These observations provide valuable information concerning the book's readership and the social setting of the Christian communities. First, the reader understands Second Temple Judaism in general and its messianic expectations in particular, *as well as* the distinctive content of early Christian witnessing. One merely familiar with Judaism or with Christianity would not have been able to understand all the allusions. Secondly, the reader is open to the possibility of God revealing Godself and/or God's will to human seers. Such a reader need not be a seer but must believe that seers exist who faithfully proclaim God's word. Thirdly, the reader expects a vision detailing Christ's imminent second coming as the Messiah of the world. The community hopes that Christ's parousia will soon end their trials (1.3). Fourthly, a basic issue, if not the basic one, is who is the 'True Israel'. Christians argue that they are the True Israel but more traditional Jewish persons disagree. Jewish persons also have misrepresented Christian doctrine to pagans (2.9; 3.9), causing Christians problems in the larger society (cf. 1 Pet. 4.12-5.11). Fifthly, these churches are also oppressed by local residents who probably resent the Christians for not participating in their religious activities. It is possible that more traditional Jews have misrepresented the Christians' beliefs and practices, identified Christians as a social threat (cf. Pliny, *Letter* 10), leading to the imprisonment of some Christians and the death of Antipas (e.g. 2.9-11, 13; 3.8-11). As noted previously, the significance of remaining faithful to the name indicates that 'Christ/Christian' had probably attained some form of public derision, a theme that recurs throughout the book (e.g. Rev. 2.17; 14.1; 19.12; 22.4). Tensions between Christians and non-Christians on this issue are aspects of the social context in which John ministers. Thus, being faithful to the name was stressed as a primary witness and means of strengthening the bond between Christ and community. Finally, several competing movements vie for followers in these churches. At least two, John's and 'Jezebel's', are prophetic movements. If the Balaam/Balak movement and the Nicolaitans are also prophetic, the Christians in Roman Asia would have been accustomed to prophetic-apocalyptic preaching. They would have attained a familiarity with its means of expression and would have been able to interpret apocalyptic visions. In any event, Revelation itself presupposes such a setting.

The letters also provide evidence of religious laxity and/or accommodation by some Christians. The hoped for response would be repentance where it is needed and continued faithfulness among the faithful. John employs mythology, theology, therapy and nihilation to achieve his ends. Within this setting, Christians experienced Jewish and Greco-Roman repression. The letters reflect the different responses that Christians in Asia gave to the socio-religio-political pressures of their day. Religious laxity became an option for some Asian Christians. For others like John, however, the only true mode of Christian deportment was a total rejection of non-Christian religio-political customs.

What is the cosmology implicit in Rev. 1.1–3.22 and 14.14-16? In brief, Christ is the Lord of the universe (i.e. heaven, earth and Hades) who has come as Jesus, who now speaks through John and will come at the end of time to protect the faithful and condemn the wicked. His primary concern is the *internal spiritual welfare* of the Christian community in order that the community might remain in accord with its Lord and be spiritually strong enough to withstand the envisioned apocalyptic trials that comprise Rev. 4.1–19.21. All people will see him as he comes to save his elect community and condemn the rest to the second death, imagery that suggests that Christians have experienced public humiliation.

What modes of behavior would this one-like-a-son-of-man Christology advance? It would make it easier for these Christians to accept their suppression as a natural consequence of witnessing faithfully in a hostile world. This would not be a docile acceptance but would require a great deal of religious commitment and inner spiritual strength. 'Faith' for these persons would not be a set of beliefs or mere doctrines, but the essence of their very existence.[158] Moreover, the very medium itself would make the life of a practicing visionary and/or prophetic figure a

158. Cf. DeSilva, 'The Revelation to John', p. 375.

live option for some persons. At the very least, one would be more open to prophetic messages and visions as a way of being religious. Finally, given the Asian context, where the imperial cult enjoyed a grassroots popularity, Christian faithful-witnessing-unto-death became a means of remaining within the sacred cosmos, defeating evil and also a form of civil disobedience within a hostile religio-political environment.

Part II

THE LAMB AND THE DIVINE WARRIOR

Chapter 5

THE CHRIST AS THE LAMB

This chapter will examine the role and function of the slain Lamb as a major, if not the major, christological image employed in Revelation. The exegetical discussions that follow will demonstrate that the most prominent christological functions center around the Lamb as the communal leader and role model whose sacrificial death provides many positive benefits for Asian Christians.[1] An important benefit is priesthood and co-regency with Christ and/or God Almighty in the New Jerusalem, a key aspect of Revelation's understanding of the relationship between Christ and community and also a major maintenance strategy in Revelation. In so doing, Revelation employs an eschatological exodus motif to portray the followers of the Lamb as the new people of God.[2] The eschatological exodus motif probably derives from Exod. 19.6: 'You will be for me a kingdom of priests and a holy nation' (NIV).

1. *The Lamb as a Symbol*

The Lamb symbol is the most pervasive means of transmitting the christological message of the book of Revelation. Several other writers have also begun with Revelation's symbols and images and come to similar conclusions.[3] Those who employ this approach work with the

1. Cf. J.D. Charles, 'An Apocalyptic Tribute to the Lamb (Rev 5:1-14)', *JETS* 34 (1991), pp. 461-73.

2. I am indebted to Professor H.W. Attridge for initially bringing this motif to my attention (Revelation seminar, SMU, summer 1978) and to the Revd John Sweet of Cambridge University for reminding me of it in private conversation. See also Bauckham, *Theology*, pp. 70-72.

3. E.g. D.M. Beck, 'The Christology of the Apocalypse of John', in E.P. Booth (ed.), *New Testament Studies: Critical Essays in New Testament Interpretation with Special Reference to the Meaning and Worth of Jesus* (New York: Abingdon–Cokesbury Press, 1942), pp. 253-77; S. Laws, *In Light of the Lamb* (GNS, 31;

understanding that the Lamb is Revelation's central christological image that controls and interprets the other major themes. Laws, for example, states that the Lamb interacts with two other major christological images: the son of man (1.12-18) and the rider on the white horse (19.11-16). Laws identifies three common elements between the son of man image and the Lamb images: (1) both are messianic images; (2) both understand Christ 'in terms of the character of God' (p. 26); (3) both the christological images relate specifically to the historical Jesus, especially the crucifixion and resurrection. The rider on the white horse shares the first two elements. However, with the rider the emphasis shifts from the present to the future, where judgment and victory will become complete, and thus this image does not display the same concern to relate specifically to the historical Jesus.

I concur with Laws for the following reasons. First, this approach recognizes that in Revelation one encounters christological images as well as christological titles and that the former are as important as the latter. This is so because Revelation is primarily a book of visions. Secondly, this approach perceives the relationship and common elements among the three major christological images. This current study will identify more common elements. Finally, the emphasis upon images, not titles, is important because images have the ability, more than titles, to grip the imagination and to represent a message succinctly. Images are symbols that enable a reader or hearer to appropriate a message quickly, both cognitively and emotively. Our discussion now turns to the different strands of Judaism that contributed to the Lamb imagery in Revelation.

2. *The Jewish Background*

The Greek word ἀρνίον appears 29 times in 27 verses in Revelation.[4] All but one appearance (13.11, which refers to the beast from the sea) refer to the Christ–Lamb figure. The Lamb as a christological image in

Wilmington, DE: Michael Glazier, 1988); cf. Farrer, *Rebirth*; Büchsel, *Christologie*; A. Läpple, 'Das Geheimnis des Lammes: Das Christbild der Offenbarung des Johannes', *BK* 39 (1984), pp. 53-58.

4. 5.6, 8, 12, 13; 6.1, 16; 7.9, 10, 14, 17; 12.11; 13.8, 11; 14.1, 4, 10; 15.3; 17.14; 19.7, 9; 21.9, 14, 22, 23, 27; 22.1, 3. See also C.K. Barrett, 'The Lamb of God', *NTS* 1 (1954–55), pp. 210-18.

Revelation has several similarities with other New Testament books (cf. Jn 1.29, 36; Acts 8.32-35; 1 Cor. 5.7; 1 Pet. 1.19).

However, some have argued that the Lamb in Revelation comes primarily from Jewish apocalyptic traditions rather than early Christian usage.[5] In *1 En.* 90.9 horned lambs represent the Maccabees and in 90.37 their leader is portrayed as a white bull with horns. However, these horned lambs are not messianic figures. In *T. Jos.* 19.8-9, a lamb, as a messianic figure, destroys the enemies of Israel. Revelation incorporates this latter motif more than the former and adds the Christian witness of faith (cf. Jn 1.29-34; 1 Pet. 1.17-21), the Lamb who conquers through suffering, a motif that is noticeably absent from the passages in *1 Enoch* and the *Testament of Joseph.*[6]

Others have argued that the names and/or titles bestowed upon Jesus provide the key to understanding the Christology of Revelation.[7] Following Charles, Mounce argues that the name 'the Lamb' derives from a merger of the traditions that portray the Lamb as victim and the Lamb as leader. The latter has been mentioned in the discussion of *1 Enoch* and the *Testament of Joseph.* While not totally disagreeing, I believe that 'the Lamb' is more than a name or a title, in fact an image, a representational symbol of something greater than what it might normally convey.[8] While a name/title carries with it definition, an image/symbol conveys definition and a pictorial concept of that which is defined. Symbols and images have the power to affect both cognition and emotion.

A final position espouses that the Lamb must be understood primarily as the focus of Christian worship.[9] Ellul, for example, argues that the

5. E.g. B. Lindars, 'A Bull, a Lamb and a Word: 1 Enoch 90:33', *NTS* 22 (1975–76), pp. 483-86; Charles, *Revelation*, I, p. 141; Lohmeyer, *Offenbarung*, pp. 54-55; Beasley-Murray, *Revelation*, pp. 124-25; Mounce, *Revelation*, p. 145; D. Guthrie, 'The Lamb in the Structure of the Book of Revelation', *Vox Evangelica* 12 (1981), pp. 64-71, esp. p. 64 n. 7. For other positions, see Swete, *Apocalypse*, p. 76, and Moffatt, 'Revelation', p. 44.

6. Cf. Holtz, *Christologie*, p. 41; Krodel, *Revelation*, p. 164; Laws, *In Light*, pp. 27-28; cf. Beasley-Murray, *Revelation*, pp. 125-26.

7. E.g. Holtz, *Christologie*, R.H. Mounce, 'The Christology of the Apocalypse', *Foundation* 11 (1968), pp. 42-51; cf. Aune, 'The Social Matrix of the Apocalypse of John', *BR* 28 (1983), pp. 5-26; Beasley-Murray, *Revelation*, pp. 124-26.

8. On the different types of symbols, see Chapter 1, this study. See also Schüssler Fiorenza, 'Followers of the Lamb: Visionary Rhetoric and Social-Political Situation', *Semeia* 36 (1986), pp. 123-46.

9. E.g. J. Ellul, *Apocalypse* (New York: Seabury, 1977).

preponderance of Lamb passages occurs in worship contexts and that this fact reflects the importance of the Lamb to the worshiping community to which the apocalypse was sent. Guthrie also sees the significance of the Lamb in worship settings and emphasizes the victory through sacrifice and suffering motif associated with the Lamb. Further, he notes other significant christological roles played by the Lamb in Revelation (eschatological judge, shepherd, redeemer figure, divine warrior, co-regent with God).[10]

Ellul and Guthrie have made some important contributions to this topic, in particular the emphasis upon the Lamb as an important symbol of victory through suffering. They are also sensitive to the other roles attributed to the Lamb in Revelation. Furthermore, they correctly note the important cultic role of the Lamb. On the other hand, they have not recognized how other christological images have contributed to the concept of the Lamb. This chapter will demonstrate how the 'one like a son of man' image has contributed to John's image of the Lamb.

As helpful as all these discussions are, only the position espoused by Laws and others correctly recognizes the shift from one image/symbol to another and thus helps the modern reader to ascertain something of the nuances and messages sent to the original readers. The christological images gave the original readers something with which to relate their own experiences in a meaningful way, that is, John has chosen particular images that have achieved a certain degree of meaning because of the experience of Asian Christians. What was that meaning and how did John employ and/or modify traditions?

The Hebrew Bible contains approximately 400 references to rams, sheep and lambs. The terms used most frequently are צאן ('sheep', 114 times); אַיִל ('ram', 106 times) and כֶּבֶשׂ, ('sheep', 100 times). The passages can be divided easily into two categories: (1) generic references to these pastoral creatures and (2) sacrificial references to religious offerings. Neither category has messianic dimensions (e.g. Gen. 30.32; Deut. 32.14; Job 31.20; Ps. 114.4, 6; Prov. 27.26; Isa. 5.17; 11.6; 40.11; 65.25).

The sacrificial references contain theological dimensions, but the rams, sheep and lambs do not cease being rams, sheep and lambs. Rather, they take on the additional role as an expiation for human sin

10. Guthrie, 'The Lamb', pp. 64-71.

(e.g. Exod. 12.5; Lev. 1.10; 1 Chron. 29.21; Isa. 1.11; 34.6). New Testament writers found the sacrificial elements appropriate to explain the role and mission of Jesus, an unprecedented development. The concept of a sacrificial lamb as an expiation for sin is an exodus motif, relates directly to the Passover lamb in Exodus and served as an aspect of the Christian concept of Jesus as a sacrificial lamb.[11]

Extant Second Temple Jewish literature in general exhibits the same two categories, the generic and the sacrificial, without any hint of messianic implications. ἀρνίον appears four times in the LXX in Ps. 113.4 and 6 (114.4 and 6 in the Hebrew Bible) for צאן and also in Jer. 11.19 for כֶּבֶשׂ and additionally in Jer. 27.45. In each instance, ἀρνίον has no messianic role. In the Apocrypha/Deuterocanonical writings, ἀρνίον is found in Sir. 46.16 and 47.3; the Pr. Azar. 17 (also known as Dan. 3.39 LXX) and 1 Esd. 6.28 (v. 29 in REB and NRSV), 7.7, 8.14 and 8.63 (8.66 in REB, NRSV). None of these passages has messianic features. For example, Sir. 46.16 reads, 'And he called upon the Sovereign Lord, when his enemies pressured [him] on all sides, by sacrificing a suckling lamb.' This passage clearly falls within the sacrificial category, as do Pr. Azar. 17 and all the passages from 1 Esdras. Only Sir. 46.16 has a solely generic, non-sacrificial context. ἀρνίον functions similarly in the Pseudepigrapha. Three (*Sib. Or.* 3.578; 3.626; 5.354) of the four (*T. Gad* 1.7) occurrences relate to animal sacrifice. Flavius Josephus, a Jewish apologist and contemporary of John the Seer, uses κριός and ἀρνίον in sacrificial contexts similar to those mentioned above and distinguishes between the adult sheep (κριός) and the less than full-grown lamb (ἀρνίον).[12] It appears that by the middle of the first Christian century ἀρνίον was used more and more by Jewish writers to refer to sacrificial animals.[13]

11. Many Christian writers have claimed that Isa. 52.13–53.13, one of the Servant Songs, predicts and/or anticipates the role of Jesus as a sacrificial lamb. For a balanced discussion of the issues surrounding the Servant Songs of Deutero–Isaiah, see J.L. McKenzie, *Second Isaiah* (AB, 20; Garden City, NY: Doubleday, 1968), pp. xxxviii-lv.

12. *Ant.* 3.221, 3.251. Compare the use of the same two terms in Dan. 3.39; 1 Esd. 6.28; 7.7; 8.14, 63 in the LXX.

13. This overview of the Hebrew Bible, the LXX and the intertestamental traditions has employed G. Lisowsky (ed.), *Konkordanz zum hebräischen Alten Testament* (Stuttgart: Deutsche Bibelgesellschaft, 2nd edn, 1966); E. Hatch and H.A. Redpath (eds.), *A Concordance to the Septuagint* (Oxford: Clarendon Press, 1897), and Albert-Marie Denis (ed.), *Concordance grecque des pseudepigraphes*

The Lamb in Revelation has developed from different traditions in Judaism. From Jewish apocalyptic traditions, it gained the concept of the messianic warrior-lamb. The sacrificial lamb has its roots in Exodus and the sacrificial system of Israel. The crucifixion and exaltation of Jesus provided a final element: *victory through suffering*.

3. *The Lamb in Revelation*

Although ἀρνίον appears 29 times in Revelation, it occurs in only 12 contexts: (1) 5.6-14; (2) 6.1-17; (3) 7.9-8.1; (4) 12.7-12; (5) 13.8; (6) 13.11; (7) 14.1-5; (8) 14.10; (9) 15.3-4; (10) 17.14; (11) 19.7-9; (12) 21.9–22.5.

It is no surprise to find parallels between the Christ-as-one-like-a-son-of-man and the Christ-as-Lamb. First, God Almighty shares divine honors with the Lamb and the Lamb possesses the seven spirits of God (5.6; cf. 1.2; 3.1). God and the Lamb receive adoration jointly and function together (e.g. 5.13; 6.16-17; 7.9; 14.1; 21.22-25; 22.1, 3). Secondly, the Lamb's blood is salvific and is the basis for his worthiness (e.g. 5.9-10; 7.14-15; 12.11; 14.1-4; cf. 1.5-6). Thirdly, the book of life is under the purview of the Lamb: he has decided who shall and shall not be saved (e.g. 13.8; 14.1; 21.26-27; 22.1; cf. 2.11; 3.5). Fourthly, the Lamb gathers to himself an elect community (e.g. 7.9-17; 14.1-4; 17.14; 21.9-22.5; cf. 1.6; 1.11, 19-20). Fifthly, as God has given the revelation to Christ (1.1) and as each letter in Rev. 2.1–3.22 contains a revelatory element in it, so too the breaking of the first six seals in Rev. 6.1-17 reveal God's plans for humanity.[14] Finally, the Lion/Lamb scene reverses expectations by replacing the mighty Lion with the slain Lamb. In addition, this scene places Christian suffering within the wider context of God's overall plan for creation.

These are but the similarities between the two christological metaphors; they demonstrate the intrinsic unity of the book as a whole and point toward its consistent Christology. However, John develops the Lamb imagery extensively and creatively. Let us now examine the key passages in more detail.

d'Ancien Testament: Concordance, corpus des textes, indices (Leiden: E.J. Brill, 1987).

14. Cf. Bauckham, *Theology*, pp. 66-67.

a. *5.6-14*

1. *Introduction.* Any examination of the introduction of the Lamb in Rev. 5.6 must begin with Rev 4.1 and continue to Rev. 5.5. Revelation 4 and 5, one of the most significant visions of Revelation, relate directly to each other and introduce the major apocalyptic sections (6.1–22.5). The setting in these two chapters moves from heaven to earth.

Although Revelation 4 and 5 provide the hermeneutical key to the remainder of the book, these chapters constitute a vision in its own right by assuring its readers that God's purpose for the universe will indeed transpire, and by asserting that the God of creation is also the God of redemption. This redemption is for the entire human community and comes not through military and/or political might but through humility, through a Lamb who has been slain.[15] While Revelation 4 focuses attention upon him who sits upon the throne (v. 3), ch. 5 shifts the focus to the Redeemer who has 'conquered', is worthy to receive the book and, in so doing, inaugurates God's plan for humankind.[16] The vision ends with all creation praising both God and the Lamb.[17]

Revelation 5 is an enthronement scene. The Lamb is exalted to God's throne over the universe, the new domain of the Lamb. The Lamb's exaltation actually began with the crucifixion.[18] Beasley-Murray correctly notes three movements from the exaltation of the Lamb (v. 5); to the presentation of the Lamb; to the enthronement of the Lamb (v. 7). He also notes a progression in praise from the four creatures and the 24 elders (vv. 8-10); to myriads of angels (vv. 11-12) and, finally, to the entire creation (vv. 13-14). The events in heaven are in the past, while those on earth are in the future.[19]

2. *Exegesis.* Revelation 5 begins with the introduction of the scroll with seven seals (v. 1). A search ensues for someone worthy (ἄξιος) to open the scroll's seals and inaugurate God's plan for the world (v. 2), but no

15. Cf. Beasley-Murray, *Revelation*, p. 108; Krodel, *Revelation*, p. 152; Sweet, *Revelation*, pp. 131-32; Mounce, *Revelation*, p. 131.

16. Cf. Beasley-Murray, *Revelation*, p. 109; Sweet, *Revelation*, pp. 113-14.

17. For a slightly different argument, see Prigent, *L'Apocalypse*, pp. 102-103.

18. Cf. Krodel, *Revelation*, pp. 149-50; Beasley-Murray, *Revelation*, p. 110.

19. Beasley-Murray, *Revelation*, pp. 110-11. As a small corrective to Beasley-Murray, the praise on earth begins and ends in 5.13. Rev. 5.14 contains the concluding praise of the four creatures and 24 elders in heaven. This establishes an *inclusio* between 4.4 and 5.14.

one is found worthy in all creation (v. 3). John weeps. One of the 24 elders (see 4.4) comforts John, saying, 'Do not cry; look, the lion of the tribe of Judah, the root of David [see Rev. 22.16; cf. *T. Jud.* 24; *4 Ezra* 11–12], has conquered in order to open the scroll and its seven seals' (v. 5). *4 Ezra* 11 and 12 also employ the lion as a symbol of the Messiah.[20] Thus, both *4 Ezra* and Revelation independently attest to this messianic symbol and the expectation in some Jewish quarters for a conquering Messiah (νικάω in v. 5; cf. 2.6, 11, 17, 26; 3.5, 12, 21; cf. 1QM 1, 15–19).[21] However, in light of the Easter experience, this expectation has been turned on its head. The Messiah is not a conquering lion but a conquered Lamb.[22] 'And I saw between the throne and the four living creatures, on one side, and the elders, on the other, a Lamb standing like it had been slain, having seven horns and seven eyes that are the seven spirits of God sent into all the earth' (v. 6; cf. 1.4, 12; 3.1).[23] This is the prime example of the reversal of the expectations mentioned previously. The Messiah is not a conqueror but the conquered. However, this is part of God's plan and leads to *victory through suffering*, an important motif in Revelation. *In order to conquer through suffering, one must first suffer.* This image strongly suggests that Asian Christians were oppressed and needed to make sense of their plight.[24]

The seven horns should probably be viewed separately from the seven eyes. If so, the seven horns would symbolize complete power, usually royal power (e.g. Num. 23.22; Deut. 33.17; Ps. 18.2; 112.9; Dan. 7.7, 20; 8.3; *1 En.* 90.12-13; Rev. 12.3; 13.1, 11; 17.3, 7, 12, 16).

20. I am aware that *4 Ezra* has been re-worked by a Christian editor, but these chapters do not exhibit such editing. For a full discussion, see Box, *Ezra-Apocalypse*, pp. xxii-xxxiii; B.M. Metzger, '4 Ezra', in *OTP*, I, pp. 516-24. On 1 Esd. 12.31, see R.J. Coggins and M.A. Knibb, *The First and Second Books of Esdras* (Cambridge: Cambridge University Press, 1979), pp. 251-52.

21. Cf. Morris, *Revelation*, pp. 93-94.

22. Cf. Lohmeyer, *Offenbarung*, pp. 56-57.

23. On my translation, see the discussion in Charles, *Revelation*, I, p. 140; Lohmeyer, *Offenbarung*, p. 54; Caird, *Revelation*, pp. 75-76; Sweet, *Revelation*, p. 128. For different views, see Mounce, *Revelation*, p. 146; Morris, *Revelation*, p. 95; Hughes, *Revelation*, p. 79.

24. Other New Testament writers also developed a rationale to explain why Christians suffered (e.g. Lk. 6.22; Jas 1.2-3; 1 Pet. 1.6-7, 4.12). See also my discussion of the social setting in Chapter 1 of this study. Cf. Mounce, *Revelation*, p. 144; Caird, *Revelation*, pp. 74-75; Ladd, *Revelation*, pp. 85-88; Morris, *Revelation*, p. 93; Reddish, 'Martyrdom', pp. 104-22, 132-60.

The seven eyes represent the Lamb's complete omniscience (1.4; cf. Zech. 3.8-10; 4.10).[25]

Rev. 5.7-8 brings a transition. The Lamb takes the scroll from the right hand of him who sits on the throne (v. 7) and this action actualizes Rev. 1.1, where the Christ becomes an authenticating revelatory figure. It also inaugurates three acts of praise directed toward the Lamb. It should be noted that prayers are offered to the Lamb in v. 8, a practice normally reserved for God.[26] These three acts of adoration reveal a good deal of information about the Christology of the book of Revelation.

The first act of praise (vv. 9-10) is described as 'a new song' (cf. Ps. 33.3; 144.9).[27] This song describes the reasons why the Lamb is worthy to open the scroll: 'for you were slain and redeemed [persons] to God from every tribe, tongue, people and race with your blood' (v. 9). As with the one-like-a-son-of-man Christology, it is Christ's sacrifice that exalts him to the status of God's eschatological agent (5.9; cf. 1.5). Rev. 5.10 follows with the same ideas that follow the reference to Christ's sacrifice in 1.5: 'and you made them a kingdom and priests to our God and they will reign on the earth' (5.10); 'And he made us a kingdom, priests to his God and father' (1.6; cf. 20.6). The ideas of Christ's sacrifice, God's kingdom, co-regency with God and/or Christ and human priesthood are inseparable for Revelation. Christ's sacrifice creates the kingdom of God wherein every person would be a priest with direct access to God, fulfilling the promise in Exod. 19.6, a promise explicitly fulfilled in Rev. 21.22-25.[28] Revelation describes an intimate and close fellowship between God and the Asian churches. This possibility would provide spiritual assurance, comfort and encouragement to the real readers/hearers. This imagery suggests a context where Christians need some assurances of their salvation. John would use another image, perhaps Christ as judge, if religious laxity were an

25. Charles probably is correct when he states that, if Rev. 5 is related to ANE magical practices, John 'has no consciousness' of it (*Revelation*, I, p. 143); cf. Bousset, *Offenbarung*, p. 259.

26. See also Krodel, *Revelation*, pp. 165-66.

27. On καινός as something qualitatively better, see Mounce, *Revelation*, pp. 147-48 n. 22; *idem*, *TDNT*, III, p. 447; cf. Prigent, *L'Apocalypse*, p. 76.

28. Cf. Ladd (*Revelation*, pp. 92-93), Sweet (*Revelation,* p. 129) and Reddish ('Martyrdom', pp. 220-22).

issue here (cf. 2.16). However, such is not the case. Roles often bestowed upon messianic figures in early Judaism are here given to the followers of the Messiah to assure them of their salvation (e.g. Zech. 4.3, 11-14; 1QS 9.8-11; *T. Jud.* 24; *T. Dan* 5.10-13; cf. Rev. 2.26-27; 20.4; 22.5).[29]

The hymn in vv. 9-10 parallels a similar one to God Almighty in 4.11. Both begin with the words ἄξιος εἶ.[30] While the hymn in 4.11 celebrates the worthiness of the Creator, the one in 5.9-10 celebrates the worthiness of the Redeemer-Lamb. The new song in 5.9-10 that ushers in a new era also parallels the new name (2.17; 3.12), the new Jerusalem (3.12; 21.2), the other new song (14.3), the new heaven and new earth (21.1) and God's proclamation to make all things new (21.5).[31] New things connote salvation and restoration in Revelation, a point noted earlier in this study. Those who sing new songs, receive new names and inhabit the New Jerusalem will experience a new quality of life free from death, illness and grief in the new age (Rev. 20.1–22.5).

The second act of praise to the Lamb begins in v. 11 and concludes in the next verse. This act of praise begins with ἄξιόν ἐστιν. This is a variation on 4.11 and 5.9, but the content of the praise is similar to the praise offered to God in 4.11. Rev. 4.11 reads,

> Worthy are you, our Lord and God,
>   to receive the glory and the honor and the power,
> for you created all things,
>   and by your will they came into being and were created.

Rev. 5.12 reads,

> Worthy is the Lamb who has been slain
>   to receive the power and riches and wisdom and might and
> honor and glory and blessing.

The Lamb receives seven attributes, or predicates, symbolic of his perfection,[32] while God Almighty only received three in 4.11.[33] However,

29. Mounce comes to similar conclusions (*Revelation*, pp. 148-49).

30. The expression 'Worthy are you' may have had a role in the imperial cult (Krodel, *Revelation*, p. 167). For a contrasting view, see Thompson, *Revelation*, pp. 95-115.

31. Prigent writes, 'Le grand moment du renouvellement attendu est venu avec le Christ' (*L'Apocalypse*, p. 101); cf. Hughes, *Revelation*, p. 82.

32. Lohmeyer correctly notes that this second hymn is in the third person while

one should not place too much weight on those numbers and deduce that the Lamb is the superior figure. Rather, John probably has intentionally overemphasized the participation of the Lamb in divine honors.[34]

Many argue that the presence of the article before the first noun in 5.12 indicates that the seven predicates should be taken together as a unit.[35] However, this argument ignores those ascriptions to God and Christ in Revelation that have more than one article (e.g. 4.11; 5.13). How are they to be taken? In fact, there is little difference. Morris suggests, correctly in my opinion, that in some cases each attribute has its own article probably to give more emphasis to them individually.[36] The first four predicates (power, riches, wisdom and strength) are qualities the Lamb possesses and relate directly to his praiseworthiness. The final three (honor, glory and blessing) constitute the nature of praise offered to the Lamb by angels and humans as an appropriate expression (cf. 1 Chron. 29.10).[37]

The third song of praise (5.13) brings the praise to a fitting conclusion in three ways. First, we note the increasing numbers from the four creatures and 24 elders (vv. 9-10), to the angelic host (vv. 11-12), to all creation (v. 13). Secondly, v. 13 refers to all creation and thus actualizes the reference to every tribe, language, people and race in v. 9.[38] Thirdly, the third hymn is a fitting conclusion for it praises both God Almighty and the Lamb together for the first time in Revelation. These two chapters have molded the hymns in a very deliberate pattern. The first two hymns praise God (4.8; 4.11), the third and fourth praise the Lamb (5.9-10; 5.12), while the last hymn praises both (5.13).[39] The

the first (vv. 9-10) was more in the second (*Offenbarung*, p. 57; cf. Beasley-Murray, *Revelation*, p. 128).

33. Cf. 7.12 where there are also seven attributes with 'thanksgiving' instead of 'riches' in that list.

34. For similar comments, see Kiddle, *Revelation*, p. 105; Ladd, *Revelation*, p. 93.

35. E.g. Charles, *Revelation*, I, p. 149; Mounce, *Revelation*, p. 149 n. 31.

36. Morris, *Revelation*, p. 99.

37. Cf. Bousset, *Offenbarung*, pp. 261-62; Charles, *Revelation*, I, p. 149; Krodel, *Revelation*, p. 167; Morris, *Revelation*, p. 98; Mounce, *Revelation*, p. 149-50; Beasley-Murray, *Revelation*, p. 128. For a different perspective, see F. Spitta, *Die Offenbarung des Johannes* (Halle: Waisenhaus, 1889), p. 285.

38. Cf. Ladd, *Revelation*, p. 93.

39. Charles (*Revelation*, I, p. 151) places the first hymn in 4.9.

close identification between God Almighty and the Lamb is a consistent dimension of the theology of Revelation.[40]

The vision ends in 5.14 with the worship of the four creatures and the 24 elders. The 4 creatures and the 24 elders symbolize all manner of living beings.[41] The 'Amen' of the four creatures and the worship of the elders establishes an *inclusio* with 4.4-8: the vision of the heavenly court in Rev. 4–5 begins and ends with the 4 creatures and 24 elders worshiping.[42] This *inclusio* attests to the unity of Rev. 4.1–5.14.

3. *Conclusion.* I have given a more detailed analysis of the first Lamb passage in Revelation because it is so crucial to understanding what follows.

Rev. 4.1–5.14 introduces what is to come and gives a focus to the book. These chapters form the theological center of the book by asserting that for God Almighty creation and redemption involve one beneficent process. The Lamb is the symbol of God's love for humanity and conveyed to the original audience that the decisive victory had already been won in heaven (5.9-12), a victory that has future consequences on earth (5.9-10, 13; cf. 1.5-6; 12.7-12). Worship then begins in heaven with the four creatures and 24 elders and continues until the entire creation joins it. In Rev. 5.6-14, the Christ-Lamb participates in divine honors with God Almighty by receiving prayers (5.8), praise (5.12) and standing at the height of the cosmos as God's co-regent (5.13). Rev. 5.13 is the first explicit statement where Christ receives honors alongside God Almighty. Others will follow. Finally, Rev. 5.6-14 promises a high status as priest-kings upon the faithful followers of God, wrought through the sacrifice of Christ. These images would convey to the hearer/reader that God Almighty desires an intimate relationship with his people in the new age (5.9-10; cf. 1.5-6; 21.3-4).[43] These features will recur in our examination of the remaining Lamb passages.

40. Morris has noted this relationship between God and Christ in 6.16; 7.9, 10, 17; 14.1, 4; 21.22, 23 (*Revelation*, p. 99); cf. Charles, *Revelation*, I, p. 151. I would add 3.21; 7.12; 22.1, 3.

41. Cf. Beasley-Murray, *Revelation*, p. 117 n. 4; also p. 129; Hughes, *Revelation*, pp. 73-76, 83.

42. Cf. Morris, *Revelation*, p. 102 and Mounce, *Revelation*, p. 150.

43. Cf. Krodel, *Revelation*, pp. 168-69.

These two chapters provide some significant social details. The victory-through-suffering motif suggests that some Christians have suffered for their beliefs. Nothing in Rev. 4.1–5.14 suggests that these passages describe a lax attitude among Christians or in some way function as examples of the judgments that await Christians. Moreover, there is little here to indicate that Christians live free of any sort of repression or discrimination. In fact, Rev. 4.1–5.14 indicate tensions between Christians and non-Christians and point toward the negative judgment awaiting non-Christians. Moreover, the worship of Christ alongside God could have been the point of pain between Christians and Jewish persons. However, the refusal of Christians to participate in the imperial cult or any other Greco-Roman religious activities, coupled with the Christian focus upon Jesus as one worthy of divine honors, would have infuriated many pagans, as it did Pliny (*Letter* 10). Thus, suffering on two fronts, the Christians in Asia would have had little social esteem and their envisioned status as priest-kings in the future might constitute an attempt to reverse their present lowly status and boost their self-esteem. Further, the seven horns and seven eyes of the Lamb and the promise of becoming priest-kings in the next age would be therapeutic means of persuading persons to remain within the sacred cosmos against external repression. Within such a social setting, the Lamb imagery could be a meaningful apologetic tool and maintenance strategy.

The exegeses of the following passages will demonstrate that the image of the Lamb functioned as a deliverer, a concerned pastor and a role model to help the churches in Asia to endure the things that will happen soon (1.3; 22.6-7).

b. *6.1-17*

Rev. 6.1-17 and 7.9–8.1 both fall within the seven seals sequence (6.1–8.1), but since they comprise distinctive types of visions, I have chosen to address them under two different headings.

The opening of the first four seals constitutes the well-known ‘four horsemen of the Apocalypse’ sequence (6.1-8). The fifth seal differs from the first four in not detailing an earthly catastrophe but a heavenly scene (6.9-11). The sixth seal returns to an earthly setting and brings more geological, cosmic and socio-political upheavals (vv. 12-17).[44]

44. See Charles (*Revelation*, I, pp. 154-61) and Walvoord (*Revelation*, pp. 124-

The opening of the seals constitutes the Lamb's only action in Rev. 6.1-17. Since the Lamb is the chief messianic figure of this section, the opening of the seals takes on more importance. Zech. 1.8-11 and 6.1-8 provide the biblical background for the first four horsemen. John characteristically transforms the images to suit his own purposes.

Verses 1-2.

> And when the Lamb opened one of the seven seals, I looked and I heard one of the four living creatures saying, like the sound of thunder, 'Come!' And I looked and behold, a white horse and he who was sitting on it had a bow; a crown was given to him and he went out conquering, in order that he might conquer.

Several argue that the rider on the white horse symbolizes Vologeses, the Parthian leader who won an impressive victory over the Romans in 62 CE. They note that Parthian kings wore crowns as a symbol of victory and rode white horses into battle. The white symbolizes purity and authority to execute judgment.[45] Others argue that the passage refers to Rome;[46] some argue that this horseman represents the advance of the Christian faith through history,[47] while others argue that the rider is the anti-Christ.[48] Still others argue that the rider is Christ and that the same rider is found in Rev. 19.11-16.[49]

The rider on the white horse does not symbolize Christ, the anti-Christ, Vologeses, or any other individual, or the Roman Empire. The rider is not the primary symbol in Rev. 6.2. The primary symbol in each of the first four seals is the horse and its color, not the rider. The rider is, at best, a secondary symbol. Each horse has a different color and brings a different aspect of the message with the breaking of the first four seals. In contrast, in 19.11-21 the rider on the white horse is the primary symbol; he and not the horse receives symbolic names and represents God in human history. White is a salvific color (see comments

38) on the various methods that have been employed in interpreting the historical meaning of the seven seals.

45. E.g. Charles, *Revelation*, I, pp. 163-64. Charles also has representative interpretations of this passage.

46. E.g. Spitta, *Offenbarung*, p. 260.

47. E.g. J. Weiss, *Offenbarung des Johannes* (FRLANT, 3; Göttingen: Vandenhoeck & Ruprecht, 1904), pp. 59-60.

48. E.g. M. Rissi, 'The Rider on the White Horse: A Study of Revelation 6,1-8', *Int* 18 (1964), pp. 413-18.

49. E.g. Sweet, *Revelation*, pp. 136-40; Ladd, *Revelation*, pp. 96-100.

on 2.17) and usually is worn by the saints (e.g. 6.9-11; 7.9-10). In 6.2, it represents righteous judgment upon the nations.[50]

Mounce correctly notes that the rider in 6.2 cannot be Christ because he wears a στέφανος, not a διάδημα, a royal symbol. 'The context in 6.2 is conquest while that in 19.11ff. is righteous retribution.'[51] Additionally, Mounce notes the confusion that would result if Christ is both the one who opens the seal and the first horseman.[52] Caird concurs and points out that John used ἐδόθη more frequently to denote 'divine permission granted to evil powers to carry out their nefarious work'[53] (see Rev. 9.1, 3, 5; 13.5, 7, 14, 15).

The first horse symbolizes the negative effects of war (e.g. the deaths of loved ones [both civilian and military]; the destruction of public and private property; the disruption of everyday life). In the Hebrew Bible, God's breaking the bow often symbolized breaking military power (e.g. Ps. 46.9; Jer. 51.56; Ezek. 39.3; Hos. 1.5). John has probably combined imagery from the Hebrew Bible and recent events to convey the image of military destruction as a means of divine judgment.[54] The white horse brings the message that war brings pain and suffering. The remaining three horses reiterate this point.[55]

Verses 3-4. A second living beast speaks with the breaking of the second seal and a red horse comes forth and removes peace from the

50. Many Romans held to the *Nero redivivus* myth that Nero was not dead but would return to defeat Rome with a Parthian army (see Suetonius, *Nero* 57; Tacitus, *Histories* 2.8; *Sib. Or.* 4-5). On the different forms of the Nero myth and their influence upon Revelation, see Bauckham, *Climax*, pp. 384-452. Also, the first horse and its rider alludes to the Parthians, fierce warriors who mastered the use of the bow and arrow in battle. The Parthians defeated the Romans in 53 BCE, 35 BCE and 62 CE.

51. Mounce, *Revelation*, p. 153.; cf. Rissi, 'The Rider', pp. 405-18.

52. Mounce, *Revelation*, p. 153.

53. Caird, *Revelation*, p. 81.

54. Cf. Mounce, *Revelation*, p. 154.

55. Cf. Charles, *Revelation*, I, pp. 163-64; Kiddle, *Revelation*, pp. 106-14; Morris, *Revelation*, pp. 100-102; Mounce, *Revelation*, pp. 152-54; Yarbro Collins, *Apocalypse*, pp. 43-45; Schüssler Fiorenza, *Vision*, pp. 62-65; Krodel, *Revelation*, pp. 171-74; Hughes, *Revelation*, pp. 84-85, 109-10. The four-horse mini-cycle may be related in some way to the synoptic apocalypse in Mk 13 *par.* (e.g. Charles, *Revelation*, I, pp. 158-61; Harrington, *Apocalypse*, p. 120; Beasley-Murray, *Revelation*, pp. 129-30), or the two passages may drawn upon the same tradition for their imagery (cf. Zech. 1.8, 6.2-6; Isa. 3–4; Jer. 14–15; Nah. 1–3; *2 Bar.* 27, 53). In either event, it has little effect upon the interpretation of Rev. 6.1-8.

earth. This horse represents the blood that will be shed by many persons during the last days. Its rider has been given a sword, not a bow. Both, however, are weapons of war and the message of the first seal continues in the second.[56] The first horse brings war; the second removes peace. The first two horses represent two halves of the same coin: war as a means of punishment.

Verses 5-6. After the breaking of the third seal, the third living creature speaks and a third horse comes forth. The third horse is black. Black usually had negative connotations in the ancient world. The rider also held a balance scale in his hand in v. 5, indicating an economic theme. That is precisely what follows in v. 6. An unidentified voice, a common mystical element in Revelation, announces that a quart of wheat will cost a denarius, a day's wage. With the same amount of money one would be able to buy barley and feed three persons. However, nothing would be left over for the next day. The price of olive oil and wine would remain the same.

This horseman and his horse symbolize economic hardships, which often accompany war, especially for the conquered. Whether buying wheat or barley, food would cost a great deal of money. This would mean that people would live constantly on the edge of deprivation.[57]

Verses 7-8. The breaking of the fourth seal brings a rider on a pale horse. The horse's color connotes death. Indeed, its rider is named 'Death' and Hades, the place of the dead, follows closely (cf. 1.18; 20.13-14). They have the authority to kill one-fourth of the earth through war, famine, pestilence and wild animals (cf. Ezek. 14.21).[58]

This is the only rider given a name and with a companion. The fourth horse and rider complete this series. Its point is that war and aggression ultimately bring suffering to all humanity and one-fourth even die. It is fitting that the fourth rider is called Death, for he personifies all the misfortune and suffering that John has envisioned in the three preceding seals. How do the opening of these four seals relate to the Christ-Lamb in Revelation?

56. Cf. Harrington, *Apocalypse*, p. 123; Ladd, *Revelation*, p. 100. On war as a form of divine judgment, see Jer. 14–15 and Nah. 1–3.

57. Charles has researched the cost of bread in the Roman Empire in the first Christian century and has shown the economic crisis that the price scale in Rev. 6.5-6 would engender (*Revelation*, I, pp. 166-68).

58. The reference to pestilence may be an exodus motif (cf. Exod. 8–11).

The Christ-Lamb has come and has inaugurated the eschaton by opening the seals. This is a prophetic act because the scroll contains the will of God for humanity. With regard to its cosmological message, it conveys to the reader that what occurs in heaven will be parallelled on earth (cf. 12.7-12; 19.11-21). Only the Lamb is worthy to open the scroll, that is, the Lamb functions as a revealer (cf. 1.1, 5, 19). By opening the scroll, the Lamb sets into motion the divine plan. The first four seals bring about the eschatological woes common to Jewish apocalyptic literature (e.g. *2 Bar.* 27, 53). Three more seals must be broken.

Verses 9-11. The opening of the fifth seal provides something of an interlude from the eschatological calamities.[59] While the first four seals relate to the future and the plight of God's enemies, the fifth seal relates to the near past and the suffering of God's elect. Sweet correctly notes that this passage employs two standard apocalyptic themes, the cry of innocent blood for revenge and the limited amount of wickedness and suffering that must transpire before the end of the world. 'To this final deliverance their sacrifice contributes invisibly, not piecemeal but as part of God's total plan: they must wait for their visible vindication till their number is complete.'[60]

1 En. 47.4, *4 Ezra* 4.33, 35-37 and *2 Bar.* 23.4-5, all written about the same time as Revelation, have very similar statements.[61] *1 En.* 47.4 states that the angels are joyful because the number of the righteous, which God has predetermined, has been reached and no more righteous ones will suffer unjustly. *4 Ezra* 4.33, 35-37 asks when will the new age come and how long will the souls of the righteous remain in their chambers. Jeremiel replies, 'When the number of those like yourselves is completed.' *2 Bar.* 23.4-5 states that God determined before time how many persons would be born and how many would die. 'No creature will live again unless the number that has been appointed is completed.'[62] In all three contexts, the seer is primarily concerned with the

59. Mounce argues that the first four seals comprise one mini-cycles the last three another (*Revelation*, p. 157). I disagree, because the sixth seal is more like the first four and also because the seventh seal relates directly to the seventh trumpet (11.15-19) and the seventh bowl (16.17-21), as will be demonstrated in the discussion of the seventh seal (8.1-5).

60. Sweet, *Revelation*, p. 141.

61. Translations are from *OTP*.

62. On the dates of *1 Enoch*, *4 Ezra* and *2 Baruch*, see *OTP*, I, pp. 6-7, 520, 616-17.

question of theodicy and how long the unjust will go on unpunished. In each case, the seer is assured that God has determined before time the extent of evil.

In Rev. 6.9-11, the saints ask a similar question and they receive a similar answer: they ask when will their deaths be avenged and are told to wait until the number of sufferers reaches a predetermined number. This apologetic tradition attempts to explain why the righteous suffer at the hands of the unrighteous, and it also attempts to assure the community its suffering will not last forever. This seal is an example of determinism, a maintenance strategy intended to assure the original audience of its ultimate liberation and salvation and to assure them that their suffering also is part of God's plan.[63] Since John had many apocalyptic motifs at his disposal, his use of this specific motif probably reflects a context where Christians are repressed.

Verses 12-17. The sixth seal shifts the scene again. These verses can be divided into two separate parts. In the first, vv. 12-14, we have another vision of the eschatological woes, which include an earthquake, a solar eclipse, a lunar eclipse (v. 12), a falling star (v. 13a) and a receding sky (v. 14a). Every mountain and island is dislodged (v. 14b). These events are signs to the reader that the end is near. Jewish and early Christian literature have many such examples (e.g. Isa. 13.10; 34.4; Hag. 2.6-7; Nah. 1.5; *Sib. Or.* 3.75-92; 8.413-28; *2 Bar.* 70.8; *4 Ezra* 5.8; Mk 13.24-25; 2 Pet. 3.11-12). In the second scene (vv. 15-17), the kings, the upper class, the generals, the rich, the strong, every slave and freedman have hidden themselves (v. 15; cf. 'the inhabitants of the earth' [v. 10]) because they have recognized the eschatological signs (vv. 12-14) and attempt to avoid the wrath of the Lamb (cf. Isa. 2.10, 19, 21; Joel 2.11, 31; Zeph. 1.14-18; Mal. 3.2-3). In most instances in the Hebrew Bible and Second Temple writings, God alone causes the end-time to come. The Messiah is merely an agent of God in the process (e.g. *4 Ezra* 11–13). In Revelation, however, the Messiah-Lamb joins God as an associate.

c. *7.9–8.1*

Rev. 7.9–8.1 concludes the opening of the seven seals begun in 6.1. Whether or not 7.9–8.1 recapitulates 7.1-8 is not a central issue for our study. Suffice it to say that both visions describe an eschatological

63. On determinism in apocalyptic literature, see Russell, *Method*, pp. 205-34.

community. While 7.1-8 describes the sealing of God's elect 144,000 persons from the 12 tribes of Israel, 7.9–8.1 contains a vision of an international exodus community.

Rev. 7.9–8.1 mentions the Lamb explicitly four times and the Lamb opens the seventh seal in 8.1. In 7.9, an innumerable, culturally inclusive eschatological Christian community stands before the heavenly co-regents, God and the Lamb. They wear white garments and receive palm branches, both emblematic of their salvific victory (cf. 1 Macc. 13.51; 2 Macc. 10.7). This might be the same group that John saw under the altar (6.9-11).[64] Rev. 7.9-17 builds upon 6.9-11 by adding that God's care for the saints, as well as God's punishment of evildoers, is part of God's plan, too. The exchange between one of the elders and John in vv. 13-17 confirms my argument.

In many prophetic and apocalyptic books, an otherworldly being guides the human seer and/or explains enigmatic visions (e.g. *1 En.* 68; *4 Ezra* 12.31-39; *Apoc. Abr.* 15-17). Often the heavenly guide does not answer questions but asks them. I refer to this feature as 'the unsolicited question'.[65] The unsolicited question is not a test for the seer but a means of imparting information to the reader/hearer. Rev. 7.13 is an example of what I refer to as 'the unsolicited question'. 'And one of the elders addressed me, saying,

> These persons who are dressed in white robes, who are they and from where have they come? And I said to him, 'My lord, you know.' And he said to me, 'These are they who have come out of the great tribulation and washed their robes and made them white by means of the blood [ἐν τῷ αἵματι] of the Lamb.'

This vision recalls to the mind of the reader the reference to Jesus 'who loved us and freed us from our sins by means of his blood' (ἐν τῷ αἵματι αὐτοῦ)' in 1.5. Rev. 5.9b reads similarly, 'for you were slaughtered and ... by means of your blood [ἐν τῷ αἵματί σου] you ransomed for God saints from every tribe and language and people and nation'. All three passages state that the Messiah died on behalf of humanity. In

64. In 6.9-11, the saints receive white garments; in 7.9, they wear white garments and receive palm branches, both symbols of their salvation. The additional details in 7.9 is a common feature in Revelation, where later visions often provide additional details not in earlier ones. In this way, the later visions are not unchanging icons but renewed media of revelation (cf. 7.1-8 and 14.1-5; 7.9-17 and 21.1-8).

65. The unsolicited question has its roots in the prophetic tradition. Ezek. 37.3 provides an excellent example: 'Son of man, can these bones live?'

all three passages, the death of the Messiah provides positive benefits for the Christian community: (1) freedom from sin; (2) founding of an international Christian community; (3) means of entry into the new age. We have already noted that the first two passages associated these benefits with the members of the community becoming priest-kings in the new age. Rev. 7.14 provides yet another means by which the followers of the Lamb who suffer identify with their Lord and his passion. In this way, suffering became for these Christians an acceptable *modus vivendi*.

Rev. 7.9–8.1 also provides another example of the reversal of expectations. Instead of the Lamb's blood staining the robes, it cleans them. Instead of death leading to defeat, it leads to victory and salvation. The saints have come through the 'great tribulation'; John employs present and past verbs in v. 14b, indicating that for John the great tribulation is ongoing.

One might counter that these images of judgment are primarily aimed at the Christian community, or at least would include wayward Christians. However, none of the critiques on Christian laxity found in the letters is found here (see 2.4-5, 14-16, 20-23; 3.1-3, 9, 15-19). Rather, 7.13-14 describes those who have died for the faith, emulating Christ's example.

John then encourages his readers to remain faithful by stating that the victim-victors of v. 14 stand before God in the heavenly court presently. This imagery may have a prophetic element in it. Verses 15-17 are prophecies. Every verb is in the future tense. God will shelter them (v. 15). They will not hunger, or thirst, or suffer from the sun's heat (v. 16) but will be led by the Lamb to springs of living water (cf. Jn 4.10-15). God will personally wipe away their tears (v. 17). These images continue the therapeutic functions identified in v. 14 by promising the readers God's providential care in the new age. It appears that the threat of social ostracism and deprivation have made accommodation, complacency and compromise appealing to some persons. Rev. 7.13-14 do not indicate that Christians lead relatively prosperous lives and want more of it. To the contrary, 7.13-14 reflect Christian suffering.

This hymn communicates several other important details. First and foremost, it states their genuine devotion to God as the protector of the community from worldly pressures (v. 14a). Conversely, it connotes that the original recipients had genuine worldly woes (v. 14b; cf. v. 17). These persons expect their sovereign God to intervene soon and bring solace soon (e.g. Rev. 1.3; 22.7-12). Moreover, the victim-victors are assured that their troubles in this age will be reversed in the next and that they will not suffer from the elements. This suggests that some Christians suffered materially and that is why protection is coupled with means of sustenance (v. 16). The Lamb/Shepherd shares a role often reserved for God Almighty (e.g. Ps. 23). Revelation has developed the concept from a distinctive Christian perspective (cf. Lk. 15.3-7; Jn 10.1-30; 21.15-17; 1 Pet. 1.19, 2.25).[66] The one who was the means of salvation now functions as the mode of protection and sustenance. Verse 16 speaks of the cessation of bodily needs, but it is the Lamb who enables this cessation to occur (v. 17a). Consequently, John manifestly conveys God's intimate and caring relationship with the victim-victors with the image of God wiping away their tears (v. 17b; see also 21.1-4). God wiping away tears would carry little weight if the crisis were only in the social location of their minds or if religious laxity were the only authentic problem for these churches.[67] Indeed, John's visions often perceive a worldwide crisis that did not transpire as John believed (e.g. 22.7-12), but this perception is based upon present realities (see, e.g., 2.8-11, 13; 6.9-11; 16.6; cf. 5.9-12), a method employed by Amos, Isaiah, Hosea, Jeremiah and Micah, to name a few. John writes to people who have shed real tears under real oppression and who desire real consolation.

Finally, Rev. 7.9-17 is a prolepsis of the fuller account in 21.1-8, the vision of the New Heaven and the New Earth. In both visions, God dwells with his people (cf. 7.15; 21.3 [twice]); wipes the tears from their eyes (cf. 7.17; 21.4) and the people of God drink from the water of life (cf. 7.17; 21.6). It is important to note that God does in 21.6 what the Messiah-Lamb did in 7.17, another example of Christ acting as God Almighty's divine agency figure. This maintenance strategy is intended to assure the original readers of the correctness of their religious convictions, God's enduring love as well as their ultimate reward in the new age, a counter to their low social status in the present age.

66. 'The idea of the Lamb as the shepherd of God's flock is an intriguing exchange of roles' (Mounce, *Revelation*, p. 175). If Mounce is correct, the Lamb/Shepherd imagery may be yet another reversal of expectation.

67. See, for example, Thompson, *Revelation*, pp. 186-97; Bauckham, *Theology*, pp. 12-17.

The seventh seal in Rev. 8.1 has brought about extensive discussions and interesting comments but no consensus among New Testament scholars. Rev. 8.1 reads, 'And when he [the Lamb] opened the seventh seal, there was silence in heaven for about half an hour.' What does this silence signify? I shall examine the major positions, evaluate them and then offer an answer to the question of the role and function of silence in Rev. 8.1.

Mounce writes that the silence forms a significant pause in a quickly moving narrative. He also argues that, during this approximately 30-minute period, the angels were preparing for their work in 8.2-5.[68] Mounce reads too much into 8.2-5. Indeed, the seventh seal creates a significant pause, but is this the totality of its function? Why are there not similar pauses after the seventh trumpet (11.15-19) and the seventh bowl (16.17-21)?

Agreeing with Mounce but going beyond him, Walvoord and Morris argue that the silence indicates an important event is about to occur. 'It may be compared to the silence before the foreman of a jury reports a verdict; for a moment... everyone awaits that which will follow.'[69] Similarly, Morris argues that the silence signifies a time of suspense before the final cataclysm.[70] Again, if silence is so important as an introduction to significant events, why is it not used more often in Revelation? Its absence indicates that silence in and of itself is not important in the manner that Walvoord, Morris and others argue.

Rissi offers a totally different explanation. In light of 2 Esdras 6–7 and *2 Baruch* 3, he argues that the silence in Rev. 8.1 represents the Jewish expectation that the world would return to its primeval chaos and from this chaos a new world would come. He points to first-century CE Jewish exegesis of Gen. 1.3 to support his argument and he notes that silence precedes creation in 2 Esdras 6.39 and 7.30 and *2 Bar.* 3.7. He also finds other works roughly contemporaneous with Revelation that give silence a significant role (Wis. 18.14-16; Jn 1.14; Ignatius, *Magn.* 8.2).[71] Though carefully argued, Rissi's position is not without its weak points. Silence in Rev. 8.1 does not precede a new creation as

68. Mounce, *Revelation*, p. 179.

69. Walvoord, *Revelation*, p. 151.

70. Morris, *Revelation*, pp. 122-23; cf. Wall, *Revelation*, p. 122; Hughes, *Revelation*, p. 101.

71. Rissi, *Time and History*, pp. 3-6; cf. Krodel, *Revelation*, p. 189.

in *2 Esd.* 6.39, 7.30 and *2 Bar.* 3.7. Rather, silence precedes the trumpets that judge and devastate the old creation. The remainder of Rissi's argument has value but fails to provide a comprehensive explanation.

Corsini argues for a theological rationale for the silence in Rev. 8.1. He states that the answer lies in John's interpretation of the death of Christ. The death of Christ established 'a line of demarcation' between Judaism and Christianity for the book of Revelation. The 30-minute silence 'corresponds to the period between the death and resurrection of Jesus'.[72] Unfortunately, Corsini does not discuss the relationship between this period of silence and the Christology of the book as a whole, nor does he identify parallel traditions in either the Jewish or Christian traditions that would support, complement or augment his argument.

Krodel[73] argues the silence might constitute a sign of reverence to God; serve as a contrast to the sixth seal (6.12-17) as well as the seven trumpets; demonstrate that the seal visions are completed (cf. *4 Ezra* 7.30) and that the trumpet visions develop from the seal visions. The seventh seal then provides a means of preparation and transition from one numbered series to another. Krodel, however, does not provide a central function that elucidates the function of silence in the entire book.

Bauckham, following Charles and yet correcting him at certain points, provides the best explanation for silence in Rev. 8.1. Charles makes two points in his analysis of this passage.[74] First, v. 1 relates directly to vv. 3-4 in that the incense burning in heaven occurs while the saints pray on earth.[75] According to Charles, v. 2 is an interpolation. Secondly, Charles notes rabbinic traditions that taught that the angels praised God by night, but they were silent by day so that God could hear the prayers of the saints. Bauckham notes several Jewish traditions that lend support to Charles's argument (*Hekhalot Rabbati, Gen. R.* 65.21, *Targ. Ezek.* 1.25; 4QShirShabb; *Targ. Cant.* 1.1; *b. Ḥag.* 12b and *T. Adam* [the Horarium]). Although most parts of the *T. Adam* have been edited

72. Corsini, *Apocalypse*, pp. 162-63.

73. Krodel, *Revelation*, pp. 188-89; cf. Wall, *Revelation*, p. 122.

74. Charles, *Revelation*, I, pp. 223-24; so too, Caird, *Revelation*, pp. 106-107; Beasley-Murray, *Revelation*, pp. 150-51; Bauckham, *Climax*, pp. 70-83; *idem*, *Theology*, pp. 40-43; cf. Harrington, *Apocalypse*, p. 133. For a different perspective, see Swete, *Apocalypse*, p. 107, who argues that the silence in heaven symbolized an eternal rest. Swete does not support his argument very well.

75. Cf. Mounce, *Revelation*, p. 179.

by a Christian, *T. Adam* 1.12 is an exception. Bauckham dates the non-Christian traditions pre-70 CE.[76] The testament mentions the burning of incense by the priests at dawn each day after the lamb has been sacrificed (see Exod. 30.7; Philo, *Spec. Leg.* 1.171, 276; *m. Tam.* 3.2; 4–7; cf. *m. Yom.* 3.5). Bauckham notes that this is the time of prayer for Jews everywhere. When the incense is burned, symbolizing the ascent of the prayers of Israel to heaven, there is no activity in heaven, according to *T. Adam* 1.12. There is silence. For Bauckham, the parallel with Rev. 8.3-4 is undeniable (cf. Tob. 12.12, 15; *1 En.* 47.1-2; 99.3). He states that worship at this time usually took about 30 minutes.

Furthermore, Bauckham argues that the seventh event in each numbered series presents the final judgment that destroys evil and gives birth to the kingdom of God. He notes that the 'flashes of lightning and rumblings and peals of thunder' in 4.5 are expanded three times in 8.5, 11.15 and 16.17-21. 'The progressive expansion of the formula corresponds to the progressive intensification of the three series of judgments.'[77]

Bauckham has shown convincingly the Jewish context of silence in heaven. Even if some of the rabbinic traditions that he cites are post-Christian, there is no reason to believe that the rabbis would appropriate a Christian belief or practice. Farrer has also noted the progression from the seventh seal to the seventh trumpet, and I had noted the progression from the seventh seal to the seventh trumpet to the seventh bowl. Additionally, I had noted a cosmic progression from heaven to earth in the seventh seal, trumpet and bowl.[78] Bauckham also states that the cosmic progression intensifies the judgment upon sinful humankind. I concur with Bauckham.

76. Bauckham, *Climax*, pp. 70-83; Cf. S.E. Robinson, '*Testament of Adam*', *OTP*, I, p. 990.

77. Bauckham, *Theology*, p. 42. I first heard a similar argument on the three numbered series as judgments in seminar lectures by Professor H.W. Attridge (Perkins School of Theology, Southern Methodist University, Dallas, TX, USA, summer 1978).

78. Farrer, *Rebirth*, p. 181. I have explored this further in a paper that I hope to publish in due course ('Silence in Heaven: An Examination of Rev 8.1', Centre for Advanced Biblical Studies, New Testament Seminar, Day Conference, King's College London, Friday, 29 October 1993).

The silence in heaven in 8.1 is part of a literary technique of Revelation. Specifically, it is part of a pattern of quantitative and cosmic progressions. These two patterns work together in the cases examined in this study. The quantitative pattern of progression raises the dramatic element of the narrative; the cosmic one conveys to the reader/hearer that what occurs in heaven must recur on earth, both the good and the bad, and touch the life of every creature in the cosmos. The progressions are part of the maintenance strategy of the book as a whole, communicating to the original audience that the divine plan will be fulfilled in heaven and also on earth.

d. *12.7-12*

Rev. 12.7-12 begins with war breaking out in heaven between the archangel Michael and his angels, on one side, and Satan and his angels, on the other (v. 7). In many Second Temple Jewish traditions, Michael served as the patron angel of Israel (e.g. Dan. 10.13, 21; *1 En.* 20.5; 1QM 13.10; 17.7-8; cf. Jude 9; *T. Dan* 6.2; *T. Levi* 5.5-6; *1 En.* 40.8; *T. Mos.* 10.1-2). Dan. 10.13, 21 refer to Michael as the heavenly 'prince' of Israel.[79] Michael and his angels defeated Satan and his angels and cast them from heaven to earth (vv. 8-9). The vision concludes with a hymn celebrating the victory in heaven but lamenting the eschatological woes to come on earth (vv. 10-12).

We focus our attention on the hymn in vv. 10-12. Verse 10 celebrates Michael's victory but attributes it not to Michael but to Christ and his followers. Verse 11 states that Michael and his angels 'were victorious [ἐνίκησαν] through the blood of the Lamb [διὰ τὸ αἷμα τοῦ ἀρνίου] and through the word of their witness [διὰ τὸν λόγον τῆς μαρτυρίας αὐτῶν]' (cf. 12.17b). It is noteworthy that νικάω is the key term in vv. 10-12, the promises in the letters (2.7, 11, 17, 26; 3.5, 12, 21) as well as Christ's victory over sin, death and evil (Rev. 5.5). Moreover, 'through the blood of the Lamb' and 'through the word of their witness' are confirmation statements, discussed earlier in Chapter 2 of this study, which would have conveyed to the reader that Christ's actions accurately and faithfully represented God's plan for humanity and those

79. See the discussion of Michael as the 'one like a son of man' of Dan. 7.13 in 'The Jewish Background', Chapter 2 of this study. On the concept of Satan in Second Temple Judaism, see Job 1–2; 1 Chron. 21.1; Zech. 3.1-2.

who lived in faithful accord with Christ would receive their reward.[80] The message is that armaments did not defeat and expel Satan from heaven but the blood of Christ and the witness of the saints. John parallels Christian witnessing and Christ's sacrificial death and then adds that Christians were willing to die for their religious beliefs. Rev. 12.10-11 admonishes the faithful on earth to persevere in the faith in the midst of the coming trials (12.13-17). Again, Christ's death, as with the one-like-a-son-of-man Christology (see 1.5-6), becomes the model for Christian behavior and also the key to understanding Christian suffering. These images communicate to the reader/hearer that faithfulness unto death has already defeated Satan in heaven and his forces, and calls upon those who yet live on earth to remain faithful if they also wish to defeat Satan on earth. This battle in heaven is a prelude to the scenes in Rev. 19.11-21 and 20.7-10, when Satan will be defeated and cast down twice.[81]

Parallellism is a central feature of Jewish poetry, where a succeeding line or two are synonymous, complementary or antithetical to the first line. In Rev. 12.11, 'through the blood of the Lamb' and 'through the word of their witness' are parallel. It is difficult to discern if they are synonymous or complementary parallels. They are not antithetical since they jointly contribute to the defeat of Satan. If they are synonymous, Jesus' death and the witness of the saints are inseparable in Revelation. If they are complementary, the two statements are closely related. The third statement strongly suggests that the first two are synonymous by mentioning the saints' willingness to die for their religious convictions. If the three lines are synonymous parallels, this is another vision that reflects a social setting where Christian lives have been lost for their confession of faith.[82]

e. *13.8*

Rev. 13.8 is an integral part of Rev. 13.1-10, the vision of the first of two beasts. This beast in 13.8 ascends from the sea. It has ten horns, symbols of its power, and ten diadems on seven heads, symbols of its

80. Cf. Sweet's connection of this passage with Paul's doctrine of justification (*Revelation*, pp. 198-202).

81. Cf. Krodel, *Revelation*, p. 242; Wall, *Revelation*, p. 162; Bauckham, *Theology*, pp. 75-76. Also, Rev. 12.7-12, 19.11-21 and 20.7-10 provide other examples of cosmic progressions discussed earlier.

82. See Pliny, *Letter* 10; see also Reddish, 'Martyrdom', pp. 217-20.

royalty.[83] The heads had a blasphemous name, or names,[84] upon them (v. 1). John compares the beast to a grotesque monster with leopard-like, bear-like and lion-like features (v. 2).[85] The first beast is not a leopard, bear or lion but has features like each of these animals and receives power from the dragon (v. 2). These grotesque features are meant to convey the beast's utterly corrupt nature.

One of the seven heads has a mortal wound that had healed and everyone on earth followed the beast in amazement (v. 3), worshiped the dragon and asked who might be compared to the beast and dare make war against him (v. 4). The beast with the mortal wound is the antitype of the Lamb who has been slain and conquers by sacrifice and suffering (5.6). The beast has spoken blasphemously toward God and those who reside in heaven. Moreover, he has made war with the saints and conquered (νικῆσαι) and ruled over every nation (vv. 5-7). Then comes the point of our interest in v. 8.

'And everyone who lives on the earth, whose name has not been written from the foundation of the world in the book of life of the Lamb who has been slain, will worship him' (v. 8). This verse contains two important christological elements: (1) the Lamb as the recorder of those to be saved; (2) apocalyptic determinism. This passage is intended to exhort the original hearers to remain within the sacred cosmos in spite of the beast's oppressive actions toward them.

References to heavenly records, an eschatological exodus motif, go back to Exod. 32.32-33, a passage that might be John's source. The Exodus passage refers to the book as God's book. Ps. 69.28 and Phil. 4.3 refer to 'the book of life' but do not attribute it to God directly. Isa. 4.3; Ezek. 13.9; Dan. 7.10; 10.21; 12.1, 4; Lk. 10.20; Heb. 12.23; *T. Abr.* 12-14 and *Mart. Isa.* 9.19-23 also mention heavenly records. Rev. 13.8 and 21.27 are two of the few extant witnesses in early Judaism and early Christianity that state that the Messiah has oversight of the heavenly records. This means that in Revelation one who was judged unjustly in this age will judge justly and decide who may be

83. The image of the seven-headed beast may go back to descriptions of Tiamat in Babylonian mythology (cf. Yarbro Collins, *Combat*).

84. The textual variants in 13.8 have no influence upon its exegesis. Those interested in the variants should consult the most recent editions of Nestle-Aland and/or GNT.

85. The presence of ὅμοιος in v. 2 supports my earlier argument in Chapter 2 of this study concerning the role of comparisons.

admitted into the next age. Giving this role to Jesus implies that the messiahship of Jesus was a key element in a dispute between Christians and non-Christians. Most probably, these non-Christians were Jews who resented the fact that Christians bestowed divine honors on Jesus, for it is difficult to imagine for whom else such a claim would matter.

Rev. 3.5; 17.8; 20.12, 15 and 21.27 also mention 'the book of life'. Many have recognized that 17.8 parallels 13.8[86] in that both refer to those whose names have not been included 'in the book of life from the foundation of the world'. While 20.12 and 20.15 refer to the book of life in contrast to 'the books' for those who meet eternal damnation, Rev. 21.27 is important because it is another negative reference. Both 13.8 and 17.8 use the same wording, with the exception that only 13.8 refers to the Lamb. It is this last aspect that 13.8 and 21.27 have in common. Both refer to the Lamb's book of life, the second important element in Rev. 13.8. This second element in 13.8 relates directly to the deterministic element in that it is the Lamb who has prerecorded the names in the book of life, conveying to Asian Christians that their place in the New Jerusalem has already been secured.

Determinism is a key element in many apocalyptic writings (e.g. *1 En.* 85–90; *As. Mos.* 2–10; *2 Bar.* 53–74).[87] This passage is deterministic by its reference to the names not in the book of life from the beginning of creation, implying that some names have been in the book since the beginning of creation. Sweet correctly argues that this passage implies that 'the Lamb's atoning death has its place in God's plan from the beginning, in contrast with the death of '"the beast that was slain" in v. 3'.[88] Charles notes cogently that according to the *As. Mos.* 1.14 Moses was ordained by God to be the mediator of God's covenant 'from the foundation of the world'. He argues that early Christianity gave a similar role to Christ (cf. 1 Pet. 1.19-20).[89]

Although many deterministic statements have as their primary goal the unwavering assertion of the sovereignty of God, the central concern in Rev. 13.8 is to assure the faithful, albeit in contrast to their oppressors, of their ultimate salvation. While this includes an underlying belief in God's sovereignty, its primary purpose is to comfort those

86. E.g. Prigent, *L'Apocalypse*, p. 206; Ladd, *Revelation*, p. 181; cf. Charles, *Revelation*, I, p. 353.

87. See also Russell, *Method*, pp. 205-34.

88. Sweet, *Revelation*, p. 212.

89. Charles, *Revelation*, I, p. 354.

suffering from oppression. The writer feels no obligation to resolve philosophical or theological tension, only to assure the elect of their victory-before-the-fact. In so doing, John allows conflicting statements to stand in the text as different witnesses to the glory of God.[90] The deterministic element finds reinforcement in vv. 9-10. First-century Jewish/Christian versions of determinism, like Roman Stoicism, did not resolve completely the tension between determinism and human responsibility.[91] Indeed, John does not perceive the tension. While John may speak of behavior affecting one's salvation (cf. 2.5; 20.12-13), in 13.8 he speaks as if human fates have been preordained 'from the foundation of the world'. Rev. 13.4 suggests that whether or not to participate in the imperial cult is the key issue in this vision. John might not have been able to separate the Roman state from the worship of the Roman emperor.[92] 'In ancient thought political institutions and the spiritual powers behind them were inseparable.'[93]

The reader of this verse must be acquainted with the concept of a heavenly record, mentioned six times in Revelation, and the soteriological meaning it conveys for one's name to be included in that record. They would find assurance in the fact that the discredited chief victim, the Lamb, would protect the other victims, the followers of the Lamb. This concept of a record book has a rather extensive history in all types of Jewish literature, the Law (e.g. Exod. 32), the Prophets (e.g. Isa. 4) and the Writings (e.g. Dan. 12). Revelation adds the Lamb's supervision to this tradition.

f. *13.11*

Rev. 13.11 reads, 'And I saw another beast coming up from the land and he had two horns like a lamb [ὅμοια ἀρνίῳ] but he spoke like a dragon.' This verse introduces the second beast of ch. 13. This beast is neither a lamb nor a dragon but possesses characteristics of those animals. Again, John employs a comparison, but in this case he intends a contrast between the one like a lamb, the beast from the land, and the

90. Cf. Krodel, *Revelation*, pp. 251-52, also p. 164; Prigent, *L'Apocalypse*, pp. 206; Sweet, *Revelation*, pp. 211-12, also p. 125.

91. On the problem of determinism within Stoicism, see C. Stough, 'Stoic Determinism and Moral Responsibility', in J.M. Rist (ed.), *The Stoics* (Berkeley: University of California Press, 1978), pp. 203-31.

92. Cf. Sweet, *Revelation*, pp. 206-209; Price, *Rituals*, pp. 197-98.

93. Sweet, *Revelation*, p. 208.

true lamb of God, the Christ. Earlier contrasts for the reader have included the first beast with the outlandish names (13.1) contrasted with the true God (1.8; 6.10); the beast with the healed mortal wound (13.3) with the slain Lamb (5.6); temporary earthly victory (13.7) with eternal, heavenly victory (5.9-14). This verse would convey to the hearer/reader that this second beast has the appearance of the Lamb but the spirit of a dragon. This beast, despite its grandeur and power, has no intention of saving the world but exploiting it. This beast cannot be trusted. Sweet notes that this beast represents pagan religion and propagandists of the imperial cult.[94] Price concurs: 'The beast from the sea clearly represents the power of Rome, and the second beast symbolizes a local authority concerned with the worship of the beast from the sea', that is, the first beast represents Roman imperial power; the second, the imperial cult in Asia.[95]

I concur with Sweet and Price. Rev. 13.4 is a reference to the imperial cult. Price suggests that the establishment of the cult of Domitian in Ephesus, 'which involved the participation of the whole province, as attested by the series of dedications by numerous cities, led to unusually great pressure on the Christians for conformity'. He lists Rev. 14.9-11, 15.2-4, 16.2, 13, 19.20 and 20.4, 10 as passages that support his argument.[96] Additionally, vv. 15-17 allude to economic and religio-political dimensions that would fit an eastern context where Nero was regarded highly, giving support to Sweet's position.

g. *14.1-5*

In this passage, John sees the Lamb and 144,000 of his disciples on Mt Zion. The Lamb's disciples 'had his name and his father's name written upon their foreheads (v. 1)'.[97] A loud, unidentified sound comes from heaven, a common feature in Revelation that lends an aura of mystery to the visions (v. 2; e.g. 1.10; 4.1; 19.6), and the saints sing a new song that only the 144,000 know, for they are those 'who have been redeemed

94. Sweet, *Revelation*, pp. 213-19.

95. Price, *Rituals*, p. 197; see also my discussion of the social setting in the introductory chapter of this study.

96. Price, *Rituals*, p. 198. Against many Christian commentators, Price argues that sorcery and trickery were not issues for these communities but are seen by John as manifestations of divine power.

97. See the discussion of the divine name in the preceding chapter's exegeses of the letters to Pergamum and Philadelphia.

from the earth' (v. 3). They are male virgins who 'follow the Lamb wherever he goes. They were redeemed from humanity as first-fruits to God and to the Lamb' (v. 4). Their veracity is unimpeachable (v. 5). This is a prophetic, eschatological exodus vision set in heaven.

As we have discussed the significance of the divine name written upon the followers in the preceding chapter of this study, suffice it to say here that the bestowal of the name establishes for the reader/hearer an unbreakable bond with the deity. We note especially that the placing of God's name upon the foreheads could mean that the saints are priests.[98] Thus, 7.3 and 14.1 express the same reality for John in different ways.

Several details make it clear that Rev. 14.1-5 is an eschatological exodus vision set in heaven. First, 'Mt Zion' symbolized the place of deliverance (e.g. Ps. 2.6-7; *4 Ezra* 13.34-38; cf. Heb. 12.22). In Rev. 21.9–22.5, the place of deliverance and God's heavenly residence descend to earth from heaven. Moreover, the followers of the Lamb number 144,000. They signify a select group that possesses knowledge, symbolized by the new song, not available to all. This is an element of mystery that elevates this group's status.[99] Their election is an example of an exodus motif: the Christians are the people of God, the new Israel on an eschatological journey to the New Jerusalem (see Rev. 7.7-14; 14.1-5; 21.1-7). Further, they have been redeemed 'as first-fruits to God and the Lamb'. 'First-fruits' carried with it a specific connotation in the Jewish tradition. It represented the best of the harvest, or of animal husbandry, or of the spoils of battle, which would be offered to God (see Exod. 23.19; Neh. 10.35; Prov. 3.9; cf. Jas 1.18). Thus, this term connotes to the reader that (1) the 144,000 constitute the best of the best and (2) their giving of their lives was an integral part of their qualitative difference. Furthermore, their distinctiveness is symbolized by their ability to sing a song that only they know (14.3; cf. 5.9), clearly setting them apart from those who do not know the song. Indeed, their purity is beyond reproach. They are 'virgins' who have not 'defiled themselves with women' (v. 4). Finally, the names upon their foreheads (v. 1) may symbolize that the 144,000 will be priests in the next age.

98. I have argued in Part I of this study that placing emblems on the foreheads is a maintenance strategy in Revelation.

99. Cf. Krodel, *Revelation*, pp. 273, 337-41.

Many have attempted to explain the ascetic element in v. 4. Caird, for example, argues that this imagery comes from a military-like consciousness that employs the regulation for holy war when soldiers abstained from sexual intercourse before a battle to maintain ceremonial purity (Deut. 23.9-14; cf. 1 Sam. 21.5; 2 Sam. 11.11).[100] Others argue that the Bible clearly endorses sexual relations in marriage (e.g. Mt. 19.1-6; 1 Cor. 7.1-7) and that, therefore, this verse must be interpreted symbolically. For example, Wall writes that the women in this passage represent only 'the evil women of Revelation'.[101]

I agree with Caird and others that 14.5 symbolizes the 144,000 as righteous, celibate soldiers prepared for a holy war. Significantly, the passage does not refer to marriage. Moreover, even married soldiers were required to abstain from sexual intercourse with their wives during a military campaign (1 Sam. 21.4-5; 2 Sam. 11.11). Exod. 19.15 is probably the source of this tradition for John, since the other elements in this passage show connections with exodus traditions. A comparison with a parallel passage might prove helpful. Rev. 14.1-5 parallels 7.1-8 in three ways. First, both refer to emblems on the saints that distinguish them from others (cf. 7.3; 14.1). These emblems might be symbols of their priesthood. Secondly, both recount the deliverance of the saints from the great tribulation (cf. 7.15-17; 5.9-10; 14.3). This is probably an eschatological exodus for John similar to the emancipation from Egypt and the deliverance from Babylon. Indeed, in Exodus 15 and Revelation 14 the liberated sing a song of deliverance. Finally, both relate how the saints have faithfully followed the Christ-Lamb and even given their lives for their religious convictions (cf. 7.14; 14.4). However, they differ in one significant way in that only 14.1-5 mentions male virgins. This is a vision of the Lamb and his followers depicted as an army on an eschatological military campaign, a prolepsis of 19.14. In neither case does the army actually engage the enemy in battle.

In order to interpret fully this passage, the reader needs a knowledge of Jewish traditions concerning 'Mt Zion', 'first-fruits', numerological speculation and spiritual purity and celibacy, all thoroughly Jewish

100. Caird, *Revelation*, p. 179; so too Sweet, *Revelation*, pp. 222-23; Yarbro Collins, *Apocalypse*, p. 100; Bauckham, *Theology*, pp. 76-80.

101. Wall, *Revelation*, p. 180; see also Hughes, *Revelation*, pp. 158-59; Krodel, *Revelation*, pp. 260-65. For a more complete listing of interpretations, see O. Boecher, *Die Johannesapokalypse* (Darmstadt: Wissenschaftliche Buchgesellschaft, 1975), pp. 56-63.

concepts that would require a broad knowledge of Judaism. Moreover, this holy war is a messianic war, with the Messiah leading his heavenly host against the forces of evil (cf. 17.14; 19.16).[102]

In Rev. 14.1-5, the Lamb gathers to himself a select community of saints whose discipleship is unquestionable and whose purity is undeniable, reiterating the message of 7.1-8, a strategy to assure the reader/ hearer that the faithful will hold positions of honor in the new dispensation.[103] Instead of suggesting Christian accommodation, the use of military imagery strongly suggests intense, and perhaps hostile, relations between Asian Christians and their pagan and/or Jewish neighbors.

h. *14.10*

Revelation 14.10 relates the torment to be suffered eternally by the followers of the beast. 'And he will drink from the wine of the wrath of God [τοῦ οἴνου τοῦ θυμοῦ τοῦ θεοῦ] which is mixed in full strength into the cup of his anger [τῆς ὀργῆς αὐτοῦ], and he will be tormented with fire and brimstone before the holy angels and before the Lamb.' 'The holy angels' could be a periphrasis for God Almighty. If this were the case, both God and the Lamb would view the punishment of the oppressors of God and the Lamb's elect.[104] However, Rev. 14.10 could mean exactly what it says, that the holy angels and the Lamb view the punishment of the damned.[105] The Christ-Lamb, in either view, will witness the punishment of those who oppressed him and his followers. The message to the Asian Christians is that the Christians who suffered in public would view the eternal suffering of their former oppressors; similarly, the evil ones who opposed the Lamb would see him and recognize too late his messianic status.[106] This vision may be a reversal of scenes in many local courts where Christians stood trial solely because of their confession of faith (cf. Pliny, *Letter* 10). This vision, a form of nihilation, does not indicate Christian laxity, but the desire to avenge Christian suffering (see 6.9-11). Rev. 14.10, and other passages that depict the suppression of Christians, also supports my argument in Part I of this study that the letters, in general, spoke to issues within the

102. Bauckham, *Theology*, pp. 67-70, 76-80.
103. Cf. Schüssler Fiorenza, 'Followers', pp. 129-34.
104. So argues Beasley-Murray, *Revelation*, p. 226.
105. So argues Mounce, *Revelation*, pp. 275-76.
106. Ellul has a similar position (*Apocalypse* [New York: Seabury], p. 176).

churches, while the apocalyptic visions, in general, reflect the plight of Christians in the broader society.

i. *15.3-4*

These verses fall within the vision of the angels with the last plagues (15.1-8). The song of Moses and the Lamb celebrates God's eschatological exodus of his people. It is similar to the song of Moses in Exodus 15 in this regard. Both songs are sung along a seashore. The reference to the Lamb could remind the reader of the Passover Lamb of the Exodus tradition (Exod. 12). However, unlike Exodus 15, which celebrates the deliverance of a single nation, the event in Rev. 15.3-4 celebrates the deliverance of a racially and culturally mixed Christian body (cf. 7.9-10). Finally, both Moses and the Lamb function as deliverers of a religious community.[107]

j. *17.14*

Rev. 17.14 falls within a larger section (17.1-17). John sees a vision 'of the great prostitute' (v. 1). The references to adultery and intoxication are metaphors for the prostitute's sinfulness (v. 2) and for the repression of Christians (v. 6). The prostitute receives the name 'Babylon the Great', a symbolic reference to Rome and its rulers (see 17.9).[108] The Roman Empire 'will make war against the Lamb and the Lamb will conquer [νικήσει] them, for he is Lord of lords and King of kings and the ones with him are called and elect and faithful' (17.14). Verses 15-18 continue with cryptic descriptions of the Roman Empire. Rev. 17.14 conveys to the Christians in Asia Minor that the victory over the Roman Empire has been won already by the Christ-Lamb. Christians remain faithful even in tribulations. These tribulations are in the future, as the verbs make clear. Thus, 17.14 is a prophecy and provides instructions to Christians on how they should behave during the coming crisis that John envisioned.

The expression 'the called and elect and faithful' confirms the elite status of the group mentioned in 17.14. This war will occur in the

107. Cf. Krodel, *Apocalypse*, pp. 178-79; Guthrie, 'Lamb', pp. 67-68.

108. 'Babylon' was a code name for Rome in other Jewish and Christian writings roughly contemporaneous with Revelation (e.g. *4 Ezra* 1.1; *Sib. Or.* 5.155-61; 1 Pet. 5.13).

future, as the future active indicative forms of πολεμέω and νικάω indicate. This vision will be realized in Rev. 19.11-21 through the Christ–Divine Warrior image, not the Christ–Lamb. Both 17.14 and 19.16 refer to the messianic figure with the same title of 'Lord of lords and King of kings'.[109] Rev. 17.14 also has a word of assurance for the community. The followers of the Lamb are special persons who have been called (κλητοὶ) and elected (ἐκλεκτοὶ) by God, terms often applied to Israel as the people of God.[110] πιστοί refers to their steadfast loyalty to God.

Those three adjectives serve important roles for the emotional well-being of the seven churches in Asia. The first two adjectives connote strong deterministic elements in John's theology. We noted earlier the priest-king status for the victors of this book and how the book's determinism assures the Christian community of its eventual salvation. In this verse, that assurance continues themes expressed earlier in Revelation (e.g. 3.5; 17.8). The term 'faithful' denotes that the saints remained true to their calling and election. These three terms tell us that the Christians saw themselves as special persons whom God will reward in a special way; their fidelity and loyalty has assured their status as God's chosen. Those terms also communicated to the hearer/reader that God cares in a special manner for the followers of the Lamb who have suffered (see 17.1-6). The passage suggests that this oppression was begun by persons who supported the imperial cult, since it depicts the beast (Rome) as the opponent of the saints.

This passage reflects a social context where the faithfulness of Christians has led to their repression. Within this type of context, the selection of the predicates 'called', 'elect' and 'faithful' are intelligible as modes of exhortation and apologetics. As exhortation, they encourage the readers to believe that their faithfulness is the proper behavior and will ultimately be rewarded. As apologetics, it explains to the Christians that their suffering is part of the divine plan. Rev. 17.14 does not convey to the reader a judgment against the Church because of its religious laxity, but, rather, the propriety of Christian fidelity that has led to trials and tribulations (see 16.6; 17.6). Rev. 17.14 addresses the oppressive context in which Asian Christians lived and suffered.

109. See also Rev. 1.5; cf. 20.4. See G.K. Beale, 'The Origin of the Title "King of kings and Lord of lords" in Revelation 17.14', *NTS* 31 (1985), pp. 618-20, and also my own '"King of Kings and Lord of Lords" Revisited', *NTS* 39 (1993), pp. 159-60.

110. Cf. Hughes, *Revelation*, p. 187.

k. *19.7-9*

Rev. 19.7-9 falls within the vision of the Lamb's marriage supper, or wedding banquet (19.5-10). The bride of the Lamb is the community of Christian saints. This is an example of the closeness of the relationship between Christ and community in the book of Revelation: a distinction or separation does not exist between Christ's witness to God and the Christian community's witness to Christ (cf. 6.9; 20.4). His word is their word; his fate theirs; his victory is theirs as well. That is to say, one link between Christ and community in Revelation is the consistency between their faithful witness to Christ and Christ's faithful witness to God. It is within this type of social context that Christ's lordship of the churches and the seven letters must also be understood.

Rev. 19.8 refers to the wedding garment as 'pure, bright, fine linen [βύσσινον λαμπρὸν καθαρόν]; for the fine linen [βύσσινον] is the righteous deeds of the saints'. Bright, radiant linen had established roles symbolizing purity and was worn most often by heavenly beings and priests in the Hebrew Bible and Jewish writings into the second century CE (e.g. Lev. 16.4; Ezek. 9.2-3, 11; 10.1-8; Dan. 10.5-6; *1 En.* 62.15-16; 104.2; *2 Bar.* 51.5, 12; *Apoc. Abr.* 13.15; *m. Yom.* 3.6-7; Philo, *Vit. Mos.* 2.17; Josephus, *War* 5.230-37). Indeed, both Philo and Josephus describe the high priest's attire with βύσσινος. Rev. 15.6 describes angels 'dressed in pure, bright linen' (λίνον καθαρὸν λαμπρὸν). Rev. 19.14 uses similar words to describe the saints who accompany the Divine Warrior (βύσσινον λευκὸν καθαρόν). Linen connotes the purity and election of the Asian Christian community. This is a significant passage since it does not depict Christian apostasy or even laxity and supports my earlier argument that the apocalyptic visions primarily concern themselves with the relationship of the church to Greco-Roman society. In this prophetic vision of the future, John sees an undefiled church entering into the new age (cf. 7.13-14; 14.1; 20.4-6). This vision presupposes that the churches have followed the instructions of their Lord (Rev. 2.1–3.22) and are thoroughly prepared to enter the New Jerusalem.

The words of assurance in Rev. 19.9 conclude with an angelic witness to the faithfulness of God: 'These are the true words of God' (see 21.5; 22.6; cf. 17.14; 19.11), affirming the authenticity and certainty of the vision.

l. *21.9–22.5*

This last vision of Revelation describes the New Jerusalem more fully than any other sections of the book[111] and mentions the Lamb six times (21.14, 22, 23, 27; 22.1, 3).[112] The Lamb plays a key role in securing and maintaining the spiritual and physical welfare of the Christian community.

Rev. 21.14 connects the ministry of the historical Jesus of Nazareth with the christological Lamb of Revelation by referring to the 12 foundations of the New Jerusalem with 'the twelve names of the twelve apostles of the Lamb'. This reference to the apostles follows mention of the 12 tribes of Israel in 21.12. It is John's way of conveying to the original recipients the antiquity of Christianity within Judaism, the elect people of God. The reference at this point to Jesus as the Lamb connotes that the Lamb who has been slain (5.6) is the primary christological image that governs Revelation (cf. Mt. 16.21; 17.22-23; 20.17-19; 26.2; Rom. 5.6-11; 1 Jn 2.1-2)[113] and that the community has longstanding traditions. Greco-Roman society respected ancient religious traditions and tended to suspect newer ones, as Pliny's *Letter* 10 attests. John's point is that Christianity is the most faithful form of Judaism.

Rev. 21.27 states that 'only those whose names that have been written in the Lamb's book of life' shall enter the New Jerusalem. The importance of the Lamb's connection with the book of life and its deterministic function have been noted repeatedly in this study. This passage conveyed to its original readers an assurance of their entry into the new age.

Rev. 21.22, 23 and 22.1, 22.3 must be discussed together, for all four passages present the Lamb as God Almighty's vice regent. This relationship between these two figures has been noted several times previously in this study. Moreover, all four passages relate Christ to the life

111. Proleptic visions of the New Jerusalem are found throughout the book (e.g. 7.1-17; 14.1-5; 19.1-10).

112. Many argue that this vision has many parallels with the description of Babylon in 17.1–19.10 (e.g. Krodel, *Revelation*, pp. 352-56); others note the parallels with Ezek. 40–47 (e.g. Harrington, *Apocalypse*, pp. 254-56), while others see links with Qumran (B. Gärtner, *The Temple and the Community in Qumran and the New Testament* [Cambridge: Cambridge University Press, 1965]; cf. Ladd, *Revelation*, pp. 283-84. Although interesting, these questions cannot detain us.

113. Cf. Caird, *Revelation*, p. 272; Mounce, *Revelation*, p. 379; Ladd, *Revelation*, p. 281; Sweet, *Revelation*, p. 304; Morris, *Revelation*, p. 243; Krodel, *Revelation*, pp. 357-58.

of the community in the New Jerusalem. These two factors tell the reader that God Almighty and the Christ are concerned deeply with the quality of their lives on earth in the present and in the New Jerusalem in the future. Moreover, it strongly suggests that the quality of life on earth for Christians has been poor. It also discloses to the reader the Lamb's concern for the well-being of the community, a link between Christ and community.

The New Jerusalem has no temple (21.22) for God Almighty and the Lamb are its temple. This is a reversal of expectations (cf. Ezek. 40–46). The New Jerusalem has no heavenly luminaries either (v. 23) for God and the Lamb provide its illumination (cf. Jn 1.4-5; 8.12; 9.5). These two verses signify that the Temple was no longer necessary because God and the Lamb, the heavenly co-regents, dwelt among humanity and have become the center of life in the community. The residents of the New Jerusalem would have direct access to God and to the Lamb, that they will be a kingdom of priests (see 1.5; 5.9; cf. 7.15). God and the Lamb will provide light for the inhabitants of the New Jerusalem.[114]

Rev. 22.1-5 confirms the preceding comments. The river of the water of life flows from the throne of God and the Lamb (v. 1). The river provides nourishment for the tree of life, which in turn heals the nations (v. 2; cf. 21.27). Only the pure will enter the city and the throne of God and the Lamb will be in it (v. 3). Verse 4 contains the key element: 'And they will see his [God's] face and his [God's] name will be upon their foreheads', that is, they will be priests (another exodus motif; see 1.5; 5.9; cf. 7.14-15) and God's emblem will be on them, designating their election and separating them from the unjust (see 3.12; 7.3; 14.1). Verse 5 reiterates 21.23. These verses provide yet another example of the Lamb's providential oversight of the Christian community.

In sum, the New Jerusalem will be the eschatological home for God, the Lamb and their faithful disciples. The eschatological exodus ends in the New Jerusalem. The New Jerusalem will establish an intimate, familial relationship among God, the Lamb and the followers of the Lamb. A symbol of this intimacy is the reference to the priestly nature of the elect in the eschatological community, which will have direct

114. Cf. Harrington, *Apocalypse*, pp. 260-63; Caird, *Revelation*, pp. 278-79; Mounce, *Revelation*, pp. 383-84; Ladd, *Revelation*, pp. 283-84.

access to God and the Lamb.[115] God and the Lamb, in turn, will provide the highest quality of life possible and the servants of God will worship them (22.4; cf. 7.14-17; Ezek. 47).[116] The New Jerusalem will be a community full of joy and without illnesses, founded by God and the Lamb. The reference to healing the nations (v. 2) might be a message of solace to the Asian Christian churches since Gen. 2.9 makes no mention of healing the nations. This passage has several eschatological exodus images in the office of priest, the end of the exodus, the New Jerusalem community and the election of the New Israel.

This ends my exegesis of the Lamb passages in Revelation and I turn now to a concluding statement.

4. *Summation*

a. *The Lamb and the Community*

The Lamb performs several important functions in Revelation, but the Lamb's most important christological function involves leading an eschatological Christian community whose destination is the New Jerusalem (e.g. 7.9-17; 14.1-5; 21.9–22.5). The numerous uses of Exodus traditions suggests that John perceives an eschatological exodus, with the Church constituting a new people of God. Moreover, the variety of functions associated with the Lamb indicates that the Lamb is the most comprehensive christological image in Revelation.

The Lamb is King of kings and Lord of lords (17.14). His domain is universal. The image of the Lamb ruling the cosmos might convey to the reader that the Lord of the universe gained the ultimate victory through suffering and that those who follow his example will be redeemed by him at the judgment. This image has a social function: it maintains the union between Christ and community through visions which enable the original readership to relate the Lamb's suffering to their own. This imagery would expect the readers to respond with a faithful conviction to remain true to the Lamb no matter what the consequences.

115. I am grateful to the Revd Peter Beetham, a British Methodist pastor in the East Anglia District, for reminding me of this fact.

116. Cf. Sweet, *Revelation*, pp. 311-12; Krodel, *Revelation*, pp. 362-68; Morris, *Revelation*, pp. 248-50; Mounce, *Revelation*, pp. 386-88; Ladd, *Revelation*, pp. 286-89.

1. The Lamb gathers, leads, provides benefits for the eschatological Christian community and protects it from Satan and his forces. First, the death of the Lamb brings salvation to the faithful. The Lamb redeems to God persons from every tribe, linguistic group, nationality and ethnic group through his sacrificial death (5.9). The Lamb saves persons, especially the saints (7.14). These two verses must be compared to the reference in 1.5 to the work of Christ in freeing persons from sin through his blood. Priest-kingship is offered in all three passages (see 1.5-6; 5.10; 7.15). Rev. 12.11 is similar in that it states that the defeat of Satan in heaven by Michael and his angels came about because of the blood of the Lamb. The sacrificial death of Jesus has positive ramifications for the righteous on earth and the expelling of the unrighteous in heaven (a part of the apologetic agenda of Revelation). The Lamb's sacrificial death is synonymous with the witness of the saints (12.10-12). Finally, the saints 'are the called and elect and faithful' (17.14). The first two predicate adjectives relate to God's action, the last to the saints' response.

Secondly, the Lamb protects the community and defeats its enemies. The community will no longer suffer from the natural elements but will find eternal sustenance under the Lamb's pastoral care (7.16-17). He seals the elect, protects them from the eschatological woes (14.1-5; cf. 7.1-8) and watches the eternal punishment of those who have persecuted the people of God (14.10), thereby assuring the earthly community of its security. He bestows positions of honor upon those who have suffered the most for their religious convictions (14.1-5; 17.14; cf. 11.18; 12.11; 16.6; 17.6).[117]

2. Revelation shows concern for the community in its initial presentation of the Lamb. Only the Lamb is worthy to open the scroll that contains God's eschatological plans. By opening the scroll, the Lamb inaugurates the events that will lead to the ultimate salvation and victory of the people of God (5.9-10; cf. 7.9-10; 19.5-10). Although the seals cycle functions as a revelatory action, it will bring about a soteriological result for Christians. Indeed, the Lamb is worthy because he has died a sacrificial death that becomes for suffering Christians a means of identification with their lord and also a symbol of victory over sin and evil. One purpose of the Lamb imagery would then be to encourage

117. Cf. Bauckham, *Theology*, pp. 94-98.

Christians to remain true to their faith and thus overcome as the Christ-Lamb overcame.[118]

3. Many Lamb passages contain a deterministic element. The Lamb's book of life, which contains the citizenship roll for the New Jerusalem, is the principal medium of determinism in Revelation. The image of the book of life assures the Christian community of its salvation and the condemnation of its opponents. At once, it connotes assurance and judgment. Names have been included in the book of life 'from the foundation of the world' (13.8; 17.8; cf. 3.5; 20.12, 15; 21.27). This would have been a reassuring message to those yet suffering for their Christian beliefs. This form of determinism indicates some type of repression that the deterministic motif attempts to nullify for the oppressed.

4. The Lamb makes war against the enemies of God on earth and defeats them (12.10-12; 17.14). These passages are prolepses of the Divine Warrior scene in 19.11-21, which underlies these visions. Suffice it to say that the Divine Warrior image is only developed fully in 19.11-21. The use of military imagery suggests two uncompromising parties in a heated conflict. Revelation's military imagery does not imply that Christians were lax in any way, but that they were suffering in some way. For John, the Roman Empire represents the threat.

5. God Almighty shares divine honors with the Lamb. All creation worships them together (e.g. 5.13; 7.10; cf. 7.15-17; 21.6). The elect are sealed with both their names (14.1; cf. 22.4). In the New Jerusalem, God Almighty and the Lamb constitute the center of life and religious activity (21.22), illumine the city (21.23; 22.5), and provide the sustenance for life and eradicate all diseases (22.1-5). John never totally separates God Almighty and the Lamb from the people of God, the followers of the Lamb (cf. 12.10-12), but relates them intimately through various symbols (e.g. the seal/emblem on the saints [14.1; cf. 7.3]; the wedding banquet [19.5-10]; God wipes away tears [7.17; 21.4]).

In Part I of this study, I identified several common messianic features of the one-like-a-son-of-man tradition in *1 Enoch, 4 Ezra* and Revelation. The Messiah (1) acts as a judge, (2) gathers to himself an elect community, (3) makes war against his enemies, (4) possesses an element of mystery and (5) is described by means of a comparison. Revelation associates the first three elements with the Christ-Lamb: (1) he judges

118. Cf. G. Rochais, 'Le règne des mille ans et la seconde mort: Origines et sens Apoc 19,11–20,6', *NRT* 103 (1981), pp. 831-56.

and determines both those who will be saved and those who will be not saved (13.8; 17.8; 21.27) and even views the punishment of the latter group (14.10); (2) he gathers to himself an elect community upon which he bestows salvific benefits (5.9; 7.9-17; 14.1-5; 17.14; 19.7-9); and (3) he makes war against his enemies and defeats them (17.14; cf. 14.10). Additionally, as with the 'one like a son of man', the Lamb functions as God's divine agent and receives adoration alongside God (5.13; 7.10; 14.1; 21.22-23; 22.1-5). Furthermore, a strong deterministic element is associated with the Lamb. The Lamb has written in the book of life the names of those who have been saved from the very moment of creation (13.8; 17.8). In this manner, Revelation joins creation and salvation as two aspects of the divine plan. Finally, the death of the Lamb provides salvific benefits for the followers of the Lamb and serves as a model for Christians to follow (e.g. 5.9; 7.9-17; 12.10-12). The Lamb as God's eschatological divine agent, the deterministic role of the Lamb, and the salvific benefits of the Lamb's death are central features of the Christology of the book of Revelation.

The use of these images suggests that John chose them because Christians were experiencing repression. The purpose would be to persuade Christians to remain faithful by depicting the slain Lamb as the Lord Supreme (17.14). Some might argue that these images refer to wayward Christians.[119] This is possible, but one would expect more explicit references if that were the case, as one finds in 2.14-16 and 2.20-23, and fewer references to the shed blood of the saints, as in 16.6 and 17.6.

b. *The Impact of the Lamb Imagery*

The image of the Lamb-Christ would have had a wide range of social possibilities for its intended readers/hearers. Some possiblities naturally overlap. I have identified six possible social dimensions. The first three are negative; the final three, positive.

1. The image of the Lamb achieving *victory through suffering* would have bolstered the faith, courage and sense of hope of many persons to whom John wrote (Rev. 5.1-14; 7.13-14; 12.7-12; 14.1-5). Revelation, as does the entire New Testament, reinterprets the cross positively. Some strands of Second Temple Judaism expected a messiah (or messiahs) who would have judicial and political powers. Revelation retains

119. E.g. Bauckham, *Theology*, pp. 11-17.

this picture in 19.11-21, but the initial presentation of the Messiah celebrates his meekness (in contrast to the lion imagery) and suffering as a means of conquering (5.7-9). His method of conquering speaks to those who would conquer in the seven churches (Rev. 2.1–3.22) and establishes the model for emulation (7.13-14). Indeed, when Michael and his heavenly entourage expel Satan from heaven, it is the blood of the Lamb and the testimony of the saints that has made their victory possible (12.7-12). 'The testimony of the saints' probably also alludes to their dying for their beliefs. Finally, those who conquer through suffering form an eschatological community beyond reproach (14.1-5).[120]

This victory-through-suffering motif tells us something of the social context from which the work comes. The Christians to whom John wrote seemed to have experienced some type of regional repression. Participants in the imperial cult probably saw Christians who refused to participate in that cult as threats to their social well-being, fearing natural disasters and/or political disorder. The only hope of the recipients of Revelation lay in the next age. No reprieve exists in this one. Thus, the punishment received in this age becomes a salvific means of entry into the next. In such a social context, Christians and the Christian message would come under suspicion, have little social value and be viewed as rather novel. To non-Christians, Christ's crucifixion was justified and necessary as a means of maintaining order in the Empire. To the Christians, it was unjustified but necessary to bring divine order into the world.

While their refusal to partipate in traditional Greco-Roman religious practices would have led to tensions with pagans, by bestowing divine honors on Jesus, Christians would have come into conflict with more traditional Jewish groups who might argue that Christianity was a form of polytheism. For both reasons, the Christian witness would have encountered hostility in Roman Asia by its very nature. Therefore, it is not surprising that at the crux of many passages is the connection between faithful witnessing and suffering that leads to one's salvation (e.g. 7.9-17; 12.7-12; 17.12-14).

2. This brings us to our second motif: *revenge upon the oppressors* (6.9-11; 14.10). Those who have already died for their religious convictions seek revenge. They receive assurance that their deaths will be avenged but only after the number of persons to die for the faith has

120. Cf. Schüssler Fiorenza, *Vision*, pp. 129-31; Reddish, 'Martyrdom', pp. 132-60.

been completed. Thus, many in John's community of churches have died and many might yet die. Their cry for retribution by God indicates the helplessness felt by those Christians. Therefore, when the saints actually witness the eternal punishment of their persecutors in 14.10, this scene is understandable. They seek a reversal. This quest for vengeance reflects a social setting where Christians have suffered public ridicule and want to see the punishment of their oppressors in the next age just as their oppressors witnessed their suffering in this one.[121] *1 En.* 47.1-2, *4 Ezra* 4.35-37 and *2 Bar.* 23.4-5 come from similar social settings and ask similar questions. In all four books, the question of theodicy and divine justice are of uppermost concern for the seer and his community. The desire to see the opposition suffer while the saints sit in heavenly bliss reflects a social context where the powerless in this dispensation seek privilege in the next. Rev. 6.9-11 and 14.10 reflect the deep enmity that exists between two groups who have mutually exclusive world-views. Conversely, it is difficult to discern how these verses reflect some form of dissonance or religious laxity. The next motif confirms this point.

3. The Lamb is often associated with *military imagery* (e.g. 12.7-12; 17.14).[122] The purpose of this imagery, developed more fully in 19.11-20.14, is to avenge the saints. Military imagery dominates the first four seals. The Lamb's control of these events is symbolized by his worthiness to open the seals. Moreover, the heavenly victory of Michael and the angelic host comes about 'because of the blood of the Lamb and because of the word of their [i.e. the saints'] witness and they did not love their lives even unto death' (12.11). The technical phrase 'because of the blood' (cf. 1.5; 5.9; 7.14) and the confirmation statement 'because of the word' create a synonymous parallel that further elucidates the fact that dying for the faith is the ultimate sacrifice that is simultaneously the ultimate victory over evil. Again, dying for the faith leads to victory, providing an unexpected reversal. However, more importantly, this reversal, coming within a warring context, provides the means for victory through victimization. At the very least, this image implies an intense struggle by Christians in Asia who are virtually defenseless. They possess no weapons. They do not resort to guerilla warfare. Their

121. Cf. G.N. Stanton, *A Gospel for a New People: Studies in Matthew* (Edinburgh: T. & T. Clark, 1992), pp. 207-31.

122. My expression 'military imagery' is similar to Bauckham's 'messianic war' (*Climax*, pp. 210-37; *Theology*, pp. 67-70).

rhetoric falls upon deaf ears. Their only defense is their shed blood. Within such a context, witnessing can become a powerful form of civil disobedience.

Rev. 17.14, which contains elements of faithfulness and determinism also set within a warring context, confirms the point just made. Those who oppose God and God's people make war with the Lamb, but the Lamb conquers them because he is the Lord Sovereign of the universe.[123] A special group of persons accompanies the Lamb on this campaign. They are the called, the elect and the faithful (cf. 19.14; 20.4). Referring to them as 'the called' and 'the elect' echoes references to Israel as the people of God (an eschatological exodus motif). Moreover, it represents God's predetermined selection of the saints for salvation, a theological feature of Revelation with an aim to exhort the community during its time of trial (cf. 13.8). 'The faithful' represents the human response to God's saving action. This passage reflects a social context where the community has been faithful to God and Christ, expects its lord to punish its oppressors and to liberate the faithful just as the Lord had done in the first (from Egypt) and second (from Babylon) exoduses. The deterministic predicates, 'called' and 'elect', probably reflect a life setting of immense suffering and deprivation where the oppressed need assurance and reassurance of the correctness of their religious convictions and the certainty of their salvation. The election imagery, coupled with the military defeat of their oppressors, provides the needed means of assurance, a form of therapy. This brings us to our next motif, determinism, and takes us from the negative to the positive aspects which accompany the Lamb imagery.

4. *Determinism* in Revelation assures the community of its salvation. Apocalypticism used determinism to convey to a community God's unending love, concern and care for it. Revelation consistently employs deterministic elements in this way. In so doing, it also joins the Lamb's sacrifice with eschatological salvation. These are maintenance strategies found principally in 13.8; 17.14 and 21.27–22.2.

In 13.8, comfort comes to the oppressed by means of the image of the slain Messiah who records the names of the saints in the book of life 'from the foundation of the world'. The slain one becomes the eschatological judge who will adjudicate on who may or may not enter the New Jerusalem. He has gained this role through his faithful witness unto

123. Cf. Malina, *Star Visions*, pp. 262-65.

death. The names of those who follow his example have been recorded before time began. Their victory is assured. No uncertainty exists concerning their status.

Since 17.14 has been discussed above, nothing more need be said and we shall move on to 21.27–22.2.

Initially, Rev. 21.27–22.2 might appear to be an appendage to the New Jerusalem section (21.9–22.5). In actuality, it serves two purposes. First, it assures the elect and faithful of their inclusion in the New Jerusalem. The purpose of this assurance would be to encourage them to remain even more steadfast in the face of oppression, a prime example of a therapeutic maintenance strategy in Revelation. Secondly, in contrast with the cowardly, the impure, the despicable and the deceitful who are excluded (21.8), the saints are courageous, pure (cf. 14.1-5), praiseworthy and honest. The image of the tree of life that heals the nations follows, symbolizing at once God's creation of the world and God's unending care for the followers of Jesus. Healing may also refer to an end of suffering by Asian Christians. Thus, these few verses communicated to the original readership/audience an unbroken divine providence from creation to ultimate salvation. That is to say, it is all part of the divine plan. Such imagery betrays a life setting of daily uncertainty and suffering and a need for reassurance of one's beliefs, giving encouragement and hope through a vision of the next age where the pain of this age would end completely and forever.

5. The Lamb *improves the quality of life*. He provides protection, leadership, nourishment, solace and promises deliverance (7.9-17; 13.8; 21.9–22.5), that is, the Lamb gives to the Christian community in the next age what Greco-Roman society has denied it in this one. The Lamb not only improves the quality of life but also liberates his people from sin, suffering and death. The Lamb is a deliverer who brings about the cessation of deprivation, protects the community and leads it to refreshing, life-giving springs where God Almighty wipes away the tears of the oppressed, a poignant vision. It would convey to the Asian Christians that God takes an interest in their woes and will attend to their sorrows personally (7.13-17; cf. 21.1-8). Such imagery connotes an intense action against Asian Christians, not accommodation to traditional religio-political practices. This community understands itself to have a close, endearing fellowship with its God. It has maintained this fellowship through trying times, symbolized by the tears, and it looks for solace only in the next age (cf. 21.1-8) when God will set apart his

people so that their status will be known to all. This will transpire because the Lamb will deliver his people from Satan and his minions through his blood (12.10-12; 15.1-4). The wedding of the Lamb and the saints reinforces the closeness of the Christian community to God and to the Lamb (19.1-9; 21.9-13). The saints constitute the Bride of the Lamb: the chaste, eschatological people of God (cf. 14.1-5; 21.9-14, 22-27). They are the called, the elect and the faithful (see 17.14). This community has remained faithful under tremendous pressures. This closeness between God and people is evidenced in the high status of priest-kings bestowed upon the faithful in the book of Revelation, our final motif.

6. The followers of the Lamb will possess a *high status as priest-kings in the next age*, which shall reverse their low status in Greco-Roman society. I also noted this same motif in Chapter 4 of this study. The Lamb enables his followers to become a kingdom of priests, a high rank in Jewish society, who will rule with Christ (5.9-10; cf. 1.5-6; 20.4-6). This is an elect, pure and elite group with unimpeachable character (14.1-5; 17.14). God and Christ share their own sovereignty with this group, those who have suffered the most (e.g. 7.13-14; cf. 20.4-6). This serves as a powerful maintenance strategy to retain persons within the community. As priests, they have direct access to God, the point of 21.22-27, and have no concerns or fears, the point of 21.1-8. The status of the saints in the coming new dispensation should be contrasted with their present lowly status in the present one where the saints are constantly under attack and their character questioned repeatedly owing to their religious convictions. Suffering without judicial reprieve shall be replaced by exaltation to a priestly co-regency with God and Christ. No higher status could be bestowed upon a human being.

Throughout this chapter, I have argued strongly that Revelation reflects an actual oppression of Asian Christians c. 95 CE. While the letters reflect the problems of religious laxity, the apocalyptic visions, as the research in this chapter has demonstrated, reflect the tensions between Christians and their oppressors in the greater society.

Chapter 6

The Image of the Divine Warrior in Revelation 19.11-21

While the christological images studied in the preceding two chapters of this study dealt primarily with the welfare of the life of the Christian community and helped the community to identify with Christ, the vision of the Divine Warrior in 19.11-21 judged the worldly institutions that had oppressed the Christian community as a way of vindicating Christians.[1] This is an example of nihilation, a maintenance technique that exhorts its readers by providing a vision of the elimination of their opponents.[2]

The present chapter will put forth four basic arguments for the interpretation of the Divine Warrior visions. First and foremost, it will argue that v. 11 contains the definitive theme for interpreting vv. 11-21: 'to judge and make war in righteousness', that is, the Divine Warrior righteously judges the world (cf. 15.3; 16.5; 19.2), administers punishment upon the guilty and, in so doing, vindicates the Christian community. While in Rev. 15.3, 16.5 and 19.2 it is God who acts, in 19.11-21 it is Christ, another example of Christ functioning as God Almighty's divine agency figure.

Secondly, in light of the thematic statement in v. 11, I shall argue that the symbolic names for Christ in vv. 11-16 signify Christ's complete faithfulness to God Almighty. Furthermore, the names prepare the reader for the images that present Christ as an eschatological judge, a role usually reserved for God Almighty in Jewish literature (e.g. Isa. 63.1-6). Some commentators have recognized the juridical dimensions of the images but few have recognized the connection between the

1. Cf. Harrington, *Apocalypse*, pp. 228-32.

2. See my discussion of nihilation in 'Symbolic Biblical Language and Sociological Interpretation', Chapter 1, this study.

names and the images.[3] These names represent Christ as the manifestation of God Almighty in human history.[4] Finally, I shall demonstrate that the significance of the names increases with each name.

Thirdly, this present chapter will demonstrate that the major images and symbols associated with the rider and the heavenly host conveyed to the reader the judgment and punishment of God's opponents, on the one hand, and the vindication of God's righteous people, on the other.

Finally, throughout this chapter, I shall note the ways in which the Divine Warrior has clear symbolic connections with the one-like-a-son-of-man and the Lamb christological images in Revelation. These connections and the consistency of functions and roles among all three major christological images attest to the unity of the Christology of Revelation.[5]

The concept of the God of Israel as a Divine Warrior has its genesis in ANE religiosity.[6] The Hebrew Bible, and Judaism in general, embraced the image of God Almighty as a Divine Warrior long before the advent of Christianity and applied it to various historical events. One finds four main motifs. First, *Yahweh Sabaoth*, 'Lord of hosts', became one of many titles for God, connoting an image of God as one who makes war against the enemies of Israel (e.g. 1 Sam. 15.2; Isa. 63.1-6; Zech. 11.1-6; Mal. 1.4-5; 4.1-3). Secondly, God also slays the sea monster and brings about order from chaos (e.g. Ps. 74.13-14; Isa. 27.1; Job 41), Jewish versions of an ancient cosmogonic myth (cf. *CTA* 2.28-30). Thirdly, God judges and punishes evil wherever it may be found (e.g. Isa. 3.1-15; Hag. 1.5-11; 2.6-9). Finally, the Divine Warrior liberates his people not once (e.g. Exod. 14.1-15) but twice (Isa. 35; 40.3-5; see

3. E.g. Lohmeyer, *Offenbarung*, p. 159; Ladd, *Revelation*, pp. 252-53; Yarbro Collins, *Apocalypse*, p. 135; Hughes, *Revelation*, pp. 203-208; C.H. Giblin, *The Book of Revelation: The Open Book of Prophecy* (GNS, 34; Collegeville, MN: Liturgical Press, 1991), pp. 180-83.

4. Cf. Corsini, *Apocalypse*, p. 351.

5. Cf. Lohmeyer, *Offenbarung*, pp. 157-58; Thompson, *Revelation*, pp. 41-46.

6. See, e.g., P.D. Hanson, *The Dawn of Apocalyptic* (Philadelphia: Fortress Press, 1975), pp. 292-334; F.M. Cross, Jr, *Canaanite Myth and Hebrew Epic* (Cambridge, MA: Harvard University Press, 1973), pp. 20, 118, 144, 229 n. 42; P.D. Miller, *The Divine Warrior in Early Israel* (HSM, 5; Cambridge, MA: Harvard University Press, 1973), pp. 18-20, 155; R.J. Clifford, *The Cosmic Mountain in Canaan and the Old Testament* (HSM, 4; Cambridge, MA: Harvard University Press 1974), p. 119 n. 23; Yarbro Collins, *Combat*, pp. 225-26.

also Isa. 51.9-11, where one finds God as Lord Sabaoth, Creator of an orderly cosmos and Liberator of the oppressed). In all four motifs, God Almighty punishes sinful behavior. Second temple Jewish writings often repeated these same themes (e.g. *1 En.* 1.3-9; Jdt. 16.15; Wis. 18.15-19). The Divine Warrior God who liberates his people also became a major theme in the Maccabean and Bar Kochba revolts.

Rev. 19.11-21 incorporates all but the second of these three traditions,[7] reinterpreting them in such a manner that they never become idolatrous icons but remain media of transmission, enabling Revelation's traditional apocalyptic imagery to remain fresh even when it is not new. Yarbro Collins may be correct when she states that the divine warrior 'is the basic principle of composition in the Apocalypse'.[8] Sweet argues that Rev. 19.11-16 contains the climax of Revelation:

> Verse 10 has prepared us to see the coming (of the Divine Warrior) in terms of the testimony of Jesus, and this is confirmed by the *white horse*, the titles *Faithful and True* and *The Word of God*, and by the *sword* issuing from his *mouth* (emphases as in the text).[9]

In Rev. 19.11-21, Isa. 63.1-6 serves as the principal divine warrior model, but it is not the only one.

1. *An Overview of Revelation 19.11-21*

Rev. 19.11-21 contains the most complete christological statement in Revelation. All the major christological themes and images can be found in this rather brief section which describes the defeat of the earthly representatives of Satan. Rev. 19.11-21 has many maintenance strategies intended to assure its readers/hearers of the final judgment of evil and the vindication of the saints (see the promise in 6.9-11). It contains three visions: (1) Christ's appearance (vv. 11-16); (2) the feast for the birds in 19.17-18 (the counterimage of the marriage feast in 19.7-9); and (3) the punishment of the beast and his followers (vv. 19-21). This pericope continues the process of the universal defeat of Satan begun by Michael and the heavenly host described in 12.7-12[10] and

7. Rev. 12.1–13.18 incorporates the second tradition. At some future date, I hope to write on the use of this tradition in Revelation, *4 Ezra* and *2 Baruch*.

8. Yarbro Collins, *Crisis*, p. 130; see also pp. 149-50; *idem*, *Combat*, pp. 130-45, 157-90, 231-34.

9. Sweet, *Revelation*, p. 281; cf. Thompson, *Revelation*, p. 45.

10. Cf. Wall, *Revelation*, p. 229.

anticipates the final defeat of Satan, Death and Hades in 20.1-3, 7-10. Rev. 17.13-14 is also a prolepsis of 19.11-21. This is evident in the reference to war (17.14; 19.11, 19; cf. 12.7) and the defeat of the Satanic forces by the 'Lord of lords and King of kings' (17.14; 19.16). The visions in 12.7-12 and 17.13-14 have prepared the readers/hearers for 19.11-21, which in turn prepares them for 20.1-3, 7-10. Within Rev. 19.11-21, Christ's symbolic names and images prepare the reader/hearer for Christ's role as a judge of the nations in God's stead (cf. Isa. 63.1-6).

In v. 11, the narrator indicates to the reader the theme of this passage by describing the Divine Warrior as one who 'judges and makes war in righteousness.' Judgment (cf. 1.16) and war (cf. 17.14) are not two tasks but two aspects of one task: the vindication of the saints (cf. 6.9-11; 12.17). John prepares the reader for a reinterpretation of God's judgment in Isa. 11.4 in v. 15. This vision also makes connections with the other major christological images, the 'one like a son of man' (cf. 19.12 with 1.14 and 2.18) and the Lamb (cf. 19.16 with 17.14). These connections assure the hearer/reader that the Divine Warrior is identical to the Christ presented by means of these other two images. In order to understand this passage fully, one first must examine the symbolic names given to Christ and then analyze the images and symbols associated with him. The names given to Christ symbolize Christ's complete unity with God Almighty and prepare the reader for Christ's role as judge, the primary role of the Divine Warrior in vv. 11-21, roles traditionally reserved for God Almighty in early Judaism.

2. *The Symbolic Names*

The purpose of the symbolic names in Rev. 19.11-16 is to present the Christ as God Almighty's eschatological judge, a divine agent.

1. The first name is 'Faithful and True' (πιστὸς καὶ ἀληθινός [v. 11]).[11] These, or similar words, occur elsewhere (ὁ μάρτυς, ὁ πιστός [1.5]; ὁ μάρτυς μου ὁ πιστός μου [2.13]; ὁ ἅγιος, ὁ ἀληθινός [3.7]; ὁ μάρτυς ὁ πιστὸς καὶ ἀληθινός [3.14]; cf. 19.9).[12] This name also

11. This passage has several textual variants, none of which alter its meaning significantly. I agree with Metzger that Sinaiticus's reading best explains the others (B.M. Metzger, *A Textual Commentary on the Greek New Testament* [Stuttgart: United Bible Societies, 1975], pp. 760-61).

12. Thompson correctly notes this as a chief feature of Revelation. 'Different

recalls the exhortations to remain faithful (e.g. 2.10; 17.14). However, the most significant occurrences are in 21.5 and 22.6, where God's words and God's apocalypse itself are πιστοὶ καὶ ἀληθινοί.

The similarity between 19.11, on the one hand, and 21.5 and 22.6, on the other, is lost in many translations because 19.11 is most often translated 'Faithful and True'; 21.5 and 22.6, 'trustworthy and true' (e.g. NRSV, NIV, NJB, NAB; cf. GNB [English]; Die Bibel in heutigem Deutsch [German]; La Bible: Ancien et Nouveau Testament [French]; La Bibbia [Italian]; but consistently, NASB [English]; Santa Biblia: Antiguo y Nuevo Testamento [Spanish]).[13] Revelation 19.9, 21.5 and 22.6 would assert God's ability to bring his words and his will into living history. Thus, Christ in his person makes God's will manifest in human history.

The first name unites God Almighty, Christ and the Christian community in two ways. First, the term 'faithful' unites Christ and community. Of its eight occurrences in Revelation, five relate to dying for the faith (1.5b; 2.10, 13; 3.14 [in light of 1.5-6]; 17.14 [in light of 7.14; 14.4]). While those five passages relate to the community and its need for staunch religious fidelity, the remaining three passages assure the community of its reward if it remains steadfast to its religious convictions (19.11; 21.5; 22.6). Secondly, the last three occurrences relate to God Almighty (21.5; 22.6) and to Christ (19.11), who has already shown his faithfulness (1.5-6): because they are faithful and true their promises to the conquerors will be honored. These passages assure the hearers/readers that, if they conquer as Christ conquered, they too shall rule during the millennium and not face judgment (see 20.4-6).[14]

'Αληθινός has a more restricted function in Revelation. It always refers to God or Christ. It describes God's nature (6.10), exemplifies God's actions (15.3; 16.7; 19.2, 9; 21.5; 22.6) and constitutes part of Christ's name (3.7, 14; 19.11). In seven instances, it functions as a synonym to other virtues (6.10, 15.3; 16.7; 19.2, 11; 21.5; 22.6).[15] In this

sections of Revelation are also connected and unified by repeated metaphors, symbols and motifs' (*Revelation*, p. 40).

13. Cf. Farrer, *Revelation*, pp. 196-97.

14. This is a therapeutic maintenance strategy aimed at instilling a renewed spiritual fervor within its recipients in order to withstand oppression ('Symbolic Biblical Language and Sociological Interpretation', Chapter 1, this study; cf. Reddish, 'Martyrdom', pp. 132-60).

15. Ladd argues that πιστος and ἀληθινός would function as synonyms in a

way, John communicates to his readers/hearers that ἀληθινός is a virtue.

Thus, in 19.11, Christ is the divine agency figure who personifies and makes manifest the fidelity and the veracity of God Almighty. Christ comes as a Divine Warrior to judge the unjust and to vindicate the righteous (see 14.13) who have remained steadfast (cf. 1.9).[16] This name might also reflect a social setting in which the Christian witness of faith has been denigrated. By employing this specific name, John might be attempting to assure the Christian community of the veracity of its witness to Christ, Christ's witness to God Almighty as well as God Almighty's salvific loyalty to the faithful.

2. The next name is not revealed (v. 12). An element of hiddenness is a key motif throughout Revelation (e.g. 2.17). This leads us to ask two questions. First, why is the name not revealed? Secondly, what is the name?

Commentators have offered several answers. Some have argued that the name is unrevealed so that no one may have power over God.[17] Others have argued that the unrevealed name symbolized that Christ's nature is unfathomable.[18] Still others have attempted to ascertain the name itself. While some argue that the unrevealed name refers to the tetragrammaton, YHWH, the name Jews believed to be too holy to speak,[19] others say it is 'Jesus',[20] or a symbolic name within Rev. 19.11-16.[21] Finally, Charles argues that the unrevealed name is an interpolation given the symbolic name in v. 13.[22]

Against the first three suggestions, one must wonder why any symbolic names are given at all in vv. 11-16. The three names are indeed revealed. These names also would be rather unusual substitutes for the

purely Jewish context (*Revelation*, p. 253). I agree. See also C.H. Giblin, 'Structural and Thematic Correlations in the Theology of Revelation', *Bib* 55 (1974), pp. 487-504 (497-98 n. 1).

16. Cf. Bauckham, *Theology*, pp. 72-73; Thompson, *Revelation*, pp. 44-45.

17. E.g. Schüssler Fiorenza, *Vision,* p. 105; Kiddle, *Revelation*, p. 385; cf. Lohmeyer, *Offenbarung*, pp. 158-59.

18. E.g. Ladd, *Revelation*, p. 254; Sweet, *Revelation*, p. 283; Morris, *Revelation*, p. 223; Thompson, *Revelation*, p. 44; cf. Lohmeyer, *Offenbarung*, pp. 158-59.

19. E.g. Farrer, *Revelation*, p. 198.

20. E.g. M. Rist, 'The Revelation of St. John the Divine', *IB*, XII, p. 513.

21. E.g. 'King of Kings and Lord of Lords' (H. Lilje, *The Last Book of the Bible* [Philadelphia: Muhlenberg, 1955], p. 244).

22. Charles, *Revelation*, II, p. 132.

tetragrammaton and perhaps be unintelligible to John's readers/hearers. Furthermore, the name in v. 16 constitutes an unnecessary repetition if one argues for 'King of kings and Lord of lords' or either of the other two revealed names as well. Finally, Charles has attributed over 22 interpolations throughout the book to a final editor who was more fluent in Greek than John, but not an orthodox Christian. His criterion for discerning interpolations were (1) passages that did not fit the context and (2) a vocabulary and/or writing style that was inconsistent with John's vocabulary and writing style. However, Bauckham, in agreeing with Charles on the background of Rev. 8.1-5, has shown that Charles could be rather subjective in his analyses even when he might be exegetically correct.[23] The presence of the reference to the unrevealed name in all surviving Greek manuscripts and versions, with witnesses across textual families and with wide geographical distribution, surely argues against Charles's interpolation theory in regard to this verse. While these theories, save the interpolation one, are not unreasonable, each leaves us with significant unanswered questions. It is important to look for parallels within Revelation itself for a consistent pattern associated with the motif of unrevealed things.

The unrevealed name in Revelation functions in a manner similar to the messianic secret motif in Mark. In Mark, the messianic secret explains to the reader why the Chosen One was not recognized by the Chosen People, while the unrevealed names in Revelation explain why the Chosen One and his followers have not been recognized by the world. Thus, in both Mark and Revelation, the authors are at pains to explain why their election is so clear to Christians but opaque to outsiders. Similarly, while the messianic secret is not a complete secret in Mark (e.g. 8.27-29; 14.61-64), neither is the name of the elect a complete secret in Revelation (e.g. 14.1). This is another example of the author providing the hearer/reader with a message of assurance. The hearer/reader is assured that his/her perception of the universe is correct. It is the outsiders, those who do not recognize the Christ, who are incorrect. In their ignorance, they have killed the 'Lord of lords and King of kings'. Instead of leading to Christ's demise, his death has led to his exaltation and the salvation of his followers (e.g. 6.9-11; 7.13-14). Oppression of the saints becomes intelligible in this scenario. Thus,

23. On Charles's interpolation hypothesis, see *Revelation*, I, pp. l-lxi; for Bauckham's critique, see *Climax*, pp. 70-83; *idem*, *Theology*, pp. 40-43. I am persuaded by Bauckham.

Asian Christians are able to decode the will of God while non-Christians cannot.[24] Similarly, since this name is only known by the Divine Warrior himself, it symbolizes the Divine Warrior's distinctive role as God Almighty's eschatological divine agent.

What is the name? It is God's name. Several passages clearly point to this. First, Rev. 14.1 states that the 144,000 on Mt Zion had God's name and the Lamb's name on their foreheads, an additional fact not mentioned in 7.1-8 and which answers the question of the new name raised in 2.17.[25] Secondly, in 2.17 and 14.3 the conquerors are associated with some new data that only they are able to appropriate. In one stroke, the reader perceives her/his distinctiveness and the reason why. Only the elect recognize who Christ is, who sent him and the truth of Christ's witness.[26] Thirdly, as noted earlier, John associates Christ with God Almighty (e.g. 5.13; 7.17; 11.15; 12.10; 14.1; 21.22). Therefore, the name in 14.1 constitutes one name for both. Fourthly, the preceding name, 'Faithful and True', describes the very nature of God (21.5; 22.6) and presents Christ as the authentic, complete manifestation of God. Fifthly, the next name, 'The Word of God' (v. 13), also presents the Christ as the full manifestation of God Almighty. Placed between these two epithets and given the manner in which John consistently depicts God sharing divine honors with Christ, the unrevealed name must be God's name, that is *God shares his name with Christ in such a way that God's name becomes Christ's name.* The unrevealed name would convey to the reader that like Christ, they have received new data (cf. 2.17) only intelligible to those few who are chosen (cf. 17.14). This is an *apologia* and the expected response would be an attitude of steadfast assurance and hopefulness. Finally, as King of kings and Lord of lords, Christ assumes a title held previously by God. Indeed, we shall see that many of the images associated with Christ were not associated with the Messiah in Jewish traditions prior to Revelation, but with God.

3. The next name, mentioned briefly above, is 'The Word of God' (ὁ λόγος τοῦ θεοῦ). Again, this name symbolizes the complete human

24. Cf. P. Minear, *New Testament Apocalyptic* (Nashville: Abingdon Press, 1981), p. 85.

25. See the exegesis of 2.17 in Chapter 4 of this study.

26. For this reason, Christianity might have been perceived by many in the first century CE as another eastern mystery religion.

manifestation of God in Christ. The development of this mode of christological expression owes much to divergent Jewish traditions.[27]

The tradition-history most often employs divine speech as a symbol of divine power and/or as a means of judging evil. For example, Hos. 6.5 reads, 'Therefore I have hewn them in pieces by the prophets; I have slain them by the words of my mouth.' This verse employs two slightly different metaphors that envision speech as a manifestation of God's power.[28] Other passages follow suit (e.g. Ps. 33.6; 147.15, 18; 148.8; Jer. 23.29). However, none of these passages present the Word in human form.

A move toward hypostasis occurs in the wisdom tradition (e.g. Prov. 1.20-22; 8.1-36; Sir. 1.6-20; Wis. 18.15-19), apocalypticism (e.g. *1 En.* 42) and Hellenistic Jewish philosophy (e.g. Philo, *Fug.* 50-51; cf. Jn 1.1-14; 1 Cor. 1.18-25). The closest parallel to Rev. 19.13 is Wis. 18.15-19.[29]

The book of Wisdom is dated in the middle of the first century BCE. In Wis. 18.15-19, Wisdom leaps from heaven to earth 'like a relentless warrior' (v. 15; cf. Rev. 19.11). Wisdom possesses a sharp sword and spreads death everywhere (v. 16; cf. Rev. 19.17-21). Nightmarish phantoms frighten the godless and they fall dead (vv. 17-18). Dream visions in the next age explain their fate (v. 19).

I see four similarities between Wis. 18.15-19 and Rev. 19.11-21. First, both give the Word of God human characteristics. Secondly, both describe the figure with military motifs. Thirdly, both specifically refer to a sword. Fourthly, both relate the downfall of sinners. However, the two passages are not without their differences. While the Word in Wisdom is a hypostasis of God, the Divine Warrior in Revelation is a divine agent. In addition, Revelation's Divine Warrior is the Messiah while Wisdom is not. Furthermore, Wisdom places the metaphor in the

27. Beasley-Murray suggests that it may refer to a cosmic mediator in connection with the logos-type Christology current in early Christianity (*Revelation*, p. 280), but he fails to develop this thesis.

28. The imagery in 19.15 functions similarly and will be discussed momentarily.

29. I am grateful to Professor Adela Collins for bringing this parallel to my attention in private discussion (cf. Lohmeyer, *Offenbarung*, p. 159; Sweet, *Revelation*, pp. 281-84). In other private discussions, Professor Carol Newsom of Emory University, Atlanta, GA, USA, and Dr David Williams of the University of Georgia, Athens, GA, USA, independently have stated that the Qumran sectarian literature has no traces of this or a similar tradition.

leaping of God's word from heaven, but Revelation uses a representative figure in the Divine Warrior.

What do these differences and similarities tell us? Judaism witnessed a variety of concepts of the innate power of God's word. While some writers spoke of heavenly hypostases as extensions of God (e.g. Prov. 8; Philo), others described the Word of God as a manifestation of God's power (e.g. Jer. 23.29; Hos. 6.5). Wisdom 18.15-19 combines these two traditions to some degree. Without explicitly stating that the Word of God became human, or assumed human likeness, it describes the Word as performing human activities. Wis. 18.15-19 therefore, anticipates the vision of Rev. 19.11-21, having several similar elements, with the exception of the messianic features and apocalyptic dimensions. Rev. 19.11-21 therefore modifies the tradition in a Christian manner, a practice identified in many earlier discussions in this study. The image of the Divine Warrior is like divine speech made manifest in human form, faithfully representing God's message to humankind: 'The Word of God' is faithful and true to God.

The Divine Warrior comes not as the convicted criminal but as God's eschatological Judge. Sweet correctly describes this figure as 'the personification of God's will suddenly made lethally present in the disobedient world'.[30] Moreover, the tradition-history behind this imagery does not indicate a social setting where religious waywardness, laxity, accommodation to or compliance with improper religious practices brings a judgment upon the people of God or a context where the people of God live in relative comfort.[31] Rather, the tradition-history suggests that this symbolic name conveys to the original recipients judgment upon their enemies and there is nothing to indicate that John employs it in any other way. This is a maintenance strategy that depicts Christ as God's divine agent who represents the authentic message of God and also comes in God's stead as an eschatological judge. Its purpose would be to convince its original readers that they who remain

30. Sweet, *Revelation*, pp. 282-83, quote from p. 283. Sweet also argues that 'The Word of God' in Rev. 19.13 probably has the prologue of the fourth Gospel in mind (p. 283). This is possible, but, given the many differences between the two books (e.g. ἀρνίον in Revelation, ἀμνός in John for Lamb; apocalyptic eschatology in Revelation, realized eschatology in John), it is probably more likely that they draw from the same tradition discussed in the body of this study.

31. Cf. Thompson, *Revelation*, pp. 186-97.

faithful to Christ's message are faithful to God Almighty and will enter the New Jerusalem.

4. 'King of kings and Lord of lords', our last epithet, is the most important name. Its tradition-history has socio-political implications. Following Beale, I have argued earlier that the probable source for 'King of kings and Lord of lords' is Dan. 4.37 LXX.[32] Both Daniel 4 and Revelation 19 remove the rule of evil kings and depict a universal defeat of God's enemies. In these two contexts and elsewhere (Deut. 10.17; 1 Tim. 6.15; *1 En.* 9.4), this title, or a similar one, denotes the sovereignty of God Almighty over all other powers. Rev. 17.14 and 19.16 are unique in associating it with the Messiah. Again, we note Revelation's Christian modification of a Jewish tradition. In this way, Revelation joins Christology and dominion.[33]

Revelation unites Christology and dominion throughout the book. Christ is the ruler of the kings of the earth and has made his followers a priestly kingdom (1.5-6; 5.10; 20.6). God, Christ and/or Christians rule together forever (11.17; 20.4; 22.5; cf. 12.10; 15.3). God Almighty also reigns alone (11.17; 15.3; 19.6). In this sacred cosmos, God Almighty rules the universe and shares dominion with Christ, who in turn shares it with an elite group of Christians (20.4-6). Once again, one notes a direct link from God to Christ to the Christian community as God Almighty shares power with those who have been the most faithful witnesses. The social impact would be to encourage communal cohesion based upon the promised future salvation (e.g. 2.11).

It is also significant that Revelation associates the title 'King of kings and Lord of lords' with two different christological images, the Lamb (17.14) and the Divine Warrior (19.16). Both passages fall within a context where the supreme King and Lord subdues his foes in battle, consistent with the tradition-history.[34] In both, the Christ wins the victory

32. See Beale, 'Origin', pp. 618-20; T.B. Slater, ' "King of Kings" ', pp. 159-60.

33. The joining of Christology and dominion throughout the book of Revelation, a topic I hope to discuss in more detail in another project, is an argument for its internal unity and one against those who would argue that the numbered series actually derive from a separate Jewish work (e.g. S.A. Edwards). J.M. Ford has recently changed her position and now believes the book is more unified than she had argued previously (SBL seminar 'Reading the Apocalypse: The Intersection of Literary and Social Methods', Philadelphia, PA, USA, 18–22 November 1995).

34. Rev. 17.14 and 19.16 are examples of the messianic military motif in Revelation. See helpful discussions in Bauckham, *Climax*, pp. 210-37; *idem*, *Theology*,

for those who cannot win it for themselves. This is a maintenance strategy exhorting its readers/hearers to stand firm in their faith until the end. This name relates directly to the stated purpose of the Divine Warrior in 19.11 'to judge and make war in righteousness'. The righteousness of the saints must be confirmed and their sacrifice must be avenged (see 6.9-11) in the vision of the next age to sustain them in the reality of the present one (cf. 14.9-13; 16.6; 17.6). Furthermore, the judgment against the beast, the false prophet and their entourage is a righteous judgment (see 19.17-21; cf. 15.3-4). The association of the title with two different christological images (17.14; 19.16) demonstrates the christological unity and consistency within Revelation.

Finally, this symbolic name may contain a political message for its original readers by conveying that Christ, not Caesar, is the true ruler of the world. Both 17.14 and 19.16 employ 'King of kings and Lord of lords' within a military context. Rev. 17.14 relates the defeat of Roman political dominance. It might be intentional that 17.14 follows rather closely the suffering mentioned in 16.6 and 17.6. Similarly, Roman political powers are defeated by the Divine Warrior in 19.17-21 after the name is given in 19.16. The tradition-history of the symbolic name supports this argument.

The discussion of the symbolic christological names in Rev. 19.11-16 concludes here. The first name, 'Faithful and True', communicated to the reader that Christ Jesus has been unswervingly faithful to God Almighty. Rev. 21.5 and 22.6 confirm this. The second name, unrevealed, communicates to the Christian community Christ's distinction and election, a status unnoticed and unacknowledged by the larger society, just as their status has gone unnoticed and unacknowledged by the larger society. Similarly, as only Christ knew the second name, a sign of Christ's exaltation, so too the saints possessed information that only they knew (e.g. 14.3). Thus, even with this name, the Christian community has a point of identification with the Christ. The third name, 'The Word of God', presents Christ as more than a witness but also as *the* full manifestation of the divine plan in human form. The definite article makes it clear that there is only one 'Word of God'. However, this name did not necessarily connote divine agency. It could merely connote hypostasis (e.g. Wis. 18.15-19). Finally, the title 'King of kings

pp. 67-70; A. Yarbro Collins, 'The Political Perspective of the Revelation to John', *JBL* 96 (1977), pp. 241-56.

and Lord of lords' gives Christ the most powerful and authoritative name. It presents Christ as the sovereign Lord of the universe, a role also associated with the one-like-a-son-of-man Christology, the Lamb and also a title usually reserved for God Almighty in earlier traditions. Thus, Christ, the cosmic King and Lord, serves as God's eschatological divine agency figure who is authorized to defeat the forces of evil and vindicate the elect.

The cumulative impact of these names, therapeutic maintenance strategies, upon John's audience/readership would be to convince Christians of the authenticity and fullness of the witness of Jesus to the will of God.[35] As God's full revelation, Jesus' testimony is completely trustworthy (v. 11) and for this reason Jesus is *The Word of God* made manifest. Against those who do not recognize him, Christ comes as a warrior-king who imposes his rule over earthly potentates (19.16). This is a key point, for the crisis pits Christ and his followers against the beast and his followers. That means that these symbolic names are not addressing issues within the church, such as complacency, complicity or accommodation to external religio-political pressures (bona fide issues in their own right), but they are reflections of a tense conflict between two unreconciling groups. For John, the opposing group is probably the Roman government, represented by the provincial governor and supporters of the imperial cult (Rev. 13.1-18). The Christians, the weaker group, seek divine intervention to rectify the situation. This position on the social genesis of this imagery is consistent with the tradition-history of the Divine Warrior image as Lord Sabaoth, one who punishes evil and liberates the oppressed, as well as being consistent with the last two symbolic names. It is also consistent with the hypothesis of the social status of Christians in the Roman Empire c. 60–120 offered in Chapter 1 of this study and the conclusions reached concerning the social role of the other christological images studied earlier in Chapters 4 and 5, respectively, of this study.

Rev. 19.11-16 presents a sacred universe with the Divine Warrior performing functions traditionally performed by God Almighty (cf. Isa. 63.1-6; Wis. 18.15-19) or Michael (cf. Dan. 10.21; Rev. 12.7-12) and acquiring a title previously held only by God Almighty (cf. Deut. 10.17; Dan. 4.37 LXX; *1 En.* 9.4). The Divine Warrior is the Deliverer sent by

35. This point supports our brief discussion of the importance of Christ's witness and the churches' witness to Christ in Chapter 1 of this study.

God who is also Lord in heaven and on earth and, as such, functions on a level with God Almighty. The saints accompany them as co-regents of the cosmos, another example of Revelation's promise of priest-kingship, the uniting of Christ and community. This would be a strong therapeutic strategy, giving its readers assurance of their own salvation, providing vindication for their faith as followers of Christ and promising the political end to the system that represses the Church.

For such believers, these symbolic names, the first three being representational images and the latter one presentational,[36] would present powerful means of therapy and messages of assurance by identifying the Divine Warrior with God Almighty and the saints; by assuring them that the 'one like a son of man', the Lamb and the Divine Warrior are one and the same Messiah; by confirming the Messiah's complete faithfulness and thorough witness to the will of God; and by preparing the reader for the judgment role of the Divine Warrior in vv. 17-21 on behalf of the saints by bestowing symbolic epithets upon him to act in God Almighty's stead.

3. *The Images*

While the symbolic names present Christ as God's human messenger *par excellence* and eschatological judge, the images in 19.11-21 are basically concerned with the judgment of the nations. These images suggest that Christians suffered extensively under regional repression. They also connect the Divine Warrior image to other christological images and themes within the book of Revelation. These images are maintenance strategies employed to retain persons within the sacred cosmos.

1. The first image is in v. 12: 'his eyes (are [like]) a flame of fire [φλὸξ πυρός].'[37] Similar words are found in 1.14 and 2.18 to describe the 'one like a son of man' (cf. Dan. 10.6). In this manner, the reader finds assurance that the figure is the same Christ found in Rev. 1.1–3.22 and 14.14-16, demonstrating once more the christological unity of the book. The fiery eyes connote the purity and powers of perception for

36. See the discussion of myths, images and symbols in Chapter 1 of this study.

37. On the textual variants, see Metzger, *Textual Commentary*, p. 761. In either case, my main point is unchanged.

judgment that Christ possesses.[38] For Christians, Christ's judgment should be more important than any human judgment.

2. The many diadems signify the Christ's royal status. John has used διαδήματα as a royal symbol previously (12.3; 13.1; cf. Diodorus Siculus 4.4.4; Philo, *Fuga* 111; 1 Macc. 11.13; *T. Jud.* 12.4). In Revelation 12 and 13, it inappropriately refers to the Roman emperors. In Rev. 19.12, it refers to the true ruler of the universe, anticipating the title in 19.16. As king, Christ has the right to judge the world. Second Temple Jewish writers used diadem as a symbol for royalty. For these Christians, Christ is the true Lord worthy of reverence and any participation in the imperial cult is unthinkable. This imagery probably reflects deep politio-religious tensions between Christians and those who supported the imperial cult.

3. In v. 13, the rider's robe 'has been dipped (or soaked, or dyed [with the REB]) in blood'. Is this the rider's blood, the saints' or his opponents'? Commentators have not reached anything near a consensus. However, most commentators accept that Isa. 63.1-6 is the background for this image.

In Isa. 63.1-6, God Almighty comes from the east in crimson apparel, robed in splendor and marching forth in majesty.[39] He has trodden the winepress and made his garment red. Trampling the winepress symbolized punishing the nations in Isaiah; the red stains, their blood. This is an act of judgment upon them which, in turn, saves Israel. However, Revelation often reinterprets traditions and it is always prudent to look internally for clues when interpreting this book.

The interpretation of Rev. 19.13a is further complicated by its textual variants. Is the robe βεβαμμένον, ἐρραντισμένον, ῥεραντισμένον, ἐρραμμένον, ῥεραμμένον, περιρεραμμένον or περιρεραντισμένον? βεβαμμένον is almost certainly the original reading. Its various meanings give it an ambiguity that might have caused some scribes to substitute a more definitive term. It also has broad geographical manuscript support.[40]

38. Cf. Ladd, *Revelation*, p. 254; Sweet, *Revelation*, p. 282; Morris, *Revelation*, p. 223.

39. See also Ezek. 40.5-16, where God returns from the east to the new, purified Temple.

40. See BAGD, pp. 132-33, 650, 733, 734; Metzger, *Textual Commentary*, pp. 761-62; see also Charles, *Revelation*, II, pp. 133-34; Mounce, *Revelation*, p. 345, esp. n. 26; cf. Swete, *Apocalypse*, p. 252, on the possible Septuagintal influences.

However, the issue does not end with reconstructing the text. One must now translate βεβαμμένον. Translation relates directly to interpretation. Many argue that the blood belongs to the warrior's enemies, as in Isaiah 63. For those who hold this position, Christ comes as God's eschatological agent of justice to execute judgment against the Parthians or against satanic earthly institutions; when John wishes to convey Christ's death, he refers to the slain Lamb.[41]

Caird represents another school of thought that argues that the saints' blood stains the robe. For example, he reads 19.13 in light of 14.18-20, where he interprets the vintage imagery as a reference to martyrdom and the gathering of the elect. 'The Rider bears on his garment the indelible traces of the death of his followers, just as he bears on his body the indelible marks of his own passion.' He continues, 'His blood has made their robes white, and theirs has made his red.'[42]

Others take a third position that the blood belongs to Christ. For example, Wall argues that John reverses the imagery of Isa. 63.1-6. He follows the patristic commentators who interpreted this image in light of 5.5-6, which represents the crucifixion.[43]

The first interpretation, that it is the blood of Christ's enemies, seems to me to be the most plausible one. The vision itself tells us in v. 11 that Christ comes to 'judge and make war in righteousness'. In keeping with that thematic statement, it makes most sense that 'the robe dipped in blood' symbolizes the blood of the opponents of Christ to be shed in vv. 15, 17-21. Some might counter that according to this interpretation their blood would appear on Christ's garments before the fact and, therefore, my interpretation must be incorrect. I would respond that John is employing a symbolic image, not literal language, and that one should not expect precision and order in a book that repeats its message several times and reinterprets religious symbols. Indeed, when Christ walks the winepress of God's wrath in v. 15, this symbolizes the defeat of God's

41. E.g. Charles, *Revelation*, II, p. 133; Swete, *Apocalypse*, p. 252; Prigent, *L'Apocalypse*, pp. 294-95; Giblin, *Revelation*, p. 181; Beasley-Murray, *Revelation*, p. 280, esp. n. 26; Lohmeyer, *Offenbarung*, p. 159; Kiddle, *Revelation*, pp. 384-85; Hughes, *Revelation*, p. 204. For a critique of this position, see Caird, *Revelation*, pp. 242-44.

42. Caird, *Revelation*, pp. 243-44; see also Krodel, *Revelation*, p. 323.

43. Wall, *Revelation*, p. 231; see also Farrer, *Revelation*, p. 197; Sweet, *Revelation*, p. 282; Morris, *Revelation*, p. 224; Boring, *Revelation*, pp. 196-97.

enemies, which will not occur until vv. 17-21.[44] Finally, the invitation to the birds (vv. 17-18) precedes the actual meal (v. 21b). I note with others the need to recognize the fluid nature of apocalyptic language.[45] Revelation 8.7-8, 11.6, 14.20, 16.6 and 17.6 provide examples of blood associated with the punishment of God's opponents because of their oppression of Christians. This eschatological vision of judgment upon their foes reverses the Christian experience in earthly courts, probably reflecting a tense conflict between Christians and non-Christians without any signs of reconciliation. Moreover, this imagery is associated with the symbolic name 'The Word of God', a phrase that our comments above demonstrated had a judgment tradition-history. Nothing in the passage suggests that John employs it in any other manner. It connotes Christian suffering and a desire to end that suffering.

4. Christ and the heavenly army accompanying him all sit on white horses and the heavenly army wears pure, white, fine linen clothing (vv. 11, 14). This is a beautiful image; it has several parallels in Revelation. It symbolizes purity.[46]

As I noted in discussing Rev. 19.7-9 in the preceding chapter of this study, bright, radiant linen clothing symbolized purity and was worn most often by heavenly beings or the high priest on Yom Kippur in the Hebrew Bible and Second Temple Jewish literature (e.g. Lev. 16.4; Ezek. 9.2-3, 11; 10.1-8; Dan. 10.5-6, 12.3-7; *1 En.* 62.15-16; 104.2; *2 Bar.* 51.5, 12; Philo, *Vit. Mos.* 2.17; Josephus, *War* 5.230-37). Thus, 19.14 presents righteous soldiers fully prepared for battle (cf. 14.1-5). These images, associated with the name 'The Word of God' with its judgmental, militaristic tradition-history, reflect a social circumstance where the elect Christian community seeks liberation from a political system that has suppressed its 'word' and denigrated its witness. The Christian community sees itself as an elect, holy community accompanying its Lord on a holy war against the enemies of the faith, the beast and his followers. This is an example of how Revelation's apocalyptic visions address the relationship between the Asian Christian community and its oppressors in the greater society by transferring the resolution to the the cosmic plane.

44. I am grateful to Richard Garside, a fellow New Testament postgraduate at King's College London, for bringing this to my attention.

45. E.g. Rissi, *Time and History*, pp. 55-62; Ladd, *Revelation*, pp. 254-55; Sweet in private conversation.

46. E.g. Seiss, *Apocalypse*, p. 240; Thompson, *Revelation*, pp. 78-79.

5. The next image in 19.15a is not what one might expect to follow. Instead of an account of the battle between the Divine Warrior and his followers, on one side, and the forces of evil,[47] on the other, the Divine Warrior defeats the nations 'with the sharp sword coming from his mouth' (19.15; cf. 1.16; 2.12, 16; see also Isa. 49.2; Hos. 6.5; Eph. 6.17; 2 Thess. 2.8; Heb. 4.12; *1 En.* 62.2). This is an example of Revelation's messianic military motif.[48] This sword imagery links the christological Divine Warrior image with the 'one like a son of man image' in 1.16, 2.12 and 2.16. The image changes but the result is the same: the nations have been judged, found wanting and punished.[49]

John employs this image consistent with tradition. In Isa. 49.2, the prophet uses the image of his mouth as a sharp sword to convey that his prophetic ministry divides fact from falsehood, good from evil. Similarly, Hos. 6.5 describes Israel's punishment as cutting them into pieces by the prophets who function as God's spokespersons (cf. Eph. 6.17; 2 Thess. 2.8; Heb. 4.12). This motif attempts to assure the original readers of the condemnation of their opponents, while conversely guaranteeing their salvation as faithful followers of the Judge. Moreover, associated with 'The Word of God', with its judgmental, militaristic elements, the image and the name together strongly suggest a *Sitz im Leben* where Christians suffered because of their witness and sought relief from their oppression. The imagery is rather intense for a minor disagreement.

6. The iron rod (v. 15b) continues the judgment theme: 'and he will lead [ποιμανεῖ] them with an iron rod'. This image has parallels with the 'one like a son of man' in 2.27 and Christ's birth recorded in 12.5, establishing a link with other christological images in the book. Again, Revelation is consistent with Jewish tradition. Ps. 2.9 reads, 'You shall break (or lead) them with an iron rod and you shall shatter them like earthenware' (translation mine). Ps. 2.9 LXX reads, 'You shall shepherd (or 'lead' [ποιμανεῖ]) them with an iron rod; you shall shatter them to pieces like earthen vessels.' Isa. 11.4b reads, 'And he will strike the earth with the rod of his mouth and with the breath of his lips he will slay the wicked.' *Ps. Sol.* 17.24, written near the middle of the first

47. Seiss has an interesting argument that explains how these evil forces came together (*Apocalypse*, pp. 252-53).

48. On this topic, see Bauckham, *Climax*, pp. 210-37; *Theology*, pp. 67-70, 76-80, 88-92.

49. Cf. Lohmeyer, *Offenbarung*, p. 159.

century BCE, interpreted Ps. 2.9 messianically[50] and reads, 'To shatter all their material possessions with an iron rod, to destroy the lawless nations with the word of his mouth.' Ps. 2.9 LXX and *Psalms of Solomon* 17 depict the Messiah ruling and judging the evil nations of the earth. At the very least, Isa. 11.4 understands God to judge the world for its evil deeds, also.

These passages share several common features. First, all present the Messiah as a righteous judge, imposing a punishing verdict upon the nations. Further, all employ the rod as the symbol of judgment. Moreover, two passages employ ποιμαίνω to describe the Messiah's leadership (Ps. 2.9 LXX; Rev. 19.15b), while two others employ the Messiah's mouth as a symbol of punishment (Isa. 11.4b; *Ps. Sol.* 17.24; cf. Rev. 19.15a). Finally, *Ps. Sol.* 17.24 and Rev 19.15 have the most similarities. Both state that the Messiah (1) will punish the nations and (2) will employ an iron rod. The overall similarities among these four works indicate a common Second Temple messianic tradition based upon Ps. 2.9. Within this tradition, the Messiah judges the nations. The reader must be acquainted with this tradition-history and be able to apply its meaning to her/his own context. This image is a therapeutic maintenance technique that presents the eschatological judgment of the nations as a means of vindicating the saints in order to bolster the religious fervor of the Christian community.[51] Conversely, Christian wavering, assimilation or some other form of religious breakdown do not appear to be primary issues here. A comparison with Rev. 2.27 confirms this argument.

Both 2.27 and 19.15 give authority to rule the evil nations. In 2.27, Christ shares this authority with the conquerors. In 19.15, God Almighty shares it with Christ, the Divine Warrior. God, Christ and the conquerors stand on one side of the cosmic battlefield; Satan and his minions, on the other.

7. The third image in 19.15c, treading the winepress (πατεῖ τὴν ληνὸν τοῦ οἴνου τοῦ θυμοῦ τῆς ὀργῆς τοῦ θεοῦ) also connotes judgment. Again, John employs an image consistent with its traditional use. In Isa. 63.3-6, God treads the winepress in anger as a symbolic act to punish the nations (cf. Isa. 28.3; Mic. 7.10). Isa. 63.3-6 LXX also use θυμός (vv. 3, 5) and ὀργή (v. 6) to convey God's judgment against the nations. Moreover, Rev. 6.14, 14.10 and 14.19 use similar expressions to

50. See Charles, *Revelation*, I, pp. 75-76.

51. For a different interpretation, see Mounce, *Revelation*, p. 347 n. 30.

describe God's anger with the sinful nations and God's punishment of them.[52] The same is true of the parallel passage in 19.15. All three refer to God's wrath as a symbol for punishing evil.

Rev. 19.15 employs three separate images for the purpose of stating that Christ will judge the nations, each reinforcing the other two and also reiterating the superscription in 19.11: 'to judge and make war in righteousness'. There is no evidence that these images deal with internal matters but, rather, with the plight of the church in Roman Asia. Finally, 19.15 might be another version of 14.17-20.

8. The next image, Rev. 19.17-18, contains the second of the three visions in this section and has its origins in Ezek. 39.4, 17-20 (cf. Ezek. 29.5; Isa. 56.9; Jer. 12.9, 46.10, 51.40; Hag. 2.22). Once again, Revelation employs an image in keeping with tradition. In prophecies against Gog, Ezek. 39.4 and 39.17 describe how those vanquished by God in battle would become food for wild animals. In Revelation, the Messiah replaces God as the Divine Warrior. Both Ezekiel and Revelation begin with a summons to eat (Ezek. 39.17; Rev. 19.17), followed by itemizations of those vanquished. Both lists include horses and horsemen (Ezek. 39.20; Rev. 19.18). There are some differences as well. While Ezekiel 39 confines its description to those of the higher socio-economic-political stratum, Rev. 19.18 includes free and slave, small and great in its indictment.[53] In brief, this vision communicated to its original audience the thoroughness of this punishment. No one will go unexamined. Favoritism will not be extended to anyone. Now the stage is set for the final image, the defeat of the unrighteous (cf. *2 Bar.* 39.7–40.4; 72.2-6; *4 Ezra* 12.31-33; 13.37-38).

9. The last two images, the feast for the birds and the lake of fire, will be discussed together because both connote the ultimate punishment of evil. They also comprise the final of the three visions in 19.11-21. First, the beast and his army assemble to make war against Christ and his army (v. 19). John does not narrate the battle. He simply states that the beast and the false prophet were seized and thrown alive into the lake of fire (v. 20), the ultimate punishment (see 20.11-14; 21.8; cf. 14.10; cf. Dan. 7.11; *Mart. Isa.* 4.14). 'The lake of fire combines the elements of punishment by fire and confinement of a rebellious foe.'[54] The sword

52. See my comments on 14.14-16 in Chapter 4 of this study.

53. Some commentators fail to note these differences (e.g. Ladd, *Revelation*, p. 257), but others do (e.g. Sweet, *Revelation*, p. 285).

54. Yarbro Collins, *Apocalypse*, p. 137.

from the Messiah's mouth kills the beast's army (v. 21a). The birds eat until they become full (v. 21b). The vindication of the saints is complete. Those who punished the saints have met their reward. Rev. 19.19-21 fulfils the expressed theme stated in v. 11 for the Messiah to judge and make war in righteousness, that is, the punishment inflicted upon the beast and his followers is just and right. Additionally, many across the hermeneutical, theological and denominational spectrum note the contrast of the marriage supper for the saved (19.7-9) and the feast for the birds.[55]

These images do not indicate judgment upon members of the Christian community, or address an internal crisis, but address the role of the Church in first-century CE Roman society. The Divine Warrior and his followers are pitted against the beast and his followers. The followers of the beast include the false prophet, kings, generals, mighty men, free men and slaves, *but no wayward Christians.* The list in 2.20-24 provides a helpful contrast. It lists (1) Jezebel, (2) her followers (her children), and (3) her sympathizers (those who commit adultery with her) and then distinguishes them from 'the rest of you in Thyatira who do not hold to [Jezebel's] teachings and have not learned Satan's deep secrets.' Therefore, 2.20-24 clearly demonstrates that John could distinguish among groups in regard to degrees of culpability. Rev. 19.11-21 does not make such distinctions, but judges the world. This passage supports my earlier argument that the letters are primarily concerned with the internal life of the churches where issues of religious laxity were relevant; the apocalyptic visions, however, describe the role of the Church in the greater Roman society, where the suffering and suppression of Christians was a central concern.

4. *Summation: Observations on Christ and Community*

a. *The Theme and its Communal Dimensions*

My analysis of Rev. 19.11-21 has shown that v. 11 contains the theme for these three visions: to judge and make war in righteousness. Both the symbolic names given to the Divine Warrior and the images and symbols associated with him confirm this thesis. The symbolic names connote Christ's right to judge the evil nations and to execute punish-

55. E.g. Sweet, *Revelation*, pp. 285-86; Lohmeyer, *Offenbarung*, pp. 160-61; Giblin, *Revelation*, p. 182; Yarbro Collins, *Apocalypse*, p. 136; Ladd, *Revelation*, p. 257; Morris, *Revelation*, p. 226; Kiddle, *Revelation*, p. 387.

ment by war in God's stead, while the images generally connote the execution of judgment. In addition, the names, with ever-increasing significance, present Christ as the complete, true representative of God in human history and the executor of divine judgment in God's stead. Finally, the study has shown the consistency of functions among all three major christological images in Revelation. Let us turn now to a more detailed exegetical summary of the different emphases set out for the original recipients.

b. *The Message of the Symbolic Names for the Community*

The names of Christ in Rev. 19.11-21 present him as the true, complete manifestation of God Almighty in human history and attest to Christ's sovereignty over human institutions. The first name, 'Faithful and True', may reflect a context where the veracity of the Christian message and the fidelity of Christians to that message has been challenged and come under fire, a setting where the basic Christian beliefs and practices have not been acknowledged but attacked viciously by non-Christians. Jews would criticize the Christians for bestowing divine honors upon Jesus; adherents of Greco-Roman religious traditions would criticize Christians for their unwillingness to participate in traditional Greco-Roman cultic practices (cf. 2.13; 6.9-11; 12.11; 16.6; 17.6; 19.10). The first name attempts to authenticate Christ's role as God's Messiah, substantiate Christ's witness to God and validate the Christian community's confession of faith. In the face of local oppression, Christians can remain firm in their beliefs because their lord is 'Faithful and True.' Again we note the possibility that the Christian confession and the importance of witnessing might have been a contributing factor leading to religious tensions. While 'faithful and true' occurs three times in Revelation (see 21.5; 22.6), only in 19.11 is it a proper name, supporting the argument that Rev. 19.11-21 constitutes the christological high point of the book.[56]

The second name, which is not revealed, plays an important intracommunal role. As a mystery, it explains the lack of acceptance by Roman authorities in particular and Roman society in general. Although this motif might come from the mystery religions, it is noteworthy that Christ *does* receive names in Revelation (e.g. 5.6; 11.15; 17.14). Thus,

56. Sweet, *Revelation*, p. 281; Yarbro Collins, *Crisis*, p. 130; *idem*, *Combat*, pp. 130-45; Reddish, 'Martyrdom', pp. 217-20.

although the motif might have originated within the mysteries, it functions quite differently in Revelation: the unrevealed element in Revelation functions as an internal motif to convey to the Christian community at once its election and its temporal circumstances. Election provides Christians with special information that only they possess, as in many mystery religions. However, unlike the mysteries, the hidden element is not withheld consistently in Revelation (see 3.12; 14.1). The unrevealed name is an example of how the Christian community has access to information that the world does not. Similarly, Christ has a relationship with God Almighty which others cannot have. Such a motif would have done much to enhance the self-esteem and commitment of its original readers by relating them in a limited way to Christ in that both he and they possessed information not available to everyone. The unrevealed name symbolizes Christ's unique role in the sacred cosmos as God's co-regent. This is a strategy employed to maintain order in the community by conveying to the readers the distinctive role that Christ plays in the symbolic universe, and it attempts to convince the readers that their loyalty to Christ is the proper religious response.

The third name, 'The Word of God', would reinforce for the original audience the first two names, yet move beyond them by asserting that Christ was in complete harmony and unity with God Almighty. The context of 19.13, a messianic military campaign, indicates an intense and fierce situation where Christian confession was a central issue. Over against these social pressures, Christians must continue to confess and profess faith in Christ, according to Revelation. It is Christ who makes manifest the will of God and makes it clear to humanity. Moreover, while 'the word of God' occurs five times in Revelation, only in 19.13 (as with the first name in v. 11) is it a proper name, supporting the argument that 19.11-21 constitutes the most developed christological passage in Revelation. This name and the imagery associated with it all have tradition-histories that connote judgment, suggesting that the original audience had experienced intensely negative relations, at the least. The intensity of the imagery suggests that the Christians suffered extensively and severely at the hands of non-Christians.

'King of kings and Lord of lords', the final name, occurs twice in Revelation (17.14; 19.16). In both passages, it functions as a title, one previously reserved for God in Jewish tradition. Both passages celebrate the messiah's sovereignty and victory over worldly institutions. The final name probably also reflects a social context where the confession of Christ as Savior of the world has been severely ridiculed and belittled. This ridicule has not discouraged some Christians but made them more adamant in their position. 'King of kings and Lord of lords' is probably a Christian reassertion of their claims against the religio-political claims of adherents to the imperial cult. In both 17.14 and 19.16, this name is a central element in the destruction of the political system that 'makes war' against the elect. Revelation 13, 17 and 18 tell us that the Roman Empire and its regional leaders are those worldly institutions for the book of Revelation.

While the first three names bolstered the resolve of the Christian community, the last name assures the community that its Lord rules the universe and its oppressors will receive a just punishment. Such enmity usually does not derive from differences among abstract theorists. It comes from world-views that are perceived by their respective adherents to be mutually exclusive. In such contexts, often the oppressed see military intervention as their only hope. The Christian desire for a military solution probably connotes the extent of the suffering by the Christian community, the depth of the need envisioned to rectify the situation, the degree of enmity that had developed between the groups and the Christian resignation that only divine intervention could alleviate their suffering. Regional tensions between Christians and Jews and/ or Christians and supporters of Greco-Roman religious traditions, as readings in the New Testament, Tacitus and Pliny attest, could result in such enmity and suffering by Christians.[57]

The appeal for a divine military intervention in 19.11-16 shows no evidence of a lack of Christian religious fervor or cognitive misapprehension, but Christian fidelity which has met with regional religio-political opposition. The envisioned resolution pits the Divine Warrior and his followers against the beast and his followers, indicating a conflict between Christians and non-Christians. John views this regional situation on a global scale, probably because Rome was the ruling international power at the time and also because Roman governors had the power to carry out capital punishment, as Pliny's letter to Trajan clearly demonstrates (*Letter* 10).[58]

57. E.g. Acts 21.27-28; 1 Pet. 4.12-19; Tacitus, *Annals* 15.44; Pliny, *Letter* 10.95-97.

58. Sweet holds a similar position (*Revelation*, pp. 22-27).

An examination of the images and symbols associated with the Divine Warrior confirms the conclusions concerning the names: every image either symbolizes the Divine Warrior's prerogative to act on behalf of the Christian community as a judge, or conveys to the reader the manner of his judgment upon his opponents. Finally, these symbolic names function as maintenance techniques to exhort Christians to remain in the Christian symbolic universe.

c. *The Message of the Images for the Community*

The images in Rev. 19.11-21 function in two ways. They convey the Divine Warrior as an eschatological judge and present the mode in which he executes judgment.

The fiery eyes (v. 12), the diadem (v. 12) and the significance of the color white (vv. 11, 14) all point to the Messiah's competence and legal right to judge humankind. The fiery eyes symbolize Christ's role as God's agent with superhuman perception; the diadem, regal authority; the color white, moral purity. In every way, John sees in the rider a being beyond reproach who by nature is worthy both to judge the nations and to execute judgment upon them. Thus, one should not be surprised to find several images of judgment within Rev. 19.11-21. These negative judgments might also constitute a mythological response to the abuse suffered by Christians in the Roman legal system.

John envisions a Divine Warrior who will come and put things aright. One purpose of these visions might be to set matters in their proper order, from the Christian perspective. The blood on the rider's robe (v. 13), the sword (vv. 15, 21), the iron rod (v. 15), the winepress (v. 15), the defeat and punishment of the beast, the false prophet and their minions (vv. 19-20) and the feast of the birds (vv. 17-18, 21) all depict horrific judgments without any reservations or considerations for mercy. These visions strongly suggest a social context where Christians have suffered and continue to suffer mercilessly without moral justification or cause. While complacency, apathy and accommodation were issues for Revelation, as the letters demonstrate, the apocalyptic visions reflect the religio-political pressures upon Asian Christians to change their views in order be more like those of the general society.[59] Other persons in Roman society felt unjustly oppressed and took military

59. Cf. Berger and Luckmann, *Social Construction*, pp. 121-34; Price, *Rituals*, pp. 197-98.

action themselves in order to redress social ills (e.g. Spartacus, the Jewish War of 66–70 CE). However, Revelation differs in projecting the conflict onto a cosmic level where the Roman Empire symbolizes all that is evil and heavenly powers must subdue this evil empire (e.g. 12.7-12; 14.14-20; 18.2-24; 20.11-15). In Revelation's world-view, God Almighty will soon judge the unrighteous and execute punishment through Christ acting as his eschatological judge.

Revelation might be criticized for espousing a 'pie-in-the-sky' eschatology with little concern for improving living conditions in this world. Such a simplistic analysis misses the point by not recognizing the dynamism of adhering to 'the word of God and the witness of Jesus' for John and his readers/hearers. First of all, a 'pie-in-the-sky' eschatology would allow injustice to continue and meekly wait indefinitely without comment until the intervention of God. Such is not the case in Revelation. Rev. 18.1-24, for example, is a severe commentary on the social injustices of John's day and time, and reminds one of the preaching of such prophets as Amos, Micah, Isaiah, Hosea and Jeremiah and also modern liberation theologians, such as Gutierrez, Cone, Ruether, Boesak, Soares-Prabhu, Segundo and Ateek, to name a few. Furthermore, John does not expect God to allow the suffering to continue indefinitely (1.1; 22.10, 12, 20). Thus, John emphasizes how Christians should behave in the brief interim:

> Let the one doing wrong still do wrong and let the one who is impure remain impure and let the one doing righteousness remain righteous and let the one being holy remain holy. Be watchful, I am coming soon and my reward (is) with me to give to each person according to his deeds (Rev. 22.11-12).

This is not a missionary statement but an exhortation to a beleaguered community to stand firmly in its religious convictions until the coming judgment (20.11-15). Finally, against a charge of docility, the perseverance which Revelation expects and demands of its readers/hearers requires a great deal of courage and inner strength. John calls his readers/hearers to a religious civil disobedience that offers no hope of an earthly reward. Living in such a way would have been difficult for the best of Christians. In our own century, Gandhi and King have demonstrated that civil disobedience can be a powerful tool in re-structuring an unjust society. They also recognized that such a stance took enormous courage. Indeed, both men lost their lives because of their devotion to their respective social agendas. The Revelation to John stands as a biblical witness for the place of civil disobedience against an unjust and oppressive state and it also reminds us of the cost of human life that civil disobedience can engender.

Against this background of the repression of the Christian community, the firm reassertion of the authenticity of the proclamation of Jesus and the truth of the Christian witness of faith concerning him become understandable and the cosmology of Revelation becomes clear. Christ Jesus is for John's hearers/readers one who is the full manifestation of God Almighty. The preceding two chapters of this study have come to this same conclusion. This is not new. What is new in Rev. 19.11-21 is the manner in which this finds expression in the Divine Warrior who comes as the eschatological judge. As with the 'one like a son of man' and the Lamb christological images, Christ takes on roles previously reserved for God Almighty. For example, he leads a heavenly host and treads the winepress in wrath (cf. Isa. 63.1-6). He is the sovereign Lord and King of the universe (19.16; cf. Dan. 4.37 LXX; Deut. 10.17; *1 En.* 9.4; 1 Tim. 6.15). The Christ is God's Anointed One who reigns over the cosmos with God Almighty. God and Christ are joined by the saints as rulers of the cosmos, the priest-kings. Although the cavalry does nothing to defeat the forces of evil, they have the honor of accompanying Christ the Conqueror on this important campaign. Undoubtedly, we should identify the cavalry with the group described in 6.9, 7.14, 14.1 and 20.4: Those who have given the most in this age, that is, their lives, will receive the most honors and privileges in the next, accompanying God and Christ wherever they may go (cf. Rev. 14.4; 22.3-4).

Chapter 7

CONCLUSIONS

In examining the three principal christological images of the book of Revelation (the 'one like a son of man', the Lamb and the Divine Warrior), this study has attempted to discern how Christ functioned as the leader of these communities, why certain christological images were important and how the images functioned in the religious life of those communities c. 95 CE.

This study has reached five general conclusions concerning these images. First and foremost, these images communicated to John's original audience that Christ Jesus was the Lord of the cosmos with whom God Almighty shared divine honors (cf. 1.8 and 1.17-18; 4.11 and 5.9-10, 12-14; 7.16-17 and 21.3-4; 19.11 and 21.5). For example, both are the beginning and the end of all things (1.8; 22.13). Both receive worship and praise (4.11; 5.9-10). Both comfort the distressed (7.16-17; 21.3-4). Additionally, Christ receives the title 'King of Kings, Lord of Lords' (17.14; 19.16) and takes on the role of the Divine Warrior (19.11-21), both of which were formerly associated with God Almighty. In almost every instance, Christ participates in divine honors and activities that previously were the sole preserve of God Almighty alone in Jewish tradition (cf. Deut. 10.17; Isa. 44.6; Dan. 4.37 LXX; *1 En.* 9.4). Throughout the visions, John stresses Christ's faithful witness to God Almighty and thus validates his worthiness to participate in divine honors.

Secondly, the slain Lamb is the most pervasive christological image in Revelation, a fact suggesting that the book comes from a social context in which Christians suffered extensively. This image derives from many different strands of Judaism: from apocalypticism came the concept of a warrior lamb; from Exodus, the sacrificial lamb, which was applied to the crucifixion. This last motif also supplied the victory-through-suffering motif that is central to both the 'one like a son of man' imagery and the Lamb imagery. This imagery provided a means for Asian Christians to understand their situation, and at the same time provided a model to emulate in order to conquer evil. Moreover, the use of the Lamb imagery explains the military imagery and rather vengeful tone of parts of Revelation as natural reactions by persons under great duress.

Thirdly, Christ performs three pastoral functions: he judges both Christians and non-Christians, gathers an elect eschatological community, and makes war with God's enemies. These are community-oriented functions with the purpose of protecting, correcting and vindicating these communities. The pastoral dimension of Revelation has often been overlooked. In this light, Jesus has a close relationship with these churches, as evidenced by his walking among the seven lampstands (1.10-20). As pastor, Jesus counsels in order that his members are able to enter the New Jerusalem as an elect fellowship (Rev. 2.1–3.22; 17.14; 20.1-4). As God Almighty's eschatological divine agent, he threatens the wayward (e.g. 3.5) and punishes those who have oppressed the Christian community (17.14; 19.11-21). The latter are acts on behalf of the Christian community to vindicate and validate its witness of faith and also to bolster the community's faith during times of disress. As pastor, Christ creates and leads an eschatological exodus community into the New Jerusalem (1.5-6; 5.9-10; 7.14-17; 12.10-11; 14.1-5; 19.6-9, 11-16; 20.4-6; 22.1-6).

Fourthly, a victory-through-suffering motif is associated with the first two images (1.5-6; 5.9-10) and possibly the third (19.13). This motif, associated with at least two of the three major christological images, strongly suggests that the Christian community has suffered for its religious beliefs and that John turns their affliction into their means of salvation. It is difficult to discern a rationale for using this motif if Christians experienced little or no duress. Moreover, Revelation was not the only early Christian writing to make this rationalization (e.g. Phil. 1.12-14; Jas 1.2-3; 1 Pet. 1.6-7). If Sherwin-White is correct that each Roman provincial governor had some freedom in dealing with Christians, it is highly probable that Christians in Asia at the time when Revelation was written lived under a regime that was not lenient toward them.

Some scholars have argued that the letters say little about a state-sponsored persecution of Christians and have thus concluded that Revelation depicts a crisis that never existed. Rather, they have argued, various forms of religious laxity were the problems John faced. Our exegeses have shown that religious laxity was indeed a problem, but it developed as a response to local pressures upon Christians to conform to and to live more moderately with regard to local pagan traditions. There were also Jewish pressures upon Christians as well for bestowing divine honors upon Jesus (2.9; 3.9). It should be noted that the letters in general address internal problems (e.g. accommodation, complacency), but the apocalyptic visions address the suppression of Christians in Roman Asia (e.g. 6.9-11; 7.13-14, 16; 12.11; 16.6; 17.6; 20.4). These two factors are not mutually exclusive but logically relate to one another. In Roman Asia, social pressures caused some Christians to become less exclusive and to take a more liberal attitude toward Asian politico-religious practices and beliefs. To say the least, John is a non-conformist.

Finally, the 'one like a son of man' and the Lamb images are more pastoral in nature than the Divine Warrior, and both promise the faithful an unbroken fellowship as priest-kings, an exodus motif, with God and Christ in the New Jerusalem (e.g. 1.5-6; 2.26-28; 5.9-10; 7.14-17; 14.1-4; 22.1-5). The reference in 19.14 to the heavenly army may be another version of this theme. On the other hand, the Divine Warrior functions primarily as an eschatological judge in God's stead to punish evil and vindicate the righteous, imagery that indicates that some Christians have experienced some type of repression and are vengefully seeking divine retribution upon their oppressors. All three images are concerned with the quality of life within the Christian community: the first two express this concern through Christ's pastoral roles; the third, by demonstrating the propriety of the community's witness to Christ. Within this context, seeking revenge and public humiliation of their oppressors is understandable (6.9-11; 14.10). Though it may not be what one expects, traditions in other apocalyptic works tell us that such requests for vindication is a natural consequence.[1]

1. The problem here is not that Jesus' love-ethic is not in force. Indeed, Jesus was not a complete pacifist (Mt. 21.12-13; 23.1-39). Rather, the problem is that the oppressed often become either insensitive or oppressive when their voices are given credence. For example, womanist theologians are African-American female academicians who often criticize African-American male liberation theologians for their sexist language and white feminists who, while espousing the need for inclusive language, employ 'black' as a negative term.

A historical-critical study of both Christian and Greco-Roman writings concluded that there was no empire-wide Roman persecution of Christians and that John's depiction of such a crisis was a prophetic perception based upon the experience of some Asian Christians. Both Christian and Greco-Roman writers of the same era when Revelation was written describe the repression of Christians. Some Christians suffered simply because of the name 'Christian'. For example, Mt. 24.9 reads, 'Then they will deliver you up to tribulation, and will kill you and you will be hated by all the nations because of my name.' One finds similar passages in Mt. 10.17-23, Jn 15.21, 1 Pet. 4.14, to name but a few early Christian writings. Roman writers provide similar comments, albeit from another perspective. Tacitus writes,

> Christus, the founder of the name [*nominis*], had undergone the death penalty in the reign of Tiberius ... and the pernicious superstition was checked ... only to break out once more, not merely in Judaea, the home of the disease, but in the capital itself (*Annals* 15.44).

Some of his contemporaries viewed Christians similarly (e.g. Pliny, *Letter* 10.96-97; Suetonius, *Nero* 16.2). Furthermore, some Jewish groups also oppressed Christians. Jews saw the Christian confession of Jesus as one worthy of divine honors as theologically inappropriate and had few scruples in seeing to it that Christians suffered: 'They [Jews] will make you outcasts from the synagogue, but an hour is coming for everyone who kills you to think that he is offering service to God' (Jn 16.2). Paul speaks as though Jewish repression of Christians was widespread (Gal. 1.13-14; see also Phil. 3.5-6; Jn 9.18-22; Acts 7.57–8.3). Indeed, Revelation depicts the repression of Christians by both Greco-Roman (e.g. Rev. 13.1-18) and Jewish groups (2.9; 3.9).

More specifically, Asian religio-political sensibilities would have been upset by the Christians' refusal to participate in Greco-Roman religious customs, especially the imperial cult. Price skillfully demonstrates that the imperial cult was deeply imbedded into Roman Asian society and that it provided a way for Asians to relate meaningfully to Roman authority. He states that Asian society would have pressured Christians to conform to their traditions, lest the gods become angry with those who repudiated them and some calamity befall society-in-general. Several recent scholars have argued that 1 Peter, written earlier to Christians in Asia (c. 80), responded to a similar situation where Jewish and pagan pressures were placed upon Christians to conform to their respective traditions. Pliny's letter, written c. 112 from the same general region, shows the extent to which non-Christians would go to attain religio-political conformity. Revelation, written c. 95, responds to similar types of social pressures.

Revelation provides evidence for a limited regional suppression of Christians in the letters in Rev. 2.1–3.22 and the apocalyptic visions in Rev. 4.1–20.15. While the primary function of the letters is to instruct each church in what it must do internally in order to enter the New Jerusalem, the letters also describe tribulation, Jewish harassment, the possibility of imprisonment, the death of Antipas and possible future trials (2.9-10, 13; 3.9-10). The reference to Satan's throne may well be yet another allusion to Pergamum's reputation as a center of the imperial cult (2.13). These passages are all the more important *because they are the only references in the letters to problems originating outside the Christian community*. Conversely, the references to the various forms of religious laxity are probably best understood as responses to the external social pressures placed upon Asian Christians to conform. It is noteworthy that the apocalyptic visions say little about religious laxity among Christians. Rather, they describe a Christian community suffering extensively for its witness of faith (6.9-11; 7.13-17; 12.17; 16.4-6; 17.6; 20.4; cf. 19.17-21; 21.4-8). John places this situation on a cosmic scale, perhaps because he could not separate the imperial cult from the imperial government.

Revelation was not the first Christian writing to place a local situation on a cosmic scale. 1 Pet. 5.9, written to Christians in the same general area, reads, 'But resist him [the Devil], be firm in your faith, knowing that the same experiences of suffering are being accomplished by your brothers who are in the world' (see also Mt. 24.9-14; Acts 28.22; Eph. 6.12). This rationale also enabled some Christians to endure their plight, while expecting an imminent cessation of their trials (e.g. 2 Cor. 4.17; 1 Thess. 5.1-4; cf. Rev. 22.6-12). Furthermore, the prophetic nature of the book would have also influenced John to envision a future that reflected his current circumstances. In this way, John emulates the Hebrew prophets well. For example, Hab. 2.2-3 reads,

> Then the Lord answered and said,
> 'Record the vision
> And inscribe it on tablets,
> That the one who reads it may run.
> For the vision is yet for the appointed time;
> It hastens toward the goal, and it will not fail.

> Though it tarries, wait for it;
> For it will certainly come, it will not delay.'[2]

Thus, while an empire-wide persecution of Christians is not historically verifiable, a regional oppression is historically intelligible, given what Christian and non-Christian writings convey concerning the social status of Christians in the first century CE. Again, religious laxity by Christians and social pressure upon Christians to conform are not mutually exclusive. Rather, they provide an intelligible rationale why certain persons took more moderate positions toward Asian customs. At the same time, the more conservative stance of John, Antipas and others becomes more understandable as well: John would not be open to a more liberal position because his suffering and Antipas's death, and the deaths of others (6.9; 20.4), would then be in vain. This would be unacceptable to John (see 12.11). It is within such a context that the christological images of the book of Revelation were developed in order to give hope to Christians who lived in Roman Asia near the end of the first century CE.

This study supplemented historical-critical research with insights from the sociology of knowledge in order to understand better the social function of Revelation's apocalyptic imagery. The 'one like a son of man' and the Divine Warrior are presentational images that are similar to their referent. The Lamb is a representational image with no natural connection with its referent and only attains meaning through traditional use. The sociological analyses showed that mythology, theology, determinism, therapy and nihilation performed significant roles as maintenance strategies. Most of these maintenance techniques were employed in association with the three major christological images of this study.

The '*one like a son of man*' is the Lord of the cosmos, God Almighty's eschatological divine agent who attains his *victory through suffering*, creating a new people of God composed of priest-kings. Having sacrificed himself on behalf of the Christian community, he now acts as Lord of the community in God's stead. Indeed, this is one major point of contact between the 'one like a son of man' image and the slain Lamb image. For Asian Christians, victory through suffering is at the center of the means of overcoming evil, attaining salvation and

2. See also, for example, Amos 5.18-27; Jer. 2.4-13; Mic. 2.1-5; Isa. 5.20-30.

becoming priest-kings (1.5-6; 5.9-10). By associating Christ's death with salvific victory and also the priestly reign of the saints in the New Jerusalem by means of two christological images, John makes a direct connection between Christ and community. Furthermore, he at once explains their plight and their means of *overcoming* it.

As the Lord of the cosmos, the 'one like a son of man' performs several pastoral functions: he judges (e.g. 2.5), gathers the elect community (e.g. 14.14-16) and makes war against God's enemies (e.g. 14.17-20). He also possesses an element of mystery (e.g. 2.17). These four elements are also found in messiah figures in *1 Enoch* and *4 Ezra*. In addition, this human-like messiah performs functions not found in Jewish literature, but found in other early Christian writings: he has cosmic authority, has power over death, is omniscient and determines who will enter the New Jerusalem. These are pastoral functions in that they relate directly to the life of the community in the present age and the next. The promise of priestly co-regency with God Almighty and Christ in the New Jerusalem and the promises to the victors of an unbroken fellowship with God and Christ (e.g. 1.5-6; 2.26-28; 3.21; cf. Exod. 19.6) are the two basic means of sustaining the bond between Christ and community associated with this image. This *pastoral* function exhorts the churches in order that they might enter the New Jerusalem.

The basic social function of the *slain Lamb image*, the most pervasive christological image in Revelation, is to lead the eschatological Christian community into the New Jerusalem (14.1-5). This community follows Christ wherever he goes and they bear the divine seal upon their persons (14.1; 22.4). The Lamb is also the Lord of the cosmos (17.14), who gathers, leads, sustains and protects an elite eschatological community of priest-kings (5.9-10; 7.15-17; 17.14; cf. 1.5-6). The Lamb, like the 'one like a son of man', judges (e.g. 13.8), gathers an elect community (14.1-5), makes war against God's enemies (17.14), shares divine honors with God Almighty and is victorious through suffering (e.g. 5.9-10; 21.22-23; 22.1-5). He also has some uniquely pastoral functions: he determines who will enter the New Jerusalem (13.18; 17.8) and his death provides salvific benefits for his followers (5.9-10; 7.13-14; 12.11; cf. 1.5-6; Jn 1.29-30; 1 Pet. 1.19-20). As with the preceding image, these *pastoral* functions relate to the life of the community in the present age and the next.

The selection of the slain Lamb image as the most pervasive christological symbol in the book suggests a social context in which Christians suffered some type of oppression and employed this image as a means of rationalizing their plight. As Christ suffered, they would suffer. As he was vindicated, so would they be. Thus, through the image of the Lamb, John developed the *victory-through-suffering* motif, as with the 'one like a son of man' image, a strategy begun in the promises in Rev. 2.1–3.22, in order to explain the religio-political repression experienced by some Christians and, at the same time, employing it to exhort those same persons to remain faithful so that they may receive their reward in the New Jerusalem. Revelation was not the only early Christian writing to do this (cf. Phil. 1.12-14; Heb. 12.3; 1 Pet. 4.12-13). Thus, Revelation should not be viewed as an aberration but as a bona fide witness to the faith and trials of early Christians. It provides a more complete picture of what first-century Christian life could be like for Christian nonconformists to Greco-Roman religious traditions.

Moreover, some Christians sought revenge against their oppressors (6.9-11; 14.10) and the Lamb is also associated with military imagery as a symbol for punishing evil and vindicating Christians (e.g. 12.7-12; 17.14). Additionally, dying for the faith often leads to victory (5.9-10; 6.9-11; 7.13-14; 12.11; cf. 20.4-6). If the book were inaccurate, it is difficult to imagine why these motifs and themes would recur so frequently in Revelation, especially in association with the image of the slain Lamb, if the Christian community were not harassed, ridiculed, held in low esteem and/or repressed in some fashion. These are not the motifs and themes that one would expect to be prominent in a setting where Christians lived free of any social pressures. Again, if the book were an inaccurate depiction of the social context, it is difficult to discern why it survived, especially given its self-designation as a prophetic book (e.g. 22.6-10). Rather, as with other early Christian writings, Revelation reflected life as Christians experienced it in Roman Asia. Indeed, the forms of religious laxity in the letters, correctly identified by many exegetes, become more understandable as attempts by some Christians to nullify Jewish and pagan coercion. In like manner, the deterministic elements, the promised status of priest-kings as well as the ways in which the Lamb improves the quality of life (e.g. 7.9-17; 21.9-22.5) strongly suggest that John's original readers were social outcasts, a minority whose religious beliefs and practices were constantly under attack by the dominant culture and whose very subsistence was often in question. Revelation spoke to them and helped them to make sense of the world.

The *Divine Warrior* (19.11-21) does not function primarily as a pastoral figure but as an eschatological divine agency figure who judges the evil worldly institutions. In so doing, he also vindicates the witness of the Christian community and assures the community of the propriety of its witness of faith. Although performing different functions, the Divine Warrior, as with the other images, is primarily concerned with the welfare of the community: his actions conveyed to the community its election through the defeat of its enemies.

The names associated with the Divine Warrior ('Faithful and True', 'The Word of God' and 'King of kings and Lord of lords') present him as the true, complete manifestation of God Almighty, a divine agent who acts as God's regent. The three given names aim at bolstering the community's religious strength and faith; the unrevealed name assures the community of its election and that its Lord rules the cosmos. In this way, John conveys to his audience that this christological figure is the same person represented by the two preceding images. Moreover, the Divine Warrior is principally a military image, suggesting a context where world-views perceived by their adherents as mutually exclusive have clashed and the weaker of the two sides seeks a heavenly intervention because it is virtually powerless against its earthly foe. This may explain why Christians never take part in any battle in Revelation. Their only weapon is their witness of faith: 'And they conquered him by means of the blood of the Lamb and because of the word of their witness; and they did not love their life even unto death' (12.11; see also 6.9; 7.13-17; 19.1-8, 14; 20.4).

The images and symbols employed to describe the work of the Divine Warrior communicate that this figure has come to judge and make war in righteousness (19.11). His white horse symbolizes purity; his crown, regal status (vv. 11-12). The sword from his mouth, the rod of iron and the trampling of the winepress in wrath represent divine judgment upon sinful institutions (v. 15). The defeat of the beast and the false prophet and the feast for the birds are rather unpleasant scenes that convey a sense of the deep enmity between opposing religious communities. The weaker Christian community seeks revenge upon its oppressors. Such attitudes normally represent a mutual animosity; the less powerful community sees itself as unjustly persecuted and appeals to the Lord of the cosmos for deliverance because its enemy controls the earthly institutions. Such a perspective would also explain why John cast a regional crisis on the cosmic stage.

Finally, the Divine Warrior performs pastoral functions found in connection with other christological images in Revelation: he acts as a judge (v. 15), gathers the elect (v. 14) and makes war against God's enemies (vv. 19-21). The motifs associated with all three christological images is an important line of evidence that points toward the unity of the book of Revelation.

This study has demonstrated that John employed the 'one like a son of man', the slain Lamb and the Divine Warrior christological images to maintain the unity between Christ and community. Christ gathers an elect community of priest-kings en route to the New Jerusalem. These are exodus motifs employed to assure the community of the correctness of its witness 'to the word of God and the testimony of Jesus' (1.2, 9; 6.9; 20.4) and to exhort it to maintain that witness regardless of the cost (12.11, 17; 17.6; 19.2, 5-9).[3] This study has also demonstrated that John employed the victory-through-suffering motif as a means of encouraging the community in its present plight to recall the crucifixion of Jesus; it also was a means of exhorting the community to remain faithful to God so that it may enter the New Jerusalem, recalling the resurrection. Finally, throughout this study we have seen how military motifs have been incorporated as symbols of judgment of Christians (2.16), but more extensively against those who repressed Christians (12.7-12; 14.1-5; 17.14; 18.24; 19.11-21; 20.7-10). These elements strongly suggest that the Revelation to John came at a time of regional oppression of Christians in Asia and that John wrote to encourage and challenge Christians to stand firm in their beliefs and wait for divine deliverance. As such, Revelation encourages passive Christian civil disobedience in the face of an unsympathetic first-century CE Roman Asian society.[4]

3. For example, on exodus motifs see my comments on Rev. 1.1-8 in Chapter 3 of this study; on the Jewish Background, Rev. 14.1-5, 15.3-4 and 21.9–22.5, Chapter 5 of this study.

4. DeSilva holds a similar view ('Apocalyptic Propaganda', p. 375).

BIBLIOGRAPHY

Aland, K., and B. Aland, *The Text of the New Testament* (Grand Rapids: Eerdmans; Leiden: E.J. Brill, 1987).

Aland, K. *et al.* (eds.), *The Greek New Testament* (New York: United Bible Societies, 3rd edn [corrected], 1983).

Anderson, R.A., *Signs and Wonders: A Commentary on the Book of Daniel* (International Theological Commentary; Grand Rapids: Eerdmans; Edinburgh: Handsel, 1984).

Attridge, H.W., *The Epistle to the Hebrews* (Hermeneia Series; Philadelphia: Fortress Press, 1989).

Aune, D.E., 'The Social Matrix of the Apocalypse of John', *BR* 26 (1981), pp. 16-32.

—'The Odes of Solomon and Early Christian Prophecy', *NTS* 28 (1982), pp. 435-60.

—'The Influence of Roman Imperial Court Ceremonial on the Apocalypse of John', *BR* 28 (1983), pp. 5-26.

—*Prophecy in Early Christianity and the Ancient Mediterranean World* (Grand Rapids: Eerdmans, 1983).

—'The Apocalypse of John and the Problem of Genre', *Semeia* 36 (1986), pp. 65-96.

—'The Prophetic Circle of John of Patmos and the Exegesis of Revelation 22.16', *JSNT* 37 (1989), pp. 103-16.

—'The Form and Function of the Proclamations to the Seven Churches (Revelation 2–3)', *NTS* 36 (1990), pp. 182-204.

Balch, D.L., *Let Wives Be Submissive* (SBLMS, 26; Chico, CA: Scholars Press, 1981).

Balthasar, H.U. von, 'Die göttlichen Gerichte in der Apokalypse', *Internationale Katholische Zeitschrift/Communio 14* (1985), pp. 28-34.

Bandstra, A.J., 'History and Eschatology in the Apocalypse', *Calvin Theological Journal* 5 (1970), pp. 180-83.

—'A Kingship and Priests: Inaugurated Eschatology in the Apocalypse', *Calvin Theological Journal* 27 (1992), pp. 10-25.

Barclay, W., *The Letters to the Seven Churches* (London: SCM Press; New York: Abingdon Press, 1957).

—*The Revelation of John* (2 vols.; Philadelphia: Westminster Press, 2nd edn, 1960).

Barnett, P., 'Polemical Parallelism: Some Further Reflections on the Apocalypse', *JSNT* 35 (1989), pp. 111-20.

Baron, D., *The Servant of Jehovah* (London: Marshall, Morgan & Scott, 1954).

Barr, D.L., 'The Apocalypse as a Symbolic Transformation of the World: A Literary Analysis', *Int* 38 (1984), pp. 39-50.

—'The Apocalypse of John as Oral Enactment', *Int* 40 (1986), pp. 243-56.

Barrett, C.K., 'The Lamb of God', *NTS* 1 (1954–55), pp. 210-18.

Bauckham, R.J., 'The Rise of Apocalyptic', *Themelios* 3 (1977–78), pp. 10-23.

—*The Climax of Prophecy: Studies in the Book of Revelation* (Edinburgh: T. & T. Clark, 1993).

—*The Theology of the Book of Revelation* (Cambridge: Cambridge University Press, 1993).

Beagley, A.J., *The 'Sitz im Leben' of the Apocalypse with Particular Reference to the Role of the Church's Enemies* (Berlin: W. de Gruyter, 1987).

Beale, G.K., 'The Problem of the Man from the Sea in IV Ezra 13 and its Relationship to the Messianic Concept in John's Apocalypse', *NovT* 25 (1983), pp. 182-88.

—'The Influence of Daniel upon the Structure and Theology of John's Apocalypse', *JETS* 27 (1984), pp. 413-23.

—*The Use of Daniel in Jewish Apocalyptic Literature and in the Revelation of St. John* (Lanham, MD: University Press of America, 1984).

—'The Origin of the Title "King of Kings and Lord of Lords" in Revelation 17.14', *NTS* 31 (1985), pp. 618-20.

—'A Reconsideration of the Text of Daniel in the Apocalypse', *Bib* 67 (1986), pp. 539-43.

—'The Interpretation Problem of Rev. 1:19', *NovT* 34 (1992), pp. 360-87.

Beare, F.W. (ed.), *The First Epistle of Peter* (Oxford: Basil Blackwell, rev. 2nd edn, 1958).

Beasley-Murray, G.R., *The Book of Revelation* (NCB; Grand Rapids: Eerdmans, 1978).

—'The Interpretation of Daniel 7', *CBQ* 45 (1983), pp. 44-58.

Beck, D.M., 'The Christology of the Apocalypse of John', in E.P. Booth (ed.), *New Testament Studies: Critical Essays in New Testament Interpretation with Special Reference to the Meaning and Worth of Jesus* (New York: Abingdon–Cokesbury Press, 1942), pp. 253-77.

Beckwith, I.T., *The Apocalypse of John* (New York: Macmillan, 1919).

Bell, A.A., Jr, 'The Date of John's Apocalypse: The Evidence of Some Roman Historians Reconsidered', *NTS* 25 (1978), pp. 93-102.

Bergant, D., 'Yahweh: A Warrior God?', *TBT* 21 (1983), pp. 156-61.

Berger, K., 'Apostelbrief und apostolische Rede: Zum Formular frühchristlicher Briefe', *ZNW* 65 (1974), pp. 212-19.

Berger, P.L., and T. Luckmann, *The Social Construction of Reality: A Treatise in the Sociology of Knowledge* (Garden City, NY: Doubleday, 1966).

Best, E. (ed.), *I Peter* (NCB; London: Marshall, Morgan & Scott, 1971).

Black, M., *An Aramaic Approach to the Gospels and Acts* (Oxford: Clarendon Press, 3rd edn, 1967).

—'The Throne-Theophany Prophetic Commission and the "Son of Man": A Study in Tradition-History', in R. Hamerton-Kelly and R. Scroggs (eds.), *Jews, Greeks and Christians: Religious Cultures in Late Antiquity: Essays in Honor of William David Davies* (Leiden: E.J. Brill, 1976), pp. 56-73.

—'Jesus and the Son of Man', *JSNT* 1 (1978), pp. 19-32.

—'Aramaic Barnåshå and the "Son of Man",' *ExpTim* 95 (1984), pp. 200-206.

Blass, F., and A. Debrunner, *A Greek Grammar of the New Testament and Other Early Christian Literature* (trans. and rev. by R.W. Funk; Chicago: University of Chicago Press, 1961).

Blevins, J.L., *Revelation as Drama* (Nashville: Broadman, 1984).

Böcher, O., 'Johanneisches in der Apokalypse des Johannes', *NTS* 27 (1981), pp. 310-21.

—*Kirche in Zeit und Endzeit: Aufsätze zur Offenbarung des Johannes* (Neukirchen–Vluyn: Neukirchener, 1983).

Bodinger, M, 'Le mythe de Neron. De l'Apocalypse de saint Jean au Talmud de Babylone', *RHR* 206 (1989), pp. 21-40.

Boecher, O., *Die Johannesapokalypse* (Darmstadt: Wissenschaftliche Buchgesellschaft, 1975), pp. 56-63.

Boesak, A.A., *Comfort and Protest* (Philadelphia: Westminster Press, 1987).

Boismard, M. E., ' "L'Apocalypse" ou "Les Apocalypse" de Jean', *RB* 56 (1949), pp. 507-41.

Boll, F., *Aus der Offenbarung Johannis* (Leipzig-Berlin: B.G. Teubner, 1914).

Boring, M.E., 'The Theology of Revelation: "The Lord Our God the Almighty Reigns",' *Int* 40 (1986), pp. 257-69.

—*Revelation* (Interpretation Commentary; Louisville, KY: Westminster/John Knox Press, 1989).

—'Narrative Christology in the Apocalypse', *CBQ* 54 (1992), pp. 702-23.

—'The Voice of Jesus in the Apocalypse of John', *NovT* 34 (1992), pp. 334-59.

Borsch, F.H., *The Son of Man in Myth and History* (Philadelphia: Westminster Press, 1967).

Botterweck, G.J., and H. Ringgren (eds.), *Theological Dictionary of the Old Testament* (6 vols.; Grand Rapids: Eerdmans, rev. edn, 1977).

Bousset, W., *Die Offenbarung Johannis* (Göttingen: Vandenhoeck & Ruprecht, 5th edn, 1906).

Bowman, J., 'The Background of the Term "Son of Man" ', *ET* 59 (1947–48), pp. 283-88.

Box, G.H. *The Ezra-Apocalypse* (ed. and trans.; London: Pitman & Sons, 1912).

Briggs, C.A., *Messianic Prophecy* (New York: Charles Scribner's Sons; Edinburgh: T. & T. Clark, 1886).

Brown, C. (ed.), *The New International Dictionary of the New Testament* (trans. and rev. L. Coenen, E. Beyreuther and H. Bietenhard; 3 vols.; Grand Rapids: Zondervan, 1978).

Brown, F., S.R. Driver and C.A. Briggs (eds.) *A Hebrew and English Lexicon of the Old Testament* (Oxford: Clarendon Press, 1907).

Büchsel, F., *Die Christologie der Offenbarung Johannis* (Halle: Druck von C.A. Kammerer, 1907).

Bultmann, R.K., *A History of the Synoptic Tradition* (Oxford: Basil Blackwell, rev. edn, 1968).

Buttrick, G.A. (ed.), *The Interpreter's Dictionary of the Bible* (4 vols.; Nashville: Abingdon Press, 1962).

Caird, G.B., *A Commentary on the Revelation of St. John the Divine* (BNTC; HNTC; London: A. & C. Black; New York: Harper & Row, 1966).

—*The Revelation of St. John the Divine* (HNTC; New York: Harper & Row, 1966).

Cambier, J., 'Les images de l'Ancien Testament dans l'Apocalypse de Saint Jean', *NRT* 77 (1955), pp. 113-22.

Camery-Hoggatt, J., *Irony in Mark's Gospel* (SNTSMS, 72; Cambridge: Cambridge University Press, 1992).

Campbell, J.Y., 'The Origin and Meaning of the Term Son of Man', *JTS* 48 (1947), pp. 145-55.

Caragounis, C.C., *The Son of Man: Vision and Interpretation* (Tübingen: Mohr-Siebeck, 1986).

Casey, M., *Son of Man: The Interpretation and Influence of Daniel 7* (London: SPCK, 1979).

—'Method in our Madness, and Madness in their Methods: Some Approaches to the Son of Man Problem in Recent Scholarship', *JSNT* 42 (1991), pp. 17-43.

—'Idiom and Translation: Some Aspects of the Son of Man Problem', *NTS* 41 (1995), pp. 448-66.

Charles, J.D., 'An Apocalyptic Tribute to the Lamb (Rev 5:1-14)', *JETS* 34 (1991), pp. 461-73.

Charles, R.H. (ed.), *The Apocrypha and Pseudepigrapha of the Old Testament* (2 vols.; Oxford: Clarendon Press, 1913).

—*A Critical and Exegetical Commentary on the Book of the Revelation of St. John* (ICC; 2 vols.; Edinburgh: T. & T. Clark, 1920).

Charlesworth, J.H., 'The SNTS Pseudepigrapha Seminars in Tübingen and Paris on the Books of Enoch', *NTS* 25 (1978–79), pp. 315-23.

—*The Old Testament Pseudepigrapha and the New Testament* (SNTSMS, 54; Cambridge: Cambridge University Press, 1985).

—'The Jewish Roots of Christology: The Discovery of the Hypostatic Voice', *SJT* 39 (1986), pp. 19-41.

Charlesworth, J.H. (ed.), *The Old Testament Pseudepigrapha* (2 vols.; Garden City, NY: Doubleday, 1983, 1985).

Charlier, J.-P., 'The Apocalypse of John: Last Times Scripture or Last Scripture', *Lumière et Vie* 40 (1985), pp. 180-92.

—*Comprendre l'Apocalypse* (Lire la Bible, 89 and 90; 2 vols.; Paris: Cerf, 1991).

Ciholas, P., ' "Son of Man" and Hellenistic Christology', *RevExp* 79 (1982), pp. 487-501.

Clifford, R.J., *The Cosmic Mountain in Canaan and the Old Testament* (HSM, 4; Cambridge, MA: Harvard University Press, 1974).

Coggins, R.J., and M.A. Knibb, *The First and Second Books of Esdras* (Cambridge: Cambridge University Press, 1979).

Collins, J.J., 'The Symbolism of Transcendence in Jewish Apocalyptic', *BR* 19 (1974), pp. 5-22.

—'Jewish Apocalyptic against its Hellenistic Near Eastern Environment', *BASOR* 220 (1975), pp. 27-36.

—'Cosmos and Salvation: Jewish Wisdom and Apocalyptic in the Hellenistic Age', *HR* (1977), pp. 121-42.

—'Pseudonymity, Historical Reviews and the Genre of the Revelation of John', *CBQ* 39 (1977), pp. 329-43.

—*The Apocalyptic Vision of the Book of Daniel* (HSM, 16; Missoula, MT: Scholars Press, 1977).

—'Introduction', *Semeia* 14 (1979), p. 9.

—'The Heavenly Representative: The "Son of Man" in the Similitudes of Enoch', in G.W.E. Nickelsburg and J.J. Collins (eds.), *Ideal Figures in Ancient Judaism* (Missoula, MT: Scholars Press, 1980), pp. 111-33.

—*Daniel, First Maccabees, Second Maccabees* (Old Testament Message, 16; Wilmington, DE: Michael Glazier, 1981).

—*Daniel, with an Introduction to Apocalyptic Literature* (FOTL, 20; Grand Rapids: Eerdmans, 1984).

—*The Apocalyptic Imagination: An Introduction to the Jewish Matrix of Christianity* (New York: Crossroad, 1984).

—'The Son of Man and the Saints of the Most High in the Book of Daniel', *JBL* 93 (1984), pp. 50-66.

—'Daniel and his Social World', *Int* 39 (1985), pp. 131-43.
—*The Apocalyptic Imagination* (New York: Crossroad, 1989).
—'The Son of Man in First-Century Judaism', *NTS* 38 (1992), pp. 448-66.
—*Daniel* (Hermeneia Series; Minneapolis: Augsburg–Fortress, 1993).
Collins, J.J. (ed.), *Apocalypse: The Morphology of a Genre* (Semeia, 14; Missoula, MT: Scholars Press, 1979).
Collins, J.J., and J.H. Charlesworth (eds.), *Mysteries and Revelations: Apocalyptic Studies since the Uppsala Colloquium* (JSPSup, 9; Sheffield: JSOT, 1991).
Collins, J.J., and G.W. Nickelsburg (eds.), *Ideal Figures in Ancient Judaism: Profiles and Paradigms* (Missoula, MT: Scholars Press, 1980).
Colpe, C., 'ὁ υἱός τοῦ ἀνθρώπου', *TDNT*, VIII, pp. 406-30.
Comblin, J., *Le Christ dans l'Apocalypse* (Paris: Desclée, 1965).
Coppens, J., *La relevée apocalyptique du messianisme royal*. III. *Le fils d'homme neotestamentaire* (Leuven: Peeters, 1981).
—*La relevée apocalyptique du messianisme royal.* II. *Le fils d'homme vetero et intertestamentaire* (Leuven: Peeters, 1983).
Corsini, E., *The Apocalypse* (GNS, 5; Wilmington, DE: Michael Glazier, 1983).
Court, J.M., *Myth and History in the Book of Revelation* (London: SPCK, 1979).
Crim, K. (ed.), *The Interpreter's Dictionary of the Bible* (sup. vol.; New York: Abingdon Press, 1976).
Cross, F.M., *Canaanite Myth and Hebrew Epic* (Cambridge, MA: Harvard University Press, 1973).
Cullmann, O., *The Christology of the New Testament* (London: SCM Press; Philadelphia: Westminster Press, 1963).
Cunningham, L.S., J. Kelsay, R.M. Barineau and H.J. McVoy, *The Sacred Quest* (Englewood, NJ: Prentice–Hall, 1995).
Dana, H.E., and J.R. Mantley, *A Manual Grammar of the Greek New Testament* (New York: Macmillan, 1927).
Davids, P.H., *The First Epistle of Peter* (Grand Rapids: Eerdmans, 1990).
Davies, P.R., *Daniel* (Sheffield: JSOT Press, 1985).
Day, J., *God's Conflict with the Dragon and the Sea: Echoes of a Canaanite Myth in the Old Testament* (University of Cambridge Oriental Publications, 35; Cambridge: Cambridge University Press, 1985).
Dehandschutter, B., 'The Meaning of Witness in the Apocalypse', in J. Lambrecht (ed.), *L'Apocalypse johannique et l'Apocalyptique dans le Nouveau Testament* (BETL, 53; Leuven: Leuven University Press, 1980), pp. 283-88.
Deissmann, G.A, *Light from the Ancient East* (Grand Rapids: Baker Book House, 1965).
Delcor, M., *Le livre de Daniel* (Paris: J. Gabalda, 1971).
Denis, Albert-Marie (ed.), *Concordance grecque des pseudepigraphes d'Ancien testament: Concordance, corpus des textes, indices* (Leiden: E.J. Brill, 1987).
Dequeker, L., 'Daniel vii et les Saints du Très-Haut', *ETL* 36 (1960), pp. 353-92.
—'The Saints of the Most High in Qumran and Daniel', *OTS* 18 (1973), pp. 108-87.
Dibelius, M., *From Tradition to Gospel* (London: Nicholson & Watson, 1934).
DiLella, A.A., 'The One in Human-Likeness and the Holy Ones of the Most High in Daniel 7', *CBQ* 39 (1977), pp. 1-19.
DeSilva, D.A., 'The Revelation to John: A Case Study in Apocalyptic Propaganda and the Maintenance of Sectarian Identity', *Sociological Analysis* 53 (1992), pp. 375-95.

—'The Social Setting of the Revelation to John: Conflicts Within, Fears Without', *WTJ* 54 (1992), pp. 273-302.

Dittenberger, W. (ed.), *Orientis graeci inscriptiones selectae* (2 vols.; Leipzig: S. Hirzel, 1903–1905).

Dodd, C.H., *The Apostolic Preaching and its Development* (London: Hodder & Stoughton, 2nd edn, 1944).

Driver, S.R., *The Book of Daniel* (Cambridge: Cambridge University Press, 1922).

D'Souza, J., 'The Lamb of God in the Johannine Writings' (Doctor of Sacred Theology [STD] Dissertation, Pontifical Institute, Rome, 1968).

Edwards, S.A., 'Christological Perspective in the Book of Revelation', in R.F. Berkey and S.A. Edwards (eds.), *Christological Perspectives: Essays in Honor of Harvey A. McArthur* (New York: Pilgrim, 1982).

Elliger, K., *et al.* (eds.), *Biblia Hebraica Stuttgartensia* (Stuttgart: Deutsche Bibelstiftung, 1984).

Ellingworth, P., 'The *marturia* Debate', *BT* 41 (1990), pp. 138-39.

Elliott, J.H., *A Home for the Homeless* (Philadelphia: Fortress Press, 1981).

—*What Is Social-Scientific Criticism?* (Minneapolis: Augsburg–Fortress, 1993).

Elliott, J.H. (ed.), *Social-Scientific Criticism of the New Testament and Its Social World* (Semeia, 35; Decatur, GA: Scholars Press, 1986).

Ellul, J., *Apocalypse* (New York: Seabury, 1977).

Ellwanger, W.H., 'The Christology of the Apocalypse', *CTM* 1 (1930), pp. 512-28.

Emerton, J.A., 'The Origin of the Son of Man Imagery', *JTS* 9 (1958), pp. 225-42.

Enroth, Anne-Marit, 'The Hearing Formula in the Book of Revelation', *NTS* 36 (1990), pp. 598-608.

Epp, E.J., and G.W. MacRae (eds.), *The New Testament and its Modern Interpreters* (Philadelphia: Fortress Press; Atlanta: Scholars Press, 1989).

Farrer, A.M., *A Rebirth of Images* (Boston: Beacon Press, 1949).

—*The Revelation of St. John the Divine* (Oxford: Clarendon Press, 1964).

Fekkes, J., ' "His Bride Has Prepared Herself": Revelation 12–21 and Isaian Nuptial Imagery', *JBL* 109 (1990), pp. 269-87.

Felder, C.H., *Troubling Biblical Waters: Race, Class, and Family* (Bishop Henry McNeal Turner Studies in North American Black Religion, 3; Maryknoll, NY: Orbis Books, 1989).

Felder, C.H. (ed.), *Stony the Road we Trod: African American Biblical Interpretation* (Minneapolis: Fortress Press, 1991).

Ferch, A.J., 'The Two Aeons and the Messiah in Pseudo-Philo, 4 Ezra, and 2 Baruch', *AUSS* 15 (1977), pp. 135-51.

—*The Son of Man in Daniel Seven* (AUSSDS, 6; Berrien Springs, MI: Andrews University Press, 1979).

—'Daniel 7 and Ugarit: A Reconsideration', *JBL* 99 (1980), pp. 75-86.

—'The Book of Daniel and the "Maccabean Thesis" ', *AUSS* 21 (1983), pp. 129-41.

Ferguson, J., *The Religions of the Roman Empire* (London: Thames & Hudson, 1970).

Feuillet, A, 'Le Fils de l'homme de Daniel et la tradition biblique', *BR* 60 (1953), pp. 170-202, 321-46.

—'Le festin des noces de l'agneau et ses anticipations', *Espirit et Vie* 97 (1987), pp. 353-62.

Ford, J.M., *Revelation* (AB, 38; Garden City, NY: Doubleday, 1975).

—'Persecution and Martyrdom in the Book of Revelation', *Bible Today* 28 (1990), pp. 141-46.

Freed, E.D., *The New Testament: A Critical Introduction* (Belmont, CA: Wadsworth Press, 1986).

Froom, L.E., *The Prophetic Faith of Our Fathers* (4 vols.; Washington, DC: Review and Herald, 1946–54).

Fuller, R.H., *The Foundations of New Testament Christology* (New York: Charles Scribner's Sons, 1965.

Funk, R.W. (ed.), *Journal for Theology and the Church 6: Apocalypticism* (New York: Herder & Herder, 1969).

Gaechter, P., 'The Role of Memory in the Making of the Apocalypse', *TS* 9 (1948), pp. 419-52.

Gager, J., *Kingdom and Community* (Englewood Cliffs, NJ: Prentice–Hall, 1975).

Gärtner, B., *The Temple and the Community in Qumran and the New Testament* (Cambridge: Cambridge University Press, 1965).

Giblin, C.H., "Structural and Thematic Correlations in the Theology of Revelation', *Bib* 55 (1974), pp. 487-504.

—*The Book of Revelation: The Open Book of Prophecy* (GNS, 34; Collegeville, MN: Liturgical Press, 1991).

Girard, M., 'Le semblant de fils d'homme de Daniel 7, un personnage du monde d'en haut: approche structurelle', *ScEs* 35 (1983), pp. 265-96.

Glasson, T.F. (ed.), *The Revelation of John* (CBCNEB; Cambridge: Cambridge University Press, 1965).

Goldingay, J.E., *Daniel* (WBC, 30; Dallas: Word Books, 1989).

Goppelt, L., *Erste Petrusbrief* (MeyerK; Göttingen: Vandenhoeck & Ruprecht, 1978).

Goulder, M.D., 'The Apocalypse as an Annual Cycle of Prophecies', *NTS* 27 (1981), pp. 342-67.

Grudem, W., *1 Peter* (TNTC; Leicester: Inter-Varsity Press; Grand Rapids: Eerdmans, 1988).

Gundry, R.H., 'The New Jerusalem: People as Place, not Place for People', *NovT* 29 (1987), pp. 254-64.

Gunkel, H., *Schöpfung und Chaos in Urzeit und Endzeit* (Göttingen: Vandenhoeck & Ruprecht, 1895).

Guthrie, D., 'The Lamb in the Structure of the Book of Revelation', *Vox Evangelica* 12 (1981), pp. 64-71.

Hahn, F., *The Titles of Jesus in Christology* (London: Lutterworth, 1969).

—'Die Sendschreiben der Johannesapokalypse: Ein Beitrag zur Bestimmung prophetischer Redeformer', in G. Jeremias, H.-W. Kuhn and H. Stegemann (eds.), *Tradition und Glaube: Das frühe Christentum in seiner Umwelt* (Göttingen: Vandenhoeck & Ruprecht, 1971), pp. 370-77.

Hall, R.G., 'Living Creatures in the Midst of the Throne: Another Look at Revelation 4.6', *NTS* 36 (1990), pp. 609-13.

Hammer, R., *The Book of Daniel* (Cambridge: Cambridge University Press, 1976).

Hanhart, K., 'The Four Beasts of Daniel's Vision in the Night in the Light of Rev. 13.2', *NTS* 27 (1981), pp. 576-83.

Hanson, A.T., *The Wrath of the Lamb* (London: SPCK, 1957).

Hanson, P.D., *The Dawn of Apocalyptic* (Philadelphia: Fortress Press, 1975).

Hardy, E.G., *Christianity and the Roman Government* (London: S. Sonnenschein, 2nd edn, 1906).

Harrington, W.J., *The Apocalypse of St. John* (London: Geoffrey Chapman, 1969).

Hartman, L.F., and A.A. DiLella, *Daniel* (AB, 23; Garden City, NY: Doubleday, 1978).

Hasel, G.F., 'The Identity of the "Saints of the Most High" in Daniel 7', *Bib* 56 (1975), pp. 173-92.

Hastings, J. (ed.), *A Dictionary of the Bible* (5 vols.; Edinburgh: T. & T. Clark, 1898–1904).

Hatch, E., and H.A. Redpath (eds.), *A Concordance to the Septuagint* (Oxford: Clarendon Press, 1897).

Heller, A., 'Towards a Sociology of Knowledge of Everyday Life', *Cultural Hermeneutics* 3 (1975), pp. 7-18.

Hellholm, D. (ed.), *Apocalypticism in the Mediterranean World and the Near East: Proceedings of the International Colloquium on Apocalypticism. Uppsala, August 12–17, 1979* (Tübingen: Mohr, 1983).

—'The Problem of Apocalyptic Genre and the Apocalypse to John', *Semeia* 36 (1986), pp. 65-96.

Hemer, C.J., *The Letters to the Seven Churches of Asia in their Local Setting* (JSNTSup, 11; Sheffield: JSOT Press, 1986).

Hengel, M., *Hellenism and Judaism* (2 vols.; Philadelphia: Fortress Press, 1981).

Hennecke, E., W. Schneemelcher and R.M. Wilson (eds.), *New Testament Apocrypha* (2 vols.; Philadelphia: Westminster Press, 1963–65).

Hill, D., 'Prophecy and Prophets in the Revelation of St. John', *NTS* 18 (1971–72), pp. 401-18.

—*New Testament Prophecy* (Atlanta: John Knox Press, 1979).

Hillyer, N., ' "The Lamb" in the Apocalypse', *EvQ* 39 (1967), pp. 228-36.

Hindley, J.C., 'Towards a Date for the Similitudes of Enoch: An Historical Approach', *NTS* 14 (1967–68), pp. 551-65.

Hindson, E.E., 'The Sociology of Knowledge and Biblical Interpretaion', *Theologica Evangelica* 17 (1984), pp. 33-38.

Hohnjec, N., *'Das Lamm: to arnion' in der Offenbarung des Johannes: Eine exegetisch-theologische Untersuchung* (Rome: Herder, 1980).

Holtz, T., *Die Christologie der Apokalypse des Johannes* (TU, 85; Berlin: Akademie-Verlag, 2nd edn, 1971).

Hooker, M.D., *The Son of Man in Mark* (Montreal: McGill University Press, 1967).

Hoyt, T., Jr, 'Interpreting Biblical Scholarship for the Black Church Tradition', in C.H. Felder (ed.), *Stony the Road we Trod: African American Biblical Interpretation* (Minneapolis: Augsburg–Fortress, 1991), pp. 34-39.

Hughes, P.E., *The Book of Revelation: A Commentary* (Leicester: Inter-Varsity Press; Grand Rapids: Eerdmans, 1990).

Hultgren, A.J., *New Testament Christology: A Critical Assessment and Annotated Bibliography* (Westport, CT: Greenwood, 1988).

Hunt, A.G., and G.C. Edgar (eds.), *Select Papyri* (2 vols.; LCL; London: Heinemann, 1932–34).

Hurtado, L.W., 'Revelation 4–5 in the Light of Jewish Apocalyptic Analogies', *JSNT* 25 (1985), pp. 105-24.

Jeske, R.L., 'Spirit and Community in the Johannine Apocalypse', *NTS* 31 (1985), pp. 452-66.

Joachim of Fiore, *Expositio in Apocalypsim* (repr.; Frankfurt: Minerva, 1964 [1519]).
—*Enchiridion super Apocalypsim* (ed. E.K. Burger; Toronto: Pontifical Institute of Mediaeval Studies, 1986).
Jones, B.W., *The Emperor Domitian* (London: Routledge, 1992).
Kang, Sa-Moon, *Divine War in the Old Testament and in the Ancient Near East* (BZAW, 177; Berlin: W. de Gruyter, 1989).
Käsemann, E., 'On the Topic of Primitive Christian Apocalyptic', in R.W. Funk (ed.), *Apocalypticism* (JTC, 6; New York: Herder & Herder, 1969).
Kearns, R., *Die Entchristologisierung des Menschensohnes: Die Übertragung des Traditionsgefüges um den Menschensohn auf Jesus* (Tübingen: Mohr-Siebeck, 1988).
Keck, L.E., 'Towards the Renewal of New Testament Christology', *NTS* 32 (1986), pp. 362-77.
Kelly, J.N.D., *A Commentary on the Epistles of Peter and Jude* (HNTC; New York: Harper & Row, 1969).
Kiddle, M., *The Revelation of St. John* (MNTC; London: Hodder & Stoughton, 1940).
Kirby, J.T., 'The Rhetorical Situations of Revelation 1–3', *NTS* 34 (1988), pp. 197-207.
Kittel, G., and G. Friedrich (eds.), *Theological Dictionary of the New Testamen*t (10 vols.; Grand Rapids: Eerdmans, 1964–76).
Knibb, M.A., *The Ethiopic Book of Enoch* (2 vols.; Oxford: Clarendon Press, 1978).
—'The Date of the Parables of Enoch: A Critical Review', *NTS* 25 (1979), pp. 345-59.
Koch, K., *Daniel* (BKAT, 22; Neukirchen–Vluyn: Neukirchener Verlag, 1986).
Kokkinos, N., *Antonia Augusta: Portrait of a Great Lady* (London: Routledge, 1992).
Köster, H., *Introduction to the New Testament* (2 vols.; Berlin: W. de Gruyter, 1987).
Kraeling, C.H., *Anthropos and Son of Man* (New York: Columbia University Press, 1927).
Kraft, H., *Die Offenbarung des Johannes* (HNT, 16a; Tübingen: J.C.B. Mohr, 1974).
Kraft, R.A., and G.W.E. Nickelsburg (eds.), *Early Judaism and its Modern Interpreters* (Philadelphia: Fortress Press, 1986).
Krodel, G.A., *Revelation* (Minneapolis: Augsburg Press, 1989).
Kümmel, W.G., *Introduction to the New Testament* (Nashville: Abingdon Press, rev. edn, 1975).
Kvanvig, H.S., *Roots of Apocalyptic. The Mesopotamian Background of the Enoch Figure and of the Son of Man* (Neukirchen–Vluyn: Neukirchener Verlag, 1988).
Lacocque, A., *The Book of Daniel* (Atlanta: John Knox Press, 1976).
Ladd, G.E., 'Why Not Prophetic-Apocalyptic?', *JBL* 76 (1957), pp. 192-200.
—*A Commentary on the Revelation of John* (Grand Rapids: Eerdmans, 1972).
Lambrecht, J. (ed.), *L'Apocalypse johannique et l'Apocalyptique dans le Nouveau Testament* (BETL, 53; Louvain: Leuven University Press, 1980).
Läpple, A., 'Das Geheimnis des Lammes. Das Christusbild der Offenbarung des Johannes', *BK* 39 (1984), pp. 53-58.
Larkin, K.J.A., *The Eschatology of Second Zechariah* (Contributions to Biblical Exegesis and Theology, 6; Kampen: Kok, 1993).
Laws, S., *In Light of the Lamb* (GNS, 31; Wilmington, DE: Michael Glazier, 1988).
Liddell, H.C., and R. Scott, *Greek–English Lexicon* (new edn by H.S. Jones; Oxford: Clarendon Press, 1940).
Lietzmann, H., *Der Menschensohn* (Freiburg: Mohr, 1896).
Lilje, H., *The Last Book of the Bible* (Philadelphia: Muhlenberg, 1955).
Lindars, B., 'Re-enter the Apocalyptic Son of Man', *NTS* 22 (1975), pp. 52-72.
—'A Bull, a Lamb and a Word: 1 Enoch 90:33', *NTS* 22 (1975–76), pp. 483-86.

Lisowsky, G. (ed.), *Konkordanz zum hebräischen Alten Testament* (Stuttgart: Deutsche Bibelgesellschaft, 1966).

Livingston, J.C., *Anatomy of the Sacred* (New York: Macmillan, 2nd edn, 1993).

Lohmeyer, E., *Die Offenbarung des Johannes* (HNT, 16; Tübingen: J.C.B. Mohr, 2nd edn, 1953).

Lohse, E., 'Der Menschensohn in der Johannesapokalypse', in R. Pesch and R. Schnackenburg, in collaboration with O. Kaiser (eds.), *Jesus und der Menschensohn: Für Anton Vögtle* (Freiburg: Herder, 1975), pp. 415-20.

—*Die Offenbarung des Johannes* (NTD; Göttingen: Vandenhoeck & Ruprecht, 1976).

Machen, J.G., *New Testament Greek for Beginners* (Toronto: Macmillan, 1923).

Magie, D., *Roman Rule in Asia Minor to the End of the Third Century after Christ* (2 vols.; Princeton, NJ: Princeton University Press, 1950).

Malherbe, A., *Social Aspects of Early Christianity* (Baton Rouge: Louisiana State University Press, 1977).

Malina, B., *On the Genre and Message of Revelation: Star Visions and Sky Journeys* (Peabody, MA: Hendrickson, 1995).

Malinowski, B., *Myth in Primitive Psychology* (New York: W.W. Norton, 1926).

Manson, T.W., 'The Son of Man in Daniel, Enoch, and the Gospels', *BJRL* 32 (1949–50), pp. 171-93.

Marxsen, W., *The Beginnings of Christology* (Oxford: Basil Blackwell, 1968).

Mazzaferri, F., '*Martyria Iesou* Revisited', *BT* 39 (1988), pp. 114-22.

—*The Genre of the Book of Revelation from a Source-Critical Perspective* (Berlin: W. de Gruyter, 1989).

McIlraith, D.A., *The Reciprocal Love between Christ and the Church in the Apocalypse* (Rome: Columban Fathers, 1989).

McKenzie, J.L., *Second Isaiah* (AB, 20; Garden City, NY: Doubleday, 1968).

Mearns, C.L., 'Dating the Similitudes of Enoch', *NTS* 25 (1978–79), pp. 36-69.

Meeks, W., *The First Urban Christians* (New Haven: Yale University Press, 1983).

Meja, V., 'The Sociology of Knowledge and the Critique of Ideology', *Cultural Hermeneutics* 3 (1975), pp. 57-68.

Metzger, B.M., *The Text of the New Testament: Its Transmission, Corruption, and Restoration* (New York: Oxford University Press, 2nd edn, 1968).

—*A Textual Commentary on the Greek New Testament* (New York: United Bible Societies, 1971).

—*The Canon of the New Testament: Its Origin, Development and Significance* (New York: Oxford University Press, 1987).

Michaels, J.R., 'Revelation 1.19 and the Narrative Voices of the Apocalypse', *NTS* 37 (1991), pp. 604-20.

Milik, J.T. (ed.), *The Books of Enoch: Aramaic Fragments from Qumran Cave 4* (Oxford: Clarendon Press, 1976).

Miller, D.G., *On This Rock: A Commentary on First Peter* (Pittsburgh: Pickwick Press, 1993).

Miller, P.D., *The Divine Warrior in Early Israel* (HSM, 5; Cambridge, MA: Harvard University Press, 1973).

Minear, P., *New Testament Apocalyptic* (Nashville: Abingdon Press, 1981).

Moffatt, J., 'The Revelation of St. John the Divine', in *The Expositor's Greek Testament* (5 vols.; Grand Rapids: Eerdmans, 1951), V, pp. 279-494.

Montgomery, J.A., *A Critical and Exegetical Commentary on the Book of Daniel* (ICC, 22; Edinburgh: T. & T. Clark, 1960).

Morgan, R., with J. Barton, *Biblical Interpretation* (Oxford: Oxford University Press, 1988).

Morgenstern, J., 'The "Son of Man" of Dan 7:13f.: A New Interpretation', *JBL* 80 (1961), pp. 65-77.

Morris, L., *The Book of Revelation: An Introduction and Commentary* (TNTC; Grand Rapids: Eerdmans, 2nd edn, 1987).

Morton, R., 'The 'One Like a Son of Man' in Daniel 7:8-13 Reconsidered in Revelation 1:13-18', *Kardia* 5 (1990), pp. 23-27.

Mosca, P.G., 'Ugarit and Daniel 7: A Missing Link', *Bib* 67 (1986), pp. 496-517.

Moule, C.F.D., 'The Nature and Purpose of I Peter', *NTS* 3 (1956–57), pp. 1-11.

—*The Origin of Christology* (Cambridge: Cambridge University Press, 1977).

—' "The Son of Man": Some of the Facts', *NTS* 41 (1995), pp. 277-79.

Moulton, J.H., *A Grammar of New Testament Greek*, I (Edinburgh: T. & T. Clark, 3rd edn, 1908).

Moulton, W.F., and A.S. Geden (eds.), *A Concordance to the Greek Testament* (rev. H.K. Moulton; Edinburgh: T. & T. Clark, 5th edn, 1978).

Mounce, R.H., 'The Christology of the Apocalypse', *Foundations* 11 (1968), pp. 42-51.

—*The Book of Revelation* (NICNT, 17; Grand Rapids: Eerdmans, 1977).

Mowinckel, S., *He That Cometh* (New York: Abingdon Press, 1954).

Muilenburg, J., 'The Son of Man in Daniel and the Ethiopic Apocalypse of Enoch', *JBL* 79 (1960), pp. 197-209.

Müller, U.B., *Messias und Menschensohn in jüdischen Apokalypsen und in der Offenbarung des Johannes* (SNT, 6. Gütersloh: Gutersloher Verlagshaus Mohn, 1972).

—*Die Offenbarung des Johannes* (Gütersloh/Würzburg: Mohn and Echter-Verlag, 1984).

Mussies, G., *The Morphology of Koine Greek as Used in the Apocalypse of St. John* (SNT, 27; Leiden: E.J. Brill, 1971).

Myers, J.M., *I and II Esdras* (AB, 42; Garden City, NY: Doubleday, 1974).

Nestle, E., and K. Aland (eds.), *Novum Testamentum Graece* (Stuttgart: Deutsche Bibelgesellschaft, 27th edn, 1993).

Neusner, J. (ed.), *Religions in Antiquity: Essays in Memory of Erwin Ramsdell Goodenough* (Leiden: E.J. Brill, 1968).

Neusner, J.. W.S. Green, and E.S. Frerichs (eds.), *Judaisms and their Messiahs at the Turn of the Christian Era* (Cambridge: Cambridge University Press, 1987).

Newman, B., 'The Fallacy of the Domitian Hypothesis: Critique of the Irenaeus Source as a Witness for the Contemporary-Historical Approach to the Interpretation of the Apocalypse', *NTS* 10 (1963–64), pp. 133-39.

Noth, M., 'Die Heiligen des Höchsten', *NorTT* 56 (1955), pp. 146-61.

Nysse, R., 'Yahweh Is a Warrior', *Word and World* 7 (1987), pp. 192-201.

Panagopoulos, J. (ed.), *Prophetic Vocation in the New Testament and Today* (Supplements to Novum Testamentum, 44; Leiden: E.J. Brill, 1977).

Peake, A.S., *The Revelation of John* (London: Halborn, 1920).

Perkins, P., *First and Second Peter, James, and Jude* (Interpretation; Atlanta: John Knox Press, 1995).

Pleket, H.W., 'Domitian, the Senate and the Provinces', *Mnemosyne* 14 (1961), pp. 296-315.

Porteous, N.W., *Daniel, a Commentary* (OTL; Philadelphia: Westminster Press, rev. edn, 1979).
Porter, S.E., 'The Language of the Apocalypse in Recent Discussion', *NTS* 35 (1989), pp. 582-603.
Poucouta, P., 'La mission prophétique de l'église dans l'Apocalypse johannique', *NRT* 110 (1988), pp. 38-57.
Preston, R.H., and A.T. Hanson, *The Revelation of Saint John the Divine* (Torch Bible Commentaries; London: SCM Press, 1949).
Price, S.R.F., *Rituals and Power: The Roman imperial cult in Asia Minor* (Cambridge: Cambridge University Press, 1984).
Prigent, P., 'Pour une théologie de l'image: Les visions de l'Apocalypse', *RHPR* 59 (1979), pp. 373-78.
—*L'Apocalypse de saint Jean* (CNT, 2nd series, 14; Paris: Delachaux & Niestlé, 1981).
Procksch, O., 'Der Menschensohn als Gottessohn', *Christentum und Wissenschaft* 3 (1927), pp. 425-43.
Rahlfs, A. (ed.), *Septuaginta* (Stuttgart: Deutsche Bibelstiftung, 1979).
Ramsay, W.M., *The Church in the Roman Empire* (London: G.P. Putnam's Sons, 1893).
—*The Letters to the Seven Churches of Asia* (Grand Rapids: Baker Book House, 1963 [1904]).
Rand, J.A. du, 'The Imagery of the Heavenly Jerusalem (Revelation 21:9–22:5)', *Neot* 22 (1988), pp. 65-86.
—'A Socio-psychological View of the Effect of Language (Parole) of the Apocalypse of John', *Neot* 24 (1990), pp. 351-65.
Reddish, M.G., 'The Theme of Martyrdom in the Book of Revelation' (PhD thesis, Southern Baptist Theological Seminary, Louisville, KY, 1982).
—'Martyr Christology in the Apocalypse', *JSNT* 33 (1988), pp. 85-95.
—*Apocalyptic Literature: A Reader* (Nashville: Abingdon Press, 1990).
Reicke, B., *The Epistles of James, Peter, and Jude* (AB, 37; Garden City, NY: Doubleday, 1964).
—*The New Testament Era* (Philadelphia: Fortress Press, 1968).
—'The Inauguration of Catholic Martyrdom According to St. John the Divine', *Aug* 20 (1980), pp. 275-83.
Remus, H.E., 'Sociology of Knowledge and Study of Early Christianity', *SR* 11 (1982), pp. 45-56.
Reynolds, J.M., 'Further Information on Imperial Cult in Aphrodisias', *St.Cl.* 24 (1986), pp. 109-17.
Rhees, R., 'A Striking Monotony in the Synoptic Gospels', *JBL* 17 (1898), pp. 87-102.
Rissi, M., 'The Rider on the White Horse: A Study of Revelation 6, 1-8', *Int* 18 (1964), pp. 413-18.
—*Time and History* (Richmond, VA: John Knox Press, 1966).
—*The Future of the World: An Exegetical Study of Revelation 19.11–22.15* (SBT, 2nd series, 23; London: SCM Press, 1972).
Rist, M., '"The Revelation of St. John the Divine", Introduction and Exegesis', *IB*, XII, pp. 345-613.
Robinson, J.A.T., *Redating the New Testament* (London: SCM Press, 1976).
Rochais, G., 'Le règne des mille ans et la seconde mort: Origines et sens Apoc 19,11–20,6', *NRT* 103 (1981), pp. 831-56.
Ross, J.M., 'The Son of Man', *IBS* 13 (1991), pp. 186-98.

Rowland, C., 'The Vision of the Risen Christ in Rev. 1.13ff.: The Debt of an Early Christian Christology to an Aspect of Jewish Angelology', *JTS* 31 (1980), pp. 1-11.

—*The Open Heaven: A Study of Apocalyptic in Judaism and Early Christianity* (New York: Crossroad, 1982).

Rowley, H.H., *The Relevance of Apocalyptic* (New York: Association Press, 1963).

Rudberg, G., 'Zu den Sendschreiben der Johannes-Apokalypse', *Eranos* 11 (1911), pp. 170-79.

Russell, D.S., *The Method and Message of Jewish Apocalyptic, 200 BC–AD 100* (OTL; Philadelphia: Westminster Press, 1964).

—*Daniel* (Philadelphia: Westminster Press, 1981).

Russell, L.M. (ed.), *The Liberating Word: A Guide to Nonsexist Interpretation of the Bible* (Philadelphia: Westminster Press, 1976).

Sahlin, H., 'Wie wurde ursprünglichlich die Benennung "Der Menschensohn" verstanden', *ST* 37 (1983), pp. 147-79.

Satake, A., *Die Gemeindeordnung in der Johannesapokalypse* (WMANT, 21; Neukirchen–Vluyn: Neukirchener Verlag, 1966).

Schmidt, D.D., 'Semitisms and Septuagintalisms in the Book of Revelation', *NTS* 37 (1991), pp. 592-603.

Schmidt, N., 'Was *bar nash* a Messianic Title?' *JBL* 15 (1896), pp. 36-53.

—' "The 'Son of Man" in the Book of Daniel', *JBL* 19 (1900), pp. 22-28.

Schneemelcher, W. (ed.), *New Testament Apocrypha*. I. *Gospels and Related Writings* (trans. and ed. of 6th German edition by R. McL. Wilson; Louisville, KY: Westminister Press/John Knox Press, rev. edn, 1991).

Schüssler Fiorenza, E., 'The Eschatology and Composition of the Apocalypse', *CBQ* 30 (1968), pp. 537-69.

—'Apocalyptic and Gnosis in the Book of Revelation', *JBL* 92 (1973), pp. 565-81.

—'Redemption as Liberation: Apoc 1:5f. and 5:9f', *CBQ* 36 (1974), pp. 220-32.

—'Followers of the Lamb: Visionary Rhetoric and Social-Political Situation', *Semeia* 36 (1986), pp. 123-46.

—*Revelation: Vision of a Just World* (Edinburgh: T. & T. Clark, 1993).

Scobie, C.H.H., 'Local References in the Letters to the Seven Churches', *NTS* 39 (1993), pp. 606-24.

Scott, E.F., *The Book of Revelation* (New York: Charles Scribner's Sons; London: SCM Press, 1939).

Scott, R.B.Y., 'Behold, He Cometh with Clouds', *NTS* 5 (1958–59), pp. 127-32.

Scroggs, R., 'The Sociological Interpretation of the New Testament: The Present State of Research', *NTS* 26 (1979–80), pp. 164-79.

Seiss, J.A., *The Apocalypse* (Grand Rapids: Zondervan, 1957 [1909]).

Selwyn, E.G., *The First Epistle of St. Peter* (Grand Rapids: Baker Book House, 1981 [repr. 1947 edn]).

Shea, W.H., 'The Covenantal Form of the Letters to the Seven Churches', *AUSS* 21 (1983), pp. 71-84.

—'The Neo-Babylonian Historical Setting for Daniel 7', *AUSS* 24 (1986), pp. 31-36.

Shepherd, M.H., *The Pastoral Liturgy and the Apocalypse* (London: Lutterworth, 1960).

Sherwin-White, A.N., *The Letters of Pliny: A Historical and Social Commentary* (Oxford: Clarendon Press, 1966).

Sim, D.C., 'Matthew 22.13a and 1 Enoch 10.4a: A Case of Literary Dependence?', *JSNT* 47 (1992), pp. 3-19.

Skehan, P.W., 'King of Kings, Lord of Lords (Apoc 19,16)', *CBQ* 10 (1948), p. 398.
Slater, T.B., 'Leading a Bible Study: Explorations in the Historical-Critical Method' (Doctor of Ministry [DMin] Thesis, Southern Methodist University, Dallas, TX, USA, 1981).
—' "King of Kings and Lord of Lords" Revisited', *NTS* 39 (1993), pp. 159-60.
—' "*Homoion huion anthropou*" in Rev 1.13 and 14.14', *BT* 44 (1993a), pp. 349-50.
—'One Like a Son of Man in First-Century CE Judaism', *NTS* 41 (1995), pp. 183-98.
—'More on Revelation 1.13 and 14.14', *BT* 47 (1996), pp. 146-49.
—'Comparisons and the Son of Man', *Bible Bhashyam* 24 (1998), pp. 67-78.
—'On the Social Setting of the Revelation to John', *NTS* 44 (1998), pp. 232-56.
Smart, N., *The Science of Religion and the Sociology of Knowledge* (Princeton, NJ: Princeton University Press, 1973).
Smith, C.R., 'Revelation 1:19: An Eschatologically Escalated Prophetic Convention', *JETS* 33 (1990), pp. 461-66.
Sparks, H.F.D. (ed.), *The Apocryphal Old Testament* (Oxford: Clarendon Press, 1984).
Spitta, F., *Die Offenbarung des Johannes* (Halle: Weisenhaus, 1889).
Spivey, R.A., and D.M. Smith, *Anatomy of the New Testament* (Englewood Cliffs, NJ: Prentice–Hall, 5th edn, 1995).
Stanton, G.N., *Jesus of Nazareth in New Testament Preaching* (Cambridge: Cambridge University Press, 1974).
—*The Gospels and Jesus* (Oxford: Oxford University Press, 1989), pp. 230-35.
—*A Gospel for a New People: Studies in Matthew* (Edinburgh: T. & T. Clark, 1992).
Stark, R., 'The Class Basis of Early Christianity from a Sociological Model', *Sociological Analysis* 47 (1986), pp. 216-25.
Stauffer, E., *Christ and the Caesars: Historical Sketches* (trans. K. and R. Gregor Smith from the 3rd rev. and enlarged German edn; London: SCM Press, 1955).
Stone, M.E., *Fourth Ezra: A Commentary on the Book of Fourth Ezra* (Hermeneia; Minneapolis: Fortress Press, 1990).
Stough, C., 'Stoic Determinism and Moarl Responsibility', in J.M. Rist (ed.), *The Stoics* (Berkeley: University of California Press, 1978), pp. 203-31.
Strack, H.L., and P. Billerbeck, *Kommentar zum Neuen Testament aus Talmud und Midrash* (Munich: Beck, 1922–61).
Strand, K.A., 'Chiastic Structure and Some Motifs in the Book of Revelation', *AUSS* 16 (1978), pp. 401-408.
—'A Further Note on the Covenantal Form in the Book of Revelation', *AUSS* 21 (1983), pp. 251-64.
—' "Overcomer": A Study in the Macrodynamic of Theme Development in the Book of Revelation', *AUSS 28* (1990), pp. 237-54.
Sturm, R.E., 'Defining the Word "Apocalyptic": A Problem in Biblical Criticism', in J. Marcus and M.L. Soards (eds.), *Apocalyptic and the New Testament: Essays in Honor of J. Louis Martyn* (JSNTSup, 24; Sheffield: JSOT Press, 1989), pp. 17-48.
Summers, R., *Worthy Is the Lamb* (Nashville: Broadman, 1951).
Surridge, R., 'Redemption in the Structure of Revelation', *ExpTim* 101 (1990), pp. 231-35.
Sweet, J.P.M., *Revelation* (TPINTC; London: SCM Press; Philadelphia: Westminister Press, 1979).
Swete, H.B., *The Apocalypse of St. John* (London: Macmillan, 3rd edn, 1909).
Tcherikover, V., *Hellenistic Civilization and the Jews* (New York: Atheneum, 1985).

Theisohn, J., *Der auswählte Richter* (SUNT, 12; Göttingen: Vandenhoeck & Ruprecht, 1975).
Theissen, G., *The Social Setting of Pauline Christianity* (Philadelphia: Fortress Press, 1982).
Thomas, R.L., 'The Glorified Christ on Patmos', *BSac* 123 (1966), pp. 334-41.
Thompson, L.L., *The Book of Revelation: Apocalypse and Empire* (New York: Oxford University Press, 1990).
Thurman, H., *Jesus and the Disinherited* (Richmond, IN: Friends United Press, 1981).
Tidball, D.J., 'On Wooing a Crocodile: An Historical Survey of the Relationship between Sociology and New Testament Studies', *Vox Evangelica* 15 (1985), pp. 95-109.
Tillich, P., *Dynamics of Faith* (World Perspectives Series; London: G. Allen & Unwin, 1957).
Toribio, J.F., 'La recepcion de Dn 7,13 en Ap 1.7', *Mayèutica* 18 (1992), pp. 9-56.
Towner, W.S., *Daniel* (Atlanta: John Knox Press, 1984).
Trites, A.A., '*Martys* and Martyrdom in the Apocalypse: A Semantic Study', *NovT* 15 (1973), pp. 72-80.
Trudinger, P., 'Some Observations Concerning the Text of the Old Testament in the Book of Revelation', *JTS* NS 17 (1966), pp. 82-88.
—'The "Nero Redivivus" Rumour and the Date of the Apocalypse of John', *St. Mark's Review* 131 (1987), pp. 43-44.
Ureta, F., 'El estado según Juan: Iglesia y estado en el libro de Apocalipsis', *Apuntes Pastorales* 4 (1983), pp. 35-42, 98.
Vanni, U., *L'Apocalisse: Ermeneutica, esegesi, teologia* (Bologna: Dehoniane, 1988).
Vassiliadis, P., 'The Translation of *Martyria Iesou* in Revelation', *BT* 36 (1985), pp. 129-34.
Vermes, G., 'The Use of *bar nas/bar nasa* in Jewish Aramaic', in M. Black, *An Aramaic Approach to the Gospels and Acts* (Oxford: Clarendon Press, 3rd edn, 1967), pp. 310-20.
Vielhauer, P., 'Introduction to Apocalypses and related Studies', in E. Hennecke, W. Schneemelcher and R.M. Wilson (eds.), *New Testament Apocrypha* (2 vols.; Philadelphia: Westminster Press, 1965), II, pp. 579-609.
Villiers, P.G.R. de, 'The Lord Was Crucified in Sodom and Egypt: Symbols in the Apocalypse of John', *Neot* 22 (1988), pp. 125-38.
Viscusi, P., 'Studies on Domitian' (PhD dissertation; Ann Arbor: University Microfilms, 1973).
Vorster, W.S., 'Genre and the Revelation of John: A Study in Text, Context and Intertext', *Neot* 22 (1988), pp. 103-23.
—'The Reader in the Text: Narrative Material', *Semeia* 48 (1990).
Walbank, F.W., *The Hellenistic World* (Cambridge, MA: Harvard University Press, 1982).
Wall, R.W., *Revelation* (NIBC, 18; Peabody, MA: Hendrickson, 1991).
Walvoord, J.F., *The Revelation of Jesus Christ* (Chicago: Moody, 1966).
—*Daniel: The Key to Prophetic Revelation* (Chicago: Moody, 1971).
Warden, D., 'Imperial Persecution and the Dating of I Peter and Revelation', *JETS* 34 (1991), pp. 203-12.
Whale, P., 'The Lamb of John: Some Myths about the Vocabulary of the Johannine Literature', *JBL* 106 (1987), pp. 289-95.
Wilson, F.M., 'The Son of Man in Jewish Apocalyptic Literature', *Studia Biblica et Theologica* 8 (1978), pp. 28-52.

Wilson, J.C., 'The Problem of the Domitianic Date of Revelation', *NTS* (1993), pp. 587-605.

Wilson, S.G., *Related Strangers* (Minneapolis: Augsburg–Fortress, 1995).

Wolff, C., 'Die Gemeinde des Christus in der Apokalypse des Johannes', *NTS* 27 (1981), pp. 186-97.

Wolff, K.H., 'Introduction to Fifty Years of "Sociology of Knowledge" ', *Cultural Hermeneutics* 3 (1975), pp. 1-5.

Wright, N.T., *Christian Origins and the Question of God.* I. *The New Testament and the People of God* (London: SPCK, 1992).

Yarbro Collins, A., *The Combat Myth in the Book of Revelation* (ed. C. Bynum and G. Rupp; HDR, 9; Missoula, MT: Scholars Press, 1976).

—'The Political Perspective of the Revelation to John', *JBL* 96 (1977), pp. 241-56.

—*The Apocalypse* (NTM, 22; Wilmington, DE: Michael Glazier, 1979).

—'Dating the Apocalypse', *BR* 26 (1981), pp. 33-45.

—'The Revelation of John: An Apocalyptic Response to a Social Crisis', *CurTM 8* (1981), pp. 4-12.

—*Crisis and Catharsis: The Power of the Apocalypse* (Philadelphia: Westminster Press, 1984).

—'Vilification and Self-Definition in the Book of Revelation', *HTR* 79 (1986), pp. 308-20.

—'Oppression from within: The Symbolisation of Rome as Evil in Early Christianity', *Concilium* 200 (1988), pp. 66-74.

Yarbro Collins (ed.), *Feminist Perspectives on Biblical Scholarship* (SBL Centennial Publications; BSNA, 10; Chico, CA: Scholars Press, 1985).

—*Early Christian Apocalypticism* (Semeia, 36; Atlanta: Scholars Press, 1986).

Zahn, T., *Die Offenbarung des Johannes* (2 vols.; Leipzig: Deichert, 1924–26).

INDEXES

INDEX OF REFERENCES

OLD TESTAMENT

PSEUDEPIGRAPHA

OTHER ANCIENT REFERENCES

INDEX OF AUTHORS

JOURNAL FOR THE STUDY OF THE NEW TESTAMENT SUPPLEMENT SERIES

1 William R. Telford, *The Barren Temple and the Withered Tree: A Redaction-Critical Analysis of the Cursing of the Fig-Tree Pericope in Mark's Gospel and its Relation to the Cleansing of the Temple Tradition*
2 E.A. Livingstone (ed.), *Studia Biblica 1978, II: Papers on the Gospels (Sixth International Congress on Biblical Studies, Oxford, 1978)*
3 E.A. Livingstone (ed.), *Studia Biblica 1978, III: Papers on Paul and Other New Testament Authors (Sixth International Congress on Biblical Studies, Oxford, 1978)*
4 Ernest Best, *Following Jesus: Discipleship in Mark's Gospel*
5 Markus Barth, *The People of God*
6 John S. Pobee, *Persecution and Martyrdom in the Theology of Paul* [Out of print]
7 Christopher M. Tuckett (ed.), *Synoptic Studies: The Ampleforth Conferences of 1982 and 1983* [Out of print]
8 Terence L. Donaldson, *Jesus on the Mountain: A Study in Matthean Theology*
9 Stephen Farris, *The Hymns of Luke's Infancy Narratives: Their Origin, Meaning and Significance*
10 R. Badenas, *Christ the End of the Law: Romans 10.4 in Pauline Perspective* [Out of print]
11 Colin J. Hemer, *The Letters to the Seven Churches of Asia in their Local Setting* [Out of print]
12 Darrell L. Bock, *Proclamation from Prophecy and Pattern: Lucan Old Testament Christology*
13 Roger P. Booth, *Jesus and the Laws of Purity: Tradition History and Legal History in Mark 7*
14 Marion L. Soards, *The Passion According to Luke: The Special Material of Luke 22*
15 Thomas E. Schmidt, *Hostility to Wealth in the Synoptic Gospels*
16 Stephenson H. Brooks, *Matthew's Community: The Evidence of his Special Sayings Material*
17 Anthony Tyrrell Hanson, *The Paradox of the Cross in the Thought of St Paul*
18 Celia Deutsch, *Hidden Wisdom and the Easy Yoke: Wisdom, Torah and Discipleship in Matthew 11.25-30*
19 L. Joseph Kreitzer, *Jesus and God in Paul's Eschatology*
20 Michael D. Goulder, *Luke: A New Paradigm*
21 Mikeal C. Parsons, *The Departure of Jesus in Luke–Acts: The Ascension Narratives in Context*
22 Martinus C. de Boer, *The Defeat of Death: Apocalyptic Eschatology in 1 Corinthians 15 and Romans 5* [Out of print]
23 Michael Prior, *Paul the Letter-Writer and the Second Letter to Timothy*

24 Joel Marcus and Marion L. Soards (eds.), *Apocalyptic and the New Testament: Essays in Honor of J. Louis Martyn*
25 David E. Orton, *The Understanding Scribe: Matthew and the Apocalyptic Ideal*
26 Timothy J. Geddert, *Watchwords: Mark 13 in Markan Eschatology*
27 Clifton C. Black, *The Disciples According to Mark: Markan Redaction in Current Debate*
28 David Seeley, *The Noble Death: Graeco-Roman Martyrology and Paul's Concept of Salvation*
29 G. Walter Hansen, *Abraham in Galatians: Epistolary and Rhetorical Contexts*
30 Frank Witt Hughes, *Early Christian Rhetoric and 2 Thessalonians*
31 David R. Bauer, *The Structure of Matthew's Gospel: A Study in Literary Design*
32 Kevin B. Quast, *Peter and the Beloved Disciple: Figures for a Community in Crisis*
33 Mary Ann Beavis, *Mark's Audience: The Literary and Social Setting of Mark 4.11-12*
34 Philip H. Towner, *The Goal of our Instruction: The Structure of Theology and Ethics in the Pastoral Epistles*
35 Alan P. Winton, *The Proverbs of Jesus: Issues of History and Rhetoric*
36 Stephen E. Fowl, *The Story of Christ in the Ethics of Paul: An Analysis of the Function of the Hymnic Material in the Pauline Corpus*
37 A.J.M. Wedderburn (ed.), *Paul and Jesus: Collected Essays*
38 Dorothy Jean Weaver, *Matthew's Missionary Discourse: A Literary Critical Analysis*
39 Glenn N. Davies, *Faith and Obedience in Romans: A Study in Romans 1–4*
40 Jerry L. Sumney, *Identifying Paul's Opponents: The Question of Method in 2 Corinthians*
41 Mary E. Mills, *Human Agents of Cosmic Power in Hellenistic Judaism and the Synoptic Tradition*
42 David B. Howell, *Matthew's Inclusive Story: A Study in the Narrative Rhetoric of the First Gospel*
43 Heikki Räisänen, *Jesus, Paul and Torah: Collected Essays*
44 Susanne Lehne, *The New Covenant in Hebrews*
45 Neil Elliott, *The Rhetoric of Romans: Argumentative Constraint and Strategy and Paul's Dialogue with Judaism*
46 John O. York, *The Last Shall Be First: The Rhetoric of Reversal in Luke*
47 Patrick J. Hartin, *James and the 'Q' Sayings of Jesus*
48 William Horbury (ed.), *Templum Amicitiae: Essays on the Second Temple Presented to Ernst Bammel*
49 John M. Scholer, *Proleptic Priests: Priesthood in the Epistle to the Hebrews*
50 Duane F. Watson (ed.), *Persuasive Artistry: Studies in New Testament Rhetoric in Honor of George A. Kennedy*

51 Jeffrey A. Crafton, *The Agency of the Apostle: A Dramatistic Analysis of Paul's Responses to Conflict in 2 Corinthians*
52 Linda L. Belleville, *Reflections of Glory: Paul's Polemical Use of the Moses–Doxa Tradition in 2 Corinthians 3.1-18*
53 Thomas J. Sappington, *Revelation and Redemption at Colossae*
54 Robert P. Menzies, *The Development of Early Christian Pneumatology, with Special Reference to Luke–Acts* [Out of print]
55 L. Ann Jervis, *The Purpose of Romans: A Comparative Letter Structure Investigation*
56 Delbert Burkett, *The Son of the Man in the Gospel of John*
57 Bruce W. Longenecker, *Eschatology and the Covenant: A Comparison of 4 Ezra and Romans 1–11*
58 David A. Neale, *None but the Sinners: Religious Categories in the Gospel of Luke*
59 Michael Thompson, *Clothed with Christ: The Example and Teaching of Jesus in Romans 12.1–15.13*
60 Stanley E. Porter (ed.), *The Language of the New Testament: Classic Essays*
61 John Christopher Thomas, *Footwashing in John 13 and the Johannine Community*
62 Robert L. Webb, *John the Baptizer and Prophet: A Socio-Historical Study*
63 James S. McLaren, *Power and Politics in Palestine: The Jews and the Governing of their Land, 100 BC–AD 70*
64 Henry Wansborough (ed.), *Jesus and the Oral Gospel Tradition*
65 Douglas A. Campbell, *The Rhetoric of Righteousness in Romans 3.21-26*
66 Nicholas Taylor, *Paul, Antioch and Jerusalem: A Study in Relationships and Authority in Earliest Christianity*
67 F. Scott Spencer, *The Portrait of Philip in Acts: A Study of Roles and Relations*
68 Michael Knowles, *Jeremiah in Matthew's Gospel: The Rejected Prophet Motif in Matthean Redaction*
69 Margaret Davies, *Rhetoric and Reference in the Fourth Gospel*
70 J. Webb Mealy, *After the Thousand Years: Resurrection and Judgment in Revelation 20*
71 Martin Scott, *Sophia and the Johannine Jesus*
72 Steven M. Sheeley, *Narrative Asides in Luke–Acts*
73 Marie E. Isaacs, *Sacred Space: An Approach to the Theology of the Epistle to the Hebrews*
74 Edwin K. Broadhead, *Teaching with Authority: Miracles and Christology in the Gospel of Mark*
75 John K. Chow, *Patronage and Power: A Study of Social Networks in Corinth*
76 Robert W. Wall and Eugene E. Lemcio (eds.), *The New Testament as Canon: A Reader in Canonical Criticism*
77 Roman Garrison, *Redemptive Almsgiving in Early Christianity*
78 L. Gregory Bloomquist, *The Function of Suffering in Philippians*
79 Blaine Charette, *The Theme of Recompense in Matthew's Gospel*

80 Stanley E. Porter and D.A. Carson (eds.), *Biblical Greek Language and Linguistics: Open Questions in Current Research*
81 In-Gyu Hong, *The Law in Galatians*
82 Barry W. Henaut, *Oral Tradition and the Gospels: The Problem of Mark 4*
83 Craig A. Evans and James A. Sanders (eds.), *Paul and the Scriptures of Israel*
84 Martinus C. de Boer (ed.), *From Jesus to John: Essays on Jesus and New Testament Christology in Honour of Marinus de Jonge*
85 William J. Webb, *Returning Home: New Covenant and Second Exodus as the Context for 2 Corinthians 6.14–7.1*
86 Bradley H. McLean (ed.), *Origins and Method—Towards a New Understanding of Judaism and Christianity: Essays in Honour of John C. Hurd*
87 Michael J. Wilkins and Terence Paige (eds.), *Worship, Theology and Ministry in the Early Church: Essays in Honour of Ralph P. Martin*
88 Mark Coleridge, *The Birth of the Lukan Narrative: Narrative as Christology in Luke 1–2*
89 Craig A. Evans, *Word and Glory: On the Exegetical and Theological Background of John's Prologue*
90 Stanley E. Porter and Thomas H. Olbricht (eds.), *Rhetoric and the New Testament: Essays from the 1992 Heidelberg Conference*
91 Janice Capel Anderson, *Matthew's Narrative Web: Over, and Over, and Over Again*
92 Eric Franklin, *Luke: Interpreter of Paul, Critic of Matthew*
93 Jan Fekkes III, *Isaiah and Prophetic Traditions in the Book of Revelation: Visionary Antecedents and their Development*
94 Charles A. Kimball, *Jesus' Exposition of the Old Testament in Luke's Gospel*
95 Dorothy A. Lee, *The Symbolic Narratives of the Fourth Gospel: The Interplay of Form and Meaning*
96 Richard E. DeMaris, *The Colossian Controversy: Wisdom in Dispute at Colossae*
97 Edwin K. Broadhead, *Prophet, Son, Messiah: Narrative Form and Function in Mark 14–16*
98 Carol J. Schlueter, *Filling up the Measure: Polemical Hyperbole in 1 Thessalonians 2.14-16*
99 Neil Richardson, *Paul's Language about God*
100 Thomas E. Schmidt and Moisés Silva (eds.), *To Tell the Mystery: Essays on New Testament Eschatology in Honor of Robert H. Gundry*
101 Jeffrey A.D. Weima, *Neglected Endings: The Significance of the Pauline Letter Closings*
102 Joel F. Williams, *Other Followers of Jesus: Minor Characters as Major Figures in Mark's Gospel*
103 Warren Carter, *Households and Discipleship: A Study of Matthew 19–20*
104 Craig A. Evans and W. Richard Stegner (eds.), *The Gospels and the Scriptures of Israel*

105 W.P. Stephens (ed.), *The Bible, the Reformation and the Church: Essays in Honour of James Atkinson*
106 Jon A. Weatherly, *Jewish Responsibility for the Death of Jesus in Luke–Acts*
107 Elizabeth Harris, *Prologue and Gospel: The Theology of the Fourth Evangelist*
108 L. Ann Jervis and Peter Richardson (eds.), *Gospel in Paul: Studies on Corinthians, Galatians and Romans for Richard N. Longenecker*
109 Elizabeth Struthers Malbon and Edgar V. McKnight (eds.), *The New Literary Criticism and the New Testament*
110 Mark L. Strauss, *The Davidic Messiah in Luke–Acts: The Promise and its Fulfillment in Lukan Christology*
111 Ian H. Thomson, *Chiasmus in the Pauline Letters*
112 Jeffrey B. Gibson, *The Temptations of Jesus in Early Christianity*
113 Stanley E. Porter and D.A. Carson (eds.), *Discourse Analysis and Other Topics in Biblical Greek*
114 Lauri Thurén, *Argument and Theology in 1 Peter: The Origins of Christian Paraenesis*
115 Steve Moyise, *The Old Testament in the Book of Revelation*
116 C.M. Tuckett (ed.), *Luke's Literary Achievement: Collected Essays*
117 Kenneth G.C. Newport, *The Sources and Sitz im Leben of Matthew 23*
118 Troy W. Martin, *By Philosophy and Empty Deceit: Colossians as Response to a Cynic Critique*
119 David Ravens, *Luke and the Restoration of Israel*
120 Stanley E. Porter and David Tombs (eds.), *Approaches to New Testament Study*
121 Todd C. Penner, *The Epistle of James and Eschatology: Re-reading an Ancient Christian Letter*
122 A.D.A. Moses, *Matthew's Transfiguration Story in Jewish–Christian Controversy*
123 David Lertis Matson, *Household Conversion Narratives in Acts: Pattern and Interpretation*
124 David Mark Ball, *'I Am' in John's Gospel: Literary Function, Background and Theological Implications*
125 Robert Gordon Maccini, *Her Testimony is True: Women as Witnesses According to John*
126 B. Hudson Mclean, *The Cursed Christ: Mediterranean Expulsion Rituals and Pauline Soteriology*
127 R. Barry Matlock, *Unveiling the Apocalyptic Paul: Paul's Interpreters and the Rhetoric of Criticism*
128 Timothy Dwyer, *The Motif of Wonder in the Gospel of Mark*
129 Carl Judson Davis, *The Names and Way of the Lord: Old Testament Themes, New Testament Christology*
130 Craig S. Wansink, *Chained in Christ: The Experience and Rhetoric of Paul's Imprisonments*

131 Stanley E. Porter and Thomas H. Olbricht (eds.), *Rhetoric, Scripture and Theology: Essays from the 1994 Pretoria Conference*
132 J. Nelson Kraybill, *Imperial Cult and Commerce in John's Apocalypse*
133 Mark S. Goodacre, *Goulder and the Gospels: An Examination of a New Paradigm*
134 Larry J. Kreitzer, *Striking New Images: Roman Imperial Coinage and the New Testament World*
135 Charles Landon, *A Text-Critical Study of the Epistle of Jude*
136 Jeffrey T. Reed, *A Discourse Analysis of Philippians: Method and Rhetoric in the Debate over Lierary Integrity*
137 Roman Garrison, *The Graeco-Roman Context of Early Christian Literature*
138 Kent D. Clarke, *Textual Optimism: A Critique of the United Bible Societies' Greek New Testament*
139 Yong-Eui Yang, *Jesus and the Sabbath in Matthew's Gospel*
140 Thomas R. Yoder Neufeld, *Put on the Armour of God: The Divine Warrior from Isaiah to Ephesians*
141 Rebecca I. Denova, *The Things Accomplished among Us: Prophetic Tradition in the Structural Pattern of Luke–Acts*
142 Scott Cunningham, *'Through Many Tribulations': The Theology of Persecution in Luke–Acts*
143 Raymond Pickett, *The Cross in Corinth: The Social Significance of the Death of Jesus*
144 S. John Roth, *The Blind, the Lame and the Poor: Character Types in Luke–Acts*
145 Larry Paul Jones, *The Symbol of Water in the Gospel of John*
146 Stanley E. Porter and Thomas H. Olbricht (eds.), *The Rhetorical Analysis of Scripture: Essays from the 1995 London Conference*
147 Kim Paffenroth, *The Story of Jesus According to L*
148 Craig A. Evans and James A. Sanders (eds.), *Early Christian Interpretation of the Scriptures of Israel: Investigations and Proposals*
149 J. Dorcas Gordon, *Sister or Wife?: 1 Corinthians 7 and Cultural Anthropology*
150 J. Daryl Charles, *Virtue amidst Vice: The Catalog of Virtues in 2 Peter 1.5-7*
151 Derek Tovey, *Narrative Art and Act in the Fourth Gospel*
152 Evert-Jan Vledder, *Conflict in the Miracle Stories: A Socio-Exegetical Study of Matthew 8 and 9*
153 Christopher Rowland and Crispin H.T. Fletcher-Louis (eds.), *Understanding, Studying and Reading: New Testament Essays in Honour of John Ashton*
154 Craig A. Evans and James A. Sanders (eds.), *The Function of Scripture in Early Jewish and Christian Tradition*
155 Kyoung-Jin Kim, *Stewardship and Almsgiving in Luke's Theology*
156 I.A.H. Combes, *The Metaphor of Slavery in the Writings of the Early Church: From the New Testament to the Begining of the Fifth Century*
158 Jey. J. Kanagaraj, *'Mysticism' in the Gospel of John: An Inquiry into its Background*

159 Brenda Deen Schildgen, *Crisis and Continuity: Time in the Gospel of Mark*
160 Johan Ferreira, *Johannine Ecclesiology*
161 Helen C. Orchard, *Courting Betrayal: Jesus as Victim in the Gospel of John*
162 Jeffrey T. Tucker, *Example Stories: Perspectives on Four Parables in the Gospel of Luke*
163 John A. Darr, *Herod the Fox: Audience Criticism and Lukan Characterization*
164 Bas M.F. Van Iersel, *Mark: A Reader-Response Commentary*
165 Alison Jasper, *The Shining Garment of the Text: Gendered Readings of John's Prologue*
166 G.K. Beale, *John's Use of the Old Testament in Revelation*
167 Gary Yamasaki, *John the Baptist in Life and Death: Audience-Oriented Criticism of Matthew's Narrative*
168 Stanley E. Porter and D.A. Carson (eds.), *Linguistics and the New Testament: Critical Junctures*
169 Derek Newton, *Deity and Diet: The Dilemma of Sacrificial Food at Corinth*
170 Stanley E. Porter and Jeffrey T. Reed (eds.), *Discourse Analysis and the New Testament: Approaches and Results*
172 Casey Wayne Davis, *Oral Biblical Criticism: The Influence of the Principles of Orality on the Literary Structure of Paul's Epistle to the Philippians*
173 Stanley E. Porter and Richard S. Hess (eds.), *Translating the Bible: Problems and Prospects*
174 J.D.H. Amador, *Academic Constraints in Rhetorical Criticism of the New Testament: An Introduction to a Rhetoric of Power*
175 Edwin K. Broadhead, *Naming Jesus: Titular Christology in the Gospel of Mark*
176 Alex T. Cheung, *Idol Food in Corinth: Jewish Background and Pauline Legacy*
177 Brian Dodd, *Paul's Paradigmatic 'I': Personal Examples as Literary Strategy*
178 Thomas B. Slater, *Christ and Community: A Socio-Historical Study of the Christology of Revelation*
179 Alison M. Jack, *Texts Reading Texts, Sacred and Secular: Two Postmodern Perspectives*
180 Stanley E. Porter and Dennis L. Stamps (eds.), *The Rhetorical Interpretation of Scripture: Essays from the 1996 Malibu Conference*
182 Johannes Nissen and Sigfred Pedersen (eds.), *New Readings in John: Literary and Theological Perspectives. Essays from the Scandinavian Conference on the Fourth Gospel in Århus 1997*
184 David Rhoads and Kari Syreeni (eds.), *Characterization in the Gospels: Reconceiving Narrative Criticism*